Brodsky in English

SRLT

Northwestern University Press
Studies in Russian Literature and Theory

Brodsky in English

Zakhar Ishov

NORTHWESTERN UNIVERSITY PRESS / EVANSTON, ILLINOIS

Northwestern University Press
www.nupress.northwestern.edu

Printed in the United States of America

10 9 8 7 6 5 4 3 2 1

Library of Congress Cataloging-in-Publication Data

Names: Ishov, Zakhar, author.
Title: Brodsky in English / Zakhar Ishov.
Other titles: Studies in Russian literature and theory.
Description: Evanston, Illinois : Northwestern University Press, 2023. | Series: Northwestern University Press studies in Russian literature and theory | Includes bibliographical references and index. | Includes poems in romanized Russian with English translation.
Identifiers: LCCN 2023010450 | ISBN 9780810145986 (paperback) | ISBN 9780810145993 (cloth) | ISBN 9780810146006 (ebook)
Subjects: LCSH: Brodsky, Joseph, 1940–1996—Translations into English—History and criticism. | Russian poetry 20th century—Translations into English. | Russian language—Translating into English. | Self–translation. | BISAC: LITERARY CRITICISM / Russian & Soviet | LITERARY CRITICISM / Poetry
Classification: LCC PG3479.4.R64 Z7285 2023 | DDC 891.7144—dc23
LC record available at https://lccn.loc.gov/2023010450

To the memory of my dear mother, Sophia Ishova

Contents

Preface

My generation came of age when the Soviet empire started to crumble. As the walls of the pyramid began to show cracks and the Iron Curtain became porous, millions of Soviet citizens streamed to the previously prohibited hemisphere in pursuit of change, opportunity, and freedom. I arrived in Berlin as a teenager, shortly after the Wall fell. Although very little in my former Soviet experience had prepared me for a new life in the West, many of us were eager to make this unfamiliar environment our home. Historically, it was a unique moment; Russian émigrés did not immediately retreat into their Slavic capsules but showed an openness and desire to rejoin the world after a prolonged severance from it.

Brodsky and Nabokov became my two Virgils who bought me the rite of passage—two cosmopolitan Russian writers from my hometown who both felt at home in the West. While Nabokov's Russian Berlin novels were closer to my new geographic setting, Brodsky was closer in time to my Soviet experience. Both had conquered America with their works composed in English and were inspirations as I started studying English philology at the university in Berlin. Brodsky's achievement was the more outstanding. Unlike Nabokov, who was raised speaking English in an aristocratic St. Petersburg household and later attended Cambridge, Brodsky grew up in Soviet-era Leningrad. It was no longer the imperial capital, Russia's window to Europe, but a "renamed city"[1] in Stalinist Russia—a country that had insulated itself from the rest of the world, severing most of its intellectual and material ties with the West. To counterbalance these mental and physical barriers, Brodsky evoked the concept of "nostalgia for world culture," passed on to him by his poetic predecessor and model, Osip Mandelstam.[2] Mandelstam, a Jewish outcast in imperial Russia, insisted that Russian culture had been ancestrally affiliated with Europe. Brodsky, himself a Jewish outsider in the Soviet context, created in his poems, essays, and interviews a universe where Russian, American, and European poets existed on an equal footing—all of them loved, internalized, and learned by heart. Brodsky's openness to other cultures reinforced my own aspirations.

While Brodsky's essays taught one to be unafraid of poetry not written in one's mother tongue, the complexity and the range of cultural references in his own poems seemed daunting, even in Russian. It was hard to imagine how the meaning and the music of his poems could ever be preserved in translation. Yet it was precisely the difficulty of his poetry in Russian that drove me to a study of the English versions of them, which I hoped might help me get closer to the originals. I have studied Brodsky's translations intermittently for more than fifteen years: digging into the archives; interviewing Brodsky's associates and friends, many of whom are no longer with us; translating his poems into English in tandem with an English poet; studying translation and versification theory; and, above all, examining various translation drafts by Brodsky and his associates. Through this work I gradually began to understand what it takes to translate poetry. It takes a miracle.

There are many hurdles in the path of the translator, ranging from the linguistic to the cultural; and there are many pitfalls related to diverging poetic traditions, properties of languages, and different expectations of a translation in the source and target cultures. These often led to irresolvable collisions, fiery battles, and real-life dramas between Brodsky and his English translators. Dealing with the translations has changed my whole perception of the originals. I have begun to see both as integral parts of one poetic oeuvre. And as I gradually discovered, this was also how Brodsky himself saw it.

Brodsky's original poems in English represented a discovery of yet another order. Following a Russian poet as he breaches the vast, forbidding grounds of a foreign idiom and watching as he trespasses upon territories where (to quote his beloved Auden) "executives would never want to tamper"[3] has become a revelatory quest. This book is my attempt to share with readers my enthusiasm for the unique phenomenon of Brodsky translating his poems, either with others or on his own, into "new originals" in English. For all its assumed merits or drawbacks, one thing is certain—the phenomenon brings the Russian and English languages and sensibilities closer together.

Acknowledgments

This book has been long in the making. Given my lifelong passion for languages, a project on the translation of poetry—which is untranslatable by definition—was bound to attract me as a young scholar. Luckily, it also inspired Russell West-Pavlov, at the Freie Universität Berlin, to immediately become, and remain, a source of continual support. I would, therefore, first like to express my sincere gratitude to him for his openness, right from the beginning, to my interest in Brodsky's English and for his unflagging support ever since.

In hindsight, I believe that two subsequent scholarly events breathed new life into this project since then. The first impulse came from the conference "Projekt Brodski," organized in December 2013 by the comparative studies students of the Jagiellonian University in Kraków, Kajo Rudziński and Monika Gromala, under the guidance of their mentor Magdalena Heydel. The genuine enthusiasm for Brodsky's experiments in English—in spite of his "Russian accent"—shown by these young Polish scholars was truly inspiring. The second impulse came from the already legendary translation studies conference in Uppsala in June 2014, organized by Susanna Witt and Julie Hansen, whose many participants, myself included, have become regular presenters at international Slavic conventions on translation. I am indebted to all my co-panelists and discussants at these events for inspirational conversations, but I want specifically to thank both Susanna and Julie for their encouragement and steadfast support over these last years. In addition, my sincerest gratitude to Adrian Wanner, whose reference to my research on Brodsky's translations in his keynote speech at the 2014 conference further convinced me that my project had promise, and whose continued support and advice have been invaluable.

This book would not have been possible without a fellowship from the Institute for Russian and Eurasian Studies (IRES) at Uppsala University, which has given me the opportunity to complete my research on this book and to pursue related projects. My separate thanks go to the former IRES scholar Julie Hansen, who was one of the first readers of my early drafts, provided useful comments, and has been encouraging throughout. I am also immensely grateful to Ann Kjellberg, Brodsky's literary executor and former editor, for her unwavering support for the project over the years, for sharing her own firsthand insights about Brodsky translations, for updating me on the whereabouts of various Brodsky materials scattered around the world, and for putting me in touch with many of Brodsky's friends and associates. This book features interviews with two of Brodsky's close associates and collaborators, both now deceased, that would not have been possible without her help: Barry Rubin, a coeditor of Brodsky's collection *A Part of Speech*; and the Pulitzer Prize–winning poet Mark Strand, Brodsky's friend and fellow US poet laureate.

I would also like to thank the Beinecke Library at Yale University, where I spent countless hours researching Brodsky-related materials graciously made available to me. I am particularly grateful to the head of access services there, Moira Fitzgerald, who was always ready to go out of her way to help with my research. I am similarly indebted to the Manuscripts and Archives Division at the New York Public Library; the Stanford University Libraries' Special Collections; the Hoover Institution Archives; the Manuscript Division at the Library of Congress; the Bakhmeteff Archive at Columbia University; and the Russian National Library in St. Petersburg for making their materials available.

I extend my deep appreciation to my first readers who, as native speakers, offered their linguistic input, their suggestions, and generously provided proofreading assistance: Marissa Grunes, Ruth Greenstein, Elizabeth Haig, Robert Lindsay, Brittany Pheiffer, and, above all, James Stotts and Ann Kjellberg. I am also most grateful to the two peer reviewers of Northwestern University Press for their constructive criticism, proofreading assistance, and feedback. The debt I owe to Kathleen Friedman, who helped me bring the manuscript into its final shape and has been my most careful and faithful reader over the past year, is beyond words.

I am grateful to Tomas Venclova, Irena Grudzińska Gross, and Ellen Hinsey for many inspirational conversations and helpful suggestions. I am also indebted to my former and current editors at Northwestern University Press, Trevor Perri and Faith Wilson Stein, as well as project editor Anne Gendler and freelance copy editor Paul Mendelson, for their help in seeing the book through. Separately, I would like to acknowledge Antonina Kalinina for helping me translate Horace's ode into English from the Latin; James Stotts for giving me a hand in translating a line from Vladimir Uflyand's poem from the Russian; and Magda Heydel for her help in translating a passage from the Polish by Stanislaw Barańczak. I would also like to express my appreciation to Natalia Movnina for providing assistance in navigating the intricate system of the Russian National Library in St. Petersburg. I also extend my gratitude to Natascha Freundel for providing the recording of the talk by Tomas Venclova on Akhmatova and Brodsky that we both attended at the Einstein Forum in Berlin in 2003.

An earlier version of chapter 6 appeared in *Wiener Slavistisches Jahrbuch* ("The Battlefield of Translation: Joseph Brodsky and Daniel Weissbort," *Wiener Slavistisches Jahrbuch* 6 (January 2018): 122–42). I thank its editor, Fedor Poljakov, for his careful and detailed engagement with the article. The French translation of the article was published as "Joseph Brodsky et Daniel Weissbort: Traduction et Contestation," in *Traduire avec l'auteur*, ed. Patrick Hersant (Paris: Sorbonne Université Presses, 2018), 195–218.

Letters from Nancy Meiselas to Brodsky and his several associates are printed with her kind permission. Letters from Richard Wilbur to Brodsky are printed with the kind permission of Christopher Wilbur. Letters of Stephen Spender to Brodsky appear with the kind permission of Matthew Spender. Letters from Anthony Hecht appear with the kind permission of Helen Hecht. Letters from W. S. Merwin to Brodsky and my interview with Mark Strand appear with the kind permission of the Wiley agency. My interview with Derek Walcott appears with the kind permission of the Derek Walcott Estate. All Brodsky letters and unpublished essays appear with the kind permission of the Brodsky Estate. I am indebted to the late Derek Walcott, Mark Strand, and Barry Rubin for their generosity and openness in my interviews with them. I am equally grateful to the late George Kline for his support of my research, and for sharing stories and documents related to Brodsky. His letters appear with the kind permission of his daughter and personal representative, Christina Hanak. My thanks go to Fausto Malcovati for permission to quote from our interview concerning his encounters with Brodsky in Leningrad and in New York. I am also extremely grateful to Barry Scherr for sharing with me his memoir on meeting with Brodsky in Leningrad in the 1970s and for allowing me to print it here. I owe a special debt of gratitude to Schamma Schahadat for inviting me to speak about Brodsky's and Nabokov's translations at a seminar in Tübingen University in October 2019. Attending two writing workshops, both organized by Julie Hansen at Uppsala University, proved to be extremely beneficial in the writing and development of the manuscript: the first, a writing workshop facilitated by Helen Sword of Auckland University in October 2018; and the second, a workshop with William Germano of New York University in August 2019.

Last but not least, I would like to thank my dear wife Joyce Noble for her angelic patience with me through the ups and downs of the writing process, especially during the pandemic. Despite my subject's remoteness from her own field—molecular biology—she has shown enthusiasm for it, accompanied me to several Slavic conferences, and has been my inspiration throughout. I would not have written this book without her.

Brodsky in English

Introduction

A Biography in the "Twists of Language"

THE TOPIC OF THIS BOOK is poetry translation—a highly contentious subject among scholars. Robert Frost memorably quipped that "poetry is what gets lost in translation."[1] Like most quips of thoughtful poets, this bon mot cleverly encapsulates a rather serious matter. Samuel Coleridge defined poetry as "the best words in the best order."[2] But what if this order were to be broken? That is surely what poetry translation entails. Can it then be adequately re-created in another language?

W. H. Auden observed that in no other art is the unity of form and meaning more evident than in poetry: "The formal structure of the poem is not something distinct from its meaning but as intimately bound up with the latter as the body is with the soul."[3] According to George Steiner, the nature of this unity is best demonstrated by the impossibility of preserving it across translation: "Traditionally, the weight of the argument [of untranslatability] bears on poetry. Here the welding of matter and form is so close that no dissociation is admissible."[4] Among the modern poets, Dante was one of the earliest skeptics of poetry translation, arguing in *Il Convivio* (*The Banquet*) that "nothing which has been musically harmonized can be transformed from its own language into another without breaking all of its sweetness and harmony."[5] Centuries later, Auden—Brodsky's poetic model—echoed the same idea: "Translation of poetry from one tongue into another is, as everybody knows, impossible, for the poetic unity of sensibility, diction, and rhythm cannot be taken apart and reassembled in exactly the same way in the new language."[6] Frost's quip expressed, in a nutshell, something that had been known to poets for centuries. Twentieth-century linguists came to similar conclusions, providing various scientific explanations for the phenomenon. Thus, Roman Jakobson argued that "poetry, governed as it is by paronomasia—by the relationship between the phonemic and the semantic unit as in a pun—is 'by definition' untranslatable."[7] Yuri Lotman similarly described the relationship between the original and the translation in poetry as asymmetrical.[8]

Yet for all its apparent untranslatability, in practice poetry has been translated since antiquity. The early twentieth-century experimental translator Franz Rosenzweig argued that in the course of the theoretically impossible, translation becomes the task of everybody: "To translate means to serve two masters—something nobody can do. Hence, as is true of all things that in theory no one can do—it becomes in practice everybody's job. Everyone must translate and everyone does translate."[9] Furthermore, translation is widely regarded as a unique and important source of cross-cultural transfer, influence, and inspiration that has enabled the spread of literary civilization throughout the world and helped each epoch witness the emergence of new national cultures.[10] In the West, the tradition is believed to have started around 250 B.C.E., when Lucius Livius Andronicus translated Homer's *Odyssey* from Greek to Latin.[11] His translation laid the groundwork for the emergence of Latin epic poetry and drama.[12] Similar patterns have been replicated in most other literary traditions throughout Europe.[13] My teacher Tomas Venclova, a Lithuanian poet and professor of Russian literature at Yale University, summed it up thus: "The literature of most nations begins with translations."[14]

Russia is certainly no exception. Russian literary history exemplifies the crucial role of poetry translation in the dissemination of literary culture. A latecomer to the Western cultural tradition, Russia started absorbing the secular Greco-Roman literary heritage only in the early eighteenth century, in the wake of a larger opening to the West instigated by Peter the Great.[15] Some scholars argue that poetry translation was vital to the process of Russia's Westernization.[16] It would not be an exaggeration to say that modern Russian literature was literally born in translation.[17] Russia's national poet, Alexander Pushkin, a fifth of whose output consisted of translations, imitations, and borrowings,[18] famously called translators the "post-horses of enlightenment."[19] By the same token, Michael Wachtel argues in his *Cambridge Introduction to Russian Poetry* that, in the case of Russian poets, it is less appropriate to speak of Harold Bloom's "anxiety of influence"[20] than of the "anxiety to be influenced."[21] The desire to be influenced by Western models through translation, imitation, and cross-border artistic inspiration continued into the early twentieth century, when Russian poetry reached the peak of its flowering; this became known as the "Silver Age."[22]

The advent of the Soviet era, however, led to Russia's gradual cultural self-insulation, bolstered by its utopian millenarianism. As Katerina Clark aptly observed: "Utopias are always closed communities."[23] The significant and centuries-old Western influence on Russian culture was, in particular, undermined and crushed in the early 1930s, when, in the words of Clark, "the Soviet Union became a closed society."[24] Russia remained closed for over seventy years, until the early 1990s, when the censorship was finally lifted and Russians were again allowed to travel abroad and have more contact with foreigners outside the Eastern Bloc.[25] Assessing the situation in retrospect, in his 1997 monograph on the history of Russian literary translation, Maurice Friedberg emphasized that the largely chauvinistic Soviet literary scholarship did not give enough credit to the historical role of Western influence on Russian literature:

> For the just emerging secular Russian literature, the eighteenth century was a period of apprenticeship at the feet of the Western European masters. Notwithstanding the jingoistic scholarship of the Stalin era, there is nothing demeaning in this fact. On the contrary, it is remarkable that within only a hundred years Russian writing was able to overcome so large a time lag.[26]

When Joseph Brodsky (1940–1996) started writing poetry in Leningrad in the late 1950s and early 1960s, he was operating in what appeared to be a culturally barren environment. Brodsky recalled, with the benefit of hindsight, the Russian literary scene of the 1950s: "We were beginning in an empty—indeed, a terrifyingly wasted—place, . . . intuitively rather than consciously, we aspired . . . to the re-creation of the effect of culture's continuity."[27] Brodsky, described by one critic as "the most outstanding individual among an exceptionally talented generation born in Russia between 1935 and 1941, [who] came to consciousness just in time for de-Stalinization,"[28] became the successor to the prerevolutionary cosmopolitan tradition of Russian poetry. Overcoming Russia's cultural isolation became the main quest for him as well as for other like-minded poets of his generation. After Brodsky's death, the Polish poet Czesław Miłosz, a friend and a fellow Nobel laureate, described Brodsky as "a builder of bridges to the past—to the great periods of Russian poetry in the nineteenth and early twentieth centuries."[29]

Brodsky's translations from English into Russian, and later in the reverse direction, were part of his quest of bridge-building to Russia's European past, and of rescuing it from Soviet provincialism. Yet this important vector of Brodsky's oeuvre has been largely omitted from the debates on the contested topic of his English translations. The aim of this book is to show that Brodsky's mission of continuing a cherished literary tradition played an important part in his active involvement in English translations of his poetry. Like every poet before him, Brodsky was well aware of poetry's untranslatability. Still, it was poetry's capacity to open a conversation between poets that transcends time, space, and cultural differences that mattered most to him. This accounts for many of his unorthodox translation decisions, which are the topic of this book.

THE ORIGINS OF THE ENGLISH-LANGUAGE BRODSKY

This is how the story begins. Or this is how the beginning is usually told. On June 4, 1972, Joseph Brodsky was exiled from the Soviet Union. The exile was a deliberate attempt to end his career as a poet. Instead, he settled in the United States, where translations of his Russian poems into English became critical to his success in his new home and abroad. Many English-language poets and translators offered their hand, but Brodsky was a demanding author and very particular about how his work was translated. He insisted that not only the meaning but also the form of his Russian poems should be preserved at all costs, especially the rhyme and meter. Some found such demands unreasonable. By the 1970s in America, very few would still be willing to preserve the rhyme and meter of a translated poem, and few even possessed the skill to do so. American poetics had by then largely switched to free verse as the medium of translation. But Brodsky would have none of this. He was uniquely well versed in English-language poetry, having translated English and American poetry into Russian and having memorized hundreds of their lines "in a previous incarnation."[30] His private pantheon of English-language poets was well structured and featured mostly, although not exclusively, poets who were masters of their craft: John Donne, Thomas Hardy, Robert Frost, W. H. Auden, and Richard Wilbur, and also T. S. Eliot, W. B. Yeats, and Robert Lowell. While many critics argued that there existed unbreachable differences between Russian and English poetics, Brodsky was confident that translations could be made to reflect his own originals more accurately. During his first few years in America, Brodsky's English made miraculous strides, emboldening him to want an even greater say in the translations of his poems. He began "fixing" translations done by native English speakers to bring them closer to the Russian. He introduced what he believed were better—that is, more sophisticated, complex, and semantically relevant—rhymes; and he would "straighten" the meter. It seemingly did not bother Brodsky that, as a result of his interventions, his English translations often lost much of "their smoothness," becoming less idiomatically correct in English.[31] Some of his translators rebelled against such practices, insisting on their authorial rights and interpretations of the English versions.

Gradually, Brodsky became a self-translator, while also composing more original poems in English. This, some have argued, ought never to have happened. Brodsky's English self-translations have been heavily criticized as inadequate, unidiomatic failures. Many have argued that it was impossible for a poet to breach the linguistic gap, and that native speakers ought to have remained in charge of "Englishing" his poems. This is the predominant view in the United States and Britain today, especially among academics. There were a few contemporaries who defended Brodsky's authorial right to interfere in the English translations of his own poems. These included such eminent American poets as Anthony Hecht and Mark Strand, as well as fellow Nobel laureates Derek Walcott and Seamus Heaney, although none of them would ever claim that Brodsky's translations were entirely unproblematic.

For decades, scholarship on Brodsky's English translations has remained at an impasse between those who resent Brodsky's English experiments and those few who defend them.[32] Some have attempted to explain, even to justify, the imperfections of the translations by emphasizing the perfection of the originals, against which any other version would inevitably pale in comparison. Others have suggested that Brodsky's English translations were aimed at bilingual readers as an auxiliary commentary.[33] This theory cannot hold, because it does not take into account the level of Brodsky's own investment in translating his poetry into English. It is highly unlikely that he would have spent such time and effort, acting against the judgment of numerous native speakers of English, just to target a handful of bilingual readers. Moreover, Brodsky never really endorsed the idea of a poet commenting on the "meaning" of his poems. In short, his translations were first and foremost aimed at speakers of English.

One unanswered question of great importance remains: What drove Brodsky to become so involved in English translation in the first place? Did he harbor an ambition to become an English-language poet? What was he trying to prove by engaging in what many saw as an impossible task?

"A poet must be judged by his intention,"[34] wrote W. H. Auden in a dedicatory poem to Lord Byron, defending his Romantic precursor from the harsh criticism of posterity. This principle should also apply to Brodsky.[35] The trouble is that there has been little consensus as to what Brodsky's intentions were regarding his Russian-English translations. It does not help that the poet himself muddied the waters. Brodsky's demands for greater accuracy from his English translators does not quite account for the fact that he eventually took the translation of his poems entirely into his own hands. Moreover, Brodsky continually denied any ambition of becoming a poet of the English language in his own right. So what prompted him to compose more and more poems each year in English?[36]

Brodsky was convinced that the real biography of a writer lies in the particular way he deals with words, rather than in the trivial facts of his life. In his autobiographical essay "Less Than One," Brodsky wrote: "A writer's biography is in his twists of language."[37] I would argue, however, that this formula cuts both ways, as some of his "twists of language" can be understood only in a biographical context. This is particularly true of the phenomenon of Brodsky as an English-language poet and is also inextricable from his Russian context. To understand Brodsky's intentions vis-à-vis his translations, it is important to first establish the nature of his relationship with the English language and what made it so unique. One archival find, a draft of an unfinished autobiographical essay from the Brodsky Papers at Yale University, located and titled "Learning English" by the archivist Lisa Conathan, sheds new light on the issue. In "Learning English," Brodsky himself attempted to put a finger on his love affair with English. It is telling that the essay remained unfinished.

"LEARNING ENGLISH": A JEWISH BOY WHO COULD NOT LEARN ENGLISH FROM A JEWISH WOMAN

> PROSPERO:
> . . . when thou didst not, savage,
> Know thine own meaning, but wouldst gabble like
> A thing most brutish, I endow'd thy purposes
> With words that made them known.
> (Shakespeare, *The Tempest*)

> Dear savages, though I've never mastered your tongue, free
> of pronouns and gerunds,
> I've learned to bake mackerel wrapped in palm leaves and
> favor raw turtle legs, with their flavor of slowness.[38]
> (Joseph Brodsky, "Infinitive")

> Choosing a foreign language as a medium of poetic expression may carry certain risks, but it also offers creative opportunities. If we assume that language shapes thinking, expanding one's linguistic repertoire entails a widening of potential poetic creativity. Writing poetry "with an accent," so to speak, can open new expressive pathways that are closed to a monolingual speaker trapped in the conventions of the native idiom. Furthermore, one could argue that the "de-automatized," slowed-down approach necessitated by a less familiar linguistic medium corresponds to a mode of reading ideally suited for poetry.[39]
> (Adrian Wanner, *The Bilingual Muse*)

Brodsky's love affair with English began in Leningrad, as he shows in "Learning English."[40] Although his love of English permeates every sentence, paradoxically, the autobiographical essay begins by mentioning the opposite sentiment: "At the age of ten I regarded this language as an unnecessary evil. So much that I was almost left for a second year in the fourth grade: on account of my poor showing in English and botany."[41] It seems hard to grasp that America's future poet laureate initially performed so poorly in English. During Stalin's rule, foreign language acquisition was not a priority of the Soviet schooling system, as Brodsky himself attested:

> Our textbooks were stuffed with the standard propaganda garbage translated into English . . . A biography of Stalin, a memoir of some party faithful meeting, Lenin in his Finnish hideout . . . there was not a single English ditty or nursery rhyme that could at least animate you to the sound of this language, because a child delights in jingle even when it's incomprehensible.[42]

Apart from the ideological indoctrination in the textbooks, Brodsky's aversion to English was apparently also colored by a fear of his first English teacher, Sophia Isaakovna: "I was petrified by her from the threshold."[43]

In "Less Than One," he alluded to his troubled relationship with authority figures within the Soviet setting—his teachers, his neighbors in the communal apartment, his supervisors during his stint at a factory, his prison guards during several imprisonments. Brodsky observed: "Your enemy in prison isn't an abstraction; he is concrete and palpable. . . . Perhaps 'enemy' is too strong a word. . . . After all, my guards or neighbors were not any different from my teachers or those workers who humiliated me during my apprenticeship at the factory."[44] Brodsky argues that repression in a totalitarian setting was channeled through everyday interactions with people vested with even minimal authority over you. In the case of his English teacher, the situation was even more psychologically complicated. On the one hand, she was an authority figure for the young Brodsky; on the other, like him she was Jewish. In the years from 1948 to 1953, the Soviet Union went through several waves of state-sponsored antisemitic campaigns, as Brodsky reminded us in "In a Room and a Half":

> The fifties were bad years for the Jews. The campaign against the "rootless cosmopolites" was in full swing; then, in 1953, came the "Doctors' Case,"[45] which didn't end in the usual bloodbath only because its instigator, Comrade Stalin himself, all of a sudden, at the case's nadir, kicked the bucket. But long before, and for some time after, the air was full of rumors of the Politburo's planned reprisals against the Jews, of relocating all those "paragraph five" creatures to Eastern Siberia, to the area called Birobidzhan, near the Chinese border.[46]

Irena Grudzinska Gross has argued that one of Brodsky's first childhood memories was a moment of awakening, when he became aware of his Jewishness in the atmosphere of institutionalized antisemitism.[47] Grudzinska Gross discusses in detail the following passage from Brodsky's "Less Than One":

> The real history of consciousness starts with one's first lie. I happen to remember mine. It was in a school library when I had to fill out an application for membership. The fifth blank was, of course, "nationality." I was seven years old and knew very well that I was a Jew, but I told the attendant that I didn't know. . . . I wasn't ashamed of being a Jew, nor was I scared of admitting it. . . . I was ashamed of the word "Jew" itself—in Russian "yevrei"—regardless of its connotations.[48]

All these different pieces of the puzzle help us understand Brodsky's apprehension surrounding his Jewish identity and shed light on the contradictory conclusion to the portrait he presents in "Learning English" of his first English teacher:

> She was all bones and knuckles and knees: with shoulder-long dark hair, usually undone, and very pronounced Semitic features. . . . I was particularly mesmerised by her razor-sharp ankles, unaware as yet, at the age of 12, of this aspect's significance. I wanted to touch them with my fingers, the way one tries a blade; but that dream was about as outlandish as the prospect of my mastery of irregular verbs or the definite article. The latter still confound [*sic*] me now and then . . . *A Jewish boy learning English from a Jewish woman: in my case it was a losing proposition* [italics mine].[49]

The account is suffused with irony. Yet his irony paves the way for serious consideration. Brodsky unexpectedly draws a connection between the caricatured Jewish-Russian accent of his teacher and the "accent" of his self-translations:

> All I've got out of Sophia Isaakovna was the notion of "the iron order of words" pertaining in my mind not so much to the English syntax as to her demeanour and complete aversion for anything beginning with "th," including the definite article, which she pronounced like "tse." Years later, though, this served me in a good stead when I found myself rhyming the English definite article with "tsetse," an African fly transmitting sleeping disease.[50]

I find the two above passages quite remarkable. The mature Brodsky, whom critics habitually accused of being "un-English," beats them to the punch by casually acknowledging his Russian accent in English. In a disarming way, he also admits to the residual struggles with English grammar that persisted into his later years. His strongest argument is the intensity of his love affair with his adopted language. It redeems the grammatical deficiencies insofar as the poet can turn them into new poetic possibilities—new rhymes. While translating his poem "Sextet"[51] from the Russian, Brodsky rhymed the name of an African fly with his pronunciation of the definite English article, "the":

> A tear falls in a vacuum without acceleration.
> The last of hotbed neu-roses, hearing the
> faint buzzing of time's tsetse,
> I smell increasingly of isolation.[52]

This is a reminder that Brodsky's accent had always haunted him, from his native tongue into his adopted language. He famously referenced his "broken Jewish r" in several of his poems.[53] The memory of his Jewish accent in Russian may have allowed Brodsky to accept his Russian accent in English, as a continuity between his former life in Russia and his English-language incarnation. One thing is certain: the mature Brodsky is clearly proud of having come up with this unique rhyme in English. He saw it as evidence that being creative in one's second language was not a privilege enjoyed solely by a handful of prose writers like Nabokov and Conrad—a poet could achieve it too.[54] Yet as Coetzee pointed out, "when a bon mot is on the horizon, Brodsky can be trusted to scamper after it . . . not unlike Nabokov."[55] A pun on the word "neurosis"—"neu-roses"—from the above poem, is a characteristic example.

Allegedly, Brodsky's fascination with English did not begin during his English classes but was triggered in a Russian literature class:

> The aura of strangeness a foreign name produces is a vehicle for imagination, and many a quest for an alien culture started out of this purely euphonic origin. . . . For me in the fifth grade the English job was done by the spondees of Lord George Gordon Byron mentioned in my Russian Literature class in connection with Pushkin and Romanticism. Like a majordomo announcing a very important guest, our Nadezhda Konstantinovna would take her sweet time over uttering every syllable of this manly, proud, sounding like three consecutive assertions name of the English bard—starting obviously with his title. In her mouth, the last two consonants of "lord" would roar majestically and resolute, making his influence on Pushkin acoustically unquestionable.[56]

Tellingly, Brodsky traced his infatuation with English back to the history of Byron's influence on Pushkin. In his unreserved and personal fascination with English-language poetry, Brodsky claimed his place as a standard bearer in the Pushkinian tradition. Writing in English allowed Brodsky to sidestep the Soviet experience. In the same essay, he calls literature "a mental abroad" that allowed him to travel in his imagination to "the illegal hemisphere"[57] long before he could do so in reality.

One can imagine that the meaning of English sounds to this Russian poet, who found himself on the wrong side of the Iron Curtain, was amplified by the almost cosmic unattainability of the illegal hemisphere to which they belonged. Hence the intensity with which he tried to endow those foreign sounds with metaphysical significance:

> I should take pity on you, the audience, since for all your colonial past, you can't have any idea as to the impact of English monosyllabics upon a psyche formed by a polysyllabic language. You can never total what a Russian or, for example, an Italian experiences at hearing something like "John Keats," "John Donne," "King James," "Robert Frost," or for that matter "Andrew Marvell," "Thomas Hardy," "Wystan Hugh Auden," "W. B. Yeats," "Thomas Stearns Eliot." For an Easterner or a Southerner there is a terrific finality to these names, abruptness, a sense of arrested destiny. They sound positively Northern, and he associates with them all those virtues of the North: the proximity to an absolute, resolve, reserve, the spirit of responsibility, grey eye.[58]

Incidentally, in his essays dedicated to Auden and Spender, Brodsky endowed the speech of his favorite British poets with similar metaphysical and moral qualities. Speaking of Auden, Brodsky mentioned "his autonomy, sanity, equipoise, irony, detachment,"[59] while Spender's speech possessed all the "nobility, civility, grace and detachment" the English language had to offer.[60] As his friend and translator Alan Myers attested, Brodsky loved the sound of well-spoken British, preferring it to the American accent, and even used to try to get people to agree that he had a British accent.[61]

Indeed, one of the chief peculiarities of the unfinished "Learning English" essay, which he must have begun in the late 1980s,[62] is that it seems to cater to a British audience. Brodsky alludes to the British colonial past of his readers, and he compares his own way of reminiscing about his Soviet schoolteachers to how the British do it: "it is very British, isn't it, to adore or malign one's tutors. So here they are, for the momentary posterity in the air they never breathed."[63] He also lists his favorite English-language poets, most of whom are British. It is not immediately clear why an American essayist reminiscing about his Russian childhood should do this. Given the extent of vitriol from Britain that was later directed at Brodsky's brand of English, it is ironic that he catered so passionately to their linguistic snobbery, nativist smugness, and proprietary feelings about their language. Indeed, his British critics accused Brodsky of such vices as "grammatical unorthodoxy, tone deafness," a lack of understanding of English idiom,[64] and "foreign ineptitude."[65] They also taunted him for being "unable to achieve more than a basic competence in his adopted language,"[66] and maliciously derided him for his alleged inability to overcome his "crippling disadvantage"—the need to resort to English because of his exilic predicament.[67] For all these alleged crimes, his British critics called Brodsky "his [own] worst translator"[68] and the "Great American Disaster,"[69] while referring to his lines as "saturated"[70] and to his American reputation as "inflated."[71]

Brodsky's chief line of defense against this vitriol was his lasting love affair with the English language and its poetry. Seamus Heaney, an Irish poet and friend of Brodsky, spoke of "his manifest love for English verse, which amounts almost to a possessiveness."[72] Incidentally, this possessive love was also Brodsky's main argument as to why his case was different from Nabokov's, to whom, to Brodsky's chagrin, he was continually compared:

> The comparison [with Nabokov] is not particularly felicitous, because English was practically Nabokov's mother tongue—he spoke it since he was a child; whereas for me—*English is my personal position*. I really enjoy writing in English and the sense of discrepancy gives me extra pleasure: because I was not supposed to speak this language by birth. On the contrary—I was born not to be able to speak it. I also believe I started writing in English for a different reason from Nabokov—simply out of *sheer excitement about this language* [italics mine].[73]

By claiming that English was his "personal position" or his "personal stance," Brodsky contested the idea that English translations became important for him only following his exile and settling in America. Instead, he insisted that writing in English was a deliberate choice, a contradiction of anti-Western Soviet jingoism. That Brodsky was not, by birth, meant to speak English turned it into a forbidden fruit for him. From the time he started learning it as an autodidact in Leningrad, until well into his American incarnation, his use of English was always tinged with an element of rebellion against Soviet monolingual determinism. Most critics of Brodsky's English have so far failed to appreciate this element of resistance. Brodsky's determination to explore anglophone territories has often been interpreted as a sign of willfulness, stubbornness, and excessive self-confidence. Instead, I interpret his hunger for foreign languages and his dogged efforts to master English as a desire to rectify the effects of "cultural disinheritance,"[74] a term coined by Bożena Shallcross in the introduction to her book *Through the Poet's Eye: The Travels of Zagajewski, Herbert, and Brodsky*. Shallcross argues the similarity in the situations of these three poets from the Communist Bloc with regard to the repositories of the Western cultural patrimony. The more alienated they had been from the art and cultural currents of the West, the more intense their encounter with it eventually became.[75]

In fact, Brodsky's acquisition of English had to happen outside a school setting, for he left school at the age of fifteen. This marked the end of his formal education. Dropping out of school at fifteen in post-Stalinist Russia was an almost unheard-of expression of independence, which Brodsky later described as his first "free act."[76] It proved to be an important step toward his intellectual freedom in a totalitarian society, for, as he argued, the ten years one spent at school, plus four in the army, would have resulted in a total loss of willpower for the average Soviet citizen.[77] Miłosz emphasized the great value of Brodsky's self-education, which allowed him and his like-minded counterparts to free themselves from the mental patterns promoted by the Soviet state:

> The surprising autonomy of Brodsky as a poet and thinker finds its explanation not only in his personal gifts of mind and heart. His essays written in English testify to a rare erudition and, indirectly, prove that in his youth he succeeded in educating himself better than in any school. The young Leningrad poets in his group were voracious readers, explorers of libraries and second-hand bookshops in their city. Their effort at self-education was sustained in spite of unfavorable circumstances—or perhaps those circumstances were favorable because they allowed them to live in complete detachment from the way of thinking promoted by the state.[78]

From then on, Brodsky acquired knowledge as an autodidact. Characteristically, toward the end of "Learning English," he named four English-language poets as his subsequent teachers: "Frost, Eliot, Hardy and Auden."[79]

The purpose of this book is to reconstruct the history of the unlikely phenomenon of the anglophone Brodsky. To cover the almost cosmic distance between the "Jewish boy" who could not learn English in a Stalinist classroom and the American poet laureate, self-translator, and essayist, this book uses autobiographical writings, letters, translation drafts, and other archival materials, as well as interviews seen through the prism of translation theory, to supply what has so far been missing in the criticism of Brodsky's English oeuvre. A synthesis of biographical, textual, and theoretical approaches should enable us to, at last, account for Brodsky's "twists of language"—in Russian and English.

The major analyses in this book focus on the process of preparing the translations for the English edition of *A Part of Speech* (1980). That collection was crucial, both in establishing Brodsky's reputation in English and in his emergence as a self-translator. It is the archival materials from the years between 1975 and 1980 that allow us to enter the "workshop" of the poet with his English-language translators and to trace the evolution of these translations from their initial versions to the final texts with which Brodsky could be satisfied. These materials—correspondence with co-translators, translation drafts, Brodsky's corrections and commentaries—reveal his general translation approach as well as the logic behind his specific decisions.

OVERVIEW

Chapter 1 places Brodsky in the historical context of a generation that led the revival of Russian poetry after Stalin. English poetic influence helped him liberate his literary idiom from years of ideological abuse and break the spell of Soviet self-isolation. Nevertheless, his interest in foreign literature, his artistic independence, and his contempt for politics brought the Soviet state's wrath down upon him.

Chapter 2 probes Brodsky's own myth about his "happy time" during his internal exile in far northern Russia, and suggests instead that his discovery of Donne, Frost, and Auden helped him "obliterate the local reality," which was rather bleak. The chapter also demonstrates that "the English destiny of his verse" had already begun to matter to Brodsky back in Leningrad.

Chapter 3 addresses the linguistic challenges of exile and unearths a fascinating psychological nuance, which has not been considered by previous scholars. Namely, in order to survive his transplantation, Brodsky developed a stratagem: America became merely a continuation of space, and English a continuation of Russian by other means.

Chapter 4 analyzes the respective translations by George Kline and Brodsky of "A Second Christmas by the Shore," exploring the discrepancies between Brodsky's demands for metrical faithfulness in translation and his own practice, which in fact followed the rhythm rather than the meter of the original. Zhirmunsky's definitions of rhythm and meter offer conceptual support in understanding the novelty but also the foreignness—of the English verse that resulted from Brodsky's self-translation.

Chapter 5 examines Brodsky's philosophy of translation. While his critics emphasized the contrasts between English and Russian grammar, as well as poetic habits, Brodsky insisted on the existence of common compositional principles that must apply to poetry in both languages. The chapter suggests an important political dimension to Brodsky's opposition to free verse as a means of translating formal Russian poetry.

Chapter 6 opens with a discussion of a major dispute between Brodsky and Daniel Weissbort, which arose in part from their diametrically opposed translation methods. The second part is devoted to a single untitled poem, "The North buckles metal," initially translated by Weissbort and subsequently revised by Brodsky. The chapter discusses the multiple layers of meaning present in the poem and shows how the translation maintains these in the English through strong rhyme assonance and alliteration. The chapter concludes that the disputes between Weissbort and Brodsky were not due merely to idiosyncratic differences but can be contextualized within a longer tradition of contrasting modes of translating poetic form.

Chapter 7 begins with a discussion of Richard Wilbur's translation of Brodsky's "Six Years Later" and then moves to Brodsky's "collaboration" with Robert Lowell on the translation of his Dantesque poem "December in Florence." Brodsky's corrections and reworkings of translations by such poetic masters in English as Wilbur and Lowell revealed his own ambition to take an active part in the process of re-creating his oeuvre in English.

Chapter 8 continues the discussion of "December in Florence," showing that in his self-translation, Brodsky availed himself not only of Lowell's draft but of the drafts by Kline in tandem with Maurice English and of those by Alan Myers. By undertaking a meticulous comparative study of various translated versions, the chapter uncovers the logic behind Brodsky's decisions. While insisting on faithfulness in his translators, Brodsky himself enjoyed remarkable creative freedom in his self-translation.

Chapter 9 shows that the success of *A Part of Speech*, which Brodsky had actively helped shape, encouraged him to be more involved in self-translation in his subsequent collections, while in his poems written directly in English, Brodsky closely followed the prosodic models provided by the anglophone poetic mentors of his youth—Auden, Frost, and Donne, as well as Hardy and Yeats.

Chapter 10 addresses the backlash against Brodsky's unidiomatic practices in English and the somewhat hostile critical reactions that placed his reputation in limbo after his death.

The conclusion proposes that in order to feel truly at home in his adoptive country, Brodsky wanted to earn and shape his reputation himself in the new linguistic milieu. Self-translation gave him a unique opportunity to engage creatively with the English language and eventually helped him to emerge as an English-language poet in his own right, albeit a poet with a Russian accent.

Chapter One

The Leningrad Literary Scene of the 1950s and 1960s

SINCE THE POET'S DEATH in 1996, the focus of Brodsky scholarship has shifted from his individual talent to his place in the postwar generation of Russian writers.[1] In his Nobel lecture, Brodsky refers to his generation as the one "born precisely at the time when the Auschwitz crematoria were working full blast, when Stalin was at the zenith of his God-like, absolute power."[2] He goes on to describe, as mentioned in the introduction, Russia's literary and artistic scene emerging in the aftermath of these catastrophes as "an empty—indeed, a terrifyingly wasted—place."[3] Scholarship of the past decades has corroborated Brodsky's account.

For instance, Herman Ermolaev's groundbreaking study of censorship in Soviet literature showed that "between the years 1917 and 1931 . . . a huge censorship machine was built" in the country, whose operation remained practically intact until the early 1990s.[4] While it is sometimes argued that Soviet censorship was a continuation of similar governmental controls in pre-revolutionary Russia,[5] Isaiah Berlin, a British philosopher of Russian-Jewish descent, clarified that, in reality, there was a difference in kind between these two types of censorship: "The censor [in tsarist Russia] was the official enemy, but unlike his modern [Soviet] successor, he was almost wholly negative. Tsarist censorship imposed silence but it did not directly tell professors what to teach; it did not dictate to authors what to say and how to say it."[6] An eminent scholar of Russian literature, Sidney Monas, likewise advised against confusing the two types of censorship:

> In spite of the complex and arbitrary censorship apparatus, dominated by fear of the Third Section, Russian literature grew during the reign of Nicholas into its golden age. . . . We are too apt to confuse the petty encumbrances of traditional societies with the withering blight of the modern totalitarian state.[7]

This Soviet type of pervasive censorship had far-reaching consequences for Russian literature.[8] As Simon Karlinsky succinctly put it, by the early 1930s, censorship had made it possible for the Soviet Union to impose "a governmental ban on all creativity and imagination."[9] The suppression worsened exponentially in the late 1930s. At the close of the Second World War, Berlin visited Leningrad and Moscow as an official of Britain's Foreign Office, meeting privately with Anna Akhmatova and Boris Pasternak, the only two major poets among the survivors of the terror.[10] Upon his return, he gave the first Western account of what he called "Stalin's war against Russian culture":[11]

> The great purges and trial of the years of 1937 and 1938 altered the literary and artistic scene beyond all recognition. The number of writers and artists exiled or exterminated during this time—particularly during the Ezhov terror—was such that Russian literature and thought emerged in 1939 like an area devastated by war, with some splendid buildings still relatively intact, but standing solitary amid stretches of ruined and deserted country.[12]

Soon after Berlin's departure, the Soviet government unleashed yet another devastating campaign against Russian culture.[13] This time, none other than Akhmatova, whom Berlin had just met in Leningrad, was one of its main targets, as his biographer reminds us: "On 4 September 1946 she was expelled from the Writer's Union, and her book of poems—the one she had promised to send Isaiah—was pulped. Once again, she had been consigned to darkness . . . with the re-arrest of Lev in 1949, once again for the crime of being her son, Akhmatova's desolation was complete."[14] The period inaugurated by this campaign, condemning so-called apolitical literature, lasted until after the death of Stalin in 1953.[15] Dubbed the Zhdanov era (Zhdanovshchina), after the Leningrad party boss and Stalin's culture czar, Andrei Zhdanov, its hallmarks were a new upsurge in xenophobia, anti-Western jingoism, and state-sponsored antisemitic campaigns.[16] Stalin also waged wars against Ukrainian, Georgian, and other cultures of the Soviet Union and the so-called Soviet bloc.[17] Berlin emphasized that during the purges, "those to fare worst were the writers and authors in closest contact with Western Europe, that is, France and England, since the turning of Soviet foreign policy . . . toward isolationism symbolized by the Russo-German Pact."[18] Gerald Smith summarized the time between 1946 and 1953 as "the most barren in the entire history of modern Russian literature,"[19] which further supports Brodsky's description.

THE THAW: A SHORT-LIVED PROMISE

The death of Stalin in 1953 was followed by what became known as "Khrushchev's Thaw"—the period of de-Stalinization and relative liberalization of the country, which initially gave many reasons for optimism.[20] Even pessimistic survivors of the Stalinist terror such as Nadezhda Mandelstam, the widow of the poet Osip Mandelstam, remained hopeful for a while.[21] Khrushchev's "secret speech" at the Party Congress in February 1956 partially denounced the regime's past crimes. Crucially, however, the crimes were never called crimes but were euphemistically referred to as "Stalin's cult of personality."[22] As a result, the liberalization was only marginal and inconsistent, and Khrushchev's cultural policy was at best a seesaw: every single step toward liberalization was followed by a step toward re-Stalinization.[23] Thus, the year 1956 witnessed a major sense of disillusionment among the young generation, who no longer remained under the spell of the old ideological incantations.[24] In his foreword to *Winter Dialogue*, a collection of poems by Tomas Venclova (b. 1937)—a fellow poet, contemporary, and friend—Brodsky recalled how their high hopes were definitively shattered with the suppression of the Hungarian Revolution in November 1956:

> The year was 1956, when hopes rose with the Hungarian revolution only to die under the treads of Soviet tanks, which literally crushed the rebellion. For Tomas Venclova's generation (and mine)—the generation of 1956—the fate of the Hungarian rebellion came to signify what the Decembrists' defeat did for Pushkin's contemporaries or what the fall of the Spanish Republic meant for W. H. Auden and his peers in the 1930s. It . . . shaped that generation's worldview . . . our generation was forever lost to the socialist idea.[25]

It is quite uncanny how Brodsky compared his own generation with two vastly different literary movements—the poets of Pushkin's Pleiade and the 1930s generation of Auden's circle of English poets. The poetic genealogy Brodsky constructed for himself while in America was deliberately Russo-English.

In his last English essay, "In Memory of Stephen Spender" (1995), Brodsky recalled how, as a young Leningrad poet, he identified with and craved belonging to the company of the British Thirties poets—Auden, Spender, MacNeice, and Day-Lewis:

> If you are born in Russia, nostalgia for an alternative genesis is inevitable. The thirties were close enough, as I was born in 1940. . . . MacNeice, Auden, and Spender—I mention them in the order I found them—made me feel at home at once. It wasn't their moral vision, since my enemy, I believe, was more formidable and ubiquitous than theirs; it was their poetics.[26]

This craving for an alternative genesis falls under the category of cultural disinheritance, which Brodsky shared with his Eastern European counterparts.

Brodsky's intuitive identification with the poets of the so-called Auden group[27] might have been based, however, on affinities running deeper than a desire for the "alternative genesis" he mentions. For instance, Spender ascribed the rapid literary success of his generation to the fact that many talented writers of the preceding one had been killed in the First World War: "I think there was a kind of gap, because many of those who should have been writing had unfortunately been killed in the war."[28] Thus, both Auden's and Brodsky's generations of poets started, as it were, with a clean slate. This psychological affinity might explain why both Auden and Brodsky attempted to revive the poetic tropes and forms of their predecessors rather than accept the further formal disintegration championed by the modernist movement.[29] Indeed, Brodsky felt that their beginning in a "terrifyingly empty place" endowed his generation with a sense of mission: "to continue what . . . was supposed to be interrupted . . . in the anonymous common graves of Stalin's archipelago."[30] No wonder that the restoration of the classicist tradition of Russian poetry became Brodsky's main poetic credo.[31] Later, when it came to the translation of Russian poetry into English, this quest for the restoration of tradition took peculiar forms: Brodsky was adamant, for instance, that it was a sacrilege to translate Akhmatova's and Mandelstam's poetry into free verse, and insisted that the original form of their Russian poems be preserved across translation.[32]

A POETIC REVIVAL THROUGH SAMIZDAT AND POLAND, THE WINDOW TO EUROPE

Notwithstanding the inconsistencies of Khrushchev's Thaw, the return of millions of inmates from Stalin's camps provoked a palpable change in the air.[33] The young started questioning the dogmas of their forefathers and showing hunger for real, not Party-controlled, poetry.[34] Despite all the efforts of the powers that be to bridle the authentic energy of the poets and to make literature subservient to ideology, the traditional importance of poetry in Russia persisted.[35] Thus, during the Second World War, soldiers going to the front had sought out "purely personal lyrical verse by Pasternak . . . [and] Akhmatova among the living, and Blok, Bely and even Bryusov, Sologub, Tsvetaeva and Mayakovsky among the (post-Revolutionary) dead."[36] Then, a decade after the end of the war, an authentic revival of interest in poetry occurred. This revival came as a complete surprise to those who, like Nadezhda Mandelstam, had lived through the decades of terror and deemed the destruction of Russian culture a fait accompli. The emergence of samizdat became crucial to that miraculous revival:[37]

> We have seen the new readers come into being before our very eyes . . . against all odds. The whole educational system was geared to preventing

> the appearance of such readers. The names of some poets were simply suppressed altogether, while others were denounced in the press and in the Party decrees, and it had begun to seem unthinkable that any of them could ever survive such massive efforts to obliterate their memory. Then, quite suddenly, everything changed, and we had samizdat. Who started it, nobody knows . . . the fact is, however, that it not only exists but also caters to its readers' actual wants.[38]

Indeed, as the two former Soviet dissidents Lyudmila Alexeyeva and Vera Lashkova recalled, the very first samizdat publications featured poetry, not politics.[39] Another channel that provided young people with access to unofficial poetry was poetry workshops, which started emerging in the mid-1950s at schools and universities.[40] Having dropped out of school, Brodsky did not attend any of them, but he later befriended several Leningrad poets who did.[41] In the first years of his adult life Brodsky changed workplaces a dozen times, working at a factory, in a morgue, and later joining geological expeditions all over the Soviet Union.[42] It was during those expeditions that he started writing poetry.[43] Very soon his poems began to be circulated in samizdat, appearing in 1959–60 in the poetry journal *Sintaksis*, edited by Alexander Ginzburg.[44] Thus, Tomas Venclova remembers:

> Alexander Ginzburg was one of the earliest Russian dissidents. His *Sintaksis* was probably the first uncensored publishing venture in the USSR since the time of the Bolshevik Revolution. Every issue consisted of fifty poems (ten authors, each represented by five texts) and nothing else . . . The poems were . . . not anti-Soviet, although . . . they would not have made it past the censor for various reasons: radical formal experiments, individualist or anguished moods, erotic content, social criticism, and so on . . . Brodsky made his debut there (he never failed to mention that Ginzburg was his very first publisher).[45]

An entire *Sintaksis* publication run amounted to only 100 copies,[46] but those who received a copy often produced further typewritten copies of their own.[47] Ginzburg, Brodsky's first unofficial publisher, was soon arrested and sentenced to two years, "the first of several such sentences in Ginzburg's life,"[48] as Venclova bitterly observed. Brodsky was summoned, interrogated, and threatened by the KGB in connection with this case but was ultimately released without charge.[49] This was the first time that he came onto the radar of the state police and was blacklisted. A dossier was opened on him, paving the way to his arrests, a political trial, and his own lengthy sentence.

Like other poets, Brodsky often projected his own circumstances onto the biographies of his poetic precursors. Thus, in a biographical note on Pushkin, written for an anglophone audience, Brodsky observed: "The popularity of his poetry grew as rapidly as his output; so did the attention paid him by the police."[50] One can see how this might have reflected Brodsky's own situation as a young poet whose increasing popularity in Leningrad had begun to attract the attention of the authorities. Venclova attributed his popularity largely to his way of performing poetry in front of an audience:

> Some people have defined it [his recitation] as "shamanistic" or compared it to synagogal chant. I believe both descriptions are inaccurate. . . . Joseph was fully in command, which is atypical for a shaman, and he avoided a singing quality: his voice was very loud, rhythmic, and monotonous, but the emphasis was on the words, not on the sound or melody. Stanza breaks, as well as enjambments, were clearly marked by a sudden change of tone. Although the poems were long, he knew everything by heart. . . . A large part of Joseph's popularity was due to his immense gift as a reader.[51]

Viktor Golyshev, another longtime friend from Moscow and translator of English prose, emphasized that, back in the day, Brodsky's popularity was strictly underground: "It's a strange kind of fame, when you don't get published and instead you go from house to house loudly reciting poetry."[52] Indeed, as Anatoly Naiman, a fellow poet from the same Leningrad circle, remembered: "One could not get anything published that would not have a thin coating of poisonous officialdom."[53]

For Brodsky and like-minded poets of his generation whose goal was to overcome the Soviet Union's cultural isolation, Poland became a window to Europe.[54] After 1956, censorship restrictions in Poland became significantly less rigid than in Russia,[55] which prompted Brodsky to call Poland "the most cheerful barrack" in the Communist prison camp:

> There was a practical side to my interest in Polish as well. In those days the bulk of Western literature, and of news about cultural events in the West, was not available in the Soviet Union, whereas Poland was even at that point the happiest and the most cheerful barrack in the entire camp.[56] People there were much better informed and they were publishing all sorts of magazines and everything was translated into Polish; the publishing house Czytelnik was printing God knows what. I remember I was reading Malcolm Lowry, some of Proust, some of Faulkner, and also Joyce I first read in Polish. So that was the practical consideration: We needed a window onto Europe, and the Polish language provided it.[57]

To gain access to the world, Brodsky and his colleagues taught themselves Polish. He later claimed that 80 percent of the modern European literature he had read was in Polish.[58] He showed great interest in all things Polish and soon began translating Polish poets. During his show trial in 1964, he described his main occupation to Judge Savelieva as a translator of Polish poetry, which had, however, little effect as the judge delivered her guilty verdict.[59]

"DRINKING VODKA WITH GENIUSES": AKHMATOVA PASSES ON THE BATON

Another way for artists to "shed the skin" of Stalinism,[60] to use Aleksander Wat's metaphor discussed below, was to "drink vodka with geniuses." This latter term, referring to the practice of searching out and frequently socializing with the surviving poets of the prerevolutionary generation, was disparagingly coined by the poet Iunna Morits, who "boasted of refusing to take part in it."[61] Two of the most prominent literary survivors in the post-Stalinist era who engaged in this intergenerational socializing were Boris Pasternak (1890–1960) and Anna Akhmatova (1889–1966).[62] Brodsky's encounter with Akhmatova, whom her admirers saw as the "torchbearer of the Great Russian Cultural Tradition,"[63] proved to be of crucial importance for the young poet.[64] Brodsky later acknowledged that Akhmatova provided him with a living link to the classical St. Petersburg tradition of Russian poetry, which had started with the poet Antioch Kantemir in the eighteenth century and ended with Akhmatova in the twentieth.[65] In the 1960s, Brodsky was known as one of "Akhmatova's boys," a group of young poets that included Anatoly Naiman, Evgeny Rein, and Dmitry Bobyshev.[66] After her death, the circle was called "Akhmatova's orphans."[67] Akhmatova held a very high opinion of the entire circle but early on singled out Brodsky, the youngest of them, as the most talented of the group. Indeed, Brodsky's first line to ever appear in the Soviet official press was a line Akhmatova chose as an epigraph for her poem "The Last Rose," which was published in January 1963 in *Novy Mir*.[68] Venclova, who also "drank vodka with geniuses," having met both Pasternak and Akhmatova even before he first met Brodsky, wrote down Akhmatova's words on this group in his diary: "The poets of Brodsky's circle form a single school, just as we Acmeists did at one point. The level of technical proficiency is quite high. There are almost no bad verses."[69] Akhmatova was hopeful that "a kind of second Silver Age was under way."[70] Unlike Akhmatova, Nadezhda Mandelstam, her close friend and comrade in suffering, herself a bearer of the literary heritage of the Silver Age and of the legacy of her husband Osip Mandelstam, was initially less impressed by Brodsky's poetic talent. Nevertheless, Nadezhda Mandelstam sympathized with Akhmatova's efforts to pass the hereditary lineage of the St. Petersburg tradition of Russian poetry on to the young:[71]

> Of all the younger friends who made life easier to bear in her [Akhmatova's] last years, he [Brodsky] was the most serious, honest and selfless in his relations with her. I think Akhmatova overestimated him as a poet—she was terribly anxious that the thread of the tradition should not be broken.[72]

Akhmatova's singling out of Brodsky from the group has been seen as a symbolic passing of the poetic baton from one epoch to another—from an honored *maîtresse* to a younger poet.[73] This image fits neatly into the body of legends concerning similar symbolic moments in Russian literary history, such as when the young Pushkin was singled out by the aging poet Derzhavin.[74] Yet their encounter does not exactly compare with the episodes from the past. In the early 1960s, Akhmatova's status was not that of an honored luminary of Russian poetry, as was Derzhavin's at the end of his life. Instead, there was something ghostlike about her existence at that time,[75] when she emerged from the preceding decades of fear, loss, and unimaginable suffering.[76] If Akhmatova seemed like a ghost after all she had gone through, perhaps there was something Hamletian about their encounter. It marked the beginning of Brodsky's quest for memory, for the preservation of his ties with the past. Venclova stresses that Akhmatova had an almost religious attitude toward memory: "Memory was the axis of her philosophy. In her opinion, preservation of the world—if only of its details—in poetic lines made a human being virtually equal to God."[77] This quest to resurrect the lost tradition and remember the past may account for Brodsky's peculiar brand of modernism, sometimes described as "rebellious classicism."[78] Thus, in his foreword to Venclova's volume of poetry, quoted earlier, Brodsky endorsed the idea of the poet as an "archaist-innovator," explaining that the term was conceived "precisely in the sense intended by Juri Tynianov in the title of his remarkable book, which contained this phrase until an editor's pen exchanged the hyphen for a fatal 'and.'"[79] Brodsky specified that in poetry "only content can be innovative and that formal innovation can occur only within the limits of form. Rejection of form is a rejection of innovation."[80]

Brodsky often repeated that Akhmatova had a greater influence on his outlook than on his poetics. Venclova observed: "Brodsky assimilated Akhmatova's disillusioned, stoic and scornful attitude toward the totalitarian Empire."[81] Akhmatova provided an example of a "code of conscience"[82]—to quote a line from Brodsky's favorite Auden poem—that was very different from that of the average *homo sovieticus*. Here is Venclova again:

> As Joseph himself confessed, Akhmatova influenced him more by her moral and civic stance than by her poetry. She was a paragon of calm yet unflinching resistance to the totalitarian state, as well as of loyalty to the ethical values

> abandoned by most people around her. . . . I shared that experience of spiritual training . . . as did everyone who visited Akhmatova.[83]

What Akhmatova's followers and disciples saw as "spiritual training," the KGB saw as her "subversive" influence on the youth[84]—the accusation also leveled at Socrates.[85]

AKHMATOVA AND BRODSKY'S ENGLISH-LANGUAGE ORIENTATION

Brodsky later explained that his discovery of foreign literatures went westward starting with Russia's neighbors to the west—the Poles, the Czechs, the Hungarians—and continued further until he eventually stumbled upon English-language poetry.[86] Venclova believes that Brodsky's westward-looking cosmopolitan orientation, and especially his lifelong fascination with the English language and literature, should also be ascribed to Akhmatova's influence on him. In her own poems, written during one of the darkest periods of Russian history, Akhmatova made a conscious effort to "preserve European standards of culture against the Soviet tide."[87] Venclova also underlines that "unlike most of her contemporaries, she [Akhmatova] was not a Francophile, but an Anglophile: I believe Joseph Brodsky inherited this characteristic from her."[88] Akhmatova worshipped Pushkin, and when most of the publications of her own poetry had been banned by Soviet censorship, she even became a professional Pushkin scholar.[89] Notably, for Pushkin, as the émigré philosopher Vladimir Veidle argued, English poetry was of even greater importance than French.[90] As for Akhmatova, her major later work "A Poem without a Hero" brimmed with allusions to Shakespeare, Byron, Keats, Shelley, and T. S. Eliot.[91] According to Venclova, these English literary connections helped her survive the worst years of Stalin's terror:

> She [Akhmatova] was extremely knowledgeable about Shakespeare and . . . Shelley. She read *Ulysses* in English four or five times and confessed to having understood it fully only during her last attempt; such endeavors helped her to endure the worst of Stalinist times. She was also very interested in T. S. Eliot and she knew his entire oeuvre, indeed some of it by heart. Together with Nadezhda Mandelstam (an opinion not shared by Pasternak) she considered Hemingway a nonentity and much preferred the work of William Faulkner.[92]

Ironically, it was the fashionable Ernest Hemingway, held in contempt by both Akhmatova and Nadezhda Mandelstam, who first attracted the young

Brodsky to John Donne—a discovery that proved to be a life-changing event for the Russian poet.[93]

"ELEGY FOR JOHN DONNE"

Brodsky's "Elegy for John Donne" (1963)—an extreme example of the nominal style of poetry, dominated by nouns and making the only verb, "to sleep," the more conspicuous by its repetition fifty-two times—is a meditation on the death of a great poet: "A part of the world dies with him."[94] Here is its opening in George Kline's English translation:

> John Donne has sunk in sleep . . . All things beside
> are sleeping too: walls, bed, and floor—all sleep.
> The table, pictures, carpets, hooks and bolts,
> clothes-closets, cupboards, candles, curtains—all
> now sleep: . . .
>   [. . .] Night everywhere . . .[95]

The elegy struck Brodsky's contemporaries as a major breakthrough in Russian poetry. Vyacheslav V. Ivanov remembered his impression on hearing it for the first time:

> I remember that winter of 1964 when the "Big Elegy for John Donne" started circulating in samizdat and became widely read in Moscow. I was at a house party at the home of a famous translator. . . . One of the guests brought along with him the poem and recited it aloud. Everybody was simply stunned. . . . We heard a text, which directly addressed the most important issues of human existence. A poet's conversation with God, which is *the main . . . content of the best of Silver Age poetry, was now being continued on the same note as it had been, before it was interrupted* [italics mine].[96]

Ivanov stresses that the diction of the elegy radically clashed with the style and subject matter of Soviet poetry, picking up, as it were, on the same note where the Silver Age poets had left off.[97] Venclova even argues that the elegy was a breakthrough not only in Russian poetry, but indeed in world poetry.[98] For one, it convinced an American professor of Russian philosophy, George L. Kline, that Brodsky was a major Russian poet, inspiring him to translate it into English. This translation paved the way to a lifelong friendship and translation cooperation between Brodsky and Kline, a central topic of this book.

In a 1965 conversation in Berkeley with his fellow poet and countryman Czesław Miłosz, the Polish-Jewish poet Aleksander Wat seems to have been the first to ascribe Brodsky's achievement of breaking the spell of Soviet literary newspeak to a foreign influence: "How delighted Joseph Brodsky was as an adolescent to discover John Donne, and what beautiful fruit that discovery bore!"[99] Later, David Bethea similarly argued that the influence of the English language helped Brodsky revive the contemporary Soviet poetic idiom: "Brodsky's anglophone (and americanophile) leanings have their source and inspiration in the Soviet history . . . of distortion and repression. . . . He looked to English . . . as a kind of 'truth serum,' a way to cleanse, reinvigorate, and discipline his own and his generation's shabby idiom."[100]

"SHEDDING THE SKIN OF STALINISM"

Indeed, as Bethea hinted, not only had the thread of tradition with previous generations of poets been broken, but the language of poetry itself had been compromised by the intrusion of ideology. During the previous decades, vast amounts of state resources were used to impose a totalitarian ideology on the language, style, and themes in Soviet literature.[101] Writers were systematically co-opted and used to lend prestige to oppression; otherwise, they were censored, exiled, or even murdered.[102] According to Wat, the young people who wanted to revive Russian literature after Stalin had to first abandon the language of ideology altogether: "In order to liberate themselves from Stalin's heritage in their souls, they must first 'detach themselves from the enemy.' Like a snake shedding its skin in the springtime, they must throw off not only any concern with Stalinism, communism, revisionism, but those ugly words themselves."[103] Wat, who had spent years in Soviet prisons and had witnessed the Stalinization of Polish literature twice—first, before his arrest in 1939 in Lvov and later in 1950[104]—was in a good position to hypothesize on the paths of literary revival in post-Stalinist Russia. Following his escape to the West, Wat argued that to liberate themselves from their Soviet heritage, Russian writers had to return to more private, personal themes, abandoning politics in their work altogether:

> The free people are not Andrei Voznesensky, Yevtushenko . . . but people like Joseph Brodsky, the Solzhenitsyn of *Matryona's House*, the Tertz-Sinyavsky of his last (apolitical!) works. Political thinking has become so distorted and corrupted during this long, long, half century that one has to begin by tearing it out, roots and all, from one's soul.[105]

However, such supposedly apolitical artistic attitudes, which Wat found so admirable in the works of Brodsky, Solzhenitsyn, and Sinyavsky, in fact constituted rather daring forms of political resistance in their totalitarian context, a phenomenon well documented by the political thinker Hannah Arendt.[106] It was, then, no coincidence that Akhmatova was accused in 1946 of writing "apolitical" poetry, which was considered a great transgression during Stalin's rule.[107] By the same token, when Wat shared with Miłosz his opinions on the future course of Russian literature, Brodsky,[108] Daniel, and Sinyavsky had already been put on trial,[109] and Solzhenitsyn would shortly find himself yet again on the receiving end of political persecution.[110]

BRODSKY'S ARREST, TRIAL, AND BANISHMENT

Most people in the West learned of Brodsky by reading the court proceedings of his Soviet trial in 1964, at which he was sentenced to five years of internal exile, and compulsory manual labor, on far-fetched charges of social parasitism. The journalist Frida Vigdorova had managed to make a transcript of the proceedings, which was then smuggled out of Russia and published in the West.[111] Commenting on the published transcript in 1965, Kline observed: "Even Brodsky's interest in foreign literature, especially English and American poetry, was held against him. Why, Judge Savelieva demanded xenophobically, didn't he pay more attention to 'our native Soviet Russian literature'?"[112] This publicity turned Brodsky into the next international cause célèbre after Pasternak's *Zhivago* debacle six years earlier, in 1958.[113] The writer Lydia Chukovskaia closely followed Brodsky's political trial and took an active part in campaigning for his release from northern exile in 1964–65.[114] In her diaries, Chukovskaia noted that Brodsky was ostensibly an apolitical person and this, according to her, should have rendered him rather harmless in the eyes of the Soviet authorities: "There are no legal grounds for his conviction. . . . And it does not even cross the mind of anyone in state power that he is actually quite innocuous, because he is not an anti-Soviet man, but simply an a-Soviet one."[115] Kline came to a similar conclusion: "Brodsky is a totally apolitical poet, no more pro-Soviet than anti-Soviet. His is a private, not a public, muse."[116] After reading Kline's English translations of Brodsky, Auden concurred: "His [Brodsky's] poems are a-political, perhaps defiantly so, which may explain why he has, so far, failed to win official approval."[117] Of all those who regarded Brodsky as an apolitical artist, only Auden surmised that Brodsky's defiantly apolitical stance might be the real reason why he fell afoul of the Soviet authorities. For, as Arendt showed, totalitarian regimes fear neutrality and creative independence more than any direct political opposition.[118] Seen from this angle, one can detect a certain, if twisted, logic in Brodsky's persecution by the Soviet authorities: his apolitical stance was perceived to be a threat to the regime. Venclova argued that even Brodsky's earlier poems clashed with Soviet literary standards:

> Joseph . . . daringly introduced tragic, philosophical, and religious topics into his verse, which countered the officially permitted "life-affirming" poetry. . . . Perhaps without even knowing it, *Brodsky continued early twentieth-century trends, interrupted by censorship following the revolution* [italics mine].[119]

In fact, the aesthetics of Brodsky's entire poetic group stood in strong contrast with the grandstanding of contemporary "topical" Soviet poets such as Evgeny Yevtushenko and Andrei Voznesensky, whom Brodsky and his circle regarded as toadies of the regime.[120] While for many Western readers, the stylistic differences seemed too subtle, in Russia their different aesthetics were reflected in their very different treatment by the Soviet state. While Yevtushenko and Voznesensky basked in international fame, were permitted to rub shoulders with world leaders, and filled stadiums with their admirers in Russia,[121] Brodsky had to serve his term in internal exile.

Chapter Two

"The Cold Had Made a Poet"

BRODSKY'S ARREST, trial, and internal exile to the Arctic village of Norenskaia is a cardinal event in his biography, and one essential for the creation of his poetic myth. Yet he seemed reluctant to discuss his exile. According to Lyudmila Sergeyeva, who knew Brodsky before his arrest, in the immediate aftermath of his release, he did not want to talk about it.[1] This is understandable. But even years later, in his American incarnation, Brodsky continued to downplay the extent of what he had endured in Norenskaia. Susan Sontag put his refusal to discuss the subject in a nutshell: "He was elegant enough always to claim that he had not really suffered during that year and a half of internal exile; that he rather liked farm work, especially shoveling manure . . . and had got quite a few poems written there."[2] By the same token, in his poetry written in America, Brodsky gave a very lyrical version of that time, referring to Norenskaia as "that village":

> . . . that village lost in the rows and rows
> of swamp in a pine-wooded territory where no scarecrows
> ever stand in orchards: the crops aren't worth it,
> and the roads are also just ditches and brushwood surface.[3]

This attitude persisted until the end of his life. In his essay "To Please a Shadow," for instance, Brodsky argued that "for a writer to mention his penal experiences . . . is like dropping names for normal folk."[4] Reviewing his two last collections of poetry and prose just days before the poet's death, J. M. Coetzee called Brodsky's "refusal to exhibit his wounds" one of his "more admirable traits."[5] Yet this refusal to peddle his suffering in the northern exile was more than just a matter of good taste or a refusal to display his wounds. Brodsky understood that, in the politically loaded context of the Cold War, an excessive focus on his persecution would inevitably divert readers' attention from his poetry. He refused to be reduced to a political sensation.[6] This accounts for his consistent efforts to diminish the extent of the adversity he had faced in Russia. Accordingly, in one of the first interviews he gave in the West, he referred to his term in the Arctic as "one of the best times of my life."[7] Brodsky later reiterated the same idea in his conversations with Solomon Volkov.[8] This latter source is particularly well liked among popular readers in Russia, despite some serious concerns about its reliability.[9] So the legend about Brodsky's "happy time" in Norenskaia lives on, although there is little evidence to back it up.

THE NORTHERN QUARANTINE

It suffices to look at the photographs taken of Brodsky in Norenskaia[10] or to read some of the poems he wrote during that period to see how bleak the entire situation was. Equally bleak is the picture painted in his letters. Following are my translations of some excerpts selected from the letters Brodsky sent during his second year in Norenskaia to a friend in Leningrad, Kira Samosiuk:

> 15 Jan. 1965, Norenskaia
> I have fallen sick; the days are flying by . . . You would like to know how I am? Well, I am surrounded by police mugs and the wind. The temperature difference between me and nature is 70 C. . . . I am all by myself in a cold hut, like a lump of mud. The last candles are burning down.[11]
>
> 23 Jan. 1965, Norinskaia [*sic*]
> . . . I have no news and no good news. Apart from possibly one longish poem titled "Felix"—a source of my personal pride, although I am too lazy to copy it out on a typewriter.[12]
>
> 31 Jan. 1965
> . . . What about my health? I'm healthy enough for an obituary. . . . The days are long. In February (12th) will be a year of my quarantine. Just think of it! A year![13]
>
> 1965 (undated)
> Had I written to you earlier, the letter would have turned out very sad. I cannot vouch for this one either.[14]

Understandably, the letters sent during the long Arctic winter are especially joyless. Brodsky marks with amazement the first anniversary of his northern confinement, referring to it with an Aesopian expression: "my quarantine." Overall, Brodsky's attitude in his letters is very composed, stoic, and dignified. He knew that the KGB was reading his letters and did not want to give them the satisfaction of knowing that they could bring him down. For example, in a letter from March 20, 1965, Brodsky mentions hearing rumors that he might be transferred to a different location in the Arctic to serve the remainder of his five-year term. The letter begins with a discussion of the usual literary matters but then makes casual mention of a possible transfer:

> 20 March 1965
>
> A.S. [Pushkin's] letters—are the best reading I know. (Perhaps also Dickens.) Last year A.A. [Akhmatova] sent me two volumes of his letters and so whenever I start feeling too lousy, I read them. . . . In parenthesis, I should mention that there is a danger of me being moved to the Nenets Autonomous region, to the tundra . . . : letters take longer to get there, while the trains it seems don't make it at all. Well, no big deal. I have already been to the tundra. Have been to the taiga too, to the deserts and the mountains. I am going to experience everything for the second time in Russia now. Something like a refrain: it's familiar—so there is no need to be afraid.[15]

Apparently, the most difficult aspect of his situation psychologically was the uncertainty of his fate. The mood of the next letter, sent a month later, is more desperate. Neither his usual matter-of-factness nor the use of Aesopian language, quite critical under the circumstances, can conceal it:

> 26 April 1965
>
> . . . As for myself my news is pretty lousy. To be honest, I am not quite used to fatum's generosity. Each time it seems the lowest point has been reached, and yet each time there is a new surprise in store. . . . My nerves are no good: my knees, pardonne, tremble when I sit down, my hands shake. I've become an old man. At one moment of semi-consciousness I was not sure whether I wanted to wake up or rather to fall back asleep. . . . poems don't come to me. The novel has been abandoned.[16]

Ahead of his twenty-fifth birthday, there seemed to be half a chance (in the end not realized) of his friend coming to pay him a visit. Brodsky felt that he had to give a detailed description of his surroundings to prevent any unnecessary shock to his prospective visitor. The picture he paints, with sardonic humor, speaks for itself:

> 17 May 1965
>
> It's a special microclimate down here. Perhaps I have not been explicit enough with you about my geography. Here it goes: the train stops—and you step outside into the mud. Then you walk, drowning in mud, toward the bus

> stop. Then the bus crawls through the mud for an hour and takes you to a heap of mud, referred to as a village. You step outside and there it is—your muddy house. By that time, you yourself look like a lump of mud. (Do this exercise for me: substitute the word "mud" with "loneliness." Then the trip becomes longer by twelve square meters—the entire area of the hut).[17]

Interestingly enough, this graphic description was followed by what seems to be his first known poem composed in English, included in the same letter. Brodsky makes apologies for his bad English, but his correspondent probably did not mind:

> I feel now like after a sleepless night: don't know well what I am saying—it's cold, it's snowing, the winter is back. Now it is high time to start speaking in English with mistakes [translation mine].
>
> My window is
> immoral kiss
> of white
> twilighte. [*sic*][18]

This example sheds light on yet another important existential function of English for Brodsky. English helped him to defamiliarize his present situation, or, as he himself put it in a later essay, "obliterate the local reality."[19] And the "local reality" was far from cheerful, as Brodsky shows with his inimitable irony in the closing part of the same letter: "It's time to finish my letter. Have to take off my jacket, crawl inside the sleeping bag with my trousers and sweater on, zip the zipper, blow out the candle and wish myself not to have too many erotic dreams. In a week I will be twenty-five."[20] Incidentally, his letters show the same penchant for detached observation as his poetry, which, according to Monas, counterbalances the "sense of solitude and desolation."[21]

BRODSKY'S DISCOVERY OF ENGLISH POETRY

Yet although Brodsky's time in Norenskaia was anything but happy, neither was it all gloom and doom. There he made his first attempts at composing poems in English and managed to discover and internalize much of English and American poetry. Against the struggle of this very Russian period, the revelation and mastery of his conquest of English becomes a bulwark that lingers after his return.

John Donne and the Metaphysical School

Brodsky's discovery of Donne, in fact, was made in Norenskaia. Equipped with only a bilingual dictionary, he used a unique approach to internalize Donne's poems by "laboriously translating the opening and closing stanzas of some poems . . . and trying to imagine how, by the as yet undeciphered intermediate stanzas, these poles might shrewdly and surprisingly be linked."[22] At this early stage, translation was a way of simply understanding the mechanisms of Donne's notoriously difficult poetry. Yet as Brodsky's beloved Auden argued, "the attempt to translate the poetry of one language into another is an invaluable training for a poet."[23] Auden believed that it is easier to accept artistic influences if they come from a distant time, culture, and sensibility: "In general the further away from you in time or feeling that poets are, the more you can get out of them for your own use. Often some piece of technique thus learnt really unchains one's own Daemon quite suddenly."[24] In Auden's case, such fecund influence came from Anglo-Saxon and Middle English poetry;[25] for Brodsky, it was the English metaphysical poets.[26] Following Donne's model unleashed something that was to remain in Brodsky's poetics until the very end.

Discovery of W. H. Auden

While Donne became a poetic model from a remote past, Auden was a contemporary not only to love and admire, but someone after whom Brodsky could model his poetry and even his life. Derek Walcott emphasized this in a poem commemorating Brodsky: "A conduct whose metre and poise were modelled on Wystan's."[27] Brodsky described his discovery of Auden in a famous essay:

> My . . . opportunity to take a closer look at Auden occurred while I was doing my . . . time in the North, in a small village lost among swamps and forests, near the Arctic Circle. . . . The anthology that I had was in English, sent to me by a friend from Moscow. . . . I was intending to read Eliot. But by pure chance the book opened to Auden's "In Memory of W. B. Yeats." . . . I soon realized that even its structure was designed to pay tribute to the dead poet.[28]

Typically, Brodsky first felt attracted to Auden on the level of form. Auden's influence was exemplified by a poem in memory of T. S. Eliot for which Brodsky adopted the meter and stanzaic design of Auden's elegy. Even more extraordinary were the circumstances in which he composed his elegy, as Susan Sontag observed:

> The young, as yet unpublished poet from Leningrad fulfilling a sentence of compulsory labor on a collective farm, in a village in the far North, near the White Sea, receives the news—it is January 1965—that T. S. Eliot has died in London, sits at a table in his icy shack, and within the next twenty-four hours composes a long elegy to Eliot, which is also an homage to the very alive W. H. Auden (the tone and swing of whose elegy on the death of Yeats he adopts).[29]

As Sontag shrewdly pointed out, the disparity between these two places, Eliot's England where he died and the Arctic kolkhoz where Brodsky was serving his term, could not have been greater. Miłosz pointed to another paradox; despite Eliot's stature, Brodsky was the only poet to elegize him: "I know of no poet in the West who mourned Eliot in a poem."[30] Auden became Brodsky's most influential poetic model among his contemporaries. His endorsement would be as important for Brodsky's reputation in English as Akhmatova's was for his Russian one.

Admiration for Robert Frost

Brodsky and his friends were fascinated by everything American and considered America their alternative motherland.[31] One example of this is his admiration for Robert Frost, who proved to be as important an influence during his Arctic exile as Auden. Brodsky had already discovered Frost before his confinement thanks to the Russian renderings by his Moscow friend and translator Andrei Sergeev.[32] Venclova remembered that Brodsky, as a young poet, competitive by nature, set out to outdo his peers by learning to produce verses that were better than theirs. With Frost he found out, however, that the trick did not work, and he had to acknowledge that he could never write better poems than his American counterpart.[33] In the United States, Brodsky went to great lengths popularizing Frost's poetry among native audiences.[34] Frost was both adulated and resented in America, but, Brodsky argued, he had been essentially misunderstood.[35] Brodsky maintained that Frost was a terrifying poet who camouflaged himself behind a mask of "quiet didacticism and rural irony."[36] What drew Brodsky to Frost, apart from his skillful use of traditional poetic technique, was his special attitude toward nature, which Brodsky thought to be peculiarly American: "When an American walks out of his house and encounters a tree it is a meeting of equals. Man and tree face each other in their respective primal power, free of references. . . . Basically, it's epidermis meeting bark. . . . Nature . . . is this poet's terrifying self-portrait."[37] Frost's non-Romantic, stoic encounters with undomesticated American nature, which in Auden's apt expression "could not possibly be imagined as a mother,"[38] as well as Frost's refusal to "wear his learning on his sleeve,"[39] became inspirational when Brodsky himself was forced to face the primal forces of nature in the Arctic circle. One example of a Brodsky verse written in the manner of Frost, which meets Frost's own definition of a poem "riding on its own melting . . . like a piece of ice on a hot stove,"[40] is Brodsky's "Autumn in Norenskaia" (1965). The following is its last stanza in an English translation by Daniel Weissbort (subsequently revised by the author):

> The sky lowers. The shouldered rake
> sees the damp roofs first, staked
> out against the ridge of a dark hill
> that's just a mound far off.
> Three versts still to cover. Rain
> lords it over this beaten plain,
> and to the crusted boots cling brown
> stubborn clods of the native earth.[41]

Brodsky's personal experience of agricultural labor in Norenskaia is presented here in terms of a meeting between human consciousness and the primal power of the elements:

"... the cold had made a poet"[42]

EFFECTS OF THE NORTHERN QUARANTINE

Although Brodsky's northern quarantine was not in the least one of the best times of his life, it was remarkable for his creative development. The discovery of English-language poets propelled Brodsky's own growth as a poet enormously. Venclova argues that his internal exile was a watershed moment: "In Norenskaya, he had undergone a veritable transformation: he produced a hundred or so poems . . . which were much more original and powerful than most of his previous work. . . . they were on par with Pasternak, Akhmatova, or anyone."[43] Given that Brodsky managed to read the many books friends had sent, discovered new poetry in English, and composed new poems in Russian, it is natural that some of his letters from Norenskaia feature normal conversations for a man of letters. At times they are even playful. He told the same friend:

> I am sending you three poems, which are perhaps not the best of the [recently] composed; yet, given the limited possibilities, I can find some merits even in them.
>
> I am writing to you as a publisher, because to feel in a fuller sense (like a

poet) I need to be corresponding with a publisher. I'd like to play this game with you, but what kind of fees can I expect from you? . . . Connoisseur of chaos, Joseph.[44]

The "publisher" reference was fanciful because there was at this point no possibility that his poems could be published. Signing off his letters with "Connoisseur of chaos" followed by an English version of his name served the function of transporting him mentally to a different place. However, when his heart condition suddenly worsened, he wrote an especially piercing letter to his friend, which also included his literary will:

> Now I feel as badly, it seems, as ever. . . . I feel like I might not see you again, so here is some information about my literary affairs for you (or whomever it may concern): I do not have an archive. Please, do not include poems from any "collections." Everything in them is topsy-turvy and there are many things I meant to destroy. . . . I only started writing for real in 1963. Starting with Kholmy [Hills]. All the rest is rubbish. Including Hills.
>
> If I get better, I will be ashamed of this letter, but now I am not. It seems this time it is not going to pass. Keep the more cheerful memories of me. . . . It's a pity you did not make it here, but perhaps, it's only for the better. . . . 8 June 1965.[45]

Brodsky recovered from that health crisis. Conversely, Frida Vigdorova, the journalist who had managed to make a stenographic transcript of his trial proceedings, drawing international attention to Brodsky's case, did not recover from hers. In the subsequent letter, which incidentally also included a poem Brodsky had composed in Polish, he mourned Vigdorova's death in a short and tragic note of gratitude and recognition: "I have been told that F.V. [Frida Vigdorova] has died in Moscow, the woman who did almost everything for my defense."[46]

OPTING AGAINST TAMIZDAT: THE PUBLICATION OF *STIKHOTVORENIIA I POEMY*

Brodsky's correspondence from Norenskaia featured one interesting episode regarding the prospect of publication of his work abroad (in so-called tamizdat).[47] In the aftermath of Brodsky's trial in 1964, two distinguished US-based Russian émigré publishers, Gleb Struve and Boris Filipoff, set out to prepare a collection of his poems distilled from samizdat editions to be published by Inter-Language Literary Associates in Washington, DC. Brodsky seemed an unlikely choice for Struve and Filipoff, who until then had collaborated on tamizdat editions of Silver Age poets.[48] Perhaps they had heard of Akhmatova's endorsement of Brodsky, or simply recognized in him a continuator of Russia's prerevolutionary poetic tradition. One thing is for sure: both were struck by Brodsky's inner dissonance with the Soviet regime, as Struve put it in a letter to Filipoff ("ego vnutrenniaia nesozvuchnost'").[49]

When the news about their plans reached Brodsky in Norenskaia in early 1965, he sent a message back to them along the same trusted channels urging them to desist.[50] Apparently, Norenskaia did not seem to be an ideal location from which to defy the already draconian authorities with a tamizdat publication. So when in April 1965 Brodsky learned that his request had been ignored and the book had come out in the United States, he was far from pleased. He suspected that this publication might have been orchestrated by the KGB and braced himself for repressions against his relatives, as he explained in a letter to a trusted correspondent in Leningrad:

> A 240-page book of mine in Russian, shorter and longer poems, has appeared in the USA. This is a KGB action: the poems were not [in circulation], but were only in their possession. Now I am afraid mayhem will break loose. They will start summoning my relatives for interrogation: was it you who provided it [the manuscript], you accomplice—but this [information] is for Anatoly [Naiman]—as to yourself, consider whether staying in touch with me might still be worth your while.[51]

Contrary to his worst expectations, the 1965 publication of *Stikhotvoreniia i poemy* (*Verses and Poems*),[52] his first poetry collection to appear in print in Russian, did not result in any new repercussions for him or his relatives. Brodsky's case had already attracted too much international attention, and the regime opted, for the time being, to minimize the damage to its reputation abroad. As Kline rightly pointed out, Brodsky's persecution had largely backfired: "As it turned out, his trial made him famous and far more influential than before."[53] When upon his return to Leningrad Brodsky saw a copy of the book, which had been smuggled into the Soviet Union, his feelings were mixed. A largely unknown poet in his own country, he must have been flattered to see a volume of his poetry printed in the United States. At the same time, having developed rapidly as a poet in Norenskaia, he was upset by the inclusion of his juvenilia and by the many misprints in *Stikhotvoreniia i poemy*.[54]

BRODSKY'S RUSSIAN TRANSLATIONS

Brodsky's internal exile ended in November 1965. He had served almost two years of his five-year sentence. Venclova's recollections indirectly refute

Brodsky's own myth about his happy time in Norenskaia, as he points to Brodsky's rather bad mental condition after his ordeal.[55] His Moscow friends recommended that he take a trip to Lithuania to quiet his nerves.[56] Still, most contemporaries, possibly somewhat anesthetized to the cruelties of the regime, thought that he had been lucky and gotten off easily, as Venclova again recalls:

> We considered it an almost incredible success. For almost the first time since 1917, the state machine went into reverse due to international protests and, what was more important, to the pressure of mounting public opinion in the USSR. Brodsky returned to his parents' flat in Leningrad, met Akhmatova . . . and started to look for translation contracts (he made a very modest living as a translator before the trial).[57]

While the regime continued to do everything in its power to make Brodsky's life difficult in Russia, friends and acquaintances provided him with translation work, allowing him to make ends meet, as he explained in his first interview to be published abroad:

> Michael Scammell: You came out of prison in 1965? Did you return to being a private person and have you been working just on your own ever since that time?
>
> Iosif Brodsky: Oh no. I worked as a translator. I am a professional translator and I was a member of the Translators' Group at the Leningrad Writers' Union. That is how I earned my living.[58]

Since the time of his political trial on trumped-up charges of parasitism, Brodsky had had to fight for the recognition of his professional status as a poet. Now his membership as a translator in a state-sanctioned literary guild provided not only a minimal source of income but also a professional identity.

It is no secret that many poets of Akhmatova's generation saw translation as mere drudge work devised by the authorities as a form of censorship, aimed at distracting them from their own original writing. Akhmatova accordingly once used a somewhat Dantesque metaphor comparing translation to "eating one's own brain."[59] Her friend and fellow acmeist poet Osip Mandelstam similarly complained about having to do translations to survive. According to Clarence Brown:

> When [Mandelstam's] own work was being systematically rejected by "vigilant" editors . . . he was driven to translating in order to live. He had to

> translate under sweatshop conditions, the texts assigned him being the trash *en vogue* at the time with the authorities. This loathsome hackwork even crowded out his own muse. He had to endure reading here and there in official reference works . . . that he had given up poetry and "gone over to translating," a legend that clung to his name for years.[60]

Friedberg even argued that the Soviet authorities approved translation as "a purgatory for authors in disfavor."[61] This characterization, which might sound like a Cold War–era oversimplification, actually contains more than a grain of truth.[62]

Brodsky's attitude toward translation was quite different from that of his poetic predecessors Akhmatova and Mandelstam,[63] who belonged to the last generation of Russians who still spoke foreign languages, had traveled abroad, and had been closely connected to the currents and influences of Western art. For Brodsky, who was dealing with the effects of cultural disinheritance, poetry became inseparable from Mandelstam's concept of a "longing for world culture," and translation in its culture-bridging and culture-spreading capacity became a natural means of fulfilling that quest.[64] Indeed, as Michael Wachtel has argued, one could say that translation served as the basis for Brodsky's entire outlook on world literature.[65] This explains why he viewed translation much more positively than his acmeist mentors. In fact, Viacheslav V. Ivanov recalled that one of the things Brodsky regretted most when given short notice that he had to leave Russia was that he would be unable to complete his project of translating the seventeenth-century English metaphysical poets for the Khudozhestvennaia Literatura publishing house.[66]

GUESTS FROM THE WEST

Back home in Leningrad after his return from internal exile, Brodsky continued his usual literary pursuits, including composing poetry in Russian, studying English, and finding new translation contracts, which were supposed to guarantee some modicum of official income and protect him from any renewed accusations of social parasitism. Venclova comments:

> After learning English in Norenskaya, Joseph began to study English-language metaphysical poetry and Modernist classics quite assiduously. . . . Donne, Auden, and Frost became his daily reading. More than once, he expressed his high opinion of Gerard Manley Hopkins, Thomas Hardy, and Wallace Stevens.[67]

Brodsky's progress in spoken English naturally lagged behind. That is why he not only continued to pursue his independent study of English but also met visitors from England and the United States, mostly exchange students. It would be a gross understatement to say that the Soviet authorities frowned upon unauthorized contacts with Westerners. As Brodsky himself later commented, "Unless . . . such contacts are initiated or encouraged by the State itself, [they are considered] in Russia an open invitation for harassment."[68] Brodsky's attitude was especially defiant, given that he himself, his house, and his visitors were under continuous surveillance by the secret police. As Venclova later pointed out, it was only a matter of time before he would be made to pay for his disregard for Soviet protocol:

> Brodsky's situation in those years did not look too bad. By Soviet standards, it could even have been seen as enviable. Yet of course he was under strict surveillance by the KGB, and remained on the margins of "normal" society, shunned by all official bodies. The fact that he became the very epitome of Leningrad's and Russia's literary underground, adored by hundreds of young people, lionized by opposition cultural figures, and frequented by Western students who managed to get into the USSR, only served to aggravate his predicament.[69]

However, it was not only Western students who visited him. In August 1967, less than two years after his release from Norenskaia, Brodsky met and befriended George Louis Kline (1921–2014), an American professor of Russian philosophy at Bryn Mawr College.[70] Kline would go on to play an essential role in Brodsky's literary career in the West. He became instrumental in bringing about two tamizdat collections of Brodsky's poetry: one in Russian, *Ostanovka v pustyne* (*A Halt in the Desert*), published in 1970 by a US-based émigré publishing house;[71] and *Joseph Brodsky: Selected Poems*, which came out in England in 1973. It was this latter collection, for which Kline did the translations and Auden wrote a foreword, that became so vital for Brodsky in the first years following his exile from Russia.[72]

GEORGE KLINE: FROM AMERICA WITH LOVE

Like most Westerners, George Kline had become aware of Brodsky after reading the transcript of his Kafkaesque trial, which appeared in the West in September 1964.[73] Kline had a good grasp of Russian, having translated Russian religious thinkers and taught courses on Russian culture. He also enjoyed Russian poetry.[74] So when in December 1964, in Warsaw, Seweryn Pollak, a Polish translator of Akhmatova, showed him a samizdat copy of Brodsky's "Elegy for John Donne," Kline was impressed and concluded that its author must be a major poet in Russian.[75] Kline managed to obtain his own copy of the poem and speedily rendered it into English. In the spring of 1965, while Brodsky was still in Norenskaia, Kline's translation appeared in Northwestern University's literary magazine *TriQuarterly*, alongside his remarks on Brodsky's trial and his poetics.[76] They reveal Kline's sensitivity to both poetry and human rights issues.[77]

Kline: The First Encounter

Kline first met Brodsky at his home in Leningrad,[78] where Brodsky had created for himself a nook in the room he shared with his parents in their communal apartment, later immortalized in his essay "In a Room and a Half."[79] There exist several detailed descriptions of the "nook," which was preserved by Brodsky's friends and admirers, who have been working for a number of years to turn the communal apartment into a museum. Brodsky's living space was very tight, crammed with suitcases and trunks piled high, along with many books. Next to a photo of Akhmatova, there was one of Frost.[80] His space brimmed with clippings from American and European magazines, humorous posters cut out in Latin letters, with some listing the series of crimes that Brodsky had supposedly committed in the United States, such as "I AM AN ENEMY OF THE STATE," "BEWARE—SEX MANIAC," "WORK IS THE CURSE OF THE DRINKING CLASS," and "WANTED DEAD (PREFERABLY) OR ALIVE J.B." While his guests would be offered vodka, Brodsky would drink gin, which was virtually unavailable in the USSR.[81] Brodsky's desk lamp was covered with labels for Camel cigarettes, his favorite American brand, while the shelf above his desk featured books by such major English and American poets as W. B. Yeats, T. S. Eliot, Dylan Thomas, Richard Wilbur, and Wallace Stevens, brought to him by various Western visitors.[82] In sum, Brodsky had created a tiny oasis of foreignness in his communal apartment where he could practically live abroad. But this was still Russia, as Kline was immediately reminded: "[Brodsky's] first words to me—as I stretched out my hand through the open door to grasp his—were 'Cherez porog nel'zia' ('Don't [greet anyone] across the threshold'), quickly followed, with a smile and in a heavy English accent, by 'Old Russian custom.'"[83] For his part, Kline had prepared a little opening speech for the occasion, comparing Brodsky to a young Akhmatova, Pasternak, and Tsvetaeva (not knowing as yet of Mandelstam's existence).[84] Kline's calculation was right: a juxtaposition with the Silver Age poets was bound to please Brodsky, for this was precisely the league he aspired to join.

Kline's Translation of the Elegies for Donne and Eliot

During their first meeting, Kline showed Brodsky his translation of the "Elegy for John Donne," which preserves the pentametric beat of the original but does not reproduce the rhymes.

We don't know how Brodsky reacted to this particular translation, but the reaction must have been favorable because Kline would soon become Brodsky's first choice of translator into English. If anything, Kline's translations managed to convince none other than Auden that Brodsky was "an excellent craftsman" in Russian:

> Knowing no Russian and therefore forced to base my judgment on English translations, I can do little more than guess about the poems of Joseph Brodsky. My chief reason for believing that Professor Kline's translations do justice to their originals is that they convince me that Brodsky is an excellent craftsman. For example, in his long poem "Elegy for John Donne" the word sleep occurs, if I have counted rightly, fifty-two times. Such repetition might very easily have become irritating and affected: in fact, it is handled with consummate art.[85]

It is rather symbolic that the first Brodsky poem which Kline translated into English was a poem so conspicuously inspired by English poetic tradition. By elegizing Donne, Brodsky was already indirectly claiming, through his muse, a spot on the genealogical tree of English poetry. In fact, in the course of his life Brodsky wrote elegies for at least five English and American poets (Donne, Frost, Eliot, Auden, and Lowell), while elegizing only three Russian poets in his verse (Pushkin, Akhmatova, and Sergei Chudakov).[86]

Surely, when he composed his elegy for T. S. Eliot in Norenskaia in January 1965, Brodsky could not have imagined that just a few years later Auden himself, who'd been friends with Eliot and wrote an obituary for him, would read his elegy and notice the resemblance to his own famous poem.[87] In his 1968 translation of Brodsky's "Verses on the Death of T. S. Eliot," Kline recognized this and did his best to imitate Auden's "In Memory of W. B. Yeats."[88] See, for instance, how Kline tries to mimic Auden's somewhat Elizabethan rhyme "lie—poetry" in his own rhyming couple, "alive—memories":

> Earth, receive an honoured guest;
> William Yeats is laid to rest:
> Let the Irish vessel lie
> Emptied of its poetry.[89]
> (W. H. Auden, "In Memory of W. B. Yeats")

and

Forest here will not forget
voice of lyre and rush of feet.
Only what remains alive
will deserve their memories.[90]
(Brodsky, "Verses on the Death of T. S. Eliot")

This was a symbolic moment, not only for Brodsky but for the entire Russian poetic tradition. For the first time in decades, Russian poetry was entering into a direct, non-party-controlled dialogue with her Western sisters, and Brodsky was at the center of this momentous event, with Kline as its facilitator. Later, in his foreword to the *Selected Poems*, Auden himself placed Brodsky firmly within the European artistic context: "Mr. Brodsky is not an easy poet, but even a cursory reading will reveal that, like Van Gogh and Virginia Woolf, he has an extraordinary capacity to envision material objects as sacramental signs, messengers from the unseen."[91]

OPTING FOR TAMIZDAT: THE PUBLICATION OF *OSTANOVKA V PUSTYNE* AND *SELECTED POEMS*

Following their first meeting, Kline and Brodsky saw each other daily for another week, disregarding the dangers this might entail for either of them. Their encounter marked the beginning of a lifelong friendship. Upon his return to the United States, Kline immediately began to arrange matters on Brodsky's behalf. He got in touch with Struve and Filipoff to settle the tricky issue of the royalties for the 1965 *Stikhotvoreniia i poemy*, thereby demonstrating an impressive knack for networking and a practical streak. During Kline's second visit to Leningrad in 1968, it was decided that he would become the unofficial editor of Brodsky's *Ostanovka v pustyne*, which was to include parts of *Stikhotvoreniia i poemy*.[92] On the same occasion, Kline offered to do translations for a new English-language collection of Brodsky's verse to be published in the West.[93]

Prior to this, only one collection of Brodsky's poetry translated into English had come out. *Elegy to John Donne, and Other Poems*, translated by Nicholas Bethell, appeared in England in 1967 without Brodsky's authorization and was, by common consent, "hasty, inaccurate and awkward."[94] After his release from Arctic exile, there was talk of a book called "Zimniaia pochta" ("Winter Mail") that Brodsky thought might come to pass. But its publication was stalled, and he soon realized that his poems would never be published in Russia and could only circulate in samizdat. So Brodsky gave

Kline his approval and, in the summer of 1968, agreed to have a book of his translated poetry published in England.[95] This became *Joseph Brodsky: Selected Poems*, published in 1973. A later comment reveals how Brodsky perceived, from Leningrad, the idea of a tamizdat publication: "The whole prospect of my book being published in England was quite unreal. The only thing that imparted a semblance of reality to this venture was its sheer illegality under Soviet law."[96] Indeed, if samizdat authors were already treated with hostility (during his politicized trial, Brodsky's poems were described as pornographic, unpatriotic, and anti-Soviet), it was even worse for writers whose works appeared in the West without official sanction.[97] But Brodsky, weathered by his penal experience, tried to live as a free person in an unfree country, for which he was greatly admired by some of his supporters, such as the Leningrad writer Sergei Dovlatov, who observed: "Brodsky created an unheard-of model of behavior. He lived not in a proletarian state, but in a monastery of his own spirit. He did not struggle with the regime. He simply did not notice it."[98]

TAMIZDAT AND ITS DIFFICULTIES

Today, it is hard to imagine what helping an unofficial Russian writer to get published in the West entailed. In 1969, two years after meeting Kline, Brodsky befriended Carl Ray Proffer (1938–1984), another American editor, translator, and professor of Russian, who would later play an equally important role in launching Brodsky's American career. Brodsky compared the methods of Ardis—a press that Carl and Ellendea Proffer established in 1971 in Ann Arbor, Michigan, to publish Russian writers who could not get published in their native land—to the tricks of the trade in famous Cold War spy novels:

> The Proffers would invariably take their kids [along on their trips to Russia] who confused the KGB surveillance by running in all possible directions, hiding important mail in their parkas and in general creating a great commotion. The crucial part of Ardis' operation was, of course, obtaining the manuscripts and getting them out of the country. Some of the schemes were more mind-boggling than any of Le Carre or Len Deighton's.[99]

Editing, translating, and compiling tamizdat books, which meant first smuggling manuscripts across extremely tight borders, like weapons or narcotics, required a rather different set of skills than those traditionally associated with translators or editors of poetry. Even frequenting a beleaguered poet's house could result in interrogation by the secret police and the eventual impossibility of revisiting the Soviet Union, a not insignificant matter of professional importance for a Russian specialist like Kline. Human integrity and courage were in high demand. Apparently, George Louis Kline, or Georgii Ludvigovich, as he introduced himself to Russians, possessed all these qualities.

Forty years after Brodsky and Kline's first encounter, in February 2007, I visited George Kline at his home in Anderson, South Carolina, and met him, his wife, and their older daughter. Already in his late eighties, and despite using a walker outside the house, George drove to the airport to pick me up in the hybrid car he had recently mastered. George was supportive of my research, sharing stories and showing me documents and Brodsky memorabilia. He was the same generous man who had visited Brodsky in Leningrad. Eleven years after Brodsky's death, the poet's name reverberated with the same urgency; Geoge's love of Brodsky and loyalty to his cause remained unwavering. One could sense that for all George's academic achievements, his involvement with Brodsky's poetry was a far more thrilling part of his life.

George's wife was also extremely kind. She looked even frailer than George but took care of the special needs of their daughter and cooked dinner for us. Unable to hold back her tears, she told me how, in 1966, a year prior to her husband's first meeting with Brodsky, their daughter, then a promising college student, had accompanied George on a trip to Moscow where they attended a performance at the Bolshoi Theater. In the middle of the show, one part of her face became paralyzed. This turned out to be the onset of multiple sclerosis, which would permanently affect her well-being, confining her to a wheelchair. To learn about this personal tragedy and to witness the stoic way her parents dealt with it was eye-opening. It showed me another side of George, his vulnerability and humanity, which sometimes remained concealed behind his somewhat formal exterior.

Indeed, I could not help thinking how temperamentally different George Kline and Joseph Brodsky were. It seemed hard to imagine how George, who was so proper, and even a bit prim, could handle the notoriously mercurial Joseph, nineteen years his junior. It was almost inevitable that sooner or later their differences would come to the fore over such a highly contested topic as poetry translation. Luckily, their bond survived those disagreements. Meeting him in person and talking to him over the phone, I discovered that Kline had a great sense of humor, the kind which people who have withstood hardships with dignity can be endowed. I concluded that it must have played a part in the durability of their friendship.

In 1968, on his next visit to Leningrad, following an interrogation by the KGB, Kline realized he had been blacklisted, essentially for his contacts with Brodsky. Despite being subjected to KGB intimidation, Kline took the risk of trying to smuggle out to the United States manuscripts of several Brodsky poems, as well as the tables of contents for both *Ostanovka v pustyne* and the *Selected Poems*. His efforts were successful, although Kline later admitted that during the checks at the airport he was "quaking in his boots."[100] The whole experience put him off traveling to the Soviet Union for more than twenty years.[101] That is why, from 1968 to 1972, communication between Kline and Brodsky was limited "to notes hand-carried by Western visitors to Leningrad, a mode of correspondence that proved frustratingly slow."[102] Kline himself later recalled:

> I sometimes sent a list of questions, which Brodsky would answer orally or in a separate note. In other cases, he jotted down his answers (often in red ink) . . . and gave this to the visitor to bring back to London or Paris or New York.[103]

Around Easter 1969, Brodsky received a little teaser from Kline: six of his poems, translated by Kline, had appeared in 1968 in a small Californian publication called the *Unicorn Journal*.[104] Presented with the first drafts of the translations, Brodsky sent Kline an ecstatic letter written characteristically half in Russian and half in English. Toward the late 1960s, bilingualism was already becoming a part of Brodsky's identity:

> Dear George, I am simply stunned: it came out brilliantly. To hell with the rhymes, if it works out this way. The only thing that upsets me is the impossibility of paying you back, as I am unable to do anything comparable for you. Forever yours, Joseph. I think that I am terribly lucky. [Translation from the Russian mine.] Excuse me, please, my terrible English. But I should like to say you the following: remember I respect and love you. . . . From my point of view, you are a big man.[105]

It is noteworthy that Brodsky at this time showed more flexibility on the issue of preserving the rhymes across translation than he would later do in America. In the notes he sent Kline on the translation of his poem "Nature Morte" in January 1972, just months before his forced emigration, Brodsky already urged his translator to work harder on the rhymes: "I put here all these notes because this poem is very important one for me; more than any other, probably. Forgive me, please. And please, don't think that I do not believe in your taste. But the rhymes are really nessesary [*sic*] here."[106] In America, Brodsky's English improved rapidly and his circumstances drastically changed, offering him a greater number of possibilities. He would become much more demanding of his English translators, in particular when it came to preserving the subtlety of his rhymes.

AUDEN'S FOREWORD

By spring 1970, Auden had completed his foreword for the *Selected Poems*, which Kline retyped "single-space . . . with narrow margins, so that it would fit on only two onion-skin pages."[107] Kline's colleague, a professor of Russian history from Ohio State University, managed to deliver it to Brodsky in Leningrad, a process which involved a few adventures. Kline recalled: "He [the professor] was subjected to a thorough body search which would undoubtedly have turned up the smuggled document if it had been in his pocket or wallet. The guard in fact slipped his fingers into the loose bottom of the canvas bag but didn't reach quite far enough to find the tiny square of folded paper."[108] That is the effort it took to deliver Auden's foreword to Leningrad. Brodsky received Auden's praise with "a mixture of astonishment, delight, and gratitude" and wrote Auden a letter expressing his thanks.[109] Brodsky later claimed that Auden's foreword mattered to him even more, in terms of recognition of his poetic achievements, than the Nobel Prize for Literature. This gives us some measure of Kline's contribution to the Brodsky cause.

THE FORBIDDEN HEMISPHERE

Now that Brodsky's book of poetry featuring Auden's foreword was about to come out in the West, the "forbidden hemisphere" was gradually becoming more real, and arguably more important to him than ever before. Brodsky's close friend, the philologist Diana Abaeva-Myers, was married to the Englishman Alan Myers, who was later to become one of Brodsky's friends and English co-translators. Diana introduced Brodsky to Faith Wigzell, a Slavic scholar from England. As one can glean from a 1969 letter to Diana, Brodsky dedicated some poems written directly in English to Faith: "Can you ask your husband to cadge from F [Faith Wigzell] some of the poems I have written in English (he'd have to be very diplomatic). In any case, they contain 12 lines, which might be considered "~~a fact~~ a feast of English culture."[110] The poems Brodsky mentions in this passage were most likely in light verse.[111] Still, however ironic his remark, the letter demonstrates Brodsky's ambition and desire, even during his Russian period, to create something in English that might be considered a "fact" or even "a feast of English culture." We find a similarly revealing remark in an earlier letter from Brodsky to Diana on April 12, 1969, in which he tries to convince her that his poems in Russian are not inferior to those by John Donne: "Do you still believe I write worse than Donne? I would not say so."[112] The often ironic Brodsky was no doubt quite serious on this occasion.

Much has been written about the importance for Brodsky and the influence of John Donne and the seventeenth-century English metaphysical poets on his work.[113] The early Brodsky scholar Mikhail Kreps argued that Brodsky's real poetic lineage should be traced back neither to the Russian Golden Age of poetry nor to the Silver Age (including Marina Tsvetaeva, whom Brodsky worshipped in his essays and interviews) but to John Donne, George Herbert, Richard Crashaw, and Andrew Marvell. One can think of many specific traits of Brodsky's poetics that point to his kinship with Donne and metaphysical poetry: his penchant for operating with metaphysical conceits (*concetti*),[114] his synthesis of feeling and intellect, his metaphysical wit, his fondness for finding resemblances between the most disparate phenomena, and his propensity to mix low and high registers in his poetry, echoing Donne's mixing of the sacred and profane.[115] One could also mention the peculiar metrics of some of Brodsky's poems, reflecting a rhythm of thought rather than creating euphony,[116] and Brodsky's knack for using his own metaphors as objects of further contemplation.[117] In a 1981 interview for Russian Radio Liberty, Brodsky himself acknowledged that the greatest lesson he learned from Donne was the use of extended stanzas, which was novel for Russian poetics at the time:

> Translating him [Donne], I learned a great deal. As it happens, the main corpus of Russian poetry is stanzaic—it operates on the basis of very simple stanzaic entities—the quatrain. Meanwhile, in Donne I discovered a much more interesting and thrilling structure. He features extremely complex stanzaic contraptions. I found his method fascinating and mastered it. Thus, unwittingly I set out to do the same thing, not as a rival, but rather as an apprentice.[118]

The technique he discovered in Donne became the cornerstone of his individual poetic style. In fact, after his release from Norenskaia, Brodsky criticized his peers for continuing to compose shorter poems that aimed to be traditional Russian small-scale masterpieces built around rhyming quatrains.[119] This brings us to a psychologically fascinating observation: when criticism was later leveled at his translations for introducing alien elements into English poetry, he must have felt that his self-translations were an exemplar of the lessons he had learned from English poetic models in the first place.

This also explains Brodsky's admission made in a letter to Proffer in November 1971, where he spoke of the importance of the "English destiny" of his poems: "You know, Carl, this is very strange and, in [*sic*] the same time, important for me: English destiny of my verses. If one man in States or in England will find in my lines at least 1/10th part of all that I did receive reading your native authors, I'll say then I am lucky person."[120] The "English destiny of his verse" had been important for Brodsky long before it became a matter of expediency after his expulsion from Russia.

Naturally, Brodsky wished one day to be able to travel to the West, to see the world, to visit the great cities of Europe: London, Paris, Venice, Rome. Yet all his attempts to obtain an exit visa from the Soviet authorities to travel (to the Poetry International Festival in London, for example, or to an analogous poetry event in Spoleto, Italy) came to naught, despite the official invitations he had received.[121] The Soviet authorities were obviously set on not making Brodsky's life any easier. His Leningrad-based Lithuanian friend Romas Katilius remembered that the powers that be even conspired, as mentioned, to thwart all Brodsky's efforts to make a modest living with translations; his friends, on the other hand, used every loophole to improve his condition.[122]

For a time, Brodsky toyed with the idea of marriage to an American citizen, a status that could provide him with the rare privilege, in the Soviet context, of freedom to travel abroad and to return at will.[123] Such was the situation of his close friend Diana Myers, as mentioned earlier. Another plan was to arrange an invitation as poet-in-residence at a Western university, but this sounded so fantastic that when he mentioned it to his friends in Moscow, they all broke out in laughter, including Brodsky. No one could believe that the Soviet authorities would ever allow this to happen. Viktor Golyshev recalled:

> I remember all three of us were sitting together, [Brodsky] and [Andrei] Sergeev and the conversation began about the possibility of becoming a poet-in-residence somewhere [at a Western college or university]. Naturally, all of us broke out in laughter—this seemed to come straight out of a fantasy land. But at one point I directly asked him: "Don't you want to emigrate?" He said: "This is out of the question." So, for me his departure was a surprise. But the choice he was really facing was that of either travelling to the West or to the East [i.e., to Siberia].[124]

Brodsky's fate was, however, decided by the so-called forces of history. When "a tyrannical and repressive regime forced him [Brodsky] into separation from his nourishing mother tongue and immediate cultural milieu,"[125] as the eminent Slavic scholar Sidney Monas so succinctly put it, this ironically allowed Brodsky to realize at least one of his initial ideas—becoming a poet-in-residence at the University of Michigan in Ann Arbor.

Chapter Three

America as a Continuation of Space

AS NOTED, on June 4, 1972, Brodsky was forced, at short notice, to leave his home country for good. He was flown to Vienna, while his elderly parents, his ex-girlfriend and their son, and his closest friends and readers stayed behind. The only familiar face he saw at the airport was Carl Proffer, who had come from the United States. Within days, Proffer and Brodsky drove to meet with Auden at his Austrian summerhouse. Later that same month, Brodsky traveled in the company of Auden to attend the Poetry International Festival in London, where they stayed in the house of Stephen and Natasha Spender, whom Brodsky would regard in the years to come as his family in the West. Brodsky had a very warm reception in London, where he recited his poems in Russian in the presence of Auden and Spender, with Robert Lowell reading the English translations. Daniel Weissbort, a British poet and translator present at the reading, was impressed by Brodsky's manner of reciting poetry:

> This must have been Joseph's first public reading in the West. Even the normally reserved British public was moved by the sight of the young poet and by his emotional if stentorian recitation. Joseph stood on the stage, textless, his hands hanging by his side, or thrust into his jacket pockets. His head thrown back, he declaimed the poems, staring into the air above his listeners, as if communing with himself rather than addressing an audience. . . . Whether you understood Russian or not, you understood Brodsky that night.[1]

Brodsky was struck by the contrast with his Russian experience, as he explained in a letter to a friend back in Leningrad. Written in Russian, the letter was characteristically interspersed with occasional expressions in English:

> Then we stayed at Stephen Spender's place and performed at the Queen Elizabeth Hall; Bobby Lowell read my poems in English, and W.H. was telling me something with tears, which I could not understand, because of the

nerves . . . and I felt lousy, because back home was no such hall and because the people around me were shaking my hand . . .[2]

Irena Grudzinska Gross has argued that while his Soviet experience toughened him up, making Brodsky capable of withstanding adversity, he would find himself at a loss whenever he encountered more sympathetic responses: "He knew how to react to hostility . . . but was totally disarmed by affection."[3]

"TO PLEASE A SHADOW": AUDEN'S BLESSING

With the benefit of hindsight, Brodsky considered his time spent with Auden during their brief friendship, which lasted a little over a year before Auden passed away, to be one of the greatest blessings of his life. When Auden died on September 28, 1973, Brodsky was devastated. He sent his editor at Penguin Books a telegram just in time to include this dedication in his *Selected Poems*: "To the Memory of Wystan Hugh Auden 1907–1973."[4] The news had reached Brodsky in New York City, where he requested a Mass in Auden's memory at the Cathedral Church of St. John the Divine, which he described in a letter to a friend back in Leningrad:

> Auden died, in Vienna, in a hotel, in his sleep, having consumed a good amount of alcohol beforehand as well as his usual sleeping pills. I was in NY then and ordered (a big—it turned out to be big) Mass in the Cathedral of St. John the Divine. Somehow no-one else had thought of it. You might find this silly, but he was the second person whom I revered: he was a great man. There are no people like him back home. Nor are there any here now. I last saw him in London in July.[5]

It is symbolic of his special relationship with English poetry that Brodsky was the only Russian poet to organize a service in memory of an English-language poet besides Pushkin, who arranged one for Byron at an Orthodox church.[6] Auden was the second person whom Brodsky revered. It is not hard to figure out who the first one was. In fact, in his unfinished memoir about Brodsky, Carl Proffer drew parallels between Brodsky's encounter with Auden and his friendship with Akhmatova in the last years of her life.[7] Brodsky was sensitive to such symbolic moments, in which the literary baton was passed from one epoch to another. If Akhmatova's approval had, as it were, consecrated him as her heir-successor on the Russian Parnassus, Auden's endorsement could be interpreted as a blessing on his future exploits in English. And while the elegy that Brodsky wrote in 1973, and did not republish,[8] indicated some unease about being left to fill Auden's shoes, with the benefit of hindsight he realized that Auden's influence and friendship helped him to develop as a poet and a prose writer. Indeed, Brodsky would later cite his wish to please Auden's "shadow" as the main reason he eventually turned to English: "In the summer of 1977 . . . [I] set out to write (essays, translations, occasionally a poem) in English. . . . My sole purpose . . . was to find myself in closer proximity to the man whom I considered the greatest mind of the twentieth century: Wystan Hugh Auden."[9]

THE UNFORESEEN CHALLENGES OF EXILE

Brodsky did not launch himself overnight into composing poetry in English. He emerged as an English-language author only gradually. In the immediate aftermath of his forced emigration, Brodsky's greatest challenge was not writing in English, but ensuring his survival as a Russian poet on foreign soil. Initially, his exile threatened to upset his entire artistic and psychological balance. In letters and conversations with close friends during his first weeks in the West, there are signs of authentic emotional turmoil.[10] He would later recall that in America he had been at first gripped by "real panic and trepidation."[11] He feared that, separated from his native tongue, he might gradually forget Russian and eventually lose his ability to compose poetry altogether.[12]

Shortly after settling in America in July 1972, Brodsky received a letter from his fellow poet-exile Czesław Miłosz which provided crucial psychological support in overcoming his initial anxiety. Miłosz, who had arguably faced even greater challenges in connection with his exile from communist Poland in 1951,[13] wrote the following: "I think that you are very worried, like all of us from our part of Europe—brought up on the myth that the life of a writer ends if he abandons his native country. But it is only a myth. . . . Everything depends on the man and on his internal health."[14] Grudzinska Gross argues that Brodsky took Miłosz's letter as a personal challenge and set out on a quest to prove that a poet worth his salt should not depend on geography.[15] He soon developed a psychological stratagem that would later crystallize into his main stance on exile. Brodsky convinced himself, and tried to convince others, that his forced emigration from the Soviet Union had not changed, nor could have changed, anything essential in his life, that his American life was merely a continuation of his former life in Leningrad. Evidently, Brodsky wanted to break the curse by which external forces could radically change the course of his existence, as had notoriously been the case with previous generations of Russian poets. Akhmatova's tragic lines from her "Northern Elegies" summed up her own experience as well as that of an entire prerevolutionary generation, as Brodsky argued in his essay in memory of his parents. He translated those lines into English:

> Just like a river,
> I was deflected by my stalwart era.
> They swapped my life: into a different valley,
> past different landscapes, it went rolling on.
> And I don't know my banks or where they are.[16]

THE POET FINDS HIS FOOTING

Brodsky's main stance on his exile in America can be illustrated by an anecdote told to me by Brodsky's Italian friend, the Slavic scholar Fausto Malcovati, who had known Brodsky in Leningrad in the late 1960s, met with his parents, and seen him in the famous "room and a half." When Malcovati visited Brodsky in his apartment in Greenwich Village in New York City, he marveled as to how the poet had been able to deal with such a change in his lifestyle and situation. Later in his essay about his parents, Brodsky himself admitted that there was an enormous difference between his Russian and American lives: "The reality I face bears . . . no correspondence to the room and a half and its two inhabitants. . . . As alternatives go, I can't think of anything more drastic than where I am at. *The difference is that . . . between night and day* [italics mine]."[17] Notably, the answer Brodsky had earlier given his Italian friend was startlingly different: "One day I noticed that the hand which puts a Mozart LP on the turntable is the same hand that used to make this movement when I lived at my parents' house in Leningrad, and the LP is the same too. At that moment I realized that nothing had essentially changed in my life."[18] The same idea is echoed in Brodsky's poem "Lullaby of Cape Cod," written on the occasion of America's bicentennial, in which he famously referred to his exile as merely "the change of Empires."[19] For all the obvious differences between the Soviet and American "empires," there was a continuity in one respect; his métier continued to occupy the same position in the poet's life as before: "For after all . . . the device in your hand is the same old pen and ink."[20] Time and again Brodsky reiterated the same idea with remarkable consistency. Here is another example from a post-Nobel interview he gave in 1988:

> Interviewer: Your exile can be seen as a sort of translation of its own. . . . Has it caused a significant schism in your writing?

Brodsky: No—if anything it involves continuity. Every land and every country is a continuation of space.[21]

It is fascinating to see how adamant Brodsky was about this notion of a "continuation of space." His letters to friends are enlightening in this regard. In them, Brodsky would often dash out his ideas in their raw state, before they got distilled into poetry or became more formulaic, as in his interviews and essays. For instance, in March 1974, during his second year in the United States, Brodsky wrote to his Leningrad friends Romas and Elvira Katilius: "From my point of view, it's in bad taste to think that space matters or that it can change anything. If one were to follow this logic, border crossings should be seen every half a mile, i.e., as soon as a person disappears out of sight."[22] In the same letter, Brodsky admitted that the only time his formula did not work was when he tried to relive the sensation of being on a tram headed to his friends' Leningrad apartment: "In this case my thesis that America is just a continuation of space somehow does not work. In all other cases (or almost all) it works."[23] Most strikingly, in a letter sent around the same time to another friend in Leningrad, Lev Losev (Loseff), Brodsky extended this principle to his main artistic tool, language: "I should tell you many things but have a block for letters. The main idea—is that America—is just a continuation of space and that English language—is merely a new set of (phonetic) synonyms. Otherwise, it can really drive you up the wall."[24]

This sounds like a stunning admission. Just eighteen months into his American life, Brodsky had begun to regard English as a mere continuation of Russian by other means. Carried to its logical conclusion, the implication is that by some magic trick English would become "merely a new set of (phonetic) synonyms" of Russian. Moreover, Brodsky described this adoption of English as a continuation of Russian as a protection from being driven up the wall—that is, it enabled him to overcome the frustration and anger he felt after being forced from his homeland.[25]

This fascinating psychological nuance has not been considered by previous scholars, critics, or even some of his friends; this includes not only native English speakers, who were ever ready to jump at Brodsky for his unidiomatic use of their language, but even his fellow Slav Czesław Miłosz, the very person whose moral support of Brodsky had been critical early on in dealing with his exilic predicament. Thus, following a joint charity reading for Amnesty International in 1984, Miłosz wrote Brodsky a letter in which he urged his friend to keep his Russian and American poetic personae apart: "After our evening for the Amnesty International I wanted to talk to you at length about your Russian way of reading your poetry and your American way. It seems to me they should be kept separated. If we are sentenced to lead a dual life, let it be. With warm feelings, Czesław."[26] Miłosz was referring to Brodsky's strikingly emphatic way of performing his poetry in front of a live audience and urging him to read less dramatically and more like American poets do. Since Miłosz was the first to point out that Brodsky "did not resemble those recent Russian immigrants who stay in their Slavic shell and are mistrustful of the evil West,"[27] he expected him to behave accordingly. But as Brodsky had tried to explain in a 1974 letter to Losev, keeping his American and Russian artistic personae separate was not part of his plan. Instead, he insisted on a continuity between his two "incarnations," including his way of delivering poetry.

This is also why Brodsky resented being continually compared with another bilingual writer from his home city, Vladimir Nabokov. What strikes nonspecialists is that Brodsky became the only Russian writer besides Nabokov who, in the words of David Bethea, "transformed the loss and pain of exile into the miracle of bilingualism."[28] Bethea himself cautioned, however, that "the similarities stop at this porous level of abstraction."[29] Indeed, as pointed out by Alexander Dolinin, following his arrival in the United States, Nabokov "chose to forsake" his "filial loyalties" to Russian literature, switching exclusively to English.[30] Brodsky's task in America was, on the other hand, much more formidable. He tried to survive as a Russian poet, while simultaneously breaching new linguistic territories as an English-language writer. Brodsky's literary executor, Ann Kjellberg, put the two men's differences in a nutshell:

> A master of an artistic medium comes to us from another language. He embraces our culture and our verse. He dedicates much of his short life to struggling mightily to rewrite his own work so that it can be read and understood by his compatriots. (This in contrast with Nabokov, an oft-mentioned comparison. Nabokov not only grew up speaking English in his aristocratic Saint Petersburg household; he abandoned composition in Russian to become an English-language writer. *Brodsky remained primarily a Russian poet, crossing over into English and crossing back and embracing a bilingual literary career.*) [Italics mine.][31]

No wonder Brodsky would be loath to let the Nabokov comparison overshadow his own artistic and linguistic ambitions.[32]

In the politically charged atmosphere of the Cold War, the arrival in 1972 of a Russian poet expelled from the Soviet Union was a noteworthy event in America. As early as 1973, many prominent American magazines and newspapers, most importantly the *New Yorker*, published several English translations of Brodsky's poems done, at that stage, mainly by Kline. The magazine's poetry editor, Howard Moss, was a poet of distinction himself and became a great supporter of Brodsky. Alongside the translations, Brodsky gave numerous interviews on television and to widely circulated magazines such as *Vogue*, whose legendary editorial director and fellow Russian émigré Alexander Liberman became another long-standing champion. In addition, in his first year in the United States Brodsky gave more than thirty poetry readings, traveling to over twenty American states. At universities and colleges, he would read in Russian accompanied by a native English speaker (in the first years it was often Kline). To sustain this rising popularity in American letters, Brodsky badly needed new translations of his verse into English; his very future in this new linguistic environment hinged on it.

ROGER STRAUS ENTERS THE SCENE

> Meet Roger W. Straus
> He runs a publishing house.
> He's so gentle at that
> that were he a cat
> I'd gladly serve as a mouse.[33]
> (Joseph Brodsky)

In 1975 Nancy Meiselas, an editor at Farrar, Straus and Giroux, introduced Brodsky to Roger Straus, head of the esteemed publishing house on Union Square in Manhattan.[34] The importance of this encounter for the phenomenon of the "English Brodsky" can hardly be overestimated. It marked a new stage, distinctly different from the translation under duress that Brodsky experienced when publishing tamizdat while he was still in the Soviet Union. With Straus's support, Brodsky soon took full control over the translation of his Russian oeuvre into English. Straus became Brodsky's ally for life and showered him with his boundless and proverbial generosity, not only organizing English publications of Brodsky's work but also serving as his agent around the world.[35]

Officially, Straus agreed to publish a new collection of English translations of Brodsky's poetry in 1977.[36] But the actual preparations for *A Part of Speech* had already begun at some point in 1975. Brodsky's role was far greater than that of the author of the original Russian texts. He had to find and commission translators for every single poem himself. He had to provide and commission interlinear translations and commentaries on the meaning and the prosodic structure of his verse for those translators who were unfamiliar with or insecure about their Russian.

Certainly, the position of Brodsky's translators in translating a living poet was special. The advantages included a kind of feedback that was unimaginable in translating the work of the deceased. They benefited, for example, from Brodsky's explanations of unclear passages and from his commentaries on the tonality of passages that he deemed important to preserve. On the other hand, Brodsky, whose English was rapidly evolving, had been a translator of poetry from Russian into English himself and held strong, idiosyncratic views about translation. Thus, the translators had to deal with the impatience of an artist in the process of reembodying his oeuvre into another language just as his expertise in English was growing. Some were stunned to discover how strongly Brodsky felt about the language. It was a painstaking process for both author and translator to scrutinize every single English line of translation, and this resulted in a series of conflicts, sometimes unnecessary, with translators and their offended egos. These conflicts significantly postponed the publication of *A Part of Speech*, which ultimately took five years to prepare (1975–80).

"DE-KLINED"

Having arrived in the United States in July 1972, Brodsky could finally meet with George Kline in person, after four years of long-distance collaboration on *Joseph Brodsky: Selected Poems*, and review the drafts of the book.[37] When eventually presented with the final set of proofs in April 1973, Brodsky appeared content with the result, as can be seen from a letter to Kline:

> It looks great. What more I might now wish for in this world I still don't know. Perhaps to marry Vanessa Redgrave? I have given the book only a cursory look, but I cannot look at it in greater detail anyway. I can only say this: despite all the talk of the difference between a translation and the original, the book has come out fairly well. I don't think anyone could have done a better job. For a poet this would have been an "ego-trip"; for a translator—a business trip. Anyway, I believe you know yourself how lucky I am. It is needless to say, I should thank your mom for giving birth to you, as it is needless to say that I thank you for what you have done for me in English.[38]

Reading those words of gratitude and appreciation, one might assume that Brodsky would commission the same man to translate his next English collection, especially since Brodsky reassuringly mentioned that he did not necessarily prefer a real poet to do the translation and that Kline's devotion had allowed him to achieve superior results. It was probably in the capacity of translator-in-chief that Kline in 1975 discussed the logistics of the next book with Nancy Meiselas, Brodsky's editor at Farrar, Straus and Giroux.[39] However, this was not how events unfolded, as is evident from Meiselas's letter in April 1976 to Barry Rubin, who became one of Brodsky's closest advisors during the preparation of *A Part of Speech*:

> Dear Barry,
>
> George [Kline] was in for lunch today, and I have to admit that seeing him was far from a delight. He did bring the re-typed version of the "Cape Cod" poem; a copy is enclosed for you. It's clear to me that he is perplexed and a little hurt that everyone but George L. Kline has been asked to work on translations. . . . Apparently, Joseph has told him to go ahead with "Mary Stuart" as well as "Cape Cod,"[40] both of which he is trying to peddle. I explained all the details and problems to him, . . . but there are bound to be conflicts . . .
>
> Nancy[41]

Apparently, Kline, to his chagrin, had been commissioned to do far fewer translations for *A Part of Speech* than he had been hoping for.[42] Even worse, one can detect a hint of irreverence toward Kline in Meiselas's tone, which must have reflected a change in Brodsky's own attitude. What could have happened in this short span of time to cause such a drastic change of heart toward his early advocate?

The question that has since troubled onlookers is why Kline, whose translations had initially shaped Brodsky's image in English, did not remain in charge of translating the poet after he had "switched Empires."[43] Some have found Brodsky's dismissal of Kline unfair, or even ungrateful, given all he had done for the poet. Barry Rubin, on the other hand, remembered that Brodsky had a strong and unwavering sense of obligation toward Kline, but he was equally concerned with the way his poetry came across in English. At some point, these two concerns would collide: "Joseph was extremely loyal to many friends. But the complication was that here was the sense of his poetry. So he was torn between his personal loyalty [toward Kline] and his loyalty to his poems, his loyalty to the language."[44]

SECOND OPINIONS: MYERS, SPENDER, AND RUBIN CRITIQUE KLINE

Shortly after his exile to the West, Brodsky sent a sample of Kline's translations for *Selected Poems* to Alan Myers, his London friend and a translator of Russian literature, to ask for a second opinion from a native speaker. Myers's assessment of Kline's work was very positive. He reassured Brodsky that Kline's translations were indeed of a high quality and pointed out that Brodsky had been very lucky with Kline, and, on the whole, the translations read very well. They "reflected the spirit of the original"; some were "splendidly witty," while others were "almost magical." Myers admitted, on the other hand, that sometimes the "rhythm jerked," and that at times "English words have been added to preserve the rhythm" (i.e., Kline had resorted to padding). Despite these minor issues, Myers believed that *Selected Poems* would do its author great credit with anglophone readers.[45]

Fifteen months later, after the book had finally come out, Stephen Spender gave a more mixed appraisal in his review of *Selected Poems*, titled "The Bread of Affliction," which appeared in the *New Statesman* on December 14, 1973. Spender's review was much more direct in its pronouncements than, for instance, Auden's 1969 foreword, when Brodsky was still living the life of a persecuted poet in the Soviet Union. Auden had had to tread very carefully so as not to aggravate the precarious situation of the already beleaguered poet, and so he had adopted a guarded tone. In contrast, when Spender was writing his review, Brodsky was living safely in the West, and the reviewer could afford to be outspoken. Among other things, Spender could now openly mention that there were many echoes of English and American poetry in Brodsky's verse, "from Donne to Byron, T. S. Eliot and W. H. Auden."[46] Back in Leningrad, such an innocuous comment alone would have rubbed against the jingoistic attitudes of Soviet officialdom and might have resulted in repercussions against Brodsky. Thereafter, Spender went over Kline's translations in great detail. Spender noted that he had derived his idea of "the technical virtuosity of brilliant rhyming" of Brodsky's poetry mainly from Kline's preface, not from the translations themselves. These featured instead some "jaw-breakers": "The road's as stubborn as / the river. / The ash-tree's shadow is / a fishnet," so that one is "never quite allowed to forget that one is reading a second-hand version." In other words, one gathers that Kline's work does not, in fact, always meet the high standards of poetic diction. On the other hand, Spender praised Kline's translations for their honesty, "which enables one to imagine the poetry that always lies just beyond it."[47] Spender also praised Kline for the literalness of his translations and for his refusal to embellish Brodsky or tailor his words to the tastes of the target audience. This literalistic accuracy had been something Brodsky himself appreciated about Kline's translations. Spender further surmised that Kline's translations conveyed "the concreteness, density, literalness of the lines of observation out of which Brodsky constructs his poems."[48] Spender's remarks offered praise but also conveyed implicit criticism of some of Kline's work, exposing Kline's insecurities as a translator. Days after Spender's review came out, Kline wrote Brodsky the following:

> Yes, the Spender review was very perceptive in some ways, though he made a rather silly error about Воротишься на родину,[49] assuming that it was written late in 1965, when in fact it dates from 1961 and has nothing to do with

> "return from prison and exile." I assume that you were returning, rather, from a geological or archaeological expedition. Since he doesn't know Russian, I'm not sure on what grounds he can speak of the "honesty" of my translations. In any case, many of the things he says about their being "near-poetry" would apply, in my judgement, to the translations of Rilke's *Duino Elegies* that he did with Leishman. . . . So, the presence of a poet on the translating team doesn't appear to guarantee success.[50]

It seems that deep down Kline sensed that he was really an amateur translator, which made him feel vulnerable. In fact, the argument that he was not really a poet was later used against him by Farrar, Straus and Giroux as an excuse to assign him only a small number of translations for *A Part of Speech*. Kline's bitterness also stemmed from the fact that Spender had allowed himself to make those categorical pronouncements without knowing any Russian. Kline had every right to be bitter. When it came to poetry in English, Spender was an authority, and his questioning of Kline's abilities clearly did not enhance Kline's chances of maintaining his status as Brodsky's translator-in-chief. One cannot rule out the possibility that Kline might later have attributed his falling from Brodsky's favor to the Spender review. Indeed, Spender's words stuck to him for almost a decade. It was then that the American poet and critic Dana Gioia, who also did not know Russian, reiterated some of Spender's criticisms of Kline's translations almost verbatim in his review of *A Part of Speech*: "When Joseph Brodsky's *Selected Poems* were published in 1973, I admired his work for its energy and imagination but still found the volume difficult to read at long stretches. . . . George Kline's translations, although quite good in some ways, also had an uncanny knack of suggesting how much the reader was missing of the original."[51]

Although some of Spender's criticisms were undoubtedly valid, Alan Myers was closer to the truth when he argued that *Selected Poems* would do its author great credit, notwithstanding its imperfections. *Selected Poems* proved to be hugely important for Brodsky's growing stature in the West. No publication, especially during his first years in the United States, would have been possible had it not been for the existence of that book. At the same time, Brodsky's new attitude toward Kline might be traced back to a dramatic change in Brodsky's own situation. After signing the contract for a new collection with Straus, Brodsky could commission poets of great stature to translate his verse, including Richard Wilbur, Anthony Hecht, and Howard Moss. In these favorable circumstances, Brodsky might understandably be tempted to give precedence to translators who were poets in their own right, rather than just translators of poetry. On the whole, it could be said that this practice of securing poets to translate poetry harkens back to the Soviet experience, where it was essentially all that poets were allowed to do, as will be further discussed in chapter 5. In the West, where poets are allowed to devote their lives to their own work, it is much less common. These poets took Brodsky on out of affection for him and enthusiasm for his project, but it was decidedly an unusual way of creating a book.

By the mid-1970s Barry Rubin, a professor of Russian at Queens College, became the de facto coeditor of *A Part of Speech*, as Kline had been the de facto editor of *Selected Poems*. In preparing *A Part of Speech*, Rubin did several interlinear translations for poets who did not know Russian. In addition, both Brodsky and Rubin went over Kline's versions of Brodsky's earlier poems with the idea of possibly including some in the new collection.[52] It was then that Rubin pointed out to Brodsky that Kline's translations often did not sound quite right, and that many of them lacked musicality or were simply "flat."[53] Kline did tend to be conservative, trying to stay close to the literal meaning of the original. While this approach worked with some poems, there were others where Rubin thought the music should be more prominent (i.e., Kline had failed to bring it out) and required something else from the translator. At the same time, Rubin also mentioned that Brodsky could often be very thoughtless. For instance, when Kline would say that he was working on a translation of this or that poem, Brodsky would not discourage him: "Instead of saying upfront: 'George, don't do it,' Joseph would give that work to somebody else. While George was very devoted to him, Joseph wanted to recognize his debt to him, so rather than hurt somebody, George in particular, he would not put things clearly, which made things even worse."[54] On one occasion, Brodsky's ambiguity led, in fact, to a rather unpleasant episode involving Kline and Anthony Hecht, an American poet of great distinction and a protégé of Auden.

THE "CAPE COD LULLABY" IMBROGLIO

In early 1977, Kline announced in the *New York Times* that he was translating "Lullaby of Cape Cod," Brodsky's long poem written on the occasion of the American bicentennial. Later the same year, in another publication, in an article titled "Working with Brodsky," Kline made a similar announcement, referring to the poem as the "powerful and original 360-line 'Cape Cod Lullaby' (1975)—which with Brodsky's generous guidance, I am now laboring to put into English."[55] This was despite the fact that Anthony Hecht had already been commissioned to translate the poem. Foreseeing a conflict, Meiselas pointed this out to Brodsky in a letter:

> I had lunch with George earlier in the month, and I told him who was translating what. Did you realize that he is still working on his version of "Cape

> Cod Lullaby"? I know we all told him at least a year ago that Anthony Hecht was doing the poem, and I'm particularly annoyed that he mentioned only his version in that *NY Times* article last month, but anyway I've reiterated that the poem cannot be published without our express permission.[56]

But despite his tendency toward self-effacement, on this occasion Kline would not be sidelined so easily. He now used all his astute networking skills to make certain that his translation would take precedence over Hecht's. Thus, in the spring of 1977, Kline got in touch with Hecht in order to persuade him to relinquish his translation of the poem in Kline's favor:

> Dear Tony Hecht,
>
> . . . Joseph tells me that you've agreed to do it, working with an interlinear version. I would be delighted to defer to you, but in this particular case the poem is very close to me, and I've already invested a great deal of time and energy in putting it into English . . . I know that Joseph would be happy to have both of us translate "Cape Cod Lullaby"; and eventually I hope that everything of his I've done can be redone by a real poet. But in the meantime it seems to me more pressing to provide English readers with a wider sampling of his work by doing what hasn't yet been done at all.[57]

Kline assumes here the tone of editor, a tone to which he had been accustomed since the days of his work on *Selected Poems*. Now, however, Brodsky had a different editor at Farrar, Straus and Giroux, Nancy Meiselas. Apparently, Kline was trying to create a back channel to get his translation published. Hecht did not take Kline's initiative lightly. It was not customary for established American poets to do translations, and Hecht would have been doing Brodsky and Farrar, Straus and Giroux a favor by having accepted such a major assignment. It was a big gift to the project, and Hecht knew it. This might explain the tantrum he threw in response to Kline's letter, as evidenced by Hecht's own account of the events in a letter to Meiselas:

> I received a quite extraordinary letter from George L. Kline, who wrote to me from England. He said that he had heard rumors (God knows how or from whom) that I was working on the "lullaby," and went on to say that it was in fact one of his favorite poems, with which he had lived and on which he had meditated for a long time, and toward which he entertained a very intimate and proprietary feeling. He therefore urged me to consider translating any other Brodsky poem I cared for, but indicated that the "lullaby" was a rather privileged preserve of his own. Inasmuch as Joseph had particularly asked me to tackle the poem, Kline's letter was provoking. But since I had not yet begun any serious work on the translation, I wrote a brusque letter to Kline,

> saying that while I was unaware of his special claims to the poem, and though Joseph had asked me to do it, . . . I washed my hands of it completely; and told him that he should get in touch with Joseph to explain how he had contrived to take over the translation.[58]

As a result of this falling-out, Brodsky had to intervene directly and explain to Hecht in a phone call that Kline had no privileges or any special entitlements regarding that particular poem, and to reassure Hecht that he was the one to do the translation. All of this added insult to injury for Kline, who was already struggling to cope with his suddenly diminished importance. Still, even after this episode, Kline continued to push his own version of "Lullaby": "If, by a stroke of luck, both he and I produce versions which satisfy both you and Nancy M., then perhaps both can be included in *A Part of Speech*. This sort of thing was done, quite successfully I think, in the Montale *Selected Poems* of 1965."[59] Ironically, when Hecht later presented his own final version of the poem, Brodsky wrote to him saying that there were about ninety-three lines too many in his translation and offered a list of amendments he thought Hecht needed to make. Hecht responded that he was done with the translation and that if Brodsky was not going to publish it, he was going to publish it himself, which he eventually did. According to both Rubin and Derek Walcott, Brodsky was very upset that he could not exercise his influence over Hecht, and he considered turning again to Kline's translation. But it was already very late; the publishing deadline was looming; and Brodsky's editor at Farrar, Straus and Giroux, as well as his collaborators Rubin and Walcott, managed to persuade Brodsky to accept Hecht's "Lullaby of Cape Cod" as it was. Nevertheless, nearly a decade later, in an interview with David Montenegro, Brodsky could still not quite get over the fact that Hecht's translation was considerably longer than the original, despite the acclaim the translation of the poem had brought him with anglophone readers.[60]

The Kline-Hecht controversy showed that translations done by famous poets could prove to be less fruitful for Brodsky in the long run. In Brodsky's experience, poets were usually less flexible than translators who were not also poets and who often didn't have well-established reputations to fall back on. The *Part of Speech* collection also acquired the traits of what Walcott later described as a "not necessarily desirable variety of an anthology of Brodsky seen through the eyes of contemporary American poets."[61] Despite, or perhaps because of, the high stature of some of the poets involved in translating *A Part of Speech*, Brodsky's own voice is arguably less audible than in his reworkings of translations done by just-translators.

Chapter Four

"A Second Christmas by the Shore"

THE AMERICAN EXCHANGES between Brodsky and Kline about translation have graced us with an especially large number of archival troves. Due to the special trust between them, rooted in their close cooperation on *Selected Poems*, Brodsky was more direct in his communications with Kline than with any of his other English-language translators, and he supplied Kline with detailed commentaries on prosody, tone, meaning, and emotion, as well as other aspects of his originals. These exchanges provide us with rare glimpses into what Brodsky deemed important in his poetry and essential in its translation. He was always ready to point out to Kline what a translator could not afford to overlook.

Furthermore, Brodsky's comments often help clarify obscure passages in his Russian poems. For his part, Kline, whether due to personal humility or out of strong devotion to Brodsky, was extremely indulgent, continually reworking his drafts as long as Brodsky found something objectionable in them. Owing to Kline's indulgence, these drafts provide a record of the earliest instances of Brodsky's involvement in self-translation.

One of the most detailed exchanges about translation between Brodsky and Kline took place in 1976 in connection with the poem "Vtoroe Rozhdestvo na beregu," translated as "A Second Christmas by the Shore." Here is my interlinear translation of the first stanza of the four-stanza poem, followed by the transliterated original poem in Russian. (All stresses in the Russian transliteration are marked in bold. Capital letters stand for a feminine ending, and the lowercase letters stand for a masculine ending, e.g., aBBa.)

A second Christmas on the shore
of an unfreezing Pontus.
The star of the kings [hangs] over the port's fence.
And I can't say I can't
live without you—because I am alive,
as follows from [this] paper. I exist,
gulp my beer, soil the leaves, and
tread on the grass.

Vtor**o**e Rozhdestv**o** na bereg**u**	enj.	a	5-foot-iambic
nezamerz**a**iushchego P**o**nta.		B	4-foot-iambic
Zvezd**a** Tsar**e**i nad **i**zgorod'iu p**o**rta.		B	5-foot-iambic
I ne mog**u** skaz**a**t', chto ne mog**u**	enj.	a	5-foot-iambic
zh**i**t' bez tebi**a**—posk**o**l'ku ia zhiv**u**.		c	5-foot-iambic
Kak v**i**dno iz bum**a**gi. Sushchestv**u**iu;		D	5-foot-iambic
glot**a**iu p**i**vo, p**a**chkaiu listv**u** i	enj.	D	5-foot-iambic
topch**u** trav**u**.[1]		c	2-foot-iambic

"A Second Christmas" is both a love elegy of retrospection and amorous nostalgia, and a Christmas poem. At Christmastime, the poem's lyrical hero revisits a sea resort in the southern province of the country—or of the empire, as Brodsky often referred to the Soviet Union in his poetry. Sitting in a café, he recalls the happy days he had spent with his beloved earlier in the same setting. The opening of the poem reads like the beginning of a Christmas postcard in which the speaker describes his circumstances and his mood.

It's worth noting that Christmas poems occupy a special place in Brodsky's oeuvre: starting with his "Christmas Ballad" in 1962, Brodsky tried to compose a poem every year around Christmas in celebration of Jesus Christ's birthday.[2] Needless to say, this custom of paying homage to the Christian Savior clashed with an ostensibly atheistic Soviet culture, dominated by a materialist ideology. In *Watermark*, his essay-cum-book dedicated to his love affair with Venice, Brodsky described himself as an agnostic, explaining that Christmas and New Year represented for him a joint holiday associated with the passage of time.[3] After his forced departure from Russia, Brodsky would travel to Venice every Christmas in a somewhat ritualistic fashion: "Every New Year's Eve, in somewhat pagan fashion, I try to find myself near water, preferably near a sea or an ocean, to watch the emergence of a new helping, a new cupful of time from it."[4] Indeed, all of Brodsky's Christmas poems, including "A Second Christmas by the Shore," deal, in one way or another, with the theme of time.

The poem contains four eight-line stanzas, rhymed aBBacDDc; the first seven lines of each stanza are in iambic pentameter, whereas the last line is a dimeter, a short two-foot iambic line. Kline and Brodsky were in full agreement that the translator had to try his best to preserve the original form across translation. Kline made this clear in an early piece about their collaboration, including the translation of "Vtoroe Rozhdestvo" (1971).[5] The poem's iambic pentameter has a direct equivalent in English. In theory, this should have facilitated the translator's task. Yet despite their unanimity on this important principle, several of Brodsky's changes concern the way the poem's meter should be rendered in English.

THE FIRST STANZA

Brodsky opened his first letter to Kline about his first draft of "Vtoroe Rozhdestvo" with a disarming compliment. Clearly anxious not to sound ungrateful for the hard work Kline had put into his translation, Brodsky tried to reassure his translator that, on the whole, he was happy with the first draft. Following this diplomatic prelude, however, he pivoted to problematic issues:

> Dear George,
>
> This is so lovely a poem in English that it's hard for me to be hard on you. Still, there are some things, which are sheer misunderstandings; also, there are certain substitutions, which hamper the meaning. So, I'll try to point out both, but care should be taken, first of all about the latter.[6]

Here is Kline's version of the first stanza with some of Brodsky's markings, followed by his comments:

A second Christmas spent beside the shore   by the shore
of that great Sea which winter does not stiffen.
The Star of Kings above a harbor cliff. And
I cannot claim that I cannot endure
your absence—since, quite clearly, I exist.
~~This paper is the witness~~. I am living;
I gulp my beer and soil the bushes, leaving
crushed clumps of grass.

I 1st line: 'spent' I think, could be omitted.
2nd line: it is 'Pontus' ('Euxinus'); 'that great Sea' doesn't produce necessary implications—slight paganistic touch
3rd line: I understand the rhyme, but the presence of 'cliff' carries on the image of 'crib', don't you think?
6th: it's much more beurocratic [*sic*] I don't think that 'exist' and 'grass' are rhymes either.[7]

Regarding the first line, Brodsky pointed out an extra word, "spent," which emerged in the translation but did not feature in the original and seemed unnecessary here. Kline introduced "spent," which adjacent to "beside" is an artificial usage, adding two feet of extraneous material, where the important elements are Christmas and the shore. This is a typical example of Kline's "padding," the practice of inserting a word into the translation purely to preserve the meter. Indeed, Kline's first line managed to reproduce most accurately the pentametric beat of the original: "A second Christmas spent beside the shore." The first line in Brodsky's redaction became two syllables shorter, turning the opening line into a tetrameter instead: "A second Christmas by the shore." In theory, Brodsky's rendition stood in conflict with the main principle of equimetrical translation—translation that strives to replicate the metrical structure of the original—a rule upon which both Kline and Brodsky seemed to agree. However, the second line of the poem in Russian, which was also two syllables shorter ("*nezamerzaiushchego Ponta*"), broke with the pentametric inertia of the first line. One might thus argue that the small metrical variation Brodsky introduced in the first line of his English translation, a substitution of tetrameter for pentameter, was not only acceptable but better reflected the prosodic balance of the entire stanza in the original. Since he was not the author, Kline could not have initiated such a bold decision. He could simply try to reproduce the metrical structure of the original verbatim, which in this case was pentametric. Moreover, having incomparably less experience with poetic practice than Brodsky, his solutions tended to be more conservative than the poet's.

Kline's omission of the word "Pontus" as a reference to the Black Sea in the second line was something that equally upset Brodsky. Finding it either too exotic or simply incompatible with the pentametric beat, Kline paraphrased the word as "that great Sea." Brodsky responded that without the word "Pontus," the poem would lose the "slight paganistic touch" it apparently required.

In his essay on Mandelstam, Brodsky argued that Russian poetry traditionally regarded the Crimea and the Black Sea as the only available approximation of the classical world, "of which these places—Taurida and Pontus Euxinus—used to be the outskirts."[8] It appears that Brodsky tried to continue this tradition in his Crimean Christmas poem. Moreover, following the model of Mandelstam's poem "Tristia," which Brodsky later translated into English, he wanted to produce an echo of the *Tristia* and the *Epistulae ex Ponto*, written in elegaic couplets by the Augustan poet Ovid during his exile at the Black Sea.[9] The echo of Ovid is important for specific reasons: on the one hand, the speaker is clearly sensitive to the reverberations of the ancient world still palpable in Soviet-era Yalta; and on the other hand, the forsaken and estranged (that is, exiled) situation of the lyrical hero himself evokes the Ovidian epistles.

Incidentally, in the same Mandelstam essay, Brodsky noted that "in almost every case when Mandelstam happens to deal with [the] theme of time, he resorts to a rather heavily caesuraed verse which echoes the [classical] hexameter either in its beat or in its content. It is usually an iambic pentameter lapsing into alexandrine verse."[10] Accordingly, in a creative writing class at Mount Holyoke College, Brodsky assigned the writing of an elegy; he described the elegy as "a lady with a very rich and colourful past;" explaining specifically that therefore his students' "choice here is not so much with how original you are going to be, but rather with whom or what you are going to imitate or echo. As to being original, your best chance here lies with the kind of rhymes you are going to use or with the meter and stanzaic design."[11]

Time and again Brodsky emphasized that the choice of formal poetic devices is part of one's expression as a poet.

The Rhymes in the First Stanza

Rhymes in poetry are the strongest instruments of euphonic and semantic emphasis, and they are also the bane of the translator. Two words that rhyme in one language almost never do in another; hence, finding words that will rhyme in translation is a notoriously difficult task. Vladimir Nabokov famously rhymed "rhyme" with "crime" in his essay on the English translation of Pushkin's *Eugene Onegin*, rebuking translators who inevitably sacrificed the meaning in an effort to maintain the rhymes. In contrast to Nabokov's "semantic absolutism,"[12] Brodsky, whom Adrian Wanner has dubbed a "formal absolutist,"[13] demanded from his translators that they try to preserve the rhymes across translation at any cost. Among his translators, George Kline was the one who never questioned Brodsky's translating expectations and always tried to come up with exact rhymes as best he could. Yet some of the rhymes Kline devised were not acceptable to Brodsky: "I don't think that 'exist' and 'grass' are rhymes."[14]

The same goes for the third line, where Kline undertook an "acrobatic" attempt to come up with a feminine rhyme in English: "stiffen/cliff. And. . . ." Curiously, it seems that Kline was imitating here the style of none other than Brodsky himself in Russian. In fact, compound rhymes with prepositions or conjunctions placed in rhyming positions are a trademark of Brodsky's own poetics.[15] This effort of looking for affinities with the poetics of the original must have, in theory, pleased Brodsky. He called for this type of approach, for instance, in his reviews of Stanley Kunitz's English translations of Akhmatova.[16] For the sake of the rhyme, however, Kline has also changed the original imagery, introducing a "cliff" instead of a port's fence. As a result, the line that literally meant "The star of kings [is hanging] over the port's fence" had become "The Star of Kings above a harbor cliff. And / . . . ." Brodsky found this a poor substitute, especially since the fence was to reappear in the poem's most crucial scene in the fourth stanza. (Not to mention the fact that cliffside locales are not also ports.) Probably wary of hurting Kline's feelings, Brodsky gave a strikingly oblique explanation as to why "cliff" would not do in this context. He suggested that in a Christmas poem the word "cliff" would create unnecessary associations with "crib," which shows how attuned Brodsky always was to the musical implications of words. Yet this remark led instead to even greater confusion. Misinterpreting Brodsky's observation, Kline introduced in his second draft the word "crib," which was even further removed from the literal meaning of the original than "cliff."

Kline's First Revision

A couple of days later, Kline produced a new revised version of the translation. Here is the first stanza of his second draft, with subsequent revisions done in Brodsky's hand:

> A second Christmas by the Euxine's shore–
> a sea whose mirror winter does not harden.
> The Star of Kings above the harbor's crib. And
> I cannot claim that I cannot endure
> your absence since, quite clearly, I am here.
> Indeed, this paper proves it. I am living;
> I trample grass and soil the bushes, heaving
> down steins of beer.

> A second Christmas by the Euxine's shore–
> a sea ~~whose mirror winter does not~~ harden.
> The Star of Kings above the harbor's ~~crib~~. And
> I cannot claim that I cannot ~~endure~~
> ~~your absence~~ ^live without you^ since, quite clearly, I am here. ^,as^
> ~~Indeed~~, this paper proves it. I ~~am living~~; ^I do live^
> I ~~trample grass~~ ^gulp my beer^ and soil ~~the bushes, heaving~~ ^and soil the leaf^
> ~~down steins of beer~~ ^and trample grass.^[17]

Literal versus Metaphorical Interpretations

Brodsky struck out from Kline's second version the expression "[a sea] whose mirror winter does not harden," which was supposed to stand for the "unfreezing Pontus" of the original.

As mentioned earlier, the sea is a repository of time in Brodsky's cosmology.[18] So the "sea that does not freeze" works as a metaphor for time, whose flow is unceasing. With Brodsky, even the images that invite metaphorical interpretations very often retain their concrete, literal, and visual meanings. Just as in Collodi's *Pinocchio*, where the continuous transformations from the wooden puppet into the boy and back again take place throughout the entirety of the book—they are fused into one person and coexist contemporaneously—so in Brodsky's poetry, the switches from literal to metaphorical meanings of the same image coexist simultaneously. For instance, the "unfreezing Pontus" of the original literally depicted the Black Sea in winter. Kline's translation, "a sea whose mirror winter does not harden," did justice only to the literal meaning of the unfrozen "sea," but neglected the metaphorical component related to time and its flow, which was especially important to Brodsky in a Christmas poem. Besides, since the sea is unfrozen, it is in motion. It never turns into a mirror; there is no reflection. The mirror introduces a different element and is simply an irrelevant image here. This is why, it seems, Brodsky crossed out Kline's mirror metaphor from the second draft.[19]

Another expression removed by Brodsky from Kline's revised draft that merits comment is "[I] soil the bushes." In Russian, "*pachkaiu listvu*" ("I soil the leaves") could, in theory, refer to the lyrical hero's treading upon leaves on the ground, although it is questionable whether there were leaves on the ground at Christmastime in Yalta. But "*pachkaiu listvu*" ("I soil the leaves") could also be interpreted figuratively as "I am covering these sheets with ink." In fact, a "list" in Russian, as in German and Italian, can mean both "leaf" and "sheet of paper." Thus, the line can be interpreted as yet another expression of self-disparagement on the part of the lyrical hero, whose purpose is to highlight his futile endeavor to win back his beloved. Those efforts would include the very composition of the poem in question. Needless to say, the "soiled bushes" proposed by Kline, especially with "beer" mentioned in the same line, would produce, in English, associations of a far less sublime nature than an image of a sheet of paper covered with lines of love poetry. At that point, Brodsky decided not to trouble Kline with further demands and simply revised the rest of the translation himself.

Brodsky's Definitive Version

A second Christmas by the shore	4-foot iamb
of Pontus, which remains unfrozen.	4-foot iamb
The Star of Kings above the sharp horizon	5-foot iamb
of harbor walls. And I can't say for sure	5-foot iamb
that I can't live without you. As	4-foot iamb
this paper proves, I do exist: I'm living	5-foot iamb
enough to gulp my beer, to soil the leaves, and	5-foot iamb
trample the grass.[20]	iambic dimeter with a choriamb

The most striking difference between Kline's translation of the first stanza of the poem and Brodsky's revision concerns the metrical structure of the poem. Surprisingly, both of Kline's translation drafts turn out to be more consistent with the metrical structure of the original poem than Brodsky's subsequent revision, as discussed earlier. In fact, the first stanza in Brodsky's revision features just four pentametric lines, three tetrametric ones, and one dimeter, as opposed to seven pentametric lines followed by one dimeter, as per the original metrical scheme. Again, this challenges Brodsky's own demands for equimetrical translation, which presents as a striking peculiarity. A brief detour to Viktor Zhirmunsky's theory of comparative versification should clarify the apparent conundrum.

Meter versus Rhythm: Zhirmunsky's Theory of Verse

Viktor Zhirmunsky was a Russian formalist scholar whom Brodsky knew personally and whose house in Leningrad he frequented. He happened to be the first Russian theorist of comparative versification to introduce a clear-cut distinction between the concepts of meter and rhythm in Russian poetry.[21] Zhirmunsky explained that most modern European nations inherited the term "metrics" from the ancient Greeks and Romans, whose systems of versification were based on a regular alternation of long and short syllables, that is, on the principle of quantity. By contrast, in modern languages, the alternation of long and short syllables of classical versification had to be replaced by a difference in quality—the alternation of stressed and unstressed syllables. Zhirmunsky shows that to adapt to an essentially alien metrical system, modern European languages, such as English, German, Italian, French, and Russian, put up what he calls a "metrical resistance." That is, in each of these modern languages, the real rhythm of poetry is a result of a compromise between their natural phonetic properties and an alien metrical system "superimposed" upon them. Zhirmunsky's crucial discovery is that each modern language, depending on its natural phonetic properties, has adapted to this ancient and alien metrical scheme differently.[22]

For instance, in the example of an iambic pentameter in English and in Russian, Zhirmunsky shows that while the "ideal" metrical scheme of distribution of strong and weak syllables might be the same for poetry written in both languages, its concrete realizations in monosyllabic English and polysyllabic Russian are very different. In Russian, iambs typically display omissions of stress in the positions prescribed by the metrical pattern ("pyrrhic foot"). Thus, a pentametric line in Russian would usually have less than five stresses per line. In contrast, English pentameters display the opposite phenomenon of "hypermetrical" stresses:

> Within metrically identical . . . iambic verse, Russian iambs display omissions of metrical stresses (on average three stresses in an iambic tetrameter), which is due to the greater word length in the Russian language. English iambs, on the other hand, because of the respective shortness of the words (predominantly monosyllables), display frequent additional stresses of the metrically weak syllables.[23]

The difference between pentameter in Russian and English is well illustrated in Brodsky's poem "Vtoroe Rozhdestvo na beregu." Because of the omissions of stress in Russian—the occurrence of the characteristic "pyrrhic foot"—the real number of rhythmical stresses per line varies between two and four, as can be seen below in the transliterated Russian version of the first stanza. (The actual rhythmical stresses are given in bold in the Latin transcription of the Russian text, and their number per line is given in parentheses at the end of each line.)

Vtor**o**ie Rozhdestv**o** na bereg**u**	enj.	a	5-foot iamb (3)
nezamerz**a**iushchego P**o**nta.		B	4-foot iamb (2)
Zvezd**a** Tsar**e**i nad **i**zgorod'iu p**o**rta.		B	5-foot iamb (4)
I ne mog**u** skaz**a**t', / chto ne mog**u**	enj.	a	5-foot iamb (3)
zh**i**t' bez tebi**a** / —posk**o**lku ia zhiv**u**.		c	5-foot iamb (4)
Kak v**i**dno iz bum**a**gi. / Sushchestv**u**iu;		D	5-foot iamb (3)
glot**a**iu p**i**vo, / p**a**chkaiu listv**u** i	enj.	D	5-foot iamb (4)
topch**u** trav**u**.		c	2-foot iamb (2)

As it turns out, Brodsky's self-translation, based on Kline's initial drafts, approximates more closely the rhythmical realization of the Russian original rather than the equivalent of its metrical scheme in English. When Brodsky spoke of "meter," what he actually had in mind was the "rhythm" of his poems, with all the peculiarities of their Russian phonetic qualities. As a consequence, some conflict between the Russianized rhythm of Brodsky's self-translations and the rhythmical expectations of English native speakers seems unavoidable. What Brodsky was after here was a replica of the rhythm of the original Russian poem rather than its metrical equivalent in English. While this musicality in Russian mattered to Brodsky, this approach was certainly problematic, as confirmed by Zhirmunsky's findings.

The Feminine Rhymes

The second interesting aspect of Brodsky's self-translation concerns the rhymes. As Barry Scherr has pointed out, "the rhymes provide one of the structural cornerstones in many of Brodsky's poems."[24] In a conversation with his friend and fellow poet Derek Walcott, Brodsky once referred to himself with pride as a "pretty good rhymer."[25] This was an area of self-translation where Brodsky felt most temped to apply his poetic skills. Thus, he characteristically changed almost all the rhymes in the first stanza of Kline's second draft of the poem in question.

TABLE 1. Rhymes in Stanza 1, "A Second Christmas by the Shore"

	Russian	Kline	Brodsky
1	**beregu**—ne mogu [<u>shore</u>—cannot]	**shore**—endure	**shore**—sure
2	Ponta—porta [Pontus—port's]	harden—crib. And	unfrozen—horizon
3	**Sushchestvuiu—listvu i** [<u>I exist</u>—<u>leaves and</u>]	**I am living**—heaving	**I'm living—leaves and**
4	Zhivu—**travu** [I'm living—<u>grass</u>]	here—beer	As—**grass**

Boldface type indicates cognates to Brodsky's original rhymes in Russian. The semantic equivalent in English is underscored.

Kline's "living" and "heaving" are not rhyming words in English, and the use of grammatical suffixes to make a rhyme is generally considered bad form in English. By slightly changing the last set of slanting rhymes in Kline's version (from "living—heaving" to "living—leaves and"), Brodsky eliminates Kline's grammatical rhymes ("I am living—heaving"), although many of these English rhymes depend on a Russian pronunciation of English vowels. The chart above also shows that Brodsky tries to rhyme the semantically analogous words in English, matching those that had rhymed in Russian. Amazingly, he often succeeds. Thus, half of the rhymes in his last revision of the first stanza have the same meaning in English as in the original poem: "leaves and," "grass," "I'm living," and "shore." Importantly, as shown by Efim Etkind, the young Pushkin used a similar approach in translating the French-language poet Évariste de Parny into Russian.[26] The range of available rhymes in English, however, differs from that in Russian, as do the rhyming habits in each language. For instance, the rhyme scheme of the poem in question, which both Kline and Brodsky attempted to preserve across translation, features alternation of feminine and masculine endings. As pointed out by Anthony Hecht, "two-syllable rhymes, favored in some poems Brodsky composed in English (Persia/inertia, Noah/spermatozoa), have struck the ears of some English readers as perilously frivolous, though such disyllabic chiming is easily available in the Russian language, and employed by Pushkin and other great poets."[27] Although Hecht was Brodsky's champion and translator, he still found his mimetic approach to translation problematic insofar as it clashed with the expectations of native speakers.

THE SECOND STANZA

Here we have the interlinear translation and the transliterated original of the second stanza:

> Now in the café, from which we,
> as is wont to happen to the temporary happy ones,
> have been thrown out by a soundless explosion
> into the future, under the assault of winter
> having fled to the South, I'm with my fingers drawing
> your face on marble for the poor;
> In distance nymphs are making leaps, on their hips
> lifting brocade.

Tepér' v koféine, // iz kotóroi mý,		e	5-foot iamb (4)
kak i pristálo vrémenno schastlívym,		F	5-foot iamb (3)
bezzvúchnym býli výbrosheny vzrývom	enj.	F	5-foot iamb (3)
v griadúshchee, // pod nátiskom zimý	enj.	e	5-foot iamb (3)
bezháv na Iúg, // ia pál'tsami cherchú		g	5-foot iamb (4)
tvoé litsó / na mrámore dlia bédnykh;		H	5-foot iamb (4)
poódal' nímfy prýgaiut, na bédrakh	enj.	H	5-foot iamb (4)
zadráv parchú.		g	2-foot iamb (2)

The stanza in Russian is one lengthy sentence, a long construction with several subordinate clauses. Metrically speaking, it features three enjambments and four syntactic pauses.[28] As early as 1964, in his note on Brodsky's poetry, Anatoly Naiman, a fellow "Akhmatova boy," argued that Brodsky had imported such bulky stanzaic constructions into Russian directly from English metaphysical poetry:

> Brodsky strips the "verse" line of its function as an independent unit. Instead, its place is taken over by verses, which are inseparably connected to the neighboring lines, first of all grammatically. . . . One minimal unit of "poetic" meaning—one poetic image—requires thus several units of form. . . . never before was it turned into a method, a poetic manner, nor did it take such proportions: some "units" might count up to twenty lines.[29]

In fact, the second stanza displays a strong kinship with the extended stanzas in Donne's poetry, as the famous Italian Donne scholar Mario Praz described them: "The poetic unit in Donne is not a line, but a stanza and . . . the rules that reign in it are not those of a song, but those of a discourse."[30] To confirm the Donne connection here, Brodsky's stanza features a metaphysical conceit. According to T. S. Eliot, who did much to popularize seventeenth-century metaphysical poetry, conceit happens to be its most natural form of expression, allowing the poet to "realize the inapprehensible in visual images."[31] He elaborated: "A conceit is the extreme limit of the simile and metaphor which is used for its own sake, and not to make clearer an idea or more definite an emotion . . . The figure does not make intelligible an idea, for there is properly no idea until you have the figure. The figure creates the idea . . ."[32]

The image of an explosion in the second stanza of Brodsky's poem illustrates what Eliot had in mind. It would not be hard to visualize two lovers suddenly blown apart by an exploding bomb. But to imagine a silent, invisible, slow-motion explosion from the past into the future demands an enhanced effort of imagination on the part of the reader. Therein lies the intellectual nature of a conceit: in order to grasp it, the reader must interrupt the natural flow of reading and focus intently. Eliot's comment that when you read Donne "your mind is continuously exercised"[33] applies equally to much of Brodsky's poetry.[34] As a "mental accelerator,"[35] to use Brodsky's own favorite descriptor of poetry, conceit is particularly effective; the affinity between such apparently disparate phenomena as an explosion and the effects of the passage of time is grasped instantly, as is the "odour of a rose,"[36] as Eliot would have put it. Brodsky's conceit succinctly conveys a number of distinctive features of time—its invisible passage and its sheer destructiveness. It also challenges the popular belief that time's passage is gradual.

Kline's First Draft

Let us see how the translator dealt with the challenges of this "metaphysical" stanza and examine the objections Brodsky raised to Kline's solutions. The following is Kline's translation of the second stanza, which includes Brodsky's comments and remarks:

> Having fled south punched ^forced^ down by winter's fist,
> I'm in that coffee-house ^café^ from which we two were
> exploded soundlessly into the future,
> our temporary happiness now past;
> my fingers trace, in ^on^ poor-man's marble, lines
> that form your face. Nymphs leap by the far roadstead; in a distance

their stiff brocaded skirts are hoisted
up to their thighs.

4th: I'd do something like: 'according to the happiness of past' or 'according to the temporary law of happiness': THIS IS VERY IMPORTANT.
5th: «Ундины»[37] ['undines'] in this case sound and imply something much more pejorative—a bit nastier than 'nymphs.' What's more, there is NO "roadstead": the whole scene takes place inside the coffee-house: those nymphs leap in the bowels of this room, on stage, in semi-dark room.[38]

Most striking here is Brodsky's comment in caps on the fourth line: "THIS IS VERY IMPORTANT." Apparently, what Brodsky thought essential about this stanza was that the lovers' fate in the elegy concerned not just their individual case but reflected a broader truth, or law, as the poet put it. Arguably, this shifted the focus from melodrama to a higher, timeless plane, allowing the poet to strike a more stoic tone.

Interpretations of Meaning: Literal versus Metaphorical

Brodsky's comment on the sixth line, which he cites as "fifth" in his comments, testifies to the special brand of Brodskian realism, a kind of "diaristic quality" which occasionally obfuscates the meaning of his poems and results in obscurity.[39] For instance, a Russian reader of the original poem might understandably wonder what kind of nymphs Brodsky could possibly be referring to here. Instead of picturing a squalid dance show in the bowels of a semi-dark provincial coffee-house (which is what was apparently meant), he might turn to a metaphorical interpretation. The metaphorical meaning is there: Brodsky would not otherwise have called the female dancers "nymphs." Also, in keeping with the poem's elegiac register, it helps to restore, in retrospect, some dignity to the dancers. Besides, the idea of cavorting nymphs invokes classical décor, underlining the classical associations the poem tried to produce, as mentioned above. At the same time, the author describes a scene he actually witnessed during a winter stay in Yalta. As often in Brodsky, a true descendant of the acmeists, the first meaning is always concrete and literal—yet another instance when his comments on the English version help clarify the meaning of Brodsky's original poem.

Kline's Revision

Here is Kline's revision of the second stanza, followed by Brodsky's definitive version of it:

Having fled south, pressed here by winter's fist,	a	5-foot iamb
I'm in that coffee-house from which we two were	B	5-foot iamb
exploded, soundlessly, into the future,	xB	5-foot iamb
by the impermanence of happiness;	xa	5-foot iamb
my fingers trace, on poor-man's marble, lines	c	5-foot iamb
that form your face. Plump nymphs cavort in clusters	X	5-foot iamb
far off; their stiff brocaded skirts are hoisted	X	5-foot iamb
up to their thighs.	c	2-foot iamb

(Kline)

Retreating south before winter's assault,	a	5-foot iamb
I sit in that café from which we two were	B	5-foot iamb
exploded soundlessly into the future	xB	5-foot iamb
according to the unrelenting law	xa	5-foot iamb
that happiness can't last. My finger tries	c	5-foot iamb
your face on poor man's marble. In the distance,	D	5-foot iamb
brocaded nymphs leap through their jerky dances,	D	5-foot iamb
flaunting their thighs.	c	2-foot iamb

(Brodsky)

Metrically speaking, the changes that Brodsky made here to Kline's translations are not substantial; Brodsky's intervention was limited to "tightening up" the rhymes ("tries/thighs") and introducing the slant rhyme "distance—dances," which is an original feminine rhyme. Similarly, the rhyme "assault—law" preserves the "au" sound and moves the 'l' from the back to the front. In fact, as Scherr has shown, in his Russian verse Brodsky often used approximate rhyming, which allowed him "to avoid 'easy' grammatical rhymes."[40] This might explain why Brodsky accepted Kline's very approximate feminine rhyme here: "two were—future." It might also be that what mattered most to him in this stanza was to bring forward the idea of the "law."

At the top of the next page is a chart showing Brodsky's changes to Kline's rhymes in the second stanza.

On the whole, it seems that while Kline was striving for a smoother flow in English, Brodsky was focused on re-creating a more literal version. For instance, Kline's "winter's fist" is figurative, whereas Brodsky uses the metaphor of a military assault to fortify the metaphor of the explosion. By literal, I also mean that Brodsky's translation strives to be closer to the original

TABLE 2. Rhymes in Stanza 2, "A Second Christmas by the Shore"

	Russian	Kline	Brodsky
1	kotoroi my—zimy [from which we—winter's]	winter's fist—happiness	assault—law
2	schastlivym—vzryvom [happy—explosion]	two were—future	two were—future
3	bednykh—**bedrakh** [poor—thighs]	clusters—hoisted	distance—dances
4	**cherchu**—parchu [I'm drawing— brocade]	lines—**thighs**	[my finger] **tries—thighs**

Boldface type indicates cognates to Brodsky's original rhymes in Russian. The semantic equivalent in English is underscored.

not only in terms of replicating the rhythm but also in reproducing a greater number of parallelisms with Russian, such as the distribution of syntactic pauses and syntactical units, even though there is no one-to-one semantic correspondence. Here are a few examples:

1st line in English (Brodsky):	Retreating south // before winter's assault
1st line in Russian:	Tepér' v koféine, // iz kotóroi mý
5th line in English (Brodsky):	that happiness can't last. // My finger tries
5th line in Russian:	bezháv na Iúg, // ia pál'tsami cherchú
6th line in English (Brodsky):	your face on poor man's marble. // In the distance
6th line in Russian:	tvoé litsó // na mrámore // dlia bédnykh

Brodsky's solution to the second line is interesting for a different reason. Kline's version, "I'm in that coffee-house from which we two were," is closer to the literal meaning of the original: "Now [sitting] in the café, from which we / were." Brodsky's line, on the other hand, seems to evoke the opening of Auden's poem "1 September 1939," to which Brodsky later dedicated a close reading. Compare:

> "I sit in one of the dives / On Fifty-second Street" (Auden)[41]
> "I sit in that café from which we two were" (Brodsky)

THE THIRD STANZA

Here we have the interlinear translation and the transliterated original of the third stanza:

> What, gods! If the brownish spot
> in the window is to symbolize you, gods,
> were you trying to convey to us after all?
> The future has arrived and it is
> endurable; an object falls down,
> a violinist leaves, the music has stopped
> and the sea and the faces get more and more creased,
> but there is no wind.

Chto, bogi, / —esli buroye piatno	enj.	a	(3)	5-foot iamb
v okne simvoliziruet vas, bogi—		B	(3)	5-foot iamb
stremilis' vy nam vyskazat' v itoge?		B	(3)	5-foot iamb
Griadushchee nastalo, / i ono	enj.	a	(3)	5-foot iamb
perenosimo; / padaet predmet,		c	(3)	5-foot iamb
skripach vykhodit, / muzyka ne dlitsia,		D	(4)	5-foot iamb
i more vse morshchinestei, i litsa.		D	(3)	5-foot iamb
A vetra net.		c	(2)	2-foot iamb

The third stanza opens with a rhetorical question addressed to some gods. Apparently, these are pagan gods, as they are plural in number. This appears to be both an effort to preserve the parallel with Ovid's setting and a veiled nod to Horace's famous ode to Leuconoë, in which Horace argued that trying to secure future good fortune through augury was futile. Instead, Horace advocated stoic endurance of one's fate. There is an echo of that sentiment in the third stanza of the Brodsky poem as well: "The future has arrived and it is / endurable." Compare this to Horace's advice:

> Don't query—we should not ask—when the gods will choose death for me or you, Leuconoë. Don't consult Babylonian numbers. Much nicer to endure whatever comes our way. No matter whether Jupiter will grant us many winters, or whether the present one, which is now wearing down the waves of the Tyrrhenian Sea against the pumice rock, will be our last one. Be wise, water down your wine, and, in anticipation, break up long whiles into smaller segments. While we are talking, sneakily life leaks away. Savor the day, and put as little hope into tomorrow as you can manage.[42]

Incidentally, Horace's ode also features a southern seascape in winter. As in Horace's ode, Brodsky's lyrical hero adopts a stoic stance toward his loss of love in the face of what apparently is a vision of eternity—a place where no wind blows. Once again, Brodsky resorts to a conceit to convey his vision: the watery sea needs the wind to become creased, but the sea of time by its very nature produces creases on the human face or on its own fabric. Its flow is perfectly effortless.

Let us now consider Kline's translation of the third stanza with Brodsky's markings, corrections, and comments.

Kline's First Draft

What is it, gods—if this small grey-brown spot,	a	5 foot iamb
glimpsed through a window, symbolizes	B	4-foot iamb
yourselves—that you would have us realize? Is	B	5-foot iamb
it, gods, that future days are here, and not	a	5-foot iamb
unbearable? Things fall apart, the fid-	c	5-foot iamb
dler leaves, the music dies, and deepening creases	D	5-foot iamb
spread over the sea's surface, and our faces.	D	5-foot iamb
But there's no wind.	c	2-foot iamb

1st: the 'spot' is not 'small'—it is essential [*sic*] sun through dirtied, dimmed window.

3rd: 'that you would have us realise' afterall. [*sic*]

4th: there is no questioning any longer. "It (the future) arrived, and it is bearable. It's much more abrupt, George, and sort of firm—THIS IS VERY IMPORTANT.

5th: not that important but: a thing falls down (on the floor) and not "things fall apart"—it's too much [of] a judgement.

6–7th: I am not that sure about 'deepening creases'—although it's quite beautiful; there are mere wrinkles—and not 'our' faces but 'faces/ the faces.'

In the first line of his draft translation, Kline introduced the qualifier "small" to the "grey-brown spot" the lyrical hero was contemplating through the window. This was an instance of "padding"—that is, of adding an extra word for the sake of the beat. Thanks to Kline's padding, we learn that the spot in the poem stood for the sun seen "through [a] dirtied, dimmed window." In his comment on the fourth line, Brodsky again uses caps to emphasize what mattered most to him. In this stanza, it was the notion that the future is here and that the lyrical hero meets it with stoic resolve. In the fifth line, Kline seems to turn to a Brodskian device in evoking a line from W. B. Yeats's famous poem "The Second Coming": "Things fall apart; the centre cannot hold."[43] Interestingly, whether he recognized the echo or not (he probably did), Brodsky tells Kline that this "poetic" rendition, "things fall apart," is unsuitable in the given context. While "things fall apart" is apocalyptic in Yeats's poem, "*padaet predmet*" sounds more banal in Russian and is decidedly self-ironic in Brodsky, which Kline seems to miss.

Brodsky's Final Version

Following is the definitive version of the third stanza as revised by Brodsky.

Just what, you gods—if this dilating blot,	a	5-foot iamb
glimpsed through a murky window, symbolizes	B	5-foot iamb
your selves now—were you trying to advise us?	B	5-foot-iamb
The future has arrived and it is not	a	5-foot iamb
unbearable. Things fall, the fiddler goes,	c	5-foot iamb
the music ebbs, and deepening creases	D	4-foot iamb
spread over the sea's surface and men's faces.	D	5-foot iamb
But no wind blows.	c	2-foot iamb

The changes to Kline's version here are again only marginal: the only major substitution is in the fourth line, where Brodsky emphasizes the lyrical hero's resolve to endure his loss. Otherwise, Brodsky appreciated quite a few of Kline's rhymes, especially the feminine ones, but eliminated the cacophonically truncated-rhyme "fid-/wind" in the fifth line and rendered the sixth line with one syllable less than the metrical scheme demanded.

TABLE 3. Rhymes in Stanza 3, "A Second Christmas by the Shore"

	Russian	Kline	Brodsky
1	**piatno**—i ono [blot—and it]	**spot**—not	**blot**—not
2	bogi—v itoge [gods—after all]	symbolizes—realize? Is	symbolize—advise us
3	ne dlitsia—**i litsa** [has stopped—and faces]	creases—**faces**	creases—**faces**
4	predmet—A **vetra net** object—but no wind	fid- —**wind**	goes— [no wind] **blows**

Boldface type indicates cognates to Brodsky's original rhymes in Russian. The semantic equivalent in English is underscored.

Of the Russian version's eight rhyming words in the stanza, two retained the same rhyming position in English as well. For the rest, it seems that Brodsky was focused on enhancing the richness of sound by introducing more assonances and alliterations into the English version. As a result, the sound that was beginning to emerge in Kline's English version acquired more resonance as the lines alluding to music began to sound like music, reproducing the rhythm of the action described: "Things fall, the fiddler goes, / the music ebbs, and deepening creases / spread over the sea's surface and men's faces. / But no wind blows" (Brodsky). In the last stanza of the poem, Brodsky continued his pursuit of greater euphony in English.

THE FOURTH STANZA

The next stanza is the most essential one of the poem, containing images of utmost beauty and terror. It is no coincidence, therefore, that Brodsky's contribution to its translation is greater than to any other part of the poem. Again, we have my interlinear translation followed by the transliterated Russian:

> One day it [the sea], but not, alas,
> we will flow over the embankment's fence
> and will advance under the exclamations '[Please], don't,'
> raising its crests over one's head,
> toward the place where you sipped your wine,
> slept in the garden, dried your blouse—
> and crashing tables will be making ready the bottom
> for a future mollusk.

Kogd***a***-nibud' on***o***, // a n***e***—uv***y***—	enj.	a	(4)	5-foot iamb
m***y***, zakhlestn***e***t resh***e***tku promen***a***da		B	(4)	5-foot iamb
i dv***i***netsia pod v***o***zglasy "ne n***a***do,"		B	(3)	5-foot iamb
vzdym***a***ia gr***e***bni v***y***she golov***y***,	enj.	a	(4)	5-foot iamb
tud***a***, gde ty pil***a*** svo***e*** vin***o***,		c	(4)	5-foot iamb
spal***a*** v sad***u***, // pros***u***shivala bl***u***zku,		D	(4)	5-foot iamb
—krush***a*** stol***y***, // griad***u***shchemu				
molli***u***sku	enj.	D	(4)	5-foot iamb
got**o**via dn**o**.[44]		c	(2)	2-foot iamb

Brodsky's friend and biographer Lev Loseff pointed to yet another feature that Brodsky shared with the English metaphysical poets: "The metaphysician seeks only the initial metaphor, expands it, and then the metaphor leads him to results which in all probability stun the poet himself."[45] In the same vein, the "time-bomb" metaphor that featured in the first stanza reemerges in the fourth—but in a different guise. Here, the conceit for time's destructiveness is not an explosion but an apocalyptic flood, with effects more powerful and devastation vastly more universal. Still, the author focuses exclusively on the destruction of the places and objects metonymically related to the lyrical hero's beloved. The depiction of these sacred objects just before they sink into ultimate oblivion creates a lyrical tension. The stanza thus conveys an uncanny mixture of lyricism and terror.

Here we have Kline's first draft of the last stanza, and Brodsky's markings and comments on it:

> Someday the sea, and not—alas—ourselves,
> will sweep across the railings of the boardwalk,
> advancing to sharp screams of "Don't!" and "Stop it!"
> to tower its breakers high above men's heads
> and flood the place where you once sipped your pale
> champagne, cat-napped, or dried a flimsy cotton
> white blouse—and crush the chairs to silt a new sea-bottom
> for future snails.
>
> 3rd: advancing "under accompaniment of exclamation(s) 'don't.'"
> Either 'don't' or 'Stop it' BUT NOT BOTH. «Не надо» sounds quite absurd, helpless, idiotic—that's the point.
> 5th: no 'pale champagne' (although cherish your memory of Crimean champagne, please)
> The ending is lovely but—wrong. What makes the impact is the word 'bottom' in the very end. The whole business of 'evolution' is stressed—and more (I think) than 'evolution' alone. 'Snails' are just charming—or just unpleasant. «Моллюск» is terrifying, and the whole notion of 'future'—changes. "For future-days mollusc (or whatever) fixing the/a bed."[46]

First, Brodsky points out that Kline's tautology, "Don't" and "Stop it," at the end of the third line diminishes the impact in English. He further objects to Kline's substitution of champagne, an exotic drink, for the much simpler and realistic wine that the lyrical hero drank in the company of his beloved, while also, in a friendly tone, urging his friend Kline to cherish his "memory of Crimean champagne." Most importantly, Brodsky argues that Kline's ending of the poem was "lovely but—wrong." As another friend and translator recalled, "cute" was one of the most damning words in Brodsky's vocabulary.[47] One might speculate that the same was true of the word "lovely." Brodsky insisted that the poem should end with the word "bottom" or "sea-bed," and that its dweller—the mollusk—was more terrifying than the "snails" Kline came up with.

Brodsky, believing in the vatic function of a poet, had idiosyncratic ideas about the way the future should be approached in poetry. This can be gleaned, for instance, from an assignment he gave in a creative writing class to compose a poem about the future:

> Whatever treatment of this theme you may choose, try to stay cool: try to keep enthusiasm out of it. Remember that you are writing about an aspect of time, and that you know nothing about it save that it will surely come. In other words, terror is more in place here than enthusiasm, yet this terror, too, must be controlled. . . . You have to sound dry, resolute, clear-eyed: you have to give your reader an impression that you know what you are talking about . . . Imagine too that your parents and in general the people who seem to you being older than yourselves will not, most likely, be around. Figure out now how you will feel about it. Avoid sounding either apocalyptic or sardonic; try to come off sober or even severe.[48]

Brodsky admonished his students to adopt a "sober or even severe" tone precisely because he associated the future with the prospect of non-being.[49] Curiously, he thought that American poetry, especially Frost's work, best supported this terrifying notion of the future, as he explained in a conversation with Miłosz:

> Tragedy, in a sense, is basically a retrospective genre. And Frost is its opposite; he deals in terror, in negative projections, for terror is always an anticipation, a projection of your own negative potential. In that respect, in that future-oriented sense, he is indeed very American, as well as every bit a catastrophist. . . . It is for this reason that I am so keen on him—because, after all, he tells me, a European, or, well, Eurasian—something qualitatively new about the species or at least something the literature of the continent failed to reveal.[50]

In Brodsky, as well as in Frost, who inspired him,[51] the future features a frightening regress of humanity to an atavistic state epitomized by the reemergence of primitive life-forms that supplant the human species in all its complexity, hurling it to the bottom of the evolutionary ladder. This idea of evolutionary regress echoes not only Frost, but some of Mandelstam's neo-Lamarckian ideas. In his explorations of Lamarck's *Philosophie zoologique* of 1809, Mandelstam treats evolution as "a reversible process, a ladder . . . that nature could well descend or even snatch away."[52] This confirms Brodsky's affinity for Mandelstam's poetic imagination and shows that his poetry was often a fusion of his Russian and anglophone influences. Hence, the importance of the word "bottom" at the end of the poem, which Brodsky insisted on in his commentary to Kline.

Kline's Revision

Having taken into account Brodsky's comments and suggestions, Kline made minor amendments and came up with a second draft of the fourth stanza:

> Someday the sea, and not, alas, ourselves,
> will sweep across the railings of the boardwalk,
> advancing to thin screams of "Stop it!"—
> to tower its breakers high above men's heads
> and flood the park where you drank wine, ate bread,
> took cat naps, and dried out your cotton
> white blouse—to crush tables and ^to^ lay a new sea-bottom
> for mollusk beds.

This time Brodsky did not suggest further changes to the ever-patient and diligent Kline. Instead, he took pen in hand himself and essentially rewrote the stanza, borrowing some words and hints from Kline's drafts:

Someday the slowly rising breakers but,	a	5-foot iamb
alas, not we, will sweep across this railing,	B	5-foot iamb
crest overhead, crush helpless screams, and roll in	B	5-foot iamb
to find the spot where you drank wine, took cat-	a	5-foot iamb
naps, spreading to the sun your wet	c	4-foot iamb
thin blouse—to batter benches, splinter boardwalks,	D	5-foot iamb
and build for future molluscs	D	3-foot iamb
a silted bed.	c	2-foot iamb

In rewriting, Brodsky attempted to re-create the music of the Russian original, specifically by introducing several assonances, consonances, and alliterations. Amazingly, he largely succeeded. While the assonances Brodsky came up with in English are built around different vowels than in Russian (in Russian, the four vowels «а», «о», «ы», «у» ['a,' 'o,' 'y,' 'u']), there are surprising overlaps in the types of alliterations and consonantal parallelisms. In Russian, alliterations involved such consonants as 'v,' 'vzd,' 'vzgl,' 'gl,' 'gr,' 'kr,' 'gd,' 'gt,' 'nd,' 'dn,' 'stl,' 'spl,' 'pl.' Conversely, in English there are more liquid ('r,' 'w,' and 'l') and plosive sounds ('b,' 'p,' 't,' and 'd'), as well as combinations with each other and combinations with some sibilants:

1) "r's" in combination with plosive sounds 'b,' 'br' ("rising," "breakers," "but," "railing")
2) "cr's" ("across," "crest," "crush," "screams")

3) "w's" ("we," "will," "sweep," "where," "wine," "wet")
4) "b's" ("blouse," "batter," "benches," "boardwalks," "build," "bed")
5) "s's" alone and in combination with other consonants ("slowly," "sweep," "screams," "spot," "-naps," "spreading," "splinter," "sun," "silted")
6) "l's" alone and in combinations ("slowly," "alas," "will," "railing," "helpless," "blouse," "splinter," "build," "molluscs," "silted")
7) "f's" ("for," "future")

The combination of these elements produces in English a harmony of its own. Some of these words, as one might observe, had already appeared in Kline's version, but they had not constituted as consistent a pattern. To achieve his euphonic effects, Brodsky made some changes that only an author could afford to make. For instance, only he could have decided that in the main metaphysical conceit of the stanza, an apocalyptic flood, the waves should be advancing slowly ("the slowly rising breakers"). The original provides no such information. Another example is a rare semantic-euphonic parallelism between a Russian word and its English translation. While Kline had rendered the expression "*krusha stoly*" ("crashing tables") as "to crush tables," Brodsky, led more by his English ear than by the meaning of the Russian, came up with a new image of "crushed screams." To do this he had to first reshuffle the entire syntax of the original, moving the image from the penultimate line in the original to the third line in English: "across this railing, / crest overhead, crush helpless screams, and roll." In the process he spotted and emphasized another parallelism between the sound and meaning of the same word in Russian and English, introducing it in his final version: "*grebni*"—"crests." This resulted in the emergence in both cases of a new image: the sea became more active, more eerie. On the other hand, the screams, which in the original had been rendered with the direct exclamation "*Ne nado!*" ("[Please], don't!"), were here simply paraphrased as "helpless screams." Similarly, Brodsky easily sacrificed the "tables," turning them into "benches," apparently to create an alliteration totaling six "b's" in just the last three lines. Furthermore, Brodsky added a new element of devastation absent from the original—"splinter boardwalks."

On the rhyme front, Brodsky tries again to eliminate what looked like banal rhymes, such as "cotton—bottom," and attempted instead to have certain words that rhyme in the original in a rhyming position in English as well.[53] At the same time, the words "wet" and "bed" rhyme only if you devoice the final consonant—very natural for a Russian, but unthinkable for a native speaker of English.

TABLE 4. Rhymes in Stanza 4, "A Second Christmas by the Shore"

	Russian	Kline's Second Draft	Brodsky's Final Version
1	uvy—golovy [alas—head]	ourselves—heads	but—cat-[naps]
2	**promenada**—ne nado [boardwalk—don't]	**boardwalk**—Stop it!	railing—roll in
3	bluzku—**mollusku** [blouse—mollusc]	cotton—**bottom**	**boardwalks—molluscs**
4	vino—**dno** [wine—sea bottom]	bread— [mollusk] **beds**	wet—[silted] **bed**

Boldface type indicates cognates to Brodsky's original rhymes in Russian. The semantic equivalent in English is underscored.

CONCLUDING OBSERVATIONS ON "A SECOND CHRISTMAS BY THE SHORE"

Brodsky's collaboration with George Kline on the translation of the poem "Vtoroe Rozhdestvo na beregu" for the new English collection *A Part of Speech* began in the same way as their past collaborations. Kline produced the first draft in English and sent it to Brodsky, who then provided comments and suggestions. The difference now was that Brodsky not only responded directly in English but also made changes to Kline's initial drafts, striking words and expressions and suggesting his own. This was a significant change from his previous practice and marked the first step toward the author's more substantial reworkings. Brodsky's comments had become more detailed too, and his translating demands became more specific. Their most conspicuous feature was Brodsky's signaling in caps: "THIS IS VERY IMPORTANT." Here a certain idea, image, or tonality of a specified line in the poem deserved the translator's special attention. Brodsky could have gone back and forth with Kline in this fashion until his demands were met, but he was clearly tempted to try his own hand at translation. This was daring since his English was still not perfect, but the risk paid off when he saw that by just slightly altering the text, he could make it better reflect his ideas of the poem. In his own reworkings, Brodsky tried to restore the general balance of the original. He tried to place certain words in rhyming position, use a specific word to finish the poem, and re-create the euphony in English through alliteration and assonance. To do this he took liberties. This creative freedom paid off as he made many discoveries. Kline, on the other hand, could not enjoy such freedoms, especially with Brodsky breathing down his neck with demands for accuracy.

Nor could Kline take too many risks and experiment, since he was not the author and lacked sufficient poetic experience of his own.

At the same time, Brodsky's recastings of Kline's drafts demonstrate that rather than re-creating English equivalents of the Russian metrical scheme, Brodsky tried to introduce the Russian rhythm of his original with some phonetic peculiarities of Russian iambs, such as the introduction of pyrrhic feet. Curiously, it seems that Kline's provision of the initial drafts held Brodsky's foreignizing tendencies at bay. This could not be said, however, about the foreignizing effect of the feminine rhymes in his self-translations. Brodsky insisted that the rhyming pattern of his originals be preserved literally. While Kline fully agreed with this position, other translators were less convinced. The next chapter will explore the origins of Brodsky's principles of equimetrical translation.

Chapter Five

Brodsky's Translation Philosophy

BRODSKY LAID DOWN his principles of Russian-English poetry translation in two reviews of English translations of verse by Anna Akhmatova and Osip Mandelstam—"Translating Akhmatova" (1973) and "Beyond Consolation" (1974). In more ways than one, Brodsky continued the acmeist poetic school, whose most prominent members were Nikolai Gumilev, Akhmatova, and Mandelstam. In contradistinction to the Russian symbolists, their predecessors and mentors, the acmeists conceived of poetry "not as . . . a source of revelation but as a craft, the art of placing words in lines, the creation of public objects independent of the private lives of their creators."[1] Brodsky's friendship with Akhmatova proved formative; moreover, she provided him with a personal link to Mandelstam.[2] In his role as acmeist ambassador and heir apparent to the traditions established by his acmeist mentors, Brodsky's reviews of their work for English readers indirectly helped to establish with his new audience his own lineage within the Russian poetic tradition. Above all, he demonstrated his loyalty toward their legacy and honored the memory of their tragic fates. Mandelstam had met his nameless death in a remote labor camp "in conditions of unutterable horror";[3] Akhmatova had witnessed the death and suffering of her loved ones while her own life "like a river, was reversed by the cruel epoch."[4] In the Soviet Union of the 1970s, their official resurrection occurred grudgingly and hence was very slow and incomplete. Their literary fate would be decided on foreign soil,[5] which is precisely why the stakes were so high: it was literally a matter of poetic justice. Much of this background, however, was lost on Brodsky's American audience. The Soviet experience did not translate well into the world of 1970s America. Brodsky's vehemence, peremptory tone, and passionate attacks on the translators of these writers, who were known only in secret back home, must have perplexed many Western readers. Still, his reviews produced quite a stir in American letters, unleashing a debate and polemics around the translation of poetry not witnessed since the translation wars caused by Nabokov's translation of Pushkin in the preceding decade.[6]

"TRANSLATING AKHMATOVA"

In her memoir, Ellendea Proffer Teasley recalls that when Brodsky arrived in the West, "he was shocked at the almost invisible status of the poet in the United States. He was determined to change all that."[7] Accordingly, in his review "Translating Akhmatova" Brodsky unfurled his translating imperatives boldly, asserting that Akhmatova's poetic legacy in English could be preserved only if certain preconditions were met:

> In translation, some loss is inevitable. But a great deal can be preserved too. One can preserve the meter, one can preserve the rhymes (no matter how difficult this may seem each time), one can and must preserve the meaning. Not one of these things, but all together.[8]

Despite the losses entailed in poetry translation, it was still possible, Brodsky argued, to preserve both the form and the meaning of the Russian poems in English. He even insisted that achieving such a unity was nothing short of an obligation of poetry translators, whom he admonished to do their duty and not to "propound fashionable theories in introductions."[9] The venom of this particular remark was directed at the celebrated American poet Stanley Kunitz, whose translations of Akhmatova Brodsky was reviewing at the time.

Kunitz had argued in his introduction to *Poems of Akhmatova* (1973) that each language has its own means, that there is no such thing as formal equivalence, and that it is therefore arbitrary "to insist on a universally rigid duplication of metrical or rhyming patterns."[10] Brodsky, on the other hand, asserted that the choice of means was not at all arbitrary and that translation should not fall victim to the fleeting fashions of the target culture. An example of this was the contemporary practice of using free verse for the translation of poetry written in strict forms—Brodsky's perennial bête noire. For Brodsky, using "free verse where the original is in sestets"[11] was a no-go. There were cultural and historical reasons for this, as Brodsky explained in "Translating Akhmatova," noting definitively: "Russian poets generally prefer the traditional verse line with rhyme and its other attributes . . . because the use of rhyme is . . . an establishment of order in chaos."[12] While this idea might have seemed obscure to his American audience, it made perfect sense to a fellow expatriate from the Soviet bloc, Stanisław Barańczak. Commenting two decades later on English translations of Akhmatova by Judith Hemschemeyer,[13] Barańczak, a Polish poet and translator, echoed Brodsky's arguments expressed in "Translating Akhmatova":

> Rhymes and regular meter were for her [Akhmatova] matters of life and death: life and death of a poem (in Stalin's Russia it was safer to preserve a

poem by memorizing it rather than writing it down; rhymes and rhythm seen from this angle are mnemonic devices); life and death of culture (in which regularity and precision of word constructions magically preserves and upholds human order imposed upon the deadly chaos of the world), and probably also her own life and death. To strip Akhmatova's poetry of the "music" that serves such purposes would be like translating every "niet" of her poetry with a "yes."[14]

Barańczak was, among other things, Brodsky's main translator into Polish and shared many of his aesthetic ideas. So his notion that rhymes and regular meter served to uphold human order against the "deadly chaos of the world" clearly harked back to Brodsky. Barańczak emphasized that at the time of the most radical denial of freedom during Stalin's rule, such mnemonic devices as rhymes and meter became key to keeping Akhmatova's poetry alive. Her close companion Lydia Chukovskaia described the extreme measures that her close circle of friends had to take to preserve Akhmatova's poetry from oblivion:

> Anna Andreevna [Akhmatova], when visiting me, recited parts of *Requiem* . . . in a whisper; suddenly, in mid-conversation, she would fall silent and, signaling to me with her eyes at the ceiling and walls, she would get a scrap of paper and a pencil; then she would loudly say something very mundane . . . , then she would cover the scrap in hurried handwriting and pass it to me. I would read the poetry and, having memorized it, would hand it back to her in silence. "How early autumn came this year," Anna Andreevna would say loudly and, striking a match, would burn the paper over an ashtray.[15]

Thus Brodsky, who later became even more entrenched in his positions, referred, in a letter to an editor, to Hemschemeyer's Akhmatova translations as "mercenary trash,"[16] since they failed to fully reflect the formal aspects of the Russian originals.

But didn't Kunitz have a point in insisting that Akhmatova's music had to be re-created by different means in English than in Russian? Richard Wilbur, one of the most lauded American poets of his generation and greatly admired by Brodsky, referred, in a 1977 interview, to Kunitz's Akhmatova translations as the best in English to date:

> Interviewer: Brodsky complained at a reading here in Louisville that Akhmatova's poems had been poorly translated. They had not been rhymed.
>
> Wilbur: He was objecting, I think, to Stanley Kunitz's translation of Akhmatova, which is probably the best book of Akhmatova around in English. . . . What Joseph minds is that Stanley didn't work hard enough to get

> the meters and get the rhymes. Maybe Stanley's reply would be, "It wasn't a matter of working hard or not working hard. I felt that some of her poems could be translated into more relaxed English forms."[17]

Wilbur suggested that Kunitz, like other American poets, believed that the rigors Brodsky insisted upon were unnecessary and that the target language offered alternative possibilities. Yet it was precisely the idea of translating Akhmatova "into more relaxed English forms," as Wilbur put it, that Brodsky most opposed. Instead, he evoked Robert Frost as a possible model for an Akhmatova translator: "Akhmatova's . . . simplicity is like the 'simplicity' of Robert Frost, to whom . . . she is extremely close stylistically."[18] To propose Frost as a poetic model in the United States of the 1970s was to display very conservative views. According to Robert Lowell, Frost was regarded as early as the 1910s as an unfashionable minority of one who went against the grain of the modernist trends advanced by Pound and Eliot.[19] Proffer Teasley observes, however, that while some of Brodsky's ideas were old-fashioned for Americans, his "personality and passion made them feel new."[20]

FORMAL RESTRICTIONS: A CURSE OR A BLESSING?

Brodsky's next argument in defense of the use of traditional forms in Russian-to-English poetry translation must have sounded even more counterintuitive to many of his readers. Commenting on Kunitz's rendition of Akhmatova's "Imitation from the Armenian," Brodsky argued that the translator had rejected the metrical structure and rhymes of the original in the hope of achieving greater creative freedom, but that the freedom, conversely, had become a burden: "Instead of the eight Russian lines we have ten English lines. And this happens despite the fact that the English words are two or three times shorter. . . . In English a line of iambic pentameter can contain up to nine words, while in Russian not more than six will fit."[21] This challenged the widespread belief that trying to replicate the form of the original makes it harder to accurately transmit the meaning. Such was the view, for instance, of those who, according to Proffer Teasley, later tried to persuade Brodsky to rethink his approach to self-translation into English: "Many, many poets and scholars told Joseph that his work would suffer in rhymed translation, that the poetic thought structure would be *deformed* in order to get the rhyme and so on [italics mine]."[22] The word "deformed" speaks volumes. Proffer Teasley herself seems to think that in his efforts to preserve their rhyme and meter, Brodsky would sacrifice the original meaning of his poems. Nabokov, working on his *Onegin* translation, would have subscribed to this opinion. In his translation of Pushkin, Nabokov famously rebelled against the "dictatorship of rhymed translations";[23] he was convinced that rhyme was an obstacle to the accurate rendition of the sense of the original, and he savagely attacked "poetical" renditions of Pushkin for being "begrimed and beslimed by rhyme."[24] While Nabokov is notorious for his strong opinions and outrageous quips, the same cannot be said of Walter Benjamin, who believed it self-evident that fidelity in reproducing the form impeded rendering the sense in translation.[25] Not only did Brodsky contest this axiom, but he also declared that focusing on the retention of form increased the translator's chances of achieving greater accuracy in rendering the meaning.

How is this possible? The answer lies in the creative potential of limitations attested to by many poets as well as some prose writers.[26] Auden, for example, emphasized that making words fit into a complicated structure always helped him refine his message. He explained that metrical restrictions were actually the aspect of poetry he most enjoyed because they helped you say "something which you haven't thought of saying, and you wouldn't have thought of if it hadn't been for these kinds of restrictions."[27] (Presumably for the same reason, Frost famously quipped: "I'd as soon write free verse as play tennis with the net down.")[28] Later, in a conversation with fellow Nobel laureate Derek Walcott, Brodsky went even further, asserting that rhymes not only help the poet discover what he has to say but also contribute to an "accelerated thinking" unattainable by other means.[29] Whether the same was applicable to translation, which, according to Benjamin, is a mode in itself, is a different matter.[30] Still, Brodsky was firm in his convictions and even invoked Pushkin to get his point across: "Pushkin called translators 'the post-horses of enlightenment.' . . . We should note that horses run as hard as they can only when a whip is whistling over them."[31] Brodsky was clearly proposing himself as whip and scourge to spur and incite English translators. He went so far as to suggest that American translators adopt as their model the accuracy controls in poetry translation that were dominant at Soviet publishing houses:

> In Soviet publishing houses there exist institutes of editors. As a rule, these are people who know the language and literature from which the translations are made. No matter how well known your name is, the editor can return your manuscript to you if he finds that you have allowed inaccuracies. One has to rework it dozens of times, but when the book is published, the author's name has full right to be on it.[32]

It might seem ironic that Brodsky advocated the strict editorial controls imposed by the notorious censorship machine that had led to the destruction of Russian literature itself. He was the first to lament its effects on

Akhmatova and Mandelstam, among many others, and would have been the last person to align himself with those repressive Soviet practices. Why was he now defending them?

TRANSLATION IN THE SOVIET CONTEXT

Comments like these served to remind Brodsky's American audience of his expertise in translating English-language poetry into Russian. According to Vyacheslav V. Ivanov, when Brodsky took to poetry translation, the general standards were very high:

> The level of translating technique that had been achieved by then [the late 1960s–early 1970s] in Russia was very high. Translation as a way of earning one's living, as opposed to verbal prostitution, had been the practice of the best poets of the older and middle-aged generation. Brodsky was aware of this work and valued it highly.[33]

It is not incidental that Ivanov linked the excellence of Russian translation technique with the talented poets of an older generation who had been forced to do translations instead of writing their own poetry. Maurice Friedberg pointed out that Soviet state propaganda tried to exploit the translation work of such "translators by necessity"[34] as Pasternak and Akhmatova, who were among the "prominent victims of Communist thought control,"[35] in order to promote its own self-congratulatory and jingoistic narratives on the superiority of the Soviet school of translation.[36] Still, the standards set by this school were indeed remarkably high.

Discussing Brodsky's Russian translations of Donne and the metaphysical poets, Ivanov summarized his approach to translation as follows: "Brodsky's translations of the metaphysical poets at their best reflect the high demands of that Russian poetic school that strived to render not only the meter, but also the rhythm, the imagery, the stanzaic design, as well as the rhyme scheme of the original."[37] Those high demands had been presented in Russia in 1919 in a brochure titled *Printsipy khudozhestvennogo perevoda* (*Principles of Artistic Translation*), which was part of an ambitious Soviet translating venture called Vsemirnaia literatura (World Literature).[38] The brochure's author, Nikolai Gumilev, who was Akhmatova's first husband and Mandelstam's friend and fellow acmeist, had formulated the "nine commandments" of poetry translation:

> Let me repeat briefly what it is obligatory to observe: 1) the number of lines, 2) the meter and measure, 3) the alternation of rhyme, 4) the nature of the

> enjambment, 5) the nature of the rhyme, 6) the nature of the vocabulary, 7) the type of similes, 8) special devices, 9) changes in tone.
>
> These are the translator's nine commandments: since there is one less than those of Moses, I hope that they will be better observed.[39]

After his murder by a Cheka firing squad in August 1921, however, Gumilev's name disappeared from the brochure.[40] The peremptory tone of Gumilev's "nine commandments" and the religious metaphors he employed echo the tone and language of Brodsky's American reviews of Akhmatova and Mandelstam to a staggering extent. In "Beyond Consolation," his notoriously scathing 1974 review of English translations of Mandelstam, Brodsky also used ecclesiastical language, speaking of verse meters as "spiritual magnitudes," arguing that "by rejecting meter in translation the translator commits sacrilege," and insisting that form and meaning "sanctify" each other as "soul and body."[41] Although no great fan of Gumilev's poetry, as far as his approaches to translation were concerned, Brodsky was clearly following the Silver Age track.

AESTHETIC DISSENT AS POLITICAL RESISTANCE

It is safe to say that building bridges to Russia's prerevolutionary past and expressing resistance to totalitarianism were two inseparable goals that nourished Brodsky's art. In keeping with the revolutionary spirit of the Soviet regime, which planned to establish its own *novus ordo seclorum* (new order of the ages), much of prerevolutionary culture would be reshaped to conform with the goals of the reigning ideology, as well as with a permanently changing party line.[42] Consequently, scores of literary figures and entire literary styles were outlawed and eradicated.[43] Then, suddenly, Brodsky's generation emerged and took up the thread of tradition exactly where the Silver Age poets had left off.[44] In fact, as Proffer Teasley pointed out, Brodsky's aesthetic preferences often had a political component: "He was . . . an enemy to the avant-garde, which was both an aesthetic and political position in his case. He saw the avant-garde as a tool of the young Soviet regime. For him the radical position was the traditional position."[45] This can also be gleaned from his Nobel lecture:

> We aspired . . . to the re-creation of the effect of culture's continuity . . . *There existed, presumably, another path: the path of further deformation*, the poetics of ruins and debris, of minimalism, of choked breath. If we rejected it, it was not at all because we thought that it was the path of self-dramatization, or because we were extremely *animated by the idea of preserving the hereditary nobility of the forms of culture we knew*, the forms that were equivalent,

in our consciousness, to forms of human dignity. *We rejected it* . . . and this choice, again, was aesthetic rather than moral [italics mine].[46]

Brodsky typically refrains from making an overtly political statement and presents the resistance of his generation in terms of their aesthetic choice. He obviously refused to politicize poetry, but in conversations with friends he was more outspoken. Once he and Venclova had settled in the United States, Brodsky admitted to his friend that resistance to totalitarianism had colored all of his actions: "You and I have been really lucky in life. There was always something unexpected ahead. There was an obvious goal—the defeat of Barmalei, Akhmatova would say. And that colored every action of mine."[47] Venclova comments: "Barmalei, the comic yet dangerous cannibal from Kornei Chukovsky's fairy-tale, was the nickname that Akhmatova's circle adopted for the powers that be."[48] The German writer Hans Christoph Buch, another friend of Brodsky's, also highlighted the political dimension of Brodsky's defense of traditional poetic forms:

> From the very start Brodsky was not aiming at the disintegration of form, as was the case with the Western avant-garde, but at the restoration of the richness of traditional art and literature in a rather classicist sense. This meant at the same time a declaration of war on the totalitarian state. Russian poets of Brodsky's generation were trying to escape its stifling influence—not through political protest, but through aesthetic dissent.[49]

Brodsky continued his aesthetic rebellion on American soil, in keeping with his idea of continuity between his Russian and American lives.

"ON RICHARD WILBUR": BRODSKY'S CRUSADE AGAINST MODERNISM

Brodsky would not have been Brodsky, however, had his anglophone poetic affiliation not played a role in his views on Russian-English translation. After all, his Russian experience had encompassed and been greatly influenced by his English-language involvement, and his special relationship with English came to the fore in his review of Mandelstam's translations. In this review, "Beyond Consolation," he explained that his main concern was not the prestige of Russian poetry in America but the impact that it might or—depending on the quality of the translations—might not have on contemporary American poets. Subpar translations, Brodsky argued, chiefly meant "plundering one's own culture, the degradation of one's own criteria, the avoidance of spiritual challenge."[50] He specified: "'OK,' the young American poet will conclude, 'the same thing goes on with them over there in Russia.' But what goes on over there is not at all the same thing."[51] Apparently he wished to repay his own strongest source of artistic influence in the same coin. The image of a "young American poet" discovering Russian poetry in translation harks back to the wish he expressed in his 1971 letter to Carl Proffer that the English versions of his verse might one day have a comparable impact on his English or American counterparts, as English-language poetry had had on him. In fact, there is a strong continuity between Brodsky's ideas on *ars poetica* (the art of poetry) expressed in his reviews of Akhmatova and Mandelstam and another review of his, "On Richard Wilbur" (1973), which discussed the poetry of the American poet Richard Wilbur.

Brodsky's review of Wilbur, whom he had translated in Russia, gave Brodsky a platform to outline for the first time his own aesthetic principles to the broader public. Brodsky explained that in Russia he had been struck by Wilbur's "dramatism, camouflaged by excellence of form."[52] "[Wilbur] speaks as a rule in a regular meter about drama of human existence, and this narration, conducted according to the rather harsh laws of his *Ars poetica*, acquires an independent value."[53] Brodsky left no doubt that he thought writing in regular meter and adhering to the harsh laws of *ars poetica* were a virtue. Having praised Wilbur for his technical skill, Brodsky rushed to his defense against the attacks of contemporary critics, who claimed that Wilbur's "excellence of form" was no more than a trademark of clichéd and outdated poetics, concealing a lack of deep feeling.[54] Under the guise of defending Wilbur, Brodsky launched into an all-out attack on "any form of free verse," which he declared to be less functional than "a regular meter and exact rhymes."[55] Brodsky emphasized that "for Wilbur attractiveness and beauty are never goals in themselves" but helped shape "an uncomfortable thought,"[56] creating an important artistic tension. Brodsky further argued, as in his subsequent Akhmatova review, that by using "a regular meter and exact rhymes,"[57] the poet resisted chaos, whereas free verse was a form of "dependence on and being determined by chaos."[58] Characteristically, Brodsky twice used the word "resistance." In a typically Russian twist, he remarked that to offer resistance was superior from "a moral point of view."[59] Years later, Brodsky would refer to Weissbort's use of more relaxed rhymes in a translation of his poems as "cowardly," presumably following a similar logic. Brodsky's concluding remarks in his Wilbur piece were equally categorical: "The laws of *Ars poetica*, when they are observed, render a greater gain in quality than any breaking of these laws . . ."[60]

Coming from a Russian poet who had just settled in their country, such strong opinions must have seemed quite remarkable to the readers of the *American Poetry Review*. But Brodsky positioned himself right from the start not as a Russian poet trying to impose his outlandish principles on the locals, but as an equal participant in a literary process with a vested interest in the fate of American poetry. This was a clever approach, for Wilbur himself soon wrote to him through a third party to express his gratitude:

> I am of course most honoured that he would care to write the piece in the first place, and (more importantly) I am gratified to have been the point of departure for such interesting and tonic remarks about form and finish in poetry: it matters greatly to me that he should see and say that in my work—as in the work of others I might name—*technical felicity is a means and a by-product rather than an end. This is an unpopular thing which needs saying nowadays*, and I admire the concision and clarity with which he puts it [italics mine].[61]

As Wilbur emphasized, these were indeed very unpopular things to say, and there came an immediate backlash from another American poet, Denise Levertov.[62] At the same time, by stating his position so forcefully, Brodsky managed to insert himself into the middle of an American debate between the proponents of loose and strict forms in poetry. Importantly, the dear shadow of Auden was on his side in this debate.

FOLLOWING IN ELIOT'S AND AUDEN'S FOOTSTEPS

In 1948, William Carlos Williams gave a lecture at the University of Washington titled "The Poem as a Field of Action."[63] Williams proposed several sweeping changes in American poetry, urging the new generation to abandon most traditional forms of poetic structure: "I say we are through with the iambic pentameter. . . ."[64] Williams instead proposed a style that would explore the vigor of American speech in its most quotidian forms. In his fervor, Williams was every bit as ideological and doctrinaire as Brodsky would become in his pursuit of the reverse cause. Williams saw his dedication to rhythms of the vernacular and to American themes as a moral choice.[65] In a curious reversal of this idea, Brodsky would describe his generation's resistance to modernism as aesthetic rather than moral.[66] Williams tried to enlist other poets in his "basic attack upon the whole realm of structure in the poem."[67] T. S. Eliot, the 1948 winner of the Nobel Prize in Literature, might have been considered a potentially important ally, but Eliot showed strong allegiance to the iambic norm even in his free verse and was likewise quite wedded to European traditions.[68] Auden, on the other hand, whom Williams described as a poet "so agile—so impressive in the use of poetic means" that he "could do anything,"[69] seemed like a better fit. Yet all Williams's attempts to convert him to his creed proved futile, and he concluded that Auden's "very skill seems to defeat him."[70] Eliot eventually turned out to be a better ally in Williams's struggle with structure, as his own comment reveals: "Eliot's experiments in the *Quartets* . . . show him to be more American in the sense I seek than, sad to relate, Auden, with his English ears and the best will in the world, will ever be able to be."[71]

Decades later, Auden's literary executor Edward Mendelson also compared Eliot with Auden in their respective attitudes toward the use of traditional forms in poetry. Yet Mendelson came to a very different conclusion:

> The poets of modernism devised their characteristic free verse as a response to the European disaster. . . . In the . . . year 1939, Eliot looked sadly back at the triumphs of modernism, and saw in them "rather the last efforts of an old world, than the first struggles of the new." In the midst of these triumphs, before modernism began its manifest decline, Auden was exuberantly at work writing in ways that modernism insisted were impossible. . . . The poets of modernism felt they could bring tradition into the present only as battered ironic fragments, or by heroic efforts to make it new. For Auden it had never grown old. . . . Where modernism had used innovative forms to speak of historical necessity, Auden . . . adopted traditional forms to speak of freedom and choice.[72]

Mendelson argued that, while the modernists believed they had to reject traditional forms as no longer suitable to describe the contemporary world, Auden continued using them quite successfully in his own poetry.[73] There was a clear similarity to Brodsky here, which explained his instinctive affinity for Auden: for neither of them had tradition ever "grown old."[74] In America, Brodsky launched his own campaign antithetical to that of Williams's fight for free verse, claiming both Auden and Eliot as allies. Evidently, Eliot could be repurposed to suit both causes, as the following passage from "Translating Akhmatova" illustrates:

> The contrast of traditional form to so-called contemporary content gives the work greater scale and tension. The principle is extremely simple: here is a normal person, with arms and legs, properly dressed, a tie and stickpin, but just look at the way he talks! Remember how the author of *The Waste Land* dressed, or imagine an automobile rushing straight toward you in your lane, and you will discover the function of the traditional verse line in Russian nineteenth-century poetry.[75]

Brodsky argued that there was an important tension between the common-looking shape of traditional verse and the contemporary relevance of its modern content. To illustrate the idea of a classically shaped poem having an ordinary appearance, Brodsky used the image of T. S. Eliot sporting a proper suit, as he is typically seen in photographs. The second image of a car rushing straight at you in your lane presents a metaphor for modern content as it confronts the reader with its metaphysical imperatives.

Later Brodsky would liken the role of the poet to an even more daunting vehicle: "The poet should charge his public like a tank, so that the reader has no escape. Poetry is an act of metaphysical and linguistic attack, not of retreat."[76] In keeping with the high stature of the poet in Russian culture, Brodsky hoped to make a strong impact on his American readers as well.

There are many traces of Eliot's criticism scattered throughout Brodsky's essays and interviews.[77] For instance, in his influential essay "Tradition and the Individual Talent," Eliot asserted that to be a traditional poet means being "judged by the standards of the past."[78] In the same vein, Venclova explained that one of the main lessons he had learned from Brodsky was "the idea that poetry is a conversation with one's predecessors and presupposes their presence," adding "my generation had to learn this anew from Brodsky."[79] Brodsky, meanwhile, had most likely learned this concept from Eliot and Auden. The latter aphoristically formulated it in a light verse poem: "I count myself a man of letters / Who writes, or hopes to, for his betters."[80] The idea of writing for his predecessors became Brodsky's idée fixe.

Eliot further argued that tradition cannot simply be inherited but must be acquired through a sustained effort on the part of the poet.[81] In "Translating Akhmatova" Brodsky echoed this, suggesting that the poet-translator also had to recapitulate in miniature the historical process. He applied this principle to translation, arguing that whoever turns to translating traditional verse ought to be "capable of using the techniques created in the original."[82] We can interpret Brodsky's ideas with an eye to Eliot's conviction that poets must secure their own place in the hierarchy of their predecessors: thus Brodsky's insistence that the English translators of Anna Akhmatova should imitate Robert Frost; those of Osip Mandelstam, W. B. Yeats; and those of Marina Tsvetaeva, a "combination of Hart Crane and [Gerard Manley] Hopkins."[83]

CONCERN FOR TRADITIONAL CONCEPTIONS OF WESTERN CULTURE

Odd as it may seem, Brodsky's opposition to free verse was not as dogmatic as it sounded. Occasionally, he himself wrote poems in free verse, provoking a witty comment in a comic poem of his friend, the Leningrad poet Vladimir Ufliand: "The moment he screws with rhyme, / He starts fucking around with verse-libre."[84] The same goes for Auden, who wrote the first part of "In Memory of W. B. Yeats," which so inspired Brodsky as a young man, in unrhymed free verse (used also in other poems). Then, of course, there were Brodsky's own bold metrical innovations in accentual verse in Russian, as well as his introduction of complicated stanzaic constructions into Russian poetics that he had borrowed from English-language poetic models. The real meeting ground for Auden and Brodsky was thus not their opposition to free verse per se, but a shared "concern for the traditional conceptions of Western culture." By extension, this also meant showing "respect for its traditions of poetic craftsmanship," as Auden put it in his introduction to W. S. Merwin's first collection, *A Mask for Janus*, which he chose in 1952 for the Yale Younger Poets Prize.[85] Describing the qualities he most cherished in a young poet and emphasizing the value of technical artistry and practice, which he saw on display in the poems of the young Merwin, Auden wrote: "Technique in itself cannot make a good poem, but the lack of it can spoil one."[86] Auden's remarks about the importance of poetic technique overlapped significantly with Brodsky's statements on its preeminence in preserving traditional form in the translation of Russian poetry. In "Translating Akhmatova," Brodsky insisted that a translator should "possess the technique of the original."[87]

Auden's praise of Merwin as a young poet stands in stark contrast to Brodsky's condemnation of Merwin's translations of Mandelstam, which he called a "product of profound moral and cultural ignorance."[88] Brodsky explained that form was central to Mandelstam's notion of tradition in poetry: "Mandelstam is a formal poet in the highest sense of the word. For him a poem began with a sound, with a 'sonorous molded shape of form,' as he himself called it. Logically, a translator should begin his work with a search for at least a metrical equivalent to the original form."[89]

It is fascinating to discover that in his translations of Andrei Voznesenky, in collaboration with Max Hayward, Auden had used precisely the approach to translation that Brodsky was so passionately advocating. Here we have Patricia Blake's description of the process:

> Wystan was exceptionally demanding. He wanted what he called prosodic models. These were transliterations of the Russian text into the English alphabet, with an interlinear English translation in the same word order as the Russian original.
>
> Every day of our stay Wystan sat out in the field studying the Russian rhyme scheme on the prosodic model we had prepared overnight, while Max read the poem to him in Russian. Then they would sort out the sense.[90]

It was simply a matter of order for Auden to study the structure of the original he intended to translate into English. For as he made clear in his foreword to Voznesensky's *Antiworlds and the Fifth Ace*, "a poem is a verbal artifact which must be as skillfully and solidly constructed as a table or a motorcycle."[91] Brodsky would have wholeheartedly subscribed to this statement. But there was one problem: Brodsky viewed Voznesensky not only as a hack but as a toady of the Soviet regime and as an archrival. He would probably have preferred to forget Auden's translation of this particular poet rather than commend Auden for it. Thus, in his Akhmatova review, Brodsky chose to extol instead a much more remote example—Auden's translations of Icelandic sagas: "To translate poetry, one has to possess some art . . . of stylistic re-embodiment. This is possible when your reserve of technical skills is varied. A good example is W. H. Auden, who is capable of translating Icelandic sagas . . . using equivalents from the languages in which they were written."[92]

Given the strong affinity between Auden and Brodsky regarding the role of form and technique in poetry, it might seem surprising that they gave two such different assessments of Merwin. The discrepancy lies in the time that had elapsed between their respective reviews. Merwin's early verse was "immensely formal" and "neoclassical in style."[93] Two decades later, however, the tide in American poetry had dramatically shifted, and Merwin's aesthetics had changed with it. By the late 1960s Merwin had switched to free verse, and in 1969 he even wrote his own manifesto advocating the use of open forms.[94] Merwin's views evidently reflected the currents of the day, for in 1970 he was awarded a Pulitzer Prize in Poetry.[95] As Merwin's case demonstrated, it was not quite true, as Brodsky had claimed, that American poets were no longer capable "of operating within traditional metrical verse."[96] Some of them, like Merwin, simply no longer wanted to. It seemed that Brodsky was fighting an already lost cause.

"I HOLD THE FORT ALONE"

But Brodsky was hardly new to fighting lost causes.[97] His fellow Slav and fellow exile Czesław Miłosz again gave him his backing. Miłosz believed that in Brodsky's resistance to the fleeting fashions of the day, the writer was "much more sober than his contemporary poets in America."[98] Brodsky's goals were ambitious. He was concerned with nothing less than the future course of poetry in English. Miłosz echoed this: "Brodsky and I may well be considered to be lingering in the rear guard, but really, we may be the avant-garde. . . . If we poets work hard at it, then we can change the direction in which poetry is headed."[99]

Brodsky's bluntness and vehemence may often have felt and looked like personal animosity. It is important to point out, however, that they were mostly a result of his commitment to safeguarding the sanctity of poetic expression, an allegiance that, for him, was detached from personal relationships. There were times, of course, when his bluntness strained friendships, which Brodsky subsequently regretted and tried to put right. As a case in point, he and Merwin became friendly after Brodsky had, ironically, recommended him as a translator of poetry.[100]

At the same time, he singled out one scholar, Harold Bloom, as his main bogeyman. In fact, when I approached the latter before a class in the fall of 2010, introducing myself as a Brodsky scholar, Bloom almost shook with rage as he heard me say the name. This reaction later became clear to me when I saw the oblique reference Brodsky had made to Bloom in a discussion with Walcott about form in poetry. Apparently, Brodsky resisted Bloom's formulation of the "anxiety of influence," finding it condescending to writers:

> There is so much garbage piled up on top of the issue. For instance, there is the entire concept of the anxiety of influence, advanced mainly by the people from Yale University. Every poet tries to say something which hasn't been said by his predecessors . . . but it doesn't necessarily mean that he doesn't like his predecessors, that he's haunted by the predecessors. I know nothing better than to write some sort of nice quatrain that would sound either like Pushkin or like Yeats, or like anybody. It's a great pleasure to do that sort of thing.[101]

Brodsky's battle against modernist poetic trends in Russian-English translation paralleled his rejection of the American academic fad for viewing the past as a burden rather than as a gift to wholeheartedly embrace. As Derek Walcott observed: "One feels that he [Brodsky] has written these many poems, most of them very long, because they serve as a bulwark, a fortress against the modern."[102]

Unlike Nabokov, whose views on translation underwent serious metamorphosis in the course of his American life,[103] Brodsky stuck to his guns until the very end. A letter sent in 1989 to his Swedish publisher, which could be regarded as his translation testament, exemplifies the way he envisioned the translation of his poetry into any language:

> Dear Jonas,
>
> In connection with the forthcoming edition of my poems . . . I would like to insist on preserving formal aspects of the original. By that I mean meter and rhymes. I do realise that in certain cases this may prove to be impossible, but I'd rather prefer my poems non-existent in Swedish than misrepresented. However, the minimum requirement that should be met by any translator is the preservation of the meter. . . . Meter is the backbone of a poem, and I'd rather appear stiff than spineless. I am a professional, and I'd like to be treated professionally. No personal philosophy of this or that trans-

> lator should be paid heed to, regardless of his or her reputation in the country. . . . It would be nice to make rhymes survive as well: not for my sake but for your readers.[104]

It is telling that Brodsky showed the same insistence on "preserving formal aspects of the original" when it came to translations into Swedish, a language he didn't even know, as he did in discussions of Russian-English poetry translation. Many of his translators, however, were not prepared for such intransigence. They felt they had been mistreated, and this led to multiple conflicts. His translator and friend Alan Myers, paraphrasing Brodsky's own metaphor from an earlier letter to him, put it in a nutshell: "You may be the only one holding the fort (poor Joseph), but at least you can choose which Indian to shoot. They have no choice."[105]

AMERICAN AND EUROPEAN RESPONSES TO THE BRODSKY CHALLENGE

The first reaction to "Translating Akhmatova" came most importantly and encouragingly from Stephen Spender, a poet whose opinion mattered very much to Brodsky. Spender was most struck by Brodsky's authoritative tone and thought that his piece could become a "turning point,"[106] changing the way people thought about poetry translation in England and America. This must have been music to Brodsky's ears. Similarly, Miłosz found Brodsky's next review, "Beyond Consolation," both "excellent" and "brutal in a salutary way."[107] As Spender rightly predicted, Brodsky's reviews of Akhmatova and later of Mandelstam inspired people to reflect more deeply on poetry translation. For a while, Brodsky even set the tone in debates around the translation of Russian poetry. Various parties sparring over the question of form in poetry translation began citing Brodsky as an authority in the pages of book reviews and in book introductions. Thus, in an introduction to his 1976 translations of Akhmatova, the British translator and poet D. M. Thomas relied on Brodsky's opinion to support his own choice of a traditional translating method, calling Brodsky's demands "stern but fair."[108]

At the other side of the spectrum stood Yves Bonnefoy, the leading French translator of Shakespeare and a distinguished French poet and scholar. In his 1979 piece "On the Translation of Form in Poetry," Bonnefoy questioned Brodsky's claim that Russian poetry had demonstrated its "moral purity" by sticking to classical forms. Bonnefoy rightly suspected that this was part of Brodsky's larger crusade against free verse, which went far beyond the specific problems of poetry translation:

> Brodsky makes it very clear that he does not limit the condemnation of free verse to its use in the translation of regular ones, but rejects every use of it, every poem written with its help. Actually, he finds in free verse the main distinction between Russian poetry and what he calls "her Western sisters" and makes us suspicious that he believes his own poetic tradition the only one inflexible, if not heroic . . . Once more, the old idea of holy Russia, whose historical misadventures could even be signs of qualities and aspirations inaccessible to our lower ones![109]

Bonnefoy's suggestion that Brodsky's attitudes were those of an old-school Slavophile, intriguing as it sounds, might be simply a rhetorical exaggeration. But as a French poet and translator, Bonnefoy had every reason to be concerned about Brodsky's demands. As Friedberg observed in a related context, requiring the re-creation of rhymes and meter "would invalidate nearly all French translations of poetry from Russian."[110] Bonnefoy next objected to Brodsky's implication that the use of traditional forms per se guaranteed a high quality of translation. In "Translating Akhmatova," Brodsky himself had argued that "the traditional line of verse puts you at a clear disadvantage; it . . . depersonalizes you . . . And then it depends on you, as a poet, whether this line of verse will become yours or remain alien, or more precisely, remain no one's. In other words, what you put into it depends on your soul."[111] But what if the translator's use of traditional lines fell short? What if the translator's "soul," as Brodsky put it, was not up to the task? Was there not a danger that translations achieved through traditional techniques might become the "absolutely impersonal product"[112] that Raffel's and Merwin's translations of Mandelstam into free verse had become, according to Brodsky? Indeed, instead of becoming "a sort of common denominator of modern verbal art,"[113] as Brodsky characterized their translations, rhymed and metered translations of Russian poetry into English might instead turn into a common denominator of hackneyed verbal art, to paraphrase Brodsky himself. In other words, Brodsky's demands could have the effect of breeding clichéd translations.

To rebut that proposition, Brodsky would have insisted that the form of the original in translation was important even as an allusion, as a way of alerting the reader that the original had employed complex compositional devices. Such a translation would at least give an idea of the poem's original architecture. In his conviction that poetic form was itself laden with meaning, Brodsky was, in fact, very close to Nadezhda Mandelstam. Much has been made lately of her effort in 1969 to defend Robert Lowell's free translations of Mandelstam from Nabokov's scathing attacks.[114] It is important to remember, however, that Nadezhda Mandelstam made those remarks in the modality of "translation under duress," as I call it. Lowell's translations, as free as they may have been, constituted a personal affirmation from a major American poet of Mandelstam's legacy, thereby providing some guarantee of a poetic afterlife for her deceased husband. Yet after both volumes of her memoirs had been published in the West and Mandelstam's archives had been transferred to Princeton, Nadezhda Mandelstam approached translation from a very different angle. In her 1976 introduction to Mandelstam's translations by the British translator James Greene, who had tried to preserve the form of the originals, Nadezhda Mandelstam's views on translation strongly overlapped with those expressed by Brodsky:

> I think that the most difficult task in the world is the translation of verses, particularly of a true poet, in whose verses there is *no discrepancy between the form and content* [italics mine]. . . . Marina Tsvetaeva said she could write as Mandel'shtam did but that she didn't want to. She was a great poet but she was greatly mistaken. . . . Mandel'shtam composed verse *in tradition*, which is far more difficult to imitate. Mr. Robert Lowell's translations are very free; Mr. Paul Celan's into German also free. But both are a very far cry from the original text. As far as I know, the translations of Mr. Greene are the best I ever saw.[115]

Similarly, Brodsky believed that even an imperfect formal translation of a Russian poem written in a traditional form was better than one done in free verse, however idiomatically smooth or appealing to the native ear it may sound. Later, Alan Myers, another convert to Brodsky's principle of mimetic translation, pointed out:

> The Merwin/Brown version of [Mandelstam's] "Insomnia," for example, is little more than the literal English prose meaning set out in lines. Who could guess that the rhyme scheme is ABBA, or that the first and last lines have twelve syllables each, the middle two thirteen—with a feminine ending? What trace is there of the poet's formal rhythmic skill which makes the verse so memorable to Russians?[116]

This also explains why, having ferociously attacked Raffel and Merwin for their translations of Mandelstam in "Beyond Consolation," Brodsky unexpectedly singled out for praise the rather inconspicuous and workmanlike translations of Mandelstam by the British translator Bernard Meares:

> I would also like to mention a cycle of translations done by Bernard Meares for the journal *Modern Poetry in Translation* published in London. (This is a remarkable journal, by the way, and regrettably not very well known in the US.) In spite of their uneven quality, one can hear Mandelstam's real voice in

> these translations. The nervous, pure voice of his love, his memory, his culture, and his faith, waverable as a candle in the wind. Naturally, Meares has trouble with his rhymes (but then again, who doesn't); yet somehow one does not notice it.[117]

Brodsky argues that Meares's unpretentious translation managed to preserve "Mandelstam's real voice," which was presumably hidden within the poetic forms Meares set out to reconstruct in his versions.

TRANSLATION BATTLES

The London-based journal *Modern Poetry in Translation*, which Brodsky praised, had been cofounded in 1965 and edited jointly by Ted Hughes and Daniel Weissbort. It published poetry from the countries of the Soviet bloc in English translation. Weissbort would later become one of the few translators who showed considerable resistance to Brodsky's iron rules of translation. He was especially opposed to the way Brodsky applied them in practice in his reworkings of Weissbort's English translations of his poems. This explains Weissbort's defense of fellow poet Elaine Feinstein in 1982 in the pages of the *New York Review of Books* after she had been criticized for her Tsvetaeva translations by the British translator and Brodsky disciple David McDuff. In a letter to the editors appropriately titled "Battle over Translation," Weissbort scathingly rebutted McDuff's criticisms of Feinstein for having failed to preserve the original form of Tsvetaeva's poems, and also attacked Brodsky:

> My professional conscience compels me . . . to defend a translator [Elaine Feinstein] whom Mr. McDuff excoriates quite unfairly. Of course, he doesn't know he is being unfair. He is . . . a man of principle, a believer in the sanctity of the word and, as far as poetry is concerned, in the sanctity of form. He is, in short, a follower of Joseph Brodsky, whose views on the translation of the great modern Russian masters have been widely disseminated . . . I feel it necessary to at least suggest an alternative approach to the absolutist one proposed by McDuff, alias Brodsky.[118]

Later the same year, Weissbort interviewed Stanley Kunitz, whose Akhmatova translations Brodsky had criticized a decade earlier. After complimenting Kunitz, Weissbort proceeds, without mentioning Brodsky by name, to characterize his position on translation in such implacable terms as to elicit from Kunitz a comparison of Brodsky to a religious extremist:

> Weissbort: There has been a view, much put around lately, that translators of formal poetry, especially formal Russian poetry, have tended to ignore the formal side. It seems to me that your Akhmatova translations represent a very nice balance between formal demands and semantic accuracy, even if not of the literal, verbal kind. . . . Do you think the absolutist demand for the "exact reconstruction of a poem," as you say, expresses the unrealistic, idealistic ambition to somehow transform English into a kind of Russian . . . ?
>
> Kunitz: There's a kind of purism in literature that is just as destructive as fanaticism in religion. I equate the two.[119]

While Weissbort alludes to Brodsky's "absolutism," Kunitz describes him as a religious fanatic of poetry translation—a label that has stuck. This mirrors a widely shared misunderstanding, especially after his death, of Brodsky's uniquely Russian relationship to poetry, which might come off as religiously extreme or absolutist when seen from the outside.

As to the battle over the actual translations, that had been fought by Weissbort and Brodsky a few years earlier. In his defense of Feinstein from McDuff, and of Kunitz from Brodsky, Weissbort was looking for an outlet for his own grievances. He certainly found a sympathetic ear in Kunitz.

Chapter Six

Translation Battlefield

DANIEL WEISSBORT met Brodsky at the Poetry International Festival in London, where Brodsky made his first appearance in 1972 in the company of Auden and Spender. Weissbort was impressed by Brodsky's manner of reciting poetry at the festival and offered to translate his verse into English. Weissbort was well versed in translation theory and knew some Russian, but since his grasp of the language was not very firm, he explicitly asked Brodsky for feedback and even insisted in one letter that the author be fussy and demanding.[1]

By 1974, however, the tone of Weissbort's letters to Brodsky began to change. Brodsky had criticized Weissbort for the way he had rendered the original meter and rhymes of his Venetian poem "Laguna" ("Lagoon"). Weissbort defended his solutions, explaining that relaxed rhyming was the method he had consciously chosen for translating Russian poetry: "To return to the translation. As I say, I'll try to absorb your notes and to revise the version. However, I'm a little concerned that you apparently did not perceive my attempt to reproduce both meter and rhymes, which you contend have totally disappeared. I had thought I'd done rather better than visual rhymes."[2] Clearly, the author's position vis-à-vis translation had become uncompromising enough to trouble the translator. Weissbort tried to persuade Brodsky that the more relaxed rhyming he had adopted was more in sync with the contemporary poetic idiom in America:

> It's a pity I couldn't have been there to read you the translation. The type of rhyme I have been using more and more in translating Russian poetry is the one based on sound, or vowel equivalence. Occasionally I use consonantal rhymes. These do not have the force of the Russian strong rhymes of course, but in my view are more appropriate in English.[3]

At the time, Weissbort, a British poet-translator, was living in the United States, teaching at the University of Iowa. His approach to translation reflected American trends. Suspecting that, despite Brodsky's impressive grasp of English, his Russian ear might still fail to catch the subtleties of more oblique rhyming in English, Weissbort went out of his way to give concrete examples of the rhyming he had in mind:

> The aa bccb scheme does not make it more difficult, though I suppose with my kind of oblique or half and quarter rhyming, it does render it more difficult to perceive the rhyme. Let me give you a few instances of this rhyming. Stanza III: chime (a) / lives (a) / chandelier (b) / duckweed (c) / with (c) / tears (b); Stanza IV: wind (a)/ brim (a) / is (b) / guard (c) / star (c) / rays (b). I don't invariably rhyme, but usually do—in this way. Also I have kept to the rhythm broadly. Does this totally fail to come across?[4]

Brodsky, holding to his principle of equimetrical translation, would probably have argued that Weissbort's approach, the use of a special metrical equivalent for translating all Russian poetry, was inherently flawed. Since Russian has all sorts of meters, Brodsky would feel that a metrical equivalent for a poem in iambic pentameter would not be equally suited to the translation of a Russian poem written in loose *dol'nik* (accentual verse), like his "Lagoon."[5]

At the same time, being far behind schedule, Brodsky could not afford to be too fussy. He had to find and commission an increasing number of translations for his forthcoming collection *A Part of Speech*, which often meant sacrificing his highest standards, the preservation of meter and rhyme. Thus, at Brodsky's request, in 1976 Nancy Meiselas of Farrar, Straus and Giroux contacted three different poets, Peter Viereck, Mark Strand, and Daniel Weissbort, asking them to translate the cycle "A Part of Speech."[6] This was a rather important commission, since the cycle gave both its title and tone to the entire collection.[7] Weissbort was the only one who agreed to do it. Once he completed the translation, Brodsky gave his initial approval in a postcard:

> Dear Danny, poems are OK, and I've already asked FS+G's editor to arrange for payment. . . . Bitterness or no bitterness, I want you to do some more and will send them to you in no time (terrific expression! Fits my modus operandi perfectly).[8]

Around the same time, however, Brodsky also wrote to Nancy Meiselas suggesting that some of the poems from the cycle translated by Weissbort had to be revised: "Danny Weissbort has translated those 19 shorts but they do need some (at times complete) revision. I'll send you those as soon as you know what. In general, I have this sinking feeling that with the present tempo we'll never make it. Try to apply some pressure if you have an appropriate device, that is. Bows J.B."[9] In the meantime, Weissbort himself moved fast. By 1978, he had published his translation of the cycle in *Poetry* magazine and was even awarded a translation prize for it.[10] Weissbort sent the issue of *Poetry* with his translation to Brodsky. The copy that can be found today among the Brodsky Papers at Yale University contains several markings in the hand of Masha Vorobiova, a first-wave Russian émigré who worked as a Russian lecturer at Vassar College. She was Brodsky's bilingual friend, New York City neighbor, and a close associate. Alongside Barry Rubin, she had produced the first interlinear translations and helped with the general editing of *A Part of Speech*. Vorobiova's markings indicate several problematic passages in Weissbort's translations, which have less to do with form and more with issues of tone and meaning.

Brodsky's next postcard to Weissbort ends with a concise note: "'A part of speech' cycle needs revisions."[11] Weissbort, however, made it clear that he was done with the translation and would not, or simply could not, undertake any more changes. Brodsky did not take no for an answer. Thus, in November 1978, he wrote to another British friend and translator, Alan Myers, asking him to translate the cycle instead:

> Dear Alan, . . . would you consider translating the cycle that gives a book its title—*A Part of Speech*. You see, *Danny did it—but it came out bloody leaden. Or wooden* [italics mine]. If you'll set for doing so, please double-check every—there are not so many of them in the cycle—line with Diana. Say "yes" or "no" but say either thing quickly. Sincerely yours, Joseph.[12]

Alan Myers did produce a translation as per Brodsky's request, which can be found among the papers at Yale University. But it was not Myers's translation that eventually made it into the definitive version of the book when it came out in 1980.

The next time Weissbort and Brodsky met was in the fall of 1979 at the International Poetry Festival in Cambridge, England. Weissbort recalled the occasion in his 2004 memoir, *From Russian with Love: Joseph Brodsky in English*: "My version [of "A Part of Speech"] was, I thought, virtually an 'official' one. I welcomed the opportunity to read it, being more than a little proud of having preserved much of the form."[13] A rude awakening awaited him instead:

> The reading took place in a rather ramshackle hall, and I was waiting in semi-darkness . . . holding my translation . . . Joseph sidled up to me, and with an uncertain smile, stretched out his hand and slowly scratched my sleeve, meowing "Danny, don't be angry" and simultaneously handing me a wad of sheets with a new version of "A Part of Speech." My response may not have been

> very gracious, but at the same time, the following despairing words formed in my head . . . : "Wait a moment! I've no right to feel this way. It's his poem. After all, I'm just a translator . . ." I did not even have the opportunity of glancing at the new version before being asked to read it to the large audience in Cambridge, whereas I had doubtless rehearsed my own version. It angered and humiliated me to hear echoes of my own work, this being about all I did hear. Did I speak to Joseph (or anyone else) afterwards? I was demoralized. And I also despised myself for not refusing to read this bowdlerized text.[14]

By the attention Weissbort pays in his memoir to the singular details of that fateful event, one can gauge the traumatizing effect it had on him. Clearly, Weissbort did not take Brodsky's revisions lightly. He felt that his effort had been underappreciated, dismissed, and altered behind his back. His insecurities were exposed, he felt robbed of his artistic achievement, and his self-confidence was dealt a severe blow. Soon after the ill-fated reading, Weissbort exploded in two embittered letters to Brodsky. Here are excerpts from them:

> Dear Joseph,
>
> First, on reflection, it was utterly within your rights to do what you did about the translation. . . . My objection to the whole affair has to do with "friendship." In my view you acted with a high-handed disregard of pretty basic rules . . . you have not really re-done the translation; you have strung it together—quite effectively—using lines and hints from my versions and . . . from that of other people, who unbeknown to me, you had evidently (contrary to the quite clear understanding I had from you that I was "commissioned" to translate this poem) engaged in trying their hands too. The result of your efforts strikes me as rather good finally (with some criticisms which I could but will not, at this stage, make) but there is a simple morality involved here. *I feel that you ought to make it clear in your introduction or whatever exactly how you arrived at a version, which though the original poem, the Russian, is obviously yours, does not wholly belong* to *you*. . . . I feel it shows a cavalier disregard for others' feelings on your part and I do have some trouble with that [italics mine].[15]

Weissbort raised an important problem of ownership of translation, challenging Brodsky in a way that Kline, for instance, had never done. Reluctantly admitting that some of Brodsky's changes might have been effective, Weissbort nevertheless disputed the author's right to having altered his translation in the first place. In his second, equally emotional, letter sent three days later, Weissbort sounded less positive that Brodsky's interventions had been for the better:

> Dear Joseph,
>
> . . . It is my humble opinion that though you have done a lot of it yourself, *you do not really understand translations* and that you are certainly not plugged into what I try to do when I aim at a translation to stand for a certain original. . . . Being a Russian, you tend to look at things absolutely—i.e., if I am not your kind of poet, nor can I be your kind of translator. *It is my work, subtly (or unsubtly) depending on your point of view, changed. They are only translations but still had a certain dynamic working for them in their pristine state, which has now been distorted* [italics mine].[16]

Accusing Brodsky of failing to appreciate what does and does not work in English translations, Weissbort argued that Brodsky's interventions destroyed the particular logic of his translations and expressed his suspicion that Brodsky harbored a certain prejudice against him as a translator because he used more open forms in his own verse.

This prompted Brodsky to write in turn a long and elaborate response to repair the damage and placate Weissbort by addressing some of his grievances. Brodsky also tried to better articulate his position:

> If I got to rework some translation in this forthcoming collection (not yours only, but also Rigsbee's, Kline's, Myers's and others . . .) it's not because that I got to aspire for a higher spot on the local Parnassus, but because I've been given the galleys and found enough time to read them. What I've found was often disagreeable and objectionable. That, in itself, wasn't a big surprise. What has surprised me really is that some of them could be easily remedied (or worsened, as you may say again). And here we are getting to the hub of the whole problem. *It's not that I believe meters and rhymes being sacred, but I'd rather look trite than slack* [italics mine].[17]

Curiously enough, the first thing Brodsky denied here was having any poetic ambition in English. He then explained that as soon as he looked at the proofs, he saw that they could easily be improved by minor tweaking, the better to render justice to the form of his Russian originals. On this latter point, Brodsky elaborated:

> Please, Danny, understand me properly: I don't dispute your notions of poetic technique. As far as I am concerned, it's extremely strong (your means, that is as they are manifested in these translations), but often it lacks that element (or device) which creates the sense of the inevitability of the statement. Sometimes, to me there is too much of this "take-it-or-leave-it." And it's not that I am afraid of being "left": I simply believe that this attitude on the whole is cowardly. I understand that this is what the poetic idiom in English has

come to, but it's simply not my cup of Earl Grey. Nor do I think that today is the last day of writing in English.[18]

Perhaps Brodsky's strongest argument was that he was writing for a future, not a present, reader and was primarily concerned with the continuity of formal tradition in poetry, which transcended the translation conventions of any given time. Indeed, history has proved Brodsky right about this; there has been a return to rhyme in English-language poetry over the past decades.[19] Brodsky found the looser, more relaxed rhymes employed by Weissbort unsatisfactory precisely because they did not convey the crucial one-way relationship between the poem's form and its meaning. It is no coincidence that this concept was best summarized by his beloved Auden in his introduction to the works of Byron. When it came to their belief in the role of poetic devices, Auden and Brodsky were clearly kindred spirits:

> In the process of composition, as every poet knows, the relation between experience and language is always dialectical, but in the finished product it must always appear to the reader to be a one-way relationship. In serious poetry thought, emotion, event, must always appear to dictate the diction, meter and rhyme in which they are embodied; vice versa, in comic poetry it is the words, meter, rhyme which must appear to create the thoughts, emotions and events they require.[20]

Brodsky felt that in Weissbort's translations his own poetic statements had lost the air of inevitability that Auden mentions. Adding insult to injury, Brodsky called this attitude cowardly, which was clearly unhelpful in healing Weissbort's wounds. In "Translating Akhmatova," Brodsky had left still other clues as to what he meant here:

> Contemporary Russian poets use a technique which seems archaic to their American colleagues. It is not just shameful for a contemporary American poet to use rhymes, it is unthinkable. It seems banal to him; he fears banality worse than anything, and therefore he uses free verse—though free verse is no guarantee against banality.[21]

Brodsky was clearly exaggerating when he said that it was unthinkable for American poets to use rhymes, but his main point was that they avoided them because rhyming technique was no longer popular. It was an accusation of a certain type of cowardice, the fear of sounding insufficiently *en vogue*, that Brodsky leveled at Weissbort. Most extraordinarily, Brodsky argued that this left him no choice but to interfere, since what was at stake here was not the English fate of his poem, but the dignity of the contemporary English poetic idiom itself: "I have an additional responsibility—that to the English language. Pathetic as it may sound, I feel . . . I am on my own not only in terms of accuracy of those translations, but also in the sense of their linguistic dignity."[22] By portraying himself as the lone defender of the poetic dignity of the English language, Brodsky trod heavily on the forbidden ground of Weissbort's native linguistic domain. At this point, it must have been clear to Weissbort that he had become entangled in Brodsky's quixotic war with modernism. Yet Weissbort dismissed Brodsky's argumentation, concentrating instead on his own creative and intellectual claims to his translation and on Brodsky's appropriation of it. However valid and lofty Brodsky's motives might be, Weissbort argued, they could not justify Brodsky's actions. In his final letter to Brodsky relating to their conflict, he wrote:

> Dear Joseph,
> Thank you for your letter. . . . I do not think you are a fool, but I do think you are misguided and wrong in most of the substantive things you say. . . .
>
> You see, frankly, your motives or whatever motive you thought you were acting under, was of no interest to me. What interested me was what you did and what it indicated in your attitude to the translation, as belonging to the translator. It is quite another matter for a translator to go on re-working his translation . . . and for someone else to rework a translator's translation, call it minor changes, adjustments, what you like. I would ask you a simple question: how minor would the changes be in one of your own poems in the original for you to accept them? Don't laugh! This may not be of the same order of magnitude—since one is only a translation, while the other is an original work—but it is, I contend, of the same kind.[23]

Eventually there came a formal reconciliation between them, though one suspects that Weissbort never recovered from the earlier blow. In his memoir about his experience translating Brodsky, Weissbort tried to give the impression that he had forgiven him, expressing a new understanding of Brodsky's position as well. By then Brodsky had been dead for almost a decade, and Weissbort's desire to forgive is very noble. Yet one can still feel his bitterness over the episode, despite his best intentions.

WEISSBORT VERSUS BRODSKY: COMPARING TRANSLATIONS OF "SEVER KROSHIT METALL"

To put the whole dispute over translation into some perspective, it might be worth taking a closer look at Brodsky's revisions of Weissbort's translation of a three-stanza poem from the cycle "A Part of Speech" that begins

"Sever kroshit metall" ("The North buckles metal"), an elegiac reminiscence of Brodsky's experience in Norenskaia.

Here we have the interlinear translation of the first stanza by Stephen White stored at the Brodsky Papers at Yale University, followed by a transliterated version of the original, and finally Weissbort's translation of the same stanza:

The North crushes metal, but it spares glass. a
It teaches the throat to pronounce "let (me) in." b
The cold brought me up and put a pen into a
(my) fingers in order to warm them, cupped. b
(White)

Sever kroshit metall, no shchadit steklo a
Uchit gortan' progovorit' «vpusti». b
Xolod menia vospital i vlozhil pero enj. a
V pal'tsy, chtob ikh sogret' v gorsti. b

The North crushes metal but leaves glass intact,
teaches the throat to utter: Let me in!
The cold raised me and placed in my hand
a pen to warm my clenched fist.
(Weissbort)

The rhyming pattern of the original poem consists of alternating masculine rhymes abab cdcd efef. Weissbort's translation instead uses what the translator himself described to Brodsky as "a kind of oblique or half and quarter rhyming": "intact—hand," "in—fist," which raised some objections from Brodsky. Leaving the rhymes aside, let us address a more serious semantic problem in Weissbort's translation of the first stanza—namely, the image of the last two lines, "placed in my hand / a pen to warm my clenched fist." Brodsky's metaphor for poetry writing, "put a pen / into my fingers, to warm them in the cup of the hand," is deliberately anti-heroic, a stance aligned with his attitude of downplaying the hardships he had endured in Norenskaia, discussed in chapter 2. Furthermore, the image in question underlines Brodsky's belief in the essential character of poetry: one needs it to obtain warmth in an existentially cold environment; one ultimately needs it to survive. The preservation of bodily warmth is the goal of every person in the Russian north; the preservation of one's soul is the challenge a human being faces in a totalitarian state. Poetry, one of the few means to this end, assumes an existential role. This explains why Brodsky time and again protested politicized interpretations of his poetry.[24] None other than Auden identified this quality in Brodsky's poetry in his introduction to *Selected Poems*: "Unlike the work of some of his contemporaries, Mr. Brodsky seems to stand outside what might be called the Mayakovsky tradition of 'public' poetry. It never uses a fortissimo."[25] It is clear, then, why it would be difficult for Brodsky to accept a heroically "clenched fist" in Weissbort's version, apart from the issue of Weissbort's rhymes.

It is also clear why Weissbort had come up with this image; the Russian word "*gorst'*," meaning "a handful" as well as "a cupped hand," has no direct equivalent in English. So a "clenched fist" seemed to come in handy. But Brodsky found a different solution.

The First Stanza: Brodsky's Version

> The North buckles metal, glass it won't harm;
> teaches the throat to say, "Let me in."
> I was raised by the cold that, to warm my palm,
> gathered my fingers around a pen.

Brodsky here paraphrased the Russian word "*gorst'*" in "gathered my fingers around a pen" and came up with arguably more emphatic rhyme pairs, "harm—palm" and "Let me in—pen."

TABLE 5. Rhymes in Stanza 1, "The North Buckles Metal"

Russian	Weissbort	Brodsky's Definitive English Version
vpustí—gorstí [Let me in—cup of hand (palm)]	**(Let me) in**—fist	**(Let me) in—pen**
steklo—**pero** [glass—pen]	intact—**hand**	harm—**palm**

Boldface type indicates cognates to Brodsky's original rhymes in Russian. The semantic equivalent in English is underscored.

As in his translation of "A Second Christmas by the Shore," we can observe a peculiar tendency of Brodsky's translations: he manages to rhyme in his English version three out of four words (above in bold) that rhyme in the original, even though some words in the English translation form part of a different rhyme pair.

The Second Stanza

Here we have the interlinear translation of the second stanza (again by Stephen White), then a transliterated version of the Russian, and finally Weissbort's translation of the second stanza:

Freezing, I see that beyond the seas		c
the sun is setting, and no one's around.		d
Either the heel slips on ice, or the earth itself		c
is becoming round under the heel.		d
(White)		

Zamerzaia, ia vizhu, kak za moria	enj.	c
solntse saditsia, i nikogo krugom.		d
To li po l'du kabluk skol'zit, to li sama zemlia	enj.	c
zakrugliaetsia pod kablukom.		d

Freezing, I see the sun going down
over the sea, and no one about.
Either the heel slips on ice, or the earth itself
arches underneath the foot.
(Weissbort)

As we can see in his translation of the second stanza, Weissbort rhymes only the even lines, so that the rhyme scheme is xaxa: "down—itself," "about—foot." On the other hand, Weissbort succeeds in finding assonances and alliterations that try to re-create the sound repetitions of the original poem: "Freezing—see—sun—sea—heel—slips—ice—itself." This created a vowel harmony with long 'e' and a consonantal harmony with combinations of voiced and voiceless 's' and the liquid sound 'l.'

As early as the 1920s, the formalist scholar Osip Brik began to focus on the repetition of consonantal groups in poetry and concluded that very often there existed a "connection between the sound structure of the verse and its rhythm and imagery."[26] The second stanza of "Sever kroshit metall," rich in consonantal repetition, seems to confirm Brik's findings, suggesting a connection between the icy and slippery imagery the stanza depicts and the liquid and plosive consonants that it features:

Zamerzaia, ia vizhu, kak za moria	(z m r z -z m r)
solntse saditsia, i nikogo krugom.	(s-ts; s-ts); (kg-kg)
To li po l'du kabluk skol'zit, to li sama zemlia	(tl-ld; lk-lk-kl; pdk; blk; lzt-tlz; lz-zl; lm–ml)
zakrugliaetsia pod kablukom.	(zkl; kl-lk; pdk; lm; blk)

Brodsky's Version of the Second Stanza

In his revision of Weissbort's translation of the second stanza, Brodsky took up and elaborated on the sound repetitions that his translator had proposed:

Freezing, I see the red sun that sets		(rz—rs; ts—ts)
behind oceans, and there is no soul	enj.	([z]—[z]; s—enj.—s)
in sight. Either my heel slips on ice, or the		
globe itself		(lp-lb sl—sl)
arches sharply under my sole.		(pl; sl)

Brodsky's version features two sets of rhymes: an assonance ("sets—itself") and a homonymic rhyme ("soul—sole"). Brodsky thought them more precise than those Weissbort had come up with. Besides, the expression "sun that sets" corresponds more literally to the original expression "*solntse saditsia.*"

TABLE 6. Rhymes in Stanza 2, "The North Buckles Metal"

Russian	Weissbort	Brodsky's Definitive English Version
za moria—zemlia [behind the seas—earth]	(going) down—itself	sets—itself
krugom—**kablukom** [(no one) around—(under my) heel]	(no one) about—**foot**	(no) soul—(under my) **sole**

Boldface type indicates cognates to Brodsky's original rhymes in Russian. The semantic equivalent in English is underscored.

In contrast with Brodsky's version of the first stanza, we do not find in his version of the second stanza, as we do in the original Russian, any rhyming of semantically identical words in English. What we find instead are three words that were not present in the original and whose main role seems to be to re-create the original interplay of meaning and sound. For instance, Brodsky introduced the descriptor "red" into the English version of the poem purely, it appears, for euphonic effect: "Freezing—red sun" was meant to produce, in my view, a sonic equivalent of "*Zamerzaya—za moriá.*" The same goes for "globe," "sharply," and "slips," which are intended to produce on an English palate the same slippery-stumbling effect that "*po l'du kabluk*" and "*zakrugliayetsia pod kablukóm*" produce on a Russian one. When asked about translation in a post-Nobel interview, Brodsky explained that he thought it to be against the rules to change a poem's original meaning.[27] Yet in revising Weissbort's translation, Brodsky obviously took some creative liberties in the meaning of the second stanza, where his main motivation most likely was to re-create in English the music and structure of the original.

Important to note is the semantically interesting plural form in the original of the expression "*za moryami*" ("beyond the seas"), which Weissbort rendered as singular, "over the sea," and Brodsky restored as a plural, "behind oceans." Arguably, the plural "oceans" better conveyed the sense of an insurmountable distance separating the lyrical hero from the rest of the world, which has shrunk to a slippery ball underneath. The whole image reinforced the feeling of the lyrical hero's absolute loneliness.

The Third Stanza

Here is White's interlinear translation of the third and last stanza, followed by a transliterated version, and below, Weissbort's translation:

And in my throat where there's supposed to be laughter e
or speech or hot tea f
ever more clearly resounds the snow e
and, like a kind of Sedov, looms the black "farewell." f
(White)

I v gortani moei, gde polozhen smekh,
ili rech', ili goriachii chai, f
vse otchetlivei razdaetsia sneg e
i cherneet, chto tvoi Sedov, «proshchai». f

As far as the Russian version of this stanza is concerned, the word "magical" seems to best describe the first rhyming couple "*smekh—sneg*" ("laughter—snow"). First, it comes as a complete surprise to the reader to find the verb "*razdaetsia*" (resounds") followed by the word "snow," even though anyone who has spent a winter in the north is, of course, familiar with the crunching sound of fresh snow under one's feet. Because it rhymes with "*smekh*" ("laughter"), one is tempted to pronounce the hard 'g' in the word "*sneg*" ("snow") as 'kh,' which would be a more colloquial pronunciation. Thus, in Russian, the rhyme quite realistically evokes the double surprise of a foot treading upon the snow: the physical surprise of the foot sinking deep into what appears to be an even and solid surface (conveyed through the passage from a hard 'g' to a soft 'kh' in "*sneg*"), and an acoustic surprise (achieved by the verb "resounds") from the unexpectedly loud screeching sound that accompanies the deepening of the foot. Needless to say, the original did not feature the "falling snow" that emerged in Weissbort's translation:

And in my throat, where laughter, or speech,
or hot tea is the norm,
the falling snow rings clear and your "farewell"
is dark as Scott wrapped in a polar storm.
(Weissbort)

In the translator's version of the third stanza, we have one set of precise rhyme ("norm—storm") that withstood the author's correcting pen; the words of the second rhyming couple, however, did not rhyme at all ("speech—farewell"). Yet one can still detect an intended internal vowel assonance between "speech" and "tea," and even between "farewell" and "wrapped," as well as what could be considered an internal rhyme between "snow" and "norm—storm." As Weissbort tried to explain to Brodsky in his letter of 1974, he believed that such oblique rhyming in English fulfilled the same function as strong rhymes in Russian. Weissbort further argued that the effect of such rhymes in English was less "intrusive" and thus more desirable. Years later in his memoir, his last and most articulate attempt to come to terms with the experience of working with Brodsky, Weissbort reiterated the same idea:

> Brodsky . . . held that the alleged paucity of full rhymes in English was simply an excuse, a cover-up for inferior skills of workmanship. Rhyming might require greater ingenuity in English, but that precisely was the challenge. He did not accept that the greater ingenuity required would tend to make the rhyme intrusive in English, and that it was not unreasonable to try to modify the impact by using slant-rhymes.[28]

Brodsky's Version of the Third Stanza

And in my throat, where a boring tale	enj.	a
or tea, or laughter should be the norm,		b
snow grows all the louder and "Farewell!"		a
darkens like Scott wrapped in a polar storm.		b

As we can see, Weissbort's translation of the last stanza suffered the fewest changes at the hand of the author. Weissbort had guessed correctly that Brodsky would wish the word "farewell" to appear at the end of a line as in the original. Brodsky also seemed satisfied with the second of the rhyming clusters Weissbort had come up with, "norm—storm." The same went for the substitution of "Scott" for "Sedov." Although Brodsky introduced many foreignizing elements into his self-translations, he seemed opposed to for-

TABLE 7. Rhymes in Stanza 3, "The North Buckles Metal"

Russian	Weissbort	Brodsky's Definitive English Version
smekh—sneg [laughter—snow]	speech—**farewell**	tale—**Farewell**
chai—**proshchai** [tea—farewell]	norm—storm	norm—storm

Boldface type indicates cognates to Brodsky's original rhymes in Russian. The semantic equivalent in English is underscored.

eignization simply to preserve local color. In other words, he wished to avoid his translations coming off as exotic to his anglophone readers. Weissbort understood this. What mattered in the stanza was the image of a polar explorer trapped in a snowy and icy wasteland, not whether he was a Russian (Sedov, a name no American would know) or an English hero (Scott), and not whether it was the North or the South Pole that he explored. With a characteristic touch of self-deprecation, Brodsky introduced a new expression into his version of the last stanza that did not exist in the original: "a boring tale," standing for the lyrical "I's" speech.

CONCLUDING OBSERVATIONS ON "THE NORTH BUCKLES METAL"

Close textual analysis has shown that Brodsky's reworking of Weissbort's translation of the poem "Sever kroshit metall" brought it closer to the original in terms of content. With the author's intervention, many shades of meanings (metaphorical vs. literal), tonalities, and various registers of speech were restored. Furthermore, his changes to Weissbort's version confirm that rhymes and verse meter were for Brodsky the most important, and indeed the essential, elements of his originals to preserve across translation.[29] His ability to find in English more precise rhymes than those proposed by his translators convinced him that the translations, after all, "could be easily remedied."[30] At the same time, Brodsky would sometimes change his own original metaphors and images, introducing new ones in English. Arguably, this was a major step toward the next phase of becoming his own English translator. That his "greater ingenuity" in finding more precise rhymes "would tend to make the rhyme intrusive in English,"[31] as Weissbort and others argued, failed to alter Brodsky's position. Brodsky maintained that he had an additional motive to rework Weissbort's translations—namely, a responsibility to the English language. Such claims may be unprecedented for a non-native speaker of English, but they make sense in light of Brodsky's stance toward his language in exile. Although he repeatedly denied that he aspired to "a higher spot on the local Parnassus,"[32] as he wrote in his letter to Weissbort, his interference told a different story.

In her memoir of Brodsky, Proffer Teasley argued that "in his stated views, contemporary American poets were weak in that many of them had given up rhyme, and they had done that because they just didn't know how to find new rhymes. He would accept no other explanations—to write poetry without rhyme was to play tennis without a net. He would translate himself and show how it should be done."[33] Indeed, it looked increasingly as though Brodsky was becoming more inclined to do the job himself. He changed the drafts even of a translator like Kline who shared his translation principles. But he intervened equally in the translation of Weissbort, who had his own firm ideas about translation and was a poet, after all, as well as a protégé of Ted Hughes, who was himself a gifted poet musically. Yet Brodsky's changes to Weissbort's work seem less dramatic than his changes to Kline's. In fact, one feels that Brodsky is just trying to make the English version his own. For obvious reasons, it was more convenient to tinker with existing translations than to begin from scratch. Weissbort was the only translator who dared directly challenge Brodsky, forcing him to defend his position more elaborately than he had ever been compelled to do. Prompted by Weissbort's indignation, Brodsky assembled a set of arguments, ranging from their clashing interpretations of the formal requirements for translation to restoring the dignity of the English language. Weissbort's response was directly personal: Brodsky had treated his hard-earned translations as his own drafts and had not been forthright about revisions. As he clearly states in the last letter between them relating to their conflict, quoted earlier:

> You have my translations, we communicate, I alter, adjust, work the changes into my scheme, and finally I say, enough, I can do no more. At that point, it is up to you to accept the version, with its imperfections, or say—not good enough, or not what I want enough. Sorry! Of course, I would have been disappointed, but it would have been far better than this surreptitious, behind-the-back, tinkering with versions I sweated long and heavily over. Is that understandable? You are right, it does not help your telling me you treated others in the same way![34]

Meanwhile, Barry Rubin, who with Derek Walcott helped to put the finishing touches on the collection before it was sent to print, sympathized with Brodsky and thought that he had made some excellent changes when amending Weissbort's translation of the cycle "A Part of Speech."[35] This positive feedback, alongside the various conflicts with translators during the preparation of *A Part of Speech*, prompted Brodsky to add a tone of gratitude and humility to the author's note that opened the 1980 edition of the book:

> I would like to thank each of my translators for his long hours of work in rendering my poems into English. I have taken the liberty of reworking some of the translations to bring them closer to the original, though perhaps at the expense of their smoothness. I am doubly grateful to the translators for their indulgence.[36]

While Brodsky thanked all his translators for their indulgence, Weissbort had indulged Brodsky the least. Brodsky noted that it was his inability to find translators willing to do his bidding that ultimately drove him to do more translations himself.[37] But the evidence of his interference shows that Brodsky felt the urge to play a more active part in the translation, shaping the "English destiny of his verse" himself, certainly more than he was willing to admit. In the end, Weissbort also acknowledged that behind Brodsky's interference in translation was his desire to leave a personal mark on his adoptive language:

> When Wilbur turned out an impeccably crafted version of a Brodsky poem, however flattering this may be, was it Brodsky? . . . It is hardly surprising that he increasingly resorted to translation of his own poetry . . . Indeed, it was perhaps preferable for him to collaborate with Russianists, who produced . . . *polufabrikaty* or half-finished products, working drafts in English for Joseph to revise and complete.[38]

While the confidence of some of his translators was left deflated—Weissbort being the most obvious case in point—Brodsky's own confidence in English grew. Rubin, as well as many others, feared that perhaps it was growing a little too fast.

Chapter Seven

Challenging the Masters

THE FALLING-OUT with Weissbort was the biggest but hardly the only conflict that erupted between Brodsky and his translators during the preparation of *A Part of Speech*. The Pulitzer Prize–winning poet Richard Wilbur remembered a minor but telling episode that sheds further light on Brodsky's involvement in his English translations. In 2005, almost a decade after Brodsky's death, Wilbur described his experience in translating two Brodsky poems, "Six Years Later" and "The Funeral of Bobò":

> When Joseph Brodsky defected to the United States or was sent over here, I hastened to do something of his because I had been told when in the Soviet Union that the best translations of my poetry into Russian had been done by Joseph. I wanted to pay him back and, because I had heard he was very choosy, very finicky about translations, I wanted to do something that he would approve of. . . . My first translation from a Brodsky poem took me a month, and the second was done slowly too, with the help of linguistic counsel and with the help of dictionaries as well. By that time, I was trying to teach myself the Russian language. Here's a poem of Brodsky's . . . called "Six Years Later" . . . and I think it's probably the best effort I've made in translating a Russian poem.[1]

Wilbur's account reveals how laborious and time-consuming the method of equimetrical translation championed by Brodsky actually was, if done properly. It took Wilbur a month to translate just thirty-six iambic pentameter lines, six stanzas of six lines each, of the poem "Six Years Later."[2] While Wilbur modestly assessed his translation as the best effort he had made in translating a Russian poem, Derek Walcott referred to it as "that miracle of adaptation."[3] Barry Rubin, who had provided Wilbur with an interlinear trot of the poem, was equally stunned by the astonishing metamorphosis it had undergone under Wilbur's pen.[4] Even Weissbort, who, as noted earlier, advocated less emphatic rhyming and less strict meter in English translation, referred to Wilbur's translation as an "an impeccably crafted version of a Brodsky poem."[5] Such unanimous appreciation by three different Brodsky associates, all of whom were involved in the preparation of *A Part of Speech*, is interesting in and of itself. One obvious reason is that Wilbur's translation is a skillfully made poem in English. To give an idea, here is Rubin's interlinear translation of the second stanza of "Six Years Later" followed by Wilbur's version. (In his interlinear version, Rubin underscored the words that were in rhyming position in Russian.)

Life together had been so long that the snow
needed only to start falling and it would seem everlasting,
that lest she would have to compress [her] eyelids
I would cover/shade them with my hand, and the eyelids,
    not believing that an attempt was being made to save them,
    would flutter about there like butterflies in the cup of [my] hand.[6]

(Rubin)

So long had life together been that once
The snow began to fall, it seemed unending;
That, lest the flakes should make her eyelids wince,
I'd shield them with my hand, and they, pretending
    Not to believe that cherishing of eyes,
    Would beat against my palm like butterflies.[7]

(Wilbur)

Compared to some of Brodsky's intricate large-scale works, "Six Years Later" is a relatively simple love elegy. The original stanza pattern in Russian is: aBaBcc in stanzas 1–2 and 4–5, but aaBccB in stanzas 3 and 6, where capital letters stand for feminine rhymes and small letters for masculine rhymes. The rhyme scheme that Wilbur received from Barry Rubin alongside the interlinear version did not distinguish between masculine and feminine rhymes and looked like this: ababcc in stanzas 1–2 and 5–6, aabccb in stanzas 3 and 4. It is unclear whether Brodsky himself had become more reasonable on that occasion, or whether it was Rubin's own initiative not to demand the impossible from Wilbur. In fact, as mentioned earlier, the use of feminine rhyme is much more unusual in English than in Russian. Indeed, according to Viktor Zhirmunsky, the Russian language, due to its polysyllabic nature and its freedom of stress, allows for a maximum diversity of verse and rhyme forms. In classical Russian poetry in particular, regular alternation of feminine and masculine rhyme is considered the norm, whereas in English there is a clear predominance of continuous masculine rhyming.[8] But even without feminine rhymes, the stanzaic design itself presented a significant challenge to the translator. Wilbur chose not to reproduce all the variations in the stanza pattern verbatim because, as he explained to Brodsky, "it was simply more convenient to keep to the form of the first stanza, once he had begun thinking in it."[9] Still, Wilbur's translation expertly reproduces the meter and flow of the original poem and comes up with precise rhyming as well. In short, it seems to do all that Brodsky expected of his translators. Wilbur even came up with one feminine rhyme in the second stanza, on his own initiative: "ending—pretending." It must be mentioned, however, that it is the tradition in English that feminine rhymes are not treated as a different category except in light verse. The poem is also rich in assonance, consonance, and alliteration. This can be seen in the example of the stanza quoted above: "l*o*ng-sn*o*w-f*a*ll; *l*e*s*t-f*l*ake*s*-eye*l*id*s*; *sh*ou*ld*-*sh*ie*ld*-cheri*sh*ing," and so on.

Wilbur's translation of this lyrical piece made Brodsky's mastery of the elegiac genre immediately apparent to his anglophone friends. It seems, however, that their unanimous approval cannot be ascribed merely to its being "a beautiful poem in English." Brodsky had been so adamant about his translation principles and had such power of persuasion that everyone around him also became convinced, sometimes even against their better judgment, that this was the way to undertake Russian-English poetry translation. Wilbur's "Six Years Later," a skillful rendition by an English-language poet, a master of the craft, embodied what Brodsky had been preaching for so long. Wilbur showed that it was, after all, possible to do Brodsky's bidding—to preserve the unity between a poem's content and its music in translation. One of the unwitting effects of this translation was thus to vindicate Brodsky's intransigence.

But what about Brodsky himself? Did he approve of Wilbur's version? As far as we can glean from Wilbur's 1977 letter to him, this time around, the demanding and hard-to-please Russian poet seemed to show genuine appreciation for the job done by a fellow poet:

> Dear Joseph, . . . I haven't yet replied to a January 20 letter from Nancy Meiselas, in which she says that you "seemed pleased" with my attempt to translate "Seven Years Later," but had "a few specific words and lines to discuss" with me. Will you let me know where you think the translation might be improved? I have, in fact, numerous alternative versions of many of the lines, and can probably amend the translation without too much difficulty. I hope you don't mind my failure to reproduce your varying of the stanza-pattern; it was simply more convenient to keep to the form of the first stanza, once I had begun thinking in it. In any case, do be frank, intolerant and insistent in your criticisms.[10]

Like Kline, but in contrast to Weissbort, Wilbur was prepared to "amend the translation" as long as it would make Brodsky happy. He even encouraged

Brodsky to be "frank, intolerant and insistent in his criticisms."[11] The fact that Wilbur's translation of "Six Years Later" opens *A Part of Speech* is a clear testimony to his success. However, during the final, and apparently rather hectic phase in preparing the collection, Brodsky and Walcott went over most translations in *A Part of Speech* in their attempt to give the book a certain stylistic and prosodic unity. That is when they decided to make a slight change in the last stanza of Wilbur's translation.[12]

With the benefit of hindsight, Wilbur was gracious enough to forgive Brodsky and to acknowledge his authorial right to make any changes to a translation of his poem, even if one can detect in Wilbur's juxtaposition of "Joseph's improved version" with his "original and perhaps mistaken lines"[13] a touch of carefully veneered irony. In actuality, Wilbur might have been less happy in the immediate aftermath of the events than he was willing to admit. We can sense this from Sven Birkerts's 1982 interview with Brodsky:

> Interviewer: . . . I was at a reading recently where Wilbur was describing to the audience—quite tartly, I thought—how you and Derek Walcott were flying in a plane over Iowa, re-correcting his translation of one of your poems—which did not make him happy . . .
>
> Brodsky: True. The poem only profited out of that. I respect him enormously. Having asked him to do certain passages three, four, or more times, I merely felt that I had no human right to bother him with that one more time, I just didn't have the guts. Even that uncorrected version was excellent. It's more or less the same thing when I said no to Wystan Auden when he volunteered to translate some poems. I thought, "Who the hell am I to be translated by Wystan?"[14]

Brodsky's response to Birkerts is puzzling in its odd combination of awe and irreverence. On the one hand, Brodsky clearly stuck to his guns, arguing that "the poem only profited" from his and Walcott's interference. On the other, he went to the opposite extreme in displaying a mock modesty toward Wilbur by comparing him to Auden, whom Brodsky deified, and in suggesting that he himself was not worthy of being translated by either of them. Brodsky had translated Wilbur into Russian, so why should Wilbur not translate him into English, especially since Farrar, Straus and Giroux had commissioned him to do so? In fact, rather than asking himself "Who the hell am I to be translated by him?" it might have been more appropriate to rephrase the question as "Who the hell am I to correct his translation?" Brodsky argues that he simply "didn't have the guts" to bother Wilbur with any further demands to alter his translation yet another time. Yet he did have the guts to change a line in Wilbur's translation without asking for his permission. Wilbur himself was equally perplexed by that interview, but for a different reason, as he explained in a letter to Brodsky written shortly after its publication:

> Dear Joseph:
> Horrors! I have just seen your interview in the new *Paris Review* and I now understand why, when we met at the Academy-Institute, you greeted me with "Sorry." Your interviewer completely misunderstood what I said before I read "Six Years Later" . . . I had no objection to collaborating in whatever manner with Derek, who is one of the best English poets in operation; and I concluded my patter by saying that translation is not an art in which the translator shows off, but a craft (a collaboration, if necessary) in which the original is got across into another language as well as possible. . . . This is not to say that I think your later change in the last stanza an improvement. I don't.[15]

Wilbur's letter illustrates his character very well: courteous, kind, but also firm when it matters. Evidently, Wilbur did not wish to allow a minor translation episode to cast a shadow over their friendship. He went out of his way to explain to Brodsky that he did not bear any grudges against him, and that there was no need to feel guilty. Moreover, Wilbur, who had won the Bollingen Prize in 1971 for his rhymed translation of Moliere's *Tartuffe*,[16] emphasized that his translation ethos had a lot in common with Brodsky's own ideas in this area. In fact, Wilbur stressed that "translation is not an art in which the translator shows off, but a craft . . . in which the original is got across into another language as well as possible."[17] Yet Brodsky's and Walcott's "tinkering" with his translation, as he later called it, was where Wilbur drew the line.[18] Unlike Weissbort, he knew his worth as an English-language poet, and no Brodsky escapade could shatter his confidence in his own ability. He remained adamant that his version worked better in English, and that Brodsky had made a mistake in correcting it. Wilbur's position precluded further discussion.

BRODSKY AND WALCOTT REVISING WILBUR

To better understand the context, let us consider Brodsky's changes to the last stanza of "Six Years Later." Here we have its interlinear translation by Rubin, followed by Wilbur's version and, finally, by the two last lines as later altered by Brodsky and Walcott:

> Life together had been so long <u>with her</u>
> that out of our own <u>shadows</u> we had made
>   a door for ourselves—<u>whether</u> one of us was at work or <u>asleep</u>,

no matter, the door halves/panels did not swing open,
and, apparently, we passed right through them
    and went out into the future by the back way.[19]

(Rubin)

So long had life together been that she   a
And I, with our joint shadows, had composed   b
A double door, a door which even if we   a
Were lost in work or sleep, was always closed: b
    Somehow, it would appear, we drifted right   c
    On through it into the future, into the night.[20]   c

(Wilbur, italics mine)

    somehow its halves were split and we went right
    through them into the future, into night.

(Brodsky and Walcott)

It is not immediately clear why Brodsky undertook these changes. He might simply have been trying to preserve the conceit of the double (Dutch) door in the last stanza, perhaps feeling guilty because it was not very clear in the original interlinear. Another conjecture is that it was because of the slight metrical variation Wilbur had introduced at the end of the stanza, which Brodsky wanted to "straighten."

Each stanza in Wilbur's translation begins with the same anaphora, "So long had life together been that . . . ," re-creating in English the lulling inertia of the original. In translation, the monotony of this beat is further enhanced through the use of the same rhyme scheme, ababcc, throughout the entirety of the poem. To break with it, and to bring the poem toward its dramatic denouement, Wilbur introduced the parallel phrases "into the future" and "into the night" that did not feature in the original. Wilbur's variation not only broke with the metrical inertia of the preceding stanzas and provided an effective ending to the poem but also managed, miraculously, to work within the context of a pentametric scheme, despite the addition of two extra syllables in the last line. This solution, however, was evidently not appreciated by Brodsky. Although in his corrected version, Brodsky preserved Wilbur's parallelism, "into the future, into the night," he was evidently determined to get rid of the extra syllables in the last line to make it conform more unequivocally to the overall iambic pentameter pattern of the poem:

So long had life together been that she
And I, with our joint shadows, had composed
A double door, a door which even if we

Were lost in work or sleep, was always closed:
somehow its halves were split and we went right
through them into the future, into night.[21]
(Brodsky, "Six Years Later"; italics mine)

As author, Brodsky was of course aware of the metrical inertia he had built up in the poem to that point. In the original, he had used a different prosodic device to guide the poem toward its resolution:

Tak d**o**lgo vm**e**ste pr**o**zhili my s n**ei**, 4
chto sd**e**lali iz s**o**bstvennykh ten**ei** 3
my dv**er**' seb**e**—rab**o**taesh' li, sp**i**sh' li, 4
no stv**o**rki ne rasp**a**khivalis' vr**o**z', 3
i m**y** proshl**i** ikh, v**i**dimo, naskv**o**z' 4
i ch**e**rnym kh**o**dom v b**u**dushchee v**y**shli. 4
(Brodsky, "Shest' let spustia"; bold added)

The last two lines of the poem had an equal number of stressed syllables: four stressed and one pyrrhic foot per line (note the accented syllables highlighted in bold). Curiously, while Wilbur tried to break with the rhythmic inertia of the poem, Brodsky instead tried to reinforce the regularity of the beat toward the very end. Now, because of the feminine rhyme in the final position, the poem ends with an exhalation: "v**y**shli" ("we exited"). In Brodsky's own reading of the poem, the ending is very abrupt, creating the effect of a train running off the rails at full speed. Characteristically, the rhythmic structure reflects the poem's imagery. While the bulk of the poem emphasizes the lovers' union, the last line, which announces their separation, becomes decidedly anticlimactic.

Ironically, Brodsky did not even attempt in his revision to reproduce the effect of the original ending. He simply tightened the last line so it corresponded more rigorously to the overall pentametric scheme of the poem, while sacrificing, in the process, Wilbur's solution. Walcott's involvement apparently served to ensure that Brodsky's correcting pen stayed within the limits of the grammatically permissible in English. The question as to whether Brodsky's and Walcott's version works better than Wilbur's remains open. Wilbur did not think it did. Indeed, Wilbur's final line seems more successful than the Brodsky-Walcott substitution, which creates a trochaic rather than iambic rhythm at the beginning of the line and has an awkward ending. This again brings to mind Stanley Kunitz, who argued in the introduction to his Akhmatova translations that "to insist on a universally rigid duplication of metrical or rhyming patterns is arbitrary and pointless, since the effects in any case are not mechanically transferable to another language."[22] Arguably,

Wilbur had already done the impossible. Some of the prosodic effects he had achieved in his translation can only be described as magical. One example is the fourth stanza, which is euphonically a high point of the poem in English:

> So long had life together been that all
> That tattered brood of papered roses went,
> And a whole birch-grove grew upon the wall,
> And we had money, by some accident . . .[23]

Brodsky himself acknowledged this in the interview with Birkerts: "Even that uncorrected version was excellent."[24] So why not simply accept Wilbur's translation as it was, given that Brodsky knew quite well that some loss in poetry translation is inevitable?

BRODSKY, VOZNESENSKY, AND AUDEN

Daniel Weissbort, who spent a long time reflecting on the question of what had motivated Brodsky's revisions, aptly observed: "When Wilbur turned out an impeccably crafted version of a Brodsky poem, however flattering this may be, was it Brodsky?"[25] One spontaneous answer that presents itself is that of course it was Brodsky—it was after all his poem, which Wilbur had translated into English. Yet Weissbort's question is more intriguing than it might initially seem. To try to answer it, we could take a closer look at the statement Brodsky made in the interview with Birkerts quoted earlier: "Who the hell am I to be translated by Wystan?"[26] Curiously enough, the same phrase reappeared almost verbatim in "To Please a Shadow," Brodsky's 1986 essay in memory of W. H. Auden. Brodsky recalled how, during one of their first encounters, Auden offered to translate him into English:

> Then he offered to translate some of my poems. This shook me considerably. Who was I to be translated by Auden? I knew that *because of his translations some of my compatriots had profited more than their lines deserved*; yet somehow I couldn't allow myself the thought of him working for me.[27]

The compatriot in question, to whom Brodsky so circuitously alluded above, was none other than Andrei Voznesensky (1933–2010)—the only Russian poet whom Auden translated, in collaboration with Max Hayward, a distinguished British translator of Russian literature.[28] In contrast to Brodsky, who was an outcast and whose poems could never appear in print in the Soviet Union, both Voznesensky and his counterpart Yevtushenko enjoyed stellar careers. They filled entire stadiums with poetry listeners in the Soviet

Union and achieved unprecedented international fame.[29] Occasionally, both Voznesensky and Yevtushenko explored risky subjects, and their works were even sometimes blocked by the Soviet censors.[30] Thus, ironically, both Yevtushenko and Voznesensky enjoyed reputations in the West as enfants terribles of Soviet literature.[31] But inside the country, they were seen very differently. Voznesensky, who was considered Pasternak's protégé, did not appear at his funeral in 1960. This, according to Venclova, was a litmus test, as the funeral "developed into a dissident demonstration, the first . . . since Leo Tolstoy's funeral, in 1910."[32] Akhmatova, for one, was skeptical of both Voznesensky and Yevtushenko, finding them "superficial, too concerned with immediate success and perfunctory innovation, and lacking in ethical backbone."[33] Brodsky and other like-minded poets of his generation saw Voznesensky and Yevtushenko as hacks and toadies of the regime and shared an aversion for their poetry.[34] Thus, in June 1972, just days after landing in Vienna, Brodsky spoke negatively about both Voznesensky and Yevtushenko with Solzhenitsyn's associate and German translator Elisabeth Markstein, inveighing especially against Voznesensky:

> As far as Yevtushenko is concerned it is not so simple. Of course, he is a very bad poet. And an even worse human being. An enormous factory for self-reproduction. But he is much better, in my opinion, than let's say Voznesensky. With Voznesensky it's always the same story—he makes me physically sick. . . . Poetry can be stupid, banal, devoid of talent, vulgar, boring, but he achieves an absolutely nauseating quality. From my point of view Yevtushenko is much better, because at the very least he writes poems in Russian, you see? But Voznesensky pretends to be God knows what—an avant-garde, a French poet and so forth.[35]

Given the dim view he held of Voznesensky, one can only imagine the shock to Brodsky when during their first encounter, his beloved Auden started showering praise on, of all people, Voznesensky. According to Carl Proffer, who had driven Brodsky to Auden's Austrian summerhouse, Auden expatiated at length on "that genius Voznesensky," paying no mind to Brodsky's admonitions to the contrary.[36] Proffer recalled that Brodsky was visibly upset and, although Auden had invited him to return for dinner the next day, Brodsky grumpily remarked to Proffer in the car that there was no need to go back and that Auden had not understood anything about him. Luckily Brodsky recovered from the shock and did return, realizing that Auden was still Auden, "even if he does like Voznesensky's poetry."[37] Furthermore, if Auden had not first translated Voznesensky, he might not have shown interest in writing a foreword for Brodsky. As to Auden's translations, Brodsky's judgment, obliquely expressed in "To Please a Shadow," echoed the assessment made two decades earlier by Simon Karlinsky in his 1966 review of Voznesensky's collection *Antiworlds*. Karlinsky had argued that in translation by the major English-language poets in the business, Voznesensky became a far better poet than he really was:

> Put into English by the likes of W. H. Auden, Robert Lowell . . . , and Richard Wilbur, Voznesensky loses the naive and provincial tone he often has in Russian, sheds his often crude and overemphatic alliteration, and indeed becomes the kind of poet he undoubtedly could be had he the literary culture and sophistication of his translators.[38]

Karlinsky's assessment thus perfectly meshes with Brodsky's own comment about "some of his compatriots" (Voznesensky) having profited from Auden's translations more than their "lines deserved."[39] This explains the logic behind Brodsky's remark: "I couldn't allow myself the thought of him working for me."[40] Unlike Voznesensky, Brodsky did not want others to do the job for him. He must have felt that profiting from the mastery of such capable craftsmen in English as Wilbur and Auden was too easy a way out. Because of his special affinity for English, Brodsky wanted to at least try to contribute to the translation process, even if he could not quite yet do the job perfectly all by himself. Competitive by nature, Brodsky must have felt that it should not require the magic of the geniuses of English poetry to turn his poems into masterpieces in English. He was convinced that the sheer power of his poems would shine through, even if the English translations became less smooth as a result of his interventions.

TO BE ADMITTED TO THE CLUB OF AMERICAN POETS

Indeed, the history of Brodsky's fascination with English-language poetry placed him in a unique position. From early on, he was eager not only to join America's literary scene, but to influence and leave his mark on her poetic legacy. This strong investment in his adoptive country's culture made him quite opinionated. Brodsky even showed pride in his strong opinions about English poetry, as though they proved how much he cared for it. Here is, for example, another excerpt from the letter in which Brodsky tried to placate Weissbort in the aftermath of their major disagreement:

> I think that the main problem between us is . . . that you never dealt with an author . . . who was so opinionated. I am not a Swede or a Hungarian who, for all their knowledge of the language into which they are translated, would

> waive the whole thing up believing that *the lads know better and that the modernism means looseness of form*, etc. [italics mine].[41]

It seems that one of the reasons Brodsky did not believe that "the lads know better" was that, steeped as he was in English poetic tradition, he could claim his own alternative version of modernism with Frost, Hardy, and Auden at the helm. Another reason was that he actually wanted to be one of the lads—to belong in their company. Such at least was the conclusion Proffer Teasley came to:

> It is also true that Joseph's close friends were now some of the most eminent of the English-language poets and he wanted to belong to their guild. He denied in one interview that he wanted to become an American poet, but as I look back, I think that is precisely what he was working toward, and in part this is connected to his sense of rejection by his own culture.[42]

It seems that Proffer Teasley might be on to something here, for the desire to belong is certainly dialectically related to the sense of rejection. I think, however, that Shallcross's concept of "cultural disinheritance"—a feeling of being isolated from the repositories of Western culture, a burden shared by the artists from the Soviet bloc that Brodsky, in particular, desperately wished to overcome—also explains his desire to be admitted to the guild of American poets, whose literary tradition itself had deep roots in the culture of the West denied to Soviet artists. In his case, the desire stems as far back as his Russian incarnation, as illustrated by one particular episode.

In the late 1960s, Brodsky wrote Robert Lowell a letter asking him some questions about his poem "For the Union Dead" that he was then translating into Russian. Toward the end of the letter, Brodsky allowed himself some general remarks about American poetry:

> Sir, I am not sure that our correspondence is going to be very lively that's why I'd like now to kill two birds with one stone. First, let me make a hypothesis and say that you are a superb poet. Second, I would like to ask you, arguably a superb poet, to send my regards to an absolutely superb one, Mr. Richard Wilbur. I hope that the impertinence of this sentence is atoned by the fact that I am translating your poetry, and not his. On the whole, I must say that I am enthralled by 20th century American poetry: Robinson, Frost, Stevens, and many others, as well as by your own generation. It's comforting to discover such a healthy condition. Sincerely yours.
>
> Where does Auden live?[43]

Brodsky was eager to show Lowell that they shared a poetic affinity and that he knew American poetry better than any other Russian poet of his generation. At the same time, it is rather odd that Brodsky should praise Wilbur so lavishly and ask about Auden's address in the same letter.[44] Evidently, Brodsky felt a strong desire to be a part of the group but feared rejection—hence the same combination of awe and irreverence that he demonstrated in his 1982 interview about Wilbur, quoted earlier. Obviously, Brodsky did not know at the time that Lowell was probably the last person to reject him, being as fascinated with Russian poetry—and strongly identifying with Boris Pasternak—as Brodsky was with English-language poetry.[45]

Brodsky's dream of being admitted to the club of British and American poets came true in July 1972 during his trip to the Poetry International in London to recite his poems at the Queen Elizabeth Hall in the company of Auden and Spender, with Lowell spontaneously offering to read Kline's English translations of Brodsky's poems. The next step was to achieve recognition from his American counterparts as a major English-language poet, on their home territory. Thus, Proffer Teasley observed: "Joseph very much wanted the other major poets—his only peers—to be able to see what his poetry was really like, and he worked very hard to show them."[46] But Brodsky's competitiveness is hardly a secret. Paradoxically, to gain the recognition of his anglophone peers, he often had to challenge them first. This was part of the game. The translation of his Russian poems, where he was at least half the expert they were, became a more level ground on which to challenge them.

BONDING OVER ITALY AND DANTE: BRODSKY AND LOWELL

It has been argued that if one poem in *A Part of Speech* marked a major breakthrough in Brodsky's development as an English-language poet, it was his elegy for Robert Lowell, the first poem written directly in English that he thought worthy of including in a collection.[47] In his review of *A Part of Speech*, Clarence Brown cited the elegy as proof of the miraculous transformation in Brodsky's English since his days in Russia: "When Brodsky first shouted an English poem by George Herbert into my ear outside a café on Gorky Street fourteen years ago, I thought he was speaking Lithuanian. Now his English suffices for this stately elegy on Lowell, and one looks forward to the sequel."[48] Not everyone agreed. Another Slavic scholar of distinction, Sidney Monas, who gave, overall, a very favorable assessment of *A Part of Speech*, found that Brodsky's English was not quite up to the task of composing original work:

> Yet one important poem Brodsky has himself written in English—partly, I suspect, to show how it should be done—did not turn out well. The elegy to

> Robert Lowell modeled in part on Lowell's own "For the Union Dead" . . . for all its intricate, assonantal rhymes and other formal arrangements, strikes me as a dead poem. Brodsky's own much freer practice of translating some of his own poems . . . seems to me more alive and to the point as an exemplar for contemporary practice.[49]

While Monas thought that "Elegy: For Robert Lowell" was "a dead poem" on arrival in English, he praised Brodsky's emerging practice of self-translation as exemplary. Monas probably did not know that Lowell had translated Brodsky's poem "December in Florence," which, oddly enough, became a breakthrough in Brodsky's self-translations.

Brodsky admired Lowell, although he regretted a shift in Lowell's poetics toward more open forms.[50] They had first met in 1972 in London, where, as mentioned, Lowell read translations of Brodsky's poems at the Poetry International, which Brodsky found "an extremely kind and moving gesture."[51] Once Brodsky had settled in the United States, Lowell introduced him to the *New York Review of Books* crowd.[52] Brodsky also became close to Lowell's ex-wife Elizabeth Hardwick, the cofounder and editor of that influential book review. Both Lowell and Hardwick were exemplars of well-traveled and cultivated Americans of their generation and established representatives of the American literary and cultural elite. Their love of Italy had a family resemblance to Brodsky's own.[53] When Brodsky came to Boston in 1975 to see Lowell, they discovered a shared appreciation of Dante:

> The time we spent was in many ways the best time I can recall having while here in the States. We talked about this and that, and finally settled on Dante. It was the first conversation about Dante since Russia which really made sense to me. He knew Dante inside out, I think, in an absolutely obsessive way. He was especially good on *Inferno*. I think he had lived for a while in Florence, or stayed there, so he felt more about *Inferno* than the other parts . . . We spent about five or six hours, more, and then we went for dinner.[54]

From both Mandelstam and Akhmatova, whom Monas aptly described as "Brodsky's cultural lodestars,"[55] he had inherited an enormous reverence for Dante.[56] During the Stalinist terror, Dante provided the stranded acmeist poets, who had grown up in a cosmopolitan pre–World War I Russia, with a connection to Europe.[57] What Dante meant to Akhmatova and Mandelstam in the Soviet Union of the 1930s, Donne, Frost, and Auden came to mean to Brodsky in the 1960s.

In December 1974, during one of his first trips to Italy, Brodsky visited Florence for the first time on a Dantesque pilgrimage.[58] The trip resulted in the poem titled "Dekabr' vo Florentsii" ("December in Florence"),[59] which is a conversation with the shadow of Dante across the centuries as well as an homage to both Akhmatova and Mandelstam.[60] "December in Florence" became an extremely important poem for Brodsky, which he may have signaled by placing it at the very end of the 1977 Russian volume titled *Chast' rechi* (*A Part of Speech*).[61] First, linking himself to Dante allowed Brodsky to put his own condition of exile into a broad perspective; as his fellow exile Miłosz would point out, Dante is "a patron saint of all poets in exile . . . But how has the number of Florences increased!"[62] Second, in dedicating a poem to this iconic Western predecessor, Brodsky continued to pledge his allegiance to the unity of Russian and European cultures.

"DECEMBER IN FLORENCE": THE POEM'S STRUCTURE AND METER

"December in Florence" was constructed both as a travelogue and as a dialogue with Dante through time. It seems to be modeled after conversations between the poets in the *Divine Comedy*: Dante and Virgil, Virgil and Statius. The lyrical hero, a poet exiled from his home city, walks around Dante's Florence, a city to which Dante could never return and which perpetually haunted him. The poem draws parallels between their respective home cities, St. Petersburg and Florence, and between the circumstances that led to their exiles.[63] To make their conversation as realistic as possible, Brodsky updates Dante on the major cultural and artistic developments in Florence, supplies him with concrete details, and imagines how Dante might interpret what the author sees as a tourist.

Numbers had a symbolic significance for Dante. His use of terza rima, as well as the overall tripartite division of the *Divine Comedy*, has been interpreted as Dante's attempt to reproduce the symmetry, order, and harmony of the universe.[64] By the same token, Brodsky's "December in Florence" consists of nine stanzas, of nine lines each. Each stanza has a tripartite rhyme scheme: AAABBBCCC. All the rhymes in "December" are feminine, and some are rather sophisticated compound rhymes.[65] The verse meter of "December" is accentual verse, or variable *dol'nik*, which became Brodsky's predominant metrical-rhythmical form during his American period, as he was gradually abandoning the classical Russian syllabo-tonic meters.[66] Brodsky's note for the translators provides an interesting insight into the semantic aura he associated with this particular verse meter:

> Meter: A kind of accentual verse; number of stresses per line not fixed; number of unstressed syllables between stresses variable. The rhythm of natural speech becomes the poem's rhythm; any rhythm that develops is natural. There is no preconceived intonation; whatever there is is neutral. There is no qualitative flavor coloring the speech.[67]

Brodsky's remarks on versification are both exacting and somewhat contradictory. He was very clear about the prosodic effects he wanted his translators to achieve, but seemed quite vague as to how they should go about it. While Barry Rubin would supply translators with a detailed prosodic model indicating the exact distribution of stressed and unstressed syllables in the original, Brodsky suggested that the poem's rhythm was that of natural speech. This sounded almost like something Williams would have advocated, but it was actually not what Brodsky was after. That became evident when he later reproached one of the translators, Alan Myers, for not keeping the "beat." On the other hand, Brodsky's remark about the neutrality of intonation in his note to the translators of "December" provides a possible clue to his real metrical intentions.

Brodsky's insistence on neutrality of tone may have been partly inspired by Eliot, who had held that the mind of a traditional artist should try to "digest and transmute the passions which are its material" so that, as a result, his emotions come out as neutral and depersonalized: "Poetry is not a turning loose of emotion, but an escape from emotion; it is not the expression of personality, but an escape from personality."[68] While Eliot cited Dante as a model for this process,[69] Brodsky attributed the same characteristics to Auden and even suggested Auden's superiority over Yeats in handling iambic trimeter: "If Yeats used this meter to express his sentiments, Auden sought to control them by the same means."[70] In a 1979 interview with John Glad, Brodsky explained that accentual verse or *dol'nik* helped him achieve precisely that effect—neutrality of intonation. "Today," he said, "I use a greater percentage of tonic verse, a lot more intonational verse, which, I believe, makes the language a bit more neutral, a bit more subtle."[71] It is fascinating that Barry Scherr sees Brodsky's highly innovative verse meter as based on anglophone models rather than on the experiments of the Russian Silver Age: "The variable *dol'nik* with longer lines has become an important meter in recent years. Brodsky may well have adapted it from modern English practice, which would indicate that it did not so much develop out of the Russian tradition as result from a sudden innovation."[72] In any case, now that his poem in *dol'nik* had to be transposed back into English, so to speak, Brodsky must have hoped that its metrical homecoming would happen without complications.

"METERS ARE METERS NO MATTER THE LANGUAGE"

It seems that Brodsky's strong affinity for the English poetic tradition led him to generally regard Russian-English metrical contrast as a much lesser hurdle in translation than is generally assumed. Unlike Nabokov, who had devised an entire prosodic terminology of his own to describe the differences between Russian and English iambs,[73] Brodsky argued in a foreword to a collection of Russian Golden Age poets, translated by Alan Myers, that "meters are meters no matter the language in which they are employed. That is what they are meters for."[74] In a 1988 interview, Brodsky reiterated a similar notion when he explained his own approach to translation: "A poem consists . . . of two or three dimensions which are significant in the translation. First of all is the content, and the second and third are structural aspects: rhyme and meter. . . . Meter is an easy aspect, since iambic pentameter in English is iambic pentameter in Russian as in German."[75] Inasmuch as meters are compositional principles based on the distribution of strong and weak syllables, it is certainly true that they work in Russian just as they do in German or English.[76] At the same time, as shown by Zhirmunsky, their concrete realizations depend directly on the natural phonetic properties of the respective languages.[77] In this second sense, Brodsky's assertion that "meters are meters" no matter what language they are employed in is clearly incorrect. Although his essays on Tsvetaeva, Mandelstam, Akhmatova, Hardy, Auden, and Frost brim with important insights into the dialectic relationship between form and content in their verse, Brodsky was clearly not a theoretician of versification. His approach to prosody was more intuitive and organic, which certainly did not make the lives of his translators any easier.

LOWELL THE TRANSLATOR

Robert Lowell, who was probably unaware of these undercurrents and pitfalls, offered himself as a translator for "December in Florence." As Brodsky himself recalled: "He was terribly generous: . . . not long before his death, he . . . suggested himself as a translator for one of my poems, a poem about Florence, 'December in Florence,' and he did several versions, about which we had our arguments."[78] Brodsky gave his English translators an undeniably hard time, including poets of such distinction as Wilbur and Hecht. Yet one can hardly be surprised that he would argue with Lowell about translation. Lowell's work represents an extreme degree of poetic appropriation. His translations are considered to be more interpretations than proper translations. In his introduction to *Imitations* (1961), a volume of loose translations of poems by classical and modern European poets, Lowell explained his idiosyncratic method: "I have dropped lines, moved lines, moved stanzas, changed images and altered meter and intent. . . . I have been almost as free as the authors themselves in finding ways to make them ring right for me."[79] Being both a person of great intellectual force and a complex and widely admired poet, Lowell got away with something few other translators ever could. His contemporaries were in awe of him.[80] In fact, in 1962 Lowell received the Bollingen Poetry Translation Prize for *Imitations*, a title suggested by Eliot himself. Likewise, just a few years later, George Steiner numbered "Robert Lowell's readings of Osip Mandelstam" among such other "great poetic translations" as Hölderlin's translations of Sophocles and Valéry's rendering of Virgil's *Eclogues*.[81]

Yet at least one writer remained utterly unfazed by this adoration of Lowell. Brodsky's bilingual doppelganger and precursor in abrasive and vitriolic attacks on anglophone translators, Vladimir Nabokov, refused to revere Lowell for his translations of Mandelstam, accusing him instead of "misinformation, mistransfiguration, and misadaptation."[82] Nabokov's attacks on Lowell were so merciless that Nadezhda Mandelstam herself felt obliged to come to Lowell's rescue, intervening on his behalf from behind the Iron Curtain.[83] But it was not just Nabokov, famous for his biting remarks at the expense of his fellow writers, who questioned Lowell's capacities as a translator.[84] Gleb Struve, who had coedited the first Russian tamizdat collection of Mandelstam,[85] felt compelled to write a letter to the editor of *Time* magazine to complain about "Robert Lowell's mistranslation" of Mandelstam's poem about Stalin that had cost the poet his life.[86] By the same token, Patricia Blake remembered that when, in 1963, Voznesensky, whose English collection she was helping to compile, expressed his wish that Lowell should translate his poetry, both she and Max Hayward became alarmed.[87] Apparently, Voznesensky hoped to please the party bosses in Moscow on the grounds that Lowell had refused an invitation to the White House. Having seen "some of Lowell's 'imitations' of Osip Mandelstam," Hayward, who had himself expertly translated Nadezhda Mandelstam's prose, tried to explain to Voznesensky that if he "had written 'horse' Lowell would render it as a 'raspberry.'"[88] This seemed to amuse Voznesensky, whose English was basic and who had very little idea about poetry in English generally.[89] One cannot help but notice again the stark contrast between Voznesensky, coopted by the Communist Party as a potential agent of international influence, and Brodsky, who shared genuine artistic affinities with such eminent American poets as Lowell, and for which "crime" he had been exiled from home. Unlike Voznesensky, Brodsky knew about the liberties Lowell allowed himself in translation. Yet Lowell's translation of "December in Florence" was undertaken in a different spirit than his other translations, which had been private encounters with poets from the past. In this case, Lowell was doing a favor for a friend to help him get a footing in America. Besides, Brodsky might have been hoping to "correct" Lowell's drafts later, as he had done with the drafts of Kline, Weissbort, Myers, and others, altering those translations just enough to be able to recognize them as his own poems in English.

LOWELL'S FIRST DRAFT OF "DECEMBER IN FLORENCE"

Lowell, who did not know Russian, worked from the literal translations provided by Barry Rubin. Let us consider Barry Rubin's interlinear translation of the first stanza, followed by Lowell's first draft:

I
[The] doors inhale [the] air and exhale steam/vapor; but
you won't come back here, where paired off in twos
the populace strolls above the shoaled/shallowed Arno,
calling to mind new quadrupeds. [The] doors
slam, wild animals come /go out onto the pavement.
There really is something from the forest in the atmosphere
of this city. This is a beautiful city,
where at a certain age you simply avert your gaze from
a person and raise your collar.[90]
(Rubin)

I
The doors take in air, exhale, steam,
Yet you won't come back here, see the populace stream
in couples, in twos, in [and] twos, along the shallow Arno—
new quadrupeds. The doors slam,
wild beasts emerge on the pavement from their hollow [old borroughs]
This city still has the tang of the forest.
Truly, it is a beautiful city;
[at a certain] age one can turn from those who follow,
and lift [raise] his collar.[91]
(Lowell)

As Michael Wachtel has shown, Lowell often "praised trots at the expense of 'poetic' translation," believing them to be "better poetry than the professor's or even the minor poet's poetic translation of a masterpiece."[92] In other words, Rubin was clearly Lowell's man. The reverse might not be true. Rubin was too much in tune with Brodsky's expectations of a translation. He was able to notice the difference between the results of Wilbur spending an entire month on "Six Years Later," trying to get its form right along with everything else, and Lowell's much less laborious effort. Lowell's approach to working with the "prose trots," as he called them, was minimalist; nor did he attempt to copy the original form exactly.

Having said that, Lowell's first stanza emerged with both an elegant flow and a steady beat. It seems that, feeling free from pressure to mold the poem into a certain shape, Lowell simply followed the interlinear trot, coming up along the way with all sorts of creative solutions: rhymes ("steam—stream—slam"; "hollow—forest—follow—collar"); internal rhymes ("take in air—come back here"; "slam—from"); parallelisms ("in couples"; "in twos, in twos"); assonances and consonances ("beasts—city—still"; "populace—couples"), and so on. The only two endings that don't rhyme in his version actually constitute a mental rhyme: "Arno—city [Florence]." Clearly, this was not something Brodsky expected from a translation. But it is still impressive, given that Lowell managed to find six out of nine feminine rhymes in the stanza, which are notoriously difficult in English, as we've discussed. Lowell's rhyme scheme aaxaBBxBB might even be said to remotely resemble the woven pattern of Dante's original tercets: aba, bcb, cdc, ded. Also, in his take on the first stanza, there is practically none of what Nabokov had described as Lowell's "hops and flutters of irresponsible invention."[93]

BRODSKY'S REVISION OF LOWELL'S FIRST DRAFT

However, Lowell's failure to replicate the exacting structure of the original triplets more accurately might have emboldened Brodsky in revising his draft. Brodsky's main concern, as always, was to maintain precise rhyming in English. As has been pointed out by Scherr, "the rhymes provide one of the structural cornerstones in many of Brodsky's poems."[94] Accordingly, in his revision of Lowell's draft, Brodsky concentrated on re-creating the original rhyming pattern:

I
The doors take in air, exhale steam; yet you won't
be back to the shallow~~ed~~ Arno where the coupled figures amount
to new quadrupeds or to a walking ant.
Beasts emerge on the pavement, as the doors bang.
This city still has the forest's tang.
It is a beautiful city where ~~before long~~ in the midst of a long
road, at a~~n average~~ certain age one may turn his hollow
eye from all those who follow
and just raise his collar.[95]
(Brodsky)

Although Brodsky did not find rhymes for Arno, he remained adamant about preserving the overall structure of the tercets, as we can see from the rhyme chart of the first stanza. "December in Florence" began with a num-

TABLE 8. Rhymes in Stanza 1, "December in Florence" (Lowell)

Rubin's Interlinear	Lowell's Draft	Brodsky's First Revision
steam but—in twos—Arno	stream—steam—Arno	won't—amount—ant
doors—wild animals—atmosphere	slam—hollow / boroughs—forest	bang—tang—long
city—gaze from—collar	city—follow—collar	hollow—follow—collar

ber of overt allusions to the opening of the *Divine Comedy* with its "wild animals" and the "dark forest." Brodsky seemed to like Lowell's phrasing in the sixth line: "This city still has the tang of the forest." But he moved words around so as to have "tang" rhyme with "bang" and "long": "Beasts emerge on the pavement, as the doors bang. / This city still has the forest's tang." He also used other hints from Lowell's version, such as the rhyme "hollow—follow."

It would be interesting to know what Lowell made of Brodsky's reworkings, whether he was annoyed as Weissbort and Wilbur had been. Or whether, having taken many liberties in translating others, he was more accepting of Brodsky's revisions. We also know that Lowell was opposed to strict metrical translations, calling them "stuffed birds" and their translators "taxidermists."[96] Since he surely recognized Brodsky as a fellow poet, not a "taxidermist," perhaps Lowell was able, after all, to acknowledge the legitimacy of his formal demands in a poem dedicated to Dante. In fact, the Brodsky Papers at Yale University contain a copy of Brodsky's first revision of Lowell's draft with subsequent markings made in Lowell's hand, including minor suggestions here and there for an alternative wording.[97] Lowell's name might well have appeared next to those who had helped shape *A Part of Speech*—a list that read like "a roll-call of an academy of English-speaking poets,"[98] according to one apt description. But tragically, Lowell died of a heart attack in September 1977, at age sixty, leaving Brodsky with an unfinished draft.

Chapter Eight

A Self-Translation with a Multitude of Sources

MEANWHILE, GEORGE KLINE was pushing his own translation of "December in Florence." Knowing Brodsky's work in detail, Kline had recognized the importance of "December in Florence" when he read it in the original in the 1977 collection *Chast' rechi* (*A Part of Speech*), published by the Proffers.[1] Having discovered Brodsky early on, and done so much to promote his career in English, Kline now sought his own share of Brodsky's American laurels. Brodsky would have observed that "it's better to share laurels than a soup seasoned with a laurel bay leaf," as he quipped, in the late 1970s, in an argument about his translations into French with Efim Etkind, who was in charge of editing them.[2] So without waiting for the go-ahead from Farrar, Straus and Giroux, which Kline knew might never materialize, he began translating "December in Florence" in collaboration with the poet and academic editor Maurice English. In bringing English on board, it seems that Kline was trying to kill two birds with one stone: for one thing, collaboration with a poet, however obscure, should dispatch the argument that Kline was not a real poet, which Farrar, Straus and Giroux had used to sideline him. And secondly, as somewhat of a poet at heart,[3] Kline might also have hoped that his collaborator's eloquent surname would send Brodsky a subconscious reminder that, notwithstanding his growing confidence in his adopted language, English was both literally and metaphorically on Kline's side.

As is clear from Kline's letter of November 4, 1978, to Brodsky, they had discussed English's participation: "Dear Iosif, Here's the latest revision of 'December in Florence.' Maurice English and I are satisfied with it *en principe*. We hope you will be too. Here are a few variants, none of which seemed good enough to put into the text. But you might want to consider them, and you might prefer one or another."[4] Initially, Brodsky went along with the Kline/English arrangement. As Kline suggested, elements of their version might appeal to Brodsky and benefit the translation process. But as Kline must have realized, Brodsky would insist on shaping the end product.

For the moment, Kline would do all in his power to see that his translation with English was selected for the Farrar, Straus and Giroux publication of *A Part of Speech*. Kline's aptitude for cunning had been clearly demonstrated during the Hecht episode in the summer of 1977, when he tried to push through his own version of "Lullaby of Cape Cod" at the expense of Hecht's. Now, in his casual, matter-of-fact letter, Kline was letting Brodsky know that his translation was ready and that two native speakers, not just one, were satisfied with it. He did not explicitly mention the looming publishing deadline, but he clearly meant to put pressure on Brodsky to accept the translation over which he and English had toiled. But, accustomed as he was to imposing his will on others, Brodsky would not, despite Kline's hopeful effort, bend to his translator's will.

ALAN MYERS TRANSLATING "DECEMBER IN FLORENCE"

In fact, Brodsky had already asked Alan Myers to translate the poem too. Unlike Kline, Myers never questioned Brodsky's decisions; he was well aware of his amateur status in a world in which Brodsky was determined to prevail as a professional.[5] At the same time, Brodsky did not owe Myers nearly as much as he owed Kline. In a somewhat vaudevillian turn of events, on the very day Kline wrote Brodsky announcing that his and English's translation was ready, Brodsky wrote Myers to discuss *his* first translation draft of the same poem:

> Speaking of "December in Florence," I haven't made any corrections as yet, for I thought there is rather a lot for me to tackle. Look, Alan, you shouldn't get disturbed by my opinions on this or that poem. Good as my ear is for the Russian, I am the last one to make pronouncements in English. Still, there are some nuances that are missing in the English version of "December," and also, something happens here and there to the beat. The drama is that there is none around who'd be capable to check the meter without resorting to counting fingers. Nobody hears anything nowadays. Poets, yjob their mom![6]

Brodsky was characteristically critical. As Myers would later remember, "Joseph used the stick always, not the carrot—I don't recall any praise."[7] Myers, however, took this in stride, being "only too glad," as he put it, "to be the handmaid of genius, and to be taken for granted."[8] Myers even later admitted that the strictures Brodsky imposed on him had been beneficial, helping him in the long run to improve his technique in translating Russian Golden Age poets.[9] Evidently, Brodsky's main objection was that Myers did not correctly reproduce the "beat" in his version. Yet, as Myers later recalled, Brodsky "would also snigger derisively if he caught me counting syllables."[10] He expected his translators to work by ear. Ultimately, it was likely his own uniquely keen Russian ear, with all its quirks, that was the judge. All indications point precisely in that direction. For instance, the bilingual expletive ("yjob [fuck] their mom!") from the passage above seems to contain a reference to Mandelstam's "Fourth Prose," a powerful text in which the beleaguered acmeist poet tried to defend himself from a vicious harassment campaign conducted by Soviet writers. Juxtaposing his authentic poetry with the sinister fabrications of the servile crowd of Soviet literati, Mandelstam wrote: "I alone in Russia work from the voice while the bitch pack writes all around."[11] If we superimpose Brodsky's phrase "Nobody hears anything nowadays" onto Mandelstam's quote, the former could be continued as "I alone work by ear." However jokingly, Brodsky was asserting his superiority over his anglophone translators. In one sense he was certainly right: none of them could have boasted of having his ear, let alone of working by it.

KLINE/ENGLISH TANDEM: THE CRISIS AND ITS RESOLUTION

By January 1979, the Kline/English duo were breathing down Brodsky's neck. Kline's main tool was, in fact, not cunning but sheer persistence. Between the two of them, Kline was the hedgehog, Brodsky the fox—to apply Isaiah Berlin's famous metaphor. Brodsky sent Myers another letter with a revised draft of Myers's translation of "December in Florence," asking him to pick up the pace with his revisions: "Dear Alan, here it is, with all its misprints and the like. It would be real nice if you found it possible to fix it, for George Kline in a tandem with another guy pushed forward their version. I hold the fort alone, everybody sides with the Indians."[12] Brodsky might have been holding the fort, but he was running out of time and ammunition. In the summer of 1979 he went to Cambridge, England, to escape from the American summer and possibly also from the heat of Kline's doggedness. But Kline was relentless and flew to England to meet with Brodsky to discuss the translation. This was probably how Kline had persuaded the editor at Penguin to sign a contract with him in 1968, rather than with the more influential Lord Nicholas Bethell, for *Selected Poems*. This was also how he had pursued Auden a year later, traveling to Austria to convince him to write a foreword for the same book.[13] Writing letters, diligently pursuing contacts, steadily prodding and wearing down people's patience—Kline had done everything in his power to promote Brodsky's cause. Now he employed the same skills to promote his and English's translation of "December in Florence." As we can glean from Kline's letter to Meiselas, another drama reached its denouement in England:

> When I asked Joseph in Cambridge if we, he and I, could do the final revision of "December in Florence" (Kline/Maurice English), he replied that it wasn't worth the while, since the basic rhyme scheme was wrong (he wasn't in a very good mood that day). Maurice English and I have worked very hard and produced what we both consider an acceptable version. (Responding to Joseph's objections in at least three thorough revisions over the past year and a half). To be sure we haven't been able to retain the tour de force of Joseph's rhymes: aaabbbccc. We tried, but couldn't make them work in English, so compromised on axabxbcxc, which seems to us to work. I think that Joseph is unrealistic in expecting the translation to retain his triple rhymes. Anyway, time is running out. Can this be offered to the *New Yorker*? And will it get into *A Part of Speech*?[14]

Brodsky's main, or at least official, objection to Kline/English's version was that they had not managed to retain the original rhyme scheme. He was resolutely adamant on this point, and Kline, who had accepted the rules of the game in general, had to grudgingly admit that he and English were failing in the rhyme department. But this was not the only objection Brodsky had to the Kline/English version. Since Kline was collaborating with English and not with him, Brodsky felt a loss of control over the translation. In the end, Kline/English's handling of his tonic meter fell below Brodsky's standards. Kline persisted. Brodsky had to say no and lost his self-control in the process. He knew what Kline had done for him and undoubtedly was remorseful about the way things had evolved. In a conversation with me, Kline hinted that the falling-out with Brodsky in Cambridge had been the lowest point in their friendship, graciously adding, however, that Brodsky later apologized profusely and tried to make it up to him. Yet Brodsky himself had effectively been cornered into a self-translation. To avert a diplomatic disaster with Kline, he had no choice but to prove that he was not "unrealistic in expecting the translation to retain his triple rhymes."[15]

BRODSKY'S SELF-TRANSLATION OF THE FIRST STANZA

Brodsky set out to do precisely this; but in the process, he helped himself amply to all the available drafts, as the following shows. Here we have Brodsky's final version of the first stanza:

I
The doors take in air, exhale steam; you, however, won't
be back to the shallowed Arno where, like a new kind
of quadruped, idle couples follow the river bend.
Doors bang, beasts hit the slabs. Indeed,
the atmosphere of this city retains a bit
of the dark forest. It
is a beautiful city where at a certain age
one simply raises the collar to disengage
from passing humans and dulls the gaze.
(Brodsky)

Brodsky's final version departs considerably from his first revision of Lowell's draft, discussed earlier. The main changes concern, as always, the rhymes.

TABLE 9. Rhymes in Stanza 1, "December in Florence"

Rubin's Interlinear	Brodsky's First Revision	Brodsky's Definitive English Version
steam but—in twos—Arno	won't—amount—ant	won't—kind—bend
doors—wild animals—atmosphere	bang—tang—long	Indeed—bit—It
city—gaze from—collar	hollow—follow—collar	age—disengage—gaze

In a post–Nobel Prize interview, Brodsky commented on his approach to translation: "Rhymes are the most entertaining aspect of translation as there are so many possibilities. The content is not terribly interesting to me, since you can't enrich or embellish it—that would be against the rules."[16]

As Brodsky's translation drafts of "December in Florence" show, rhymes were the driving force and the main creative mechanism of his translating technique in English. In his second and final revision of the first stanza, Brodsky had changed eight out of nine rhymes from an earlier draft but still managed to retain the triple rhymes of his original. He decided to discard the "ant" that had crept into his first version: "to new quadrupeds or to a walking ant." He was seemingly not keen on ad-libbing without a good reason—that would be "against the rules." The diction of his second version also became more straightforward. In the fifth line he replaced "This city still has the forest's tang," suggested by Lowell's draft, with a much more prose-like line: "the atmosphere of this city retains a bit / of the dark forest." The colloquialism "a bit" might seem jarring in a Dantesque poem. The same goes for another colloquialism he added in the fourth line—"beasts hit the slabs"—in place of the more neutral "Beasts emerge on the pavement" from an earlier revision. The use of slang in serious poems, however, was a trademark of Brodsky's poetics in Russian, a conscious artistic device to achieve a special effect by switching between colloquial and elevated registers. Subsequently, Brodsky tried to smuggle this feature into his English self-translations. But as has been noted, his ear for colloquialisms in English was not as refined as in Russian. The frequent use of enjambments was also typical of his style in Russian and was a practice he would import into English. In the sixth line he got rid of another instance of improvisation from his earlier draft, "in the middle of a long / road," which would have been an obvious reference to the opening of the *Divine Comedy*. But since in the Russian original there was no such allusion, it would also have been "against the rules."

The seventh line, on the other hand, reproduces Barry Rubin's literal translation almost verbatim, with only the characteristic addition of an enjambment following the pronoun "it" ("It // is a beautiful city, / where at a certain age//"). Conversely, the last rhyme of the cluster, "age—disengage—gaze," seems to have been suggested by the final line in the Kline/English version: "shutting out its people from your gaze." This was, it appears, their only contribution to the final version of the first stanza:

I
The doors inhale air and exhale steam;
but you will not return here. Breaking into pairs,
the crowds go strolling by the Arno's failing stream
like some new breed of quadruped that's strayed,
doors slamming behind them, down the pavement.
Truly, there's something of the forest glade
About this handsome city. Yet at a certain age
you simply turn up your collar,
shutting out its people from your gaze.
(Kline/Maurice English)

On the whole, apart from the internal slant rhymes "strolling—failing—slamming," the Kline/English version lacked the musicality of Kline's previous translations done in collaboration with Brodsky. It would appear that, in the absence of a clear pentametric pattern, Kline and English tried to follow Brodsky's instructions on how to render into English the poem's innovative meter. Taking clues from Brodsky, they came up with the rhythm "of natural speech," as they understood it, which ended up sounding more like prose. As it turned out, Brodsky was after something else. Myers's translation of the same stanza displayed, on the other hand, a much more sustained rhythm:

I
The doorways inhale air and exhale steam,
But you won't come back where the people teem
in pairs close by the shoaling Arno's stream,
like some new kind of beast. The heavy doors
slam shut. They pad the pavement on all fours;
the air's alive with forest noise and claws!
Here in this city, beautiful, no doubt,
at a certain age you don't look about
for people—raise your collar, shut them out.
(Myers)

Yet Brodsky was still unimpressed. One problem with Myers's version, it appears, was its tone, which failed to capture the world-weariness of Brodsky's voice. His couples don't "teem" in a crowded city center; rather, they have somehow agglomerated into a single beastlike creature, amplifying the speaker's solitude. Similarly, the sixth line—"the air's alive with forest noise and claws!"—is wrong. Dante's dark forest was a journey away from daily existence. By likening the city to a forest, Brodsky dehumanizes it, drawing it into metaphor, which increases the speaker's alienation. In other words, while Brodsky makes a sad observation, Myers interprets it in a cheerful key.

Another problem with both the Kline/English and Myers versions was that they failed to satisfy Brodsky's intent to re-create in translation the same tension between the inertia of the beat and the prose-like qualities of his *dol'nik*.

According to Zhirmunsky's definition, "pure tonic verse is based on a count of the stressed syllables," while "the number of unstressed syllables between stresses is a variable quantity."[17] Zeroing in more concretely on *dol'nik*, Barry Scherr specified that while in the regular *dol'nik* "there are both one- and two-syllable intervals between the ictuses,"[18] in the variable *dol'nik*—as used by Brodsky—"the number of ictuses from line to line fluctuates."[19] Again, Zhirmunsky observed: "The organizing principle of such verse is the recurrence of a strong syllable following a more or less extended group of weak ones; rhythmical attention is directed toward catching the strong syllables which recur after groups of varying lengths."[20] However, the sharper the fluctuations in the number of unstressed syllables between stresses, or ictuses, "the more difficult it is to hold the unstressed groups together by means of the stress."[21] Thus, while discussing the qualities of the Silver Age precursors of Brodsky's *dol'niki*, Zhirmunsky noted that readers unaccustomed to them could easily confuse them with prose:

> The stronger are the variations in the syllabic structure of the inter-accentual spaces . . . the greater the number of unaccented syllables between the

> ictuses, the more difficult it becomes for the main accent to maintain unity with the unstressed syllables; as a result *the verse becomes less ordered rhythmically, approximating colloquial speech or literary prose* whose main characteristic is natural freedom in the distribution of accents [italics mine].[22]

Some Silver Age poets intentionally explored such prose-like qualities of *dol'nik* for their artistic effect. Thus, while comparing the *dol'niki* of Alexander Blok, who was responsible for popularizing *dol'niki* in Russian poetry by using them in his own poems, with those of Akhmatova, Zhirmunsky pointed out that, in contrast to the singing style of Blok, Akhmatova's *dol'niki* "acquire the character of intentionally casual, intimate, colloquial speech: the poetry strives, as it were, to approximate the free rhythm of prose."[23] I believe that in "December in Florence," Brodsky was striving to achieve a similar kind of artistic effect. While the Kline/English version sounded too much like prose, Myers's version sounded too singsong. Brodsky wanted meter, but meter that would re-create the tension between the musical and prose-like qualities of his original poem. Indeed, as Myers once remarked: "My own versions were too smooth, light and regular ('cute') for his taste."[24] Curiously, in this opposition to smoothness, Brodsky draws closer to Walter Benjamin's foreignizing approach to translation:[25] "For Benjamin, translation does not transform a foreign language into one we may call our own, but rather renders radically foreign that language we believe to be ours."[26] If Brodsky's aim was to import the difficulty of his original *dol'nik* into English, he could be said to have succeeded. The problem with this approach in Brodsky's case was that he was translating into a language that was not his own: he was a foreigner foreignizing English.

THE SIXTH STANZA

In the sixth stanza, which is important in the context of Dantesque tripartite symbolism, Brodsky sharpens the main message of the poem—the connection between a poet's vocation and his exile. Elsewhere, in his essays on Frost and Hardy, he suggested that in poetry, birds and poets can often be equated.[27] In "December in Florence," Brodsky took this metaphor to its logical conclusion, equating the exiled Dante, who found his refuge and ended his days in the city of Ravenna,[28] with a caged bird in a coffee-house. The bard resembles a bird in that neither requires much to produce a song: the bird/bard can sing—and sing beautifully—even if confined to a cage in a dusty café. In 1976, a year after finishing "December in Florence," Brodsky expanded on this idea in the talk "Language as Otherland," delivered at Amherst College and Hunter College.[29] Brodsky argued that, if only in terms of writing, exile is bearable. While Dante the man undoubtedly longed for Florence, Dante the poet did not need it to write his poetry: "Dante Alighieri left his Florence, and because of that we have *La Divina Commedia* . . . There are many other instances, and many of them, however tragic, prove that if anything, exile is bearable in terms of writing. For any country is but a continuation of space."[30] It is quite symbolic that Brodsky reiterated here his "continuation of space" mantra, which had helped him cope with his own exile, while at the same time elevating Dante as a model of a poet's triumph over displacement. From poetry's vantage point, Ravenna with its "salty bread" and "steep stairs" did just as well as Florence.[31] The same applied to Brodsky who, as the result of his exile, could travel to Florence, sit in a dusty café, and write a poem in homage to Dante. Here we have Rubin's interlinear translation of the sixth stanza, followed by Lowell's draft:

VI
In a dusty coffee-house [one's] eye under the partial shade of a cap
gets used to the nymphs on the ceiling, the cupids, [and] the sculpture;
sensing/feeling the lack of terza rima, in a cage
[a] decrepit goldfinch executes its [melodic] figures.
A ray of sunlight splattering against the palazzo, against
the dome of the cathedral in which Lorenzo lies,
penetrates the blind [i.e., the shutter] and warms up the veins
of dirty marble, [and] the tub of verbena;
and the goldfinch sings [sweetly] / pours forth a song in the middle of his
wire Ravenna.
(Rubin)

VI
In a dusty coffee house, under one's cap's twilight,
one gets used to the frescoes, nymphs and cupids;
the caged goldfinch, since terza rima is out of fashion,
cheeps its jagged, controlled improvisation.
A ray of sunlight splatters the pietra serena
of the sacristy where Lorenzo abides [sleeps] his night,
pierces the shutters and warms the veins
of dirty marble, the tub of verbena—
the goldfinch chirping sweetly thru its wire-Ravenna.
(Lowell)

In this stanza, Lowell could not help departing from the original in a way typical of his *Imitations*. Ironically, the randomly introduced phrase "controlled improvisation" reminds one of the uncontrollable improvisations typical of Lowell's translations. The Italian phrase "pietra serena," which did not appear in the original, is a case in point, although Lowell might simply have been trying to come up with feminine rhymes to mirror the original, and "serena" and "Ravenna" seemed like a good choice. The rhyme scheme in Lowell's sixth stanza is AXBBCaxCC, which deviates from Brodsky's original triplets. Brodsky was unconvinced, and, as we will see later, his final version of the stanza bears little resemblance to Lowell's draft. The Kline/English attempt came with its own problems.

> VI
> In a dusty café, an eye out of a cap's shadow takes in
> the nymphs on the painted ceiling, the cupids, the stucco molding.
> A goldfinch, out of the tremble of wires he's caged in
> feebly runs through the *terzinas* of his tune.
> A ray of the sun, breaking against the palace and against
> the cupola of the sacristy that holds Lorenzo's tomb,
> warms, through the shutters, a tub of flowering verbena
> and the veins of the dirty marble.
> A goldfinch's voice flows out from its cage in Ravenna.
> (Kline/English)

It is easy to see how Brodsky would have frowned at such manufactured grammatical rhymes as "takes in—caged in," particularly since Klein and English failed to preserve the original triplet rhymes. To be fair, they tried to compensate with the internal rhyme "ceiling—molding" in the second line, but the rhythm of their version was presumably too unemphatic for Brodsky. Moreover, despite Kline's knowledge of Brodsky's poetics, their fourth line contained a significant misreading: "A goldfinch . . . feebly runs through the *terzinas* of his tune" as opposed to "feeling the lack of terza rima, in a cage / [a] decrepit goldfinch executes its [melodic] figures" (Rubin). For Brodsky the distinction is crucial. His lyrical hero is often self-deprecating about his persona, health, and appearance, but he would never disparage his poetic gift. In other words, the goldfinch could be "decrepit" or "seedy," but he would never sing "feebly." Had they collaborated as in the past, Brodsky would surely have pointed this out to Kline. But striking out on his own with English as his collaborator, Kline lost the advantage of receiving direct feedback from Brodsky, which had contributed to the semantic accuracy of his versions in the past.

Myers's Translation

Myers's translation of the sixth stanza opened with the phrase "A dusty coffee-bar." Brodsky suggested an alternative beginning: "Why not: 'In a dusty café;'—since the beat is ruined all the same."[32] Despite the critical note (ruined beat), Brodsky actually borrowed quite substantially from Myers's final version of this stanza:

VI
A dusty coffee-bar. Eyes shaded from the glare
can pick out putti, molded ceilings, nymphs everywhere;
sensing lack of *terza rima* in his cage, in despair,
a draggled goldfinch trills his thin cadenza.
The sunlight breaking over the palazzo,
the duomo's dome wherein lies old Lorenzo!
Now pierces drapes and titillates the veinous
filthy marble, sprays of white verbena;
the bird's ablaze within his wire Ravenna.
(Myers)

Brodsky reproduced the last three lines from Myers's version almost verbatim. He also incorporated two-thirds of the rhymes proposed by Myers in his published version. This was quite unusual, considering Brodsky's enjoyment in coming up with new rhymes for his self-translations:

VI
In a dusty café, in the shade of your cap,
Eyes pick out frescoes, nymphs, cupids on their way up.
In a cage, making up for the sour terza-rima crop,
a seedy goldfinch juggles his sharp cadenza.
A chance ray of sunlight splattering the palazzo
And the sacristy where lies Lorenzo
Pierces thick blinds and titillates the veinous
filthy marble, tubs of snow-white verbena;
and the bird's ablaze within his wire Ravenna.
(Brodsky)

The explanation may lie in the difficulty of finding rhymes for Italian words in English. In fact, in six out of the nine stanzas of "December" in Russian, Brodsky put Italian names into rhyming position—Arno, Signoria, Cellini, Brunelleschi, Ravenna, Lorenzo—where each had to rhyme with two other words in their respective triplets. In the third line, Brodsky introduced an aphoristic paraphrase, "sour terza-rima crop," which shows that

TABLE 10. Rhymes in Stanza 6, "December in Florence"

Rubin's Interlinear	Myers's Draft	Brodsky's Definitive English Version
of a cap—sculpture—cage	glare—everywhere—despair	cap—way up—crop
[melodic] figures–palazzo, against [the dome]—Lorenzo	cadenza—palazzo—Lorenzo!	cadenza—palazzo—Lorenzo
veins—of verbena—Ravenna	veinous—verbena—Ravenna	veinous—verbena—Ravenna

Brodsky felt tempted to flex his poetic muscles in English. As a result, the line sounds more hermetic than in Russian or in Rubin's interlinear "feeling the lack of *terza rima*."

THE LAST STANZA OF "DECEMBER IN FLORENCE"

The last stanza is the most lyrical in tone and was clearly the most important one for the author. It certainly contains vital clues to the poem's meaning. No wonder it was the one Brodsky rewrote most substantially. It begins with a prophecy of no return, which was a reference both to Cacciaguida's prophecy in *Paradiso* XVII and to Akhmatova's 1936 poem "Dante," quoted in the epigraph to "December": "He has not returned to his old Florence, / even after having died. . . ." In 1975, when the poem was written, it was axiomatic that Brodsky would never again see his home city. Fourteen years later, the double blessing of receiving the Nobel Prize shortly before the fall of communism suddenly turned his refusal to return into a highly discussed topic, as Sontag observed:

> Perhaps no decision he made in the later part of his life was as startling (to many), as emblematic of who he was, as his refusal, after the dismantling of the Soviet empire and in the face of countless worshipful solicitations, to go back even for the briefest visit. And so he lived most of his adult life elsewhere: here. And Russia, the source of everything that was most subtle and audacious and fertile and doctrinaire about his mind and gifts, became the great elsewhere to which he could not, would not, out of pride, out of anger, out of anxiety, ever return.[33]

To the long list of reasons why Brodsky would not want to return to Russia even when the opportunity arose—the most obvious being that his parents had died after his departure without ever again seeing their beloved son—one could add faithfulness to the prophecy made in his Dantesque poem of never returning. This crucial detail has entirely eluded those who participated in endless discussions about the motives for his refusal. The lyrical hero of "December" looked back at his native city and compared his memory of it with what was now before his eyes. The bridges over the Arno reminded him of the six bridges across the Neva. In remembrance, he evoked the most sacred aspects connecting him to the place of his birth: the waters of St. Petersburg's seascape, his love, his poetry. Crucially, Dante would have been able to relate to it all, had he read the poem. The final two lines of the poem express in essence both the exile's greatest losses and his hope for poetic justice.

Brodsky's first published piece after setting foot on American soil in 1972 was titled "A Writer Is a Lonely Traveller, and No One Is His Helper." There he summarized his greatest linguistic challenge as a Russian poet in America: "In order to write well in a language, you have to hear it—in taverns, buses and grocery stores. I have not yet invented a way to fight this. But I hope . . . that I will take the Russian language wherever I go."[34] This passage reveals Brodsky's lingering fear that his muse might not survive his transplantation. Four years later, one could hear a tectonic shift in his tone, which, although it harbored some of the same concerns, has become more defiant:

> It is true, though, that in order to write and to write well—poetry especially—it is better to hear your language spoken every day—in grocery, in street-cars, in bed. That is, one should be in constant touch with the current idiom. But it is too bad when the idiom creates a writer. Because it is precisely a writer who creates the idiom. Mind this—however solemn it may sound—people in Rome today speak Dante's Italian.[35]

In his 1976 talk "Language as Otherland," Brodsky paraphrased what he had succinctly formulated earlier in the last two lines of "December." The greatest challenge for a poet—being cut off from his native language as spoken in streetcars and grocery stores—could be overcome. Because the poet is the one "by whom language lives," as per Brodsky's favorite Auden line. It is the poet who creates the idiom, while those who have remained at home will of necessity eventually adopt the language coined by the exile. The poet thus becomes a part of speech of those at home, which is essentially the leitmotif of the entire *A Part of Speech* collection.

Lowell's Draft

Let us now turn to Rubin's interlinear translation and to Lowell's draft of the last stanza. (The boldface, italics, and underlining serve to distinguish the three different sets of endings forming rhyme triplets in the original.)

IX
There are cities to which there is no **return**.
The sun beats against their windows, as if they were smooth **mirrors.**
That
is, there is no penetrating them—not for any amount of **gold**.
There a river always flows under six *bridges*.
There are places there where there was occasion to press *lips*
Against other lips and pen to *[sheets of] paper*. And
there is a blur of arcades, colonnades, iron scarecrows;
there the crowd speaks, as it besieges the trolley corner,
in the tongue of a person who has departed.
(Rubin)

IX
There are cities to which one cannot return,
the sun beats on a window, as if it were a mirror–
that is, there's no penetration,
There six bridges always arch a local river, [clear/clean]
there are places where lip first pressed against a lip,
and a pen first marked a ~~piece~~ shoot of scrap–
a blur of arcades there, colonnades, scarecrows—
there a crowd speaks, as it besieges the trolley-top,
in the tongue of a person departed, elsewhere.
(Lowell)

Lowell tries to preserve the feminine endings but uses alternate rhyming instead of triplets; some of his endings hardly rhyme at all—for example, "return—penetration." In the fourth line Lowell comes up with the colloquialism "a pen first marked a shoot of scrap" instead of "pen pressed to sheets of paper" (Rubin). But this seems to fall within the realm of poetic expression rather than "irresponsible invention," as Nabokov would have maliciously put it. Moreover, Lowell creates a symmetrical opposition between the pronoun "there" in the anaphora of four lines in the stanza and the word "elsewhere" at its end. Lowell's last stanza has a rather pleasant flow; after all, Lowell was not Lowell for nothing. Had Brodsky been able to accept anything less than what he felt was the exact shape of his poem in English, he would probably have been happy with Lowell's version of the last stanza.

The Kline/English Draft

In contrast to the pleasant flow in Lowell's draft, Kline/English's last stanza feels decidedly heavy:

IX
There are cities in this world to which one can't return.
The sun beats on their windows as though on polished mirrors.
And no amount of gold will make their hinged gates turn.
Rivers in those cities always flow beneath six bridges.
There are places in those cities where lips first pressed on lips
and pen on paper. In those cities there's a richness
of scarecrows cast in iron, of colonnades, arcades.
There the crowds besieging trolley stops are speaking
In the language of a man who's been written off as dead.
(Kline/English)

The repetition of the word "cities" four times instead of the pronoun "there" as an anaphora feels cumbersome. Rhymes such as "return—turn" do not seem original. Yet because Kline knew Brodsky's circumstances so well, he could more accurately interpret the meaning, especially of the lines written in a diaristic tone. Thus, in the last line, the Kline/English translation reads "a man who's been written off as dead" instead of "a person who has departed," as per Rubin's literal translation from the Russian. Kline's interpretation was later echoed in Brodsky's 1976 talk. There Brodsky referred to his exile as "a light execution,"[36] implying that the real intention of those who had forced him out of Russia had been to destroy him as a poet. He was now set to prove them wrong.

Myers versus Brodsky

Because Brodsky collaborated more directly with Myers than with the other translators on "December," Myers's draft received the lion's share of his criticism and marginal comments. Next to Myers's first line, Brodsky wrote, "Should have a trifle more epic swing"; next to the third line, "The idea of *gold* is crucial: implies sun itself"; next to the fourth and sixth lines, just one word—"beat." Brodsky was clearly dissatisfied with the way Myers had rendered the stanza's rhythm. Next to the seventh line he noted that it should open with the same demonstrative pronoun in the anaphora, "there." And next to the last triplet, he briskly added, "It should rhyme better than that." Here we have Myers's draft:

IX
Cities there are to which there's no returning.
The sun beats on their mirror windows, a sign to the discerning
that they stay shut in face of wealth or learning.
There six bridges span a running river.

There those places, where lips touched lover's
Lips and pen pressed paper in a fever.
The eye is dazed, arcades, columns, cast-iron bugbears;
There the populace surging round the tramcars
Speak the tongue of one long since departed.
(Myers)

For all his criticism, Brodsky took more hints from Myers's draft for his final version of the last stanza than from any other of the translations. Compare, for example, the rhymes in the second triplet: "river—lover's—fever" (Myers) versus "river—ever—fervor" (Brodsky):

IX
There are c**i**ties **o**ne won't s**ee** ag**ai**n. The s**u**n 5
thr**o**ws its g**o**ld at their fr**o**zen w**i**ndows. But **a**ll the s**a**me enj. 6
There is no **e**ntry, no pr**o**per s**u**m. 3
There are **a**lways s**i**x br**i**dges sp**a**nning the sl**u**ggish r**i**ver. 6
There are pl**a**ces where l**i**ps t**o**uched l**i**ps for the f**i**rst time **e**ver, enj. 6
Or p**e**n pr**e**ssed p**a**per with r**e**al f**e**rvor. 5
There are arc**a**des, colonn**a**des, **i**ron **i**dols that bl**u**r your·l**e**ns. 6
There the str**ee**tcar's m**u**ltitudes, j**o**stling, d**e**nse, enj. 4
Sp**e**ak in the t**o**ngue of a m**a**n who's dep**a**rted th**e**nce. 5
(Brodsky)

In his own take on the last stanza, Brodsky got closer than in any previous versions to the style of his later self-translations. Crucially, this style has been not only the target of the strongest criticism and misunderstanding, but also the reason for some valiant attempts to defend him, coming mostly from native Russian speakers. The explanation for both types of reactions is that Brodsky's achievement can be best appreciated by bilingual readers, not that he was aiming for that sort of audience. While clearly seeking to engage anglophone readers, Brodsky himself was undoubtedly developing a bilingual sensibility. His translation of the last stanza of "December in Florence" impressively mimics the movements and syntactic units of the original, striving, ultimately, to reproduce its real rhythm. Guided by his authorial ear, Brodsky rewrote the same stanza in English. Here is the transliterated original:

Est' gorod***a***, v kot***o***rye n***e***t vozvr***a***ta. 5
S**o**lntse b'***e***tsia v ikh ***o***kna, kak v gl***a***dkie zerkal***a***. To enj. 5
est', v n***i***kh ne pron***i***knesh' ni za kak***o***e zl***a***to. 4
T***a***m vsegd***a*** protek***a***et rek***a*** pod shest'i***u*** most***a***mi. 5
T***a***m est' mest***a***, gde pripad***a***l ust***a***mi enj. 5

t***o***zhe k ust***a***m i per***o***m k list***a***m. I	enj.	4
t***a***m riab***i***t ot ark***a***d, kolonn***a***d, ot chug***u***nnykh p***u***gal;		6
t***a***m tolp***a*** govor***i***t, osazhd***a***ia tramv***a***inyi ***u***gol,	enj.	6
n***a*** iazyk***e*** chelov***e***ka, kot***o***ryi ***u***byl.		5

The first striking feature of his translation is that the total number of stressed positions in Russian is almost identical (45) to that in English (46). Although there is no line-by-line correspondence, the net acoustic weight of the Russian poem and its translation is analogous. There is also a similar number of enjambments: 4 in Russian and 3 in English. Then there are several lines that directly mimic the movement and sometimes even the vowels of the respective line in the original:

1 "***É***st' gorod***á***, | v kot***ó***rye | n***é***t vozvr***á***ta"	[e—a | o | e—a]
1 "There are c**i**ties **o**ne | won't s**ee** ag**ai**n. | The s**u**n"	$[{}_{s}\text{i}_{t—w}\Lambda_{n} \mid {}_{w}\text{əʊ}_{nt}—{}_{s}\text{i:–ei}_{n} \mid {}_{s}\Lambda_{n}]$
2 "S**o**lntse b'***e***tsia v ikh **o**kna":	[o—o—i—o]
2 "thr**o**ws its g**o**ld at their fr**o**zen w**i**ndow":	[əʊ—əʊ—əʊ—i]
4 "There are **al**ways s**i**x br**i**dges sp**a**nning the sl**u**ggish r**i**ver."	6
4 "T**a**m vsegd**a** protek**a**et rek**a** pod shest'**iu** most**a**mi."	6

The correspondences in each of the quoted lines are of a different kind. In the first line it is the movement of the phrase boundaries. In the second half-line, the parallelism is in the imagery and in the similarity between the vowels employed in both languages. In the fourth line it is the number of stressed syllables matched by the correspondence in the imagery. Similarly, in line five there is parallelism between the consonances employed in English and in Russian: "*mes*t*a*—us*t*a*mi*" and "*pl*aces . . . *lips* . . . *lips*." And in the eighth line, there is a more subtle onomatopoeic correspondence between "m*u*ltitudes, *jostl*ing" and "*osa*zhd*aia* . . . ug*ol*" ("besieging . . . the corner").

Alongside this mimetic approach Brodsky engages in self-commentary, adding epithets to several nouns that didn't have any in the original. Thus, in the second line the windows become "frozen";[37] in the fourth line, the river is "sluggish," whereas the Russian gives no such information. Similarly, in line six in English, we learn that "pen pressed paper *with real fervor*." At the same time, there are instances where the translation obfuscates the meaning of the original. Thus, in the third line in Russian, it is implied that no amount of gold would buy you entry into the city, whereas in English, the ellipsis seems too strong to be able to convey this meaning: "There is no entry, no proper sum." The reason for the ellipsis is evident—to fit the third rhyme of the cluster, "sun—same—sum." Myers later recalled that Brodsky was often prepared to alter his drafts considerably just for the sake of rhyme: "The line-length, (my) rhythm, even the meaning might all undergo change. Indeed, on one occasion, he went so far as to say that everything should be sacrificed to the rhyme! For a sharp increase in energy level, 'smoothness' was well lost."[38] Indeed, the sharp caesura before the phrase "But all the same" at the end of the second line, followed by an enjambment, produces in Brodsky's version an effect of breathlessness. By the same token, ending the poem on such a dated word as "thence" sounds awkward: "Speak in the tongue of a man who's departed thence." In comparison, Lowell's last line, "in the tongue of a person departed, elsewhere," sounds more idiomatic.

GENERAL OBSERVATIONS ON "DECEMBER IN FLORENCE"

The structure of the original was essential for Brodsky. It was the sticking point, but it was also an excuse for Brodsky to interfere and try his own hand at the translation process. He would start with the invention of rhymes in English and gradually move on to those aspects of translation that concerned meaning, tone, and euphony. Obviously, it was important to have an effective ending for a poem. This was true of his co-translation of "A Second Christmas by the Shore" with Kline, where he took over the translator's job in the last stanza. The same was true of his reworking of Weissbort's translation of "The North buckles metal," in which Brodsky rewrote the last stanza more heavily than others. Even his minor revisions of Wilbur's impeccable translation of "Six Years Later" concerned the last two lines. With "December in Florence," Brodsky became even more daring. Rather than re-creating the single structural and euphonic elements of the Russian poem in English, he effectively wrote it anew in English, using the hum of his Russian original as his main compositional principle. Weissbort described it as follows:

> The point is that Brodsky tries to bring the two languages closer together, encouraging Russian, as it were, to speak English—syntax, accent, and all. It is not a question of verbally or syntactically literal translation, but of a far more radical, synthetic process, the result at this point being so novel that it is almost bound to be misunderstood.[39]

Given Brodsky's idea that English was a continuation of Russian by other phonetic means, such an approach might not have been as outlandish as it sounds. It is doubtful, however, that Brodsky would have thought that "encouraging Russian . . . to speak English" was what he was up to, aware as he surely was that the accentual verse meter employed in the poem resulted from the influence of English on his Russian poetics in the first place.[40] Moreover, in his own versions, Brodsky was able to create authentic harmonies in English, even if those harmonies were largely based on unfamiliar phonetic principles. One could not easily substitute a line or even a word in his translation without breaking its whole structure. One reason for such drastic experiments was that the delivery of his poetry was extremely important to Brodsky. In fact, Weissbort himself observed that when Brodsky recited them, the rhythm of his self-translations "projected the poems as highly formal structures."[41] Weissbort wondered, however, whether "this formality was an illusion dependent on the author's own performance."[42] Be that as it may, Brodsky's wish to perform them alone, before an audience, and in both languages certainly played a part in his motivation to shape them according to his wish and ear. His ability to captivate an audience and shape its reception of his work had been a crucial part of his poetic experience in Russia and was intended to protect his self-worth as a poet in his new linguistic environment.

Brodsky's translators' understanding was that they had been commissioned to do the job. His persistent revisions of their work were disappointing—and in some cases, infuriating. While Brodsky repeatedly tried to placate his disillusioned partners, he clearly benefited from what became a dress rehearsal for his later practice of self-translation. Given what he was after, it is hardly surprising that none of the translators could entirely satisfy him. Weissbort, who dared to air his grievances vocally, lamented that such a practice promoted "the translator's invisibility," to use Venuti's term:

> Given his circumstance, Brodsky can hardly be blamed for wanting to be the one to define his English profile. That being so, he took over from his translators what is generally regarded as an essential part of the job. Gradually (quite rapidly, in fact) his translators were reduced to hired hands, which is more or less how the law treats them anyway.[43]

One cannot help thinking that there was an element of Dantesque justice in Brodsky's cavalier treatment of Lowell's translation draft, given what Lowell had done to many poems by great European poets. But the same cannot be said about his other translators—Kline/English, Myers, Weissbort. It is true that Brodsky tried to compensate his translators for their many hours of work, as he explained in a letter to Myers: "The reason I am trying to put them into the well-paying magazines is that the translators should have some sort of incentive to work, because the royalties, apart from being extremely meager, are usually paid to the author."[44] Yet, as he himself admitted, the handsome fees paid by the *New Yorker* and *Vogue* were still "crumbs, peanuts,"[45] given the long hours, days, weeks, and months the translators had toiled. In reality, the service provided to him by his translators was priceless. Thus, Weissbort aptly observed: "Unfortunately, . . . he appeared to be demanding slavishness of his translators. Arguably, though, . . . his 'translators' had unwittingly participated not only in getting his poetry into English, but in getting Brodsky himself into English."[46]

Chapter Nine

Going It Alone

ROBERT LOWELL'S sudden death in September 1977, just four years after Auden's, left Brodsky with a sense of loss. Two major English-language poets who had become his friends and champions during the toughest period of his displacement had now departed in quick succession. It may have felt like déjà vu, evoking his all too brief friendship with Akhmatova, which was further truncated by the years of his Arctic exile. Yet it seems that he once again interpreted the death of a poetic precursor as a summons to step in and fill the void as his continuator:

> He was a lovely man . . . Lowell . . . The age difference wasn't that big between us—well, some twenty years, so I felt in a sense somewhat more comfortable with him than with Auden. But then again, I felt most comfortable with Akhmatova. . . . while they were alive . . . I felt as a young boy. They were the elders, so to speak, the masters. Now that they are gone, I think of myself as terribly old all of a sudden. . . . This is what civilization means, carrying on.[1]

As he had following Auden's death, Brodsky managed to channel his grief into an elegy for Lowell written directly in English. While he later regretted publishing the Auden poem, he felt more confident including the one for Lowell in *A Part of Speech*. Regardless of whether we find it a major breakthrough in his command of English poetics, as Brown and Bethea did,[2] or a "dead poem,"[3] as Monas claimed, this elegy is still revealing of Brodsky's approach to writing poetry directly in English.

In a 1991 interview, Brodsky described what gave him the initial impulse to compose poems in any language: "The poem always starts with the first line or with a line anyway. And from that you go. It is something in the line, a certain hum to which you try to fit the line. . . . some tune, which has oddly enough some sort of psychological weight or denomination."[4] What Brodsky referred to as the "psychological weight" of certain verse meters, Mikhail Gasparov called their "semantic aura,"[5] referring to the notion that certain verse forms can often be strongly associated with particular moods or subject matter. By the same token, the process of fitting a line to a tune or a hum, as Brodsky put it, was described by Zhirmunsky as "the unity of a creative task," which is the practice of subjugating all the "contrasting facts of meaning, of sound and of syntax" to a single metrical law.[6] While in his self-translations the initial "hum" stemmed from the real rhythm of his Russian originals, the poems Brodsky wrote directly in English began with a "hum" borrowed from lines by his favorite English-language poets, often committed to memory. Here we have a short excerpt from his Lowell elegy as an illustration:

In the republic of ends
and means that counts each deed
poetry represents
the minority of the dead.

Now you become a part
of the inanimate, plain
terra of disregard
of the common pain.[7]

The "hum" that Brodsky followed here is that of Auden's trimeters from his poem "1 September 1939":

Exiled Thucydides knew
All that a speech can say
About Democracy,
And what dictators do,
The elderly rubbish they talk
To an apathetic grave;
Analysed all in his book,
The enlightenment driven away,
The habit-forming pain,
Mismanagement and grief:
We must suffer them all again.[8]

It's notable that both poems feature democracy, which also appears in the opening remarks of Brodsky's Nobel lecture: "It is better to be a total failure in democracy than a martyr or the crème de la crème in tyranny."[9] Though he embraced democracy, Brodsky lamented the marginal position occupied in it by poets ("In the republic . . . poetry represents / the minority of the dead").

Even though the rhythm of Brodsky's elegy for Lowell is perhaps less subtle in its English prosody than that of its celebrated model, to fail by such high standards as set by Auden was already a great achievement, especially for someone who, by birth, was not meant to speak English. Apart from the "hum" of Auden's poem "1 September 1939" (which so gripped Brodsky that he dedicated an entire essay to a line-by-line analysis of it), it is possible to find in his Lowell elegy echoes of his other favorite lines in English. Thus, "terra of disregard" harks back to Brodsky's favorite line from the much-anthologized Frost poem "Provide, Provide": "No memory of having starred / Atones for later disregard / Or keeps the end from being hard."[10] Similarly, the beginning of the stanza "Now you become a part . . ." evokes another stanza from the first part of Auden's elegy "In Memory of W. B. Yeats": "Now he is scattered among a hundred cities," which famously ends with the phrase "The words of a dead man / Are modified in the guts of the living."[11] At the same time, Brodsky's self-commentary in an interview with Tom Vitale from New York Public Radio reveals the elegy's intertextual connections to Lowell's own verse: "If it's good, it is partly because it exploits several of Lowell's own tropes."[12] Because he was conscious of his position within the hierarchy established by time and tradition, Brodsky felt honored to be regarded as an Auden, Frost, or Lowell imitator. Pastiche was a way to pay homage to a dear poet, especially in an elegy.

Thus, when Brodsky, already accomplished as a craftsman in his first language, set out to compose poems in English, he re-embraced his apprenticeship to his favorite English-language poets. This was the practicum he had taken up as a young poet in adopting tropes, verse structures, and other poetic devices from Donne, Auden, and Frost—although one gets the impression that Donne and Eliot faded in the later years as Hardy and Frost became more influential. In fact, judging from his essays, Hardy and Frost brought a more modern English prosody than the metaphysicals, one he would have been unable to hear before becoming a fluent English speaker.[13] Still, one cannot but marvel at Brodsky's industry and patience as manifested in his willingness to go through the same process of apprenticeship again.

But displacement was all about starting from scratch. Nabokov too had gone through the process of reinventing himself as an English-language writer when he came to America.[14] Brodsky's self-reinvention, however, was an ongoing process that was also strongly based on his belief in and commitment to continuity. He remained largely faithful to his early poetic influences. The only difference was that now those predecessors helped him write poetry not in Russian but in English—with a Russian accent, as it were. Perhaps because of that accent, Brodsky continued to remain coy about his ambitions in English. When asked in 1984 why he had written the elegy for Lowell in English, Brodsky explained that he did so to please Lowell's shadow. Later, he gave the same reason for switching to English in his essays—to please the shadow of Auden:

> I thought about writing it in Russian, of course, but then I thought that he would like it better if I did it in English. I've done it simply to please him . . . I've written several poems in English, but *I have no ambition to do that in any kind of substantial way. I have no aspiration to become a poet of the English language* [italics mine]. That is, I translate quite a lot of my own into English, and that's enough for me.[15]

Brodsky claimed that, in terms of his creative engagement with English, doing self-translations was already more than enough. All indications suggest, however, that his translations, essays, and poems written in English sprang from the desire to secure his self-respect as a writer in his immediate linguistic environment. Occasionally, a typically unpredictable Brodsky would admit so himself, as he did in a 1979 interview he gave in Russian: "I, for one, [wrote poetry in English] several times, to at least persuade myself that I am capable of it, so I wouldn't have any complexes."[16]

DEREK WALCOTT: AN ENCOUNTER WITH A POETIC SIBLING

The loss of Lowell was alleviated by Brodsky's encounter at the funeral with Derek Walcott. Brodsky recalled in an interview: "I met Derek . . . at Lowell's funeral. Lowell had told me about Derek and showed me some poems which impressed me a great deal. . . . I'd put him somewhere between Marlowe and Milton . . . He's astonishing. The critics want to make him a regional poet from the West Indies, and it's a crime."[17]

In Walcott, Brodsky found not another master but a near contemporary, an equal. In fact, in 2007, exactly thirty years after their first meeting, I myself serendipitously encountered Walcott on a New Haven street and explained to him that I was a Brodsky scholar. The first thing he told me was "Joseph was a brother." By the reverence with which Walcott spoke, one could tell that Brodsky was perhaps the *bigger* brother. Thus, not surprisingly, in 1983 Brodsky persuaded Walcott to write what would become Walcott's "Eulogy to W. H. Auden" for a commemoration of the tenth anniversary of Auden's death, which Brodsky organized, as he had in 1973, at the Cathedral of St. John the Divine. Walcott recalls:

> Joseph who was a friend of Auden's—Joseph Brodsky—wanted a commemoration of Auden in New York City. I remember him telling me at some point, this is going to be done in the church, and that I *had* to write something. So, I said, "Joseph, you're crazy, I can't do that," and he said, "Well, no, you *have* to." And I remember when I showed him something close to a final draft—or what I thought was a final draft—and he said, "Well, you know, it's okay, but it

> has to go 'up' at the end." Meaning it had to get, at some point, a bit seraphic at the end. Which I did.[18]

Not only did Brodsky succeed in convincing Walcott to write a poem in Auden's memory, but he also gave him specific instructions for how to go about it. Evidently, Brodsky tried to share with Walcott a piece of his own technique; he would himself introduce a kind of upward gravity toward the end of his own poems. Brodsky's devotion to Auden and understanding of poetic craft made quite an impression on Walcott. He therefore accepted the challenge and did as the other poet suggested. It seems, on the whole, that Brodsky's contemporaries had less trouble than did posterity in recognizing his stature in English.

THE STRUGGLES OF TRANSLATION

Walcott's appearance in Brodsky's life was truly serendipitous. For all his mastery of English poetry, Walcott, a black man from the Caribbean, was an outsider in America and easily identified with Brodsky's struggles in exile. He appeared just in time to help see Brodsky through the final stages of the proofreading process for *A Part of Speech*, during which, as mentioned, they slightly revised Wilbur's translation and altered much more substantially some of Weissbort's translations. Toward the end of 1979, they spent an entire afternoon at the house of Pat Strachan from Farrar, Straus and Giroux going over the last proofs of *A Part of Speech*. Since Walcott did not know Russian, Barry Rubin had also been invited to supervise their accuracy vis-à-vis the Russian originals. It was the only time such a three-way collaboration ever took place, which Walcott recounted to me in an interview:

> We were looking through the proofs, these were the last proofs. Each of us was proposing something, and the other guy would say . . . nah. You know, Joseph was very dismissive too, very exact in terms of the rhythm being right. He did not want it to sound too much like English poetry, like a common meter. He worked like hell. I don't know what time it was, but by the end or somewhere in the middle, Joseph got tired and he said, "Fuck you, fuck you, fuck me, and fuck poetry!" Of the whole poem, in about six hours, he did about three lines. I don't know the rhythm of translators, but I would imagine that is the kind of rhythm they go by. It's an unappreciated occupation, underappreciated.[19]

Brodsky had every right to be exasperated; the translation method he pushed for was excruciatingly laborious and time-consuming. Myers described doing mimetic versions of rhymed poetry as "the ideal prison occupation," as whole days can pass unnoticed. He also quoted the eminent British historian of the Soviet Union, and a poet and translator of Russian poetry, Robert Conquest, who had once remarked that "translating Russian rhymed poetry into English rhymed poetry is the most difficult of all arts."[20] Even such an unrivaled master of English as Auden, whose command of poetic technique presumably allowed him to do almost anything he desired, admitted in his comments on translating Voznesensky, his only experience of translating from Russian: "The question of preserving the Russian rhythms and rhymes is *frightfully* difficult."[21] Given that Auden himself found the problem of rendering a Russian poem into English "frightfully difficult," how could Brodsky, a poet with an accent, dream of achieving this? The answer is that these were his own poems, and he accepted that some loss would be inevitable. "What you arrive at in a translation," he noted, "is about 85% of the original, at best."[22] Besides, it seems that for Brodsky, the whole challenge transcended the question of Russian poetry's translatability per se.

Life was providing him with a great experiment; from his vantage point, there was not much difference between writing poetry in Russian while separated from his nurturing mother tongue, self-translating into English, and writing his essays and poetry directly in English. In each case, he had to prove himself—to himself—a writer able to create anywhere, asserting art's independence from one's position in space. Brodsky thrived on challenges; they spurred him on. During his first years in America, marked by his fear of losing Russian, Brodsky wrote his Leningrad friends a letter telling them that he experienced moments of panic whenever he encountered difficulties finding a rhyme in Russian. He then concluded rather optimistically: "But what is progress if not a complication of one's task?"[23] By the same token, he saw his English translations simply as a new challenge to be confronted, a continuation of Russian by other phonetic means. Besides, his mimetic approach to translation was not a matter of whim, as has often been opined. For Brodsky, it revolved around a fundamental artistic principle, and he was prepared to sacrifice for his aesthetic ideals.

A PART OF SPEECH: THE FINISH LINE

The publication of *A Part of Speech* in 1980 mattered greatly to Brodsky. After all, his American reputation was at stake, and it was the only reputation he had. After his departure from Russia, even his name became taboo there, and friends who merely dared to compile samizdat collections of his poems were subjected to severe persecution.[24] Yet, oddly enough, some of Brodsky's best Russian friends in America did not recognize how much his English translations mattered to him. Even his biographer Lev Loseff observed in his *Literary Life* that 1979, when Brodsky did not publish anything in Russian, was a lean year for the poet. Loseff suggested several reasons for this lacuna: Brodsky's depression after a bypass operation, personal reasons, a desire to develop a different poetic style.[25] Any, or all, of these considerations might have played a role. Yet 1979 was above all else the year of Brodsky's most intensive work on translations for *A Part of Speech*, an endeavor of primary consequence that consumed much of his energy and time. The Iron Curtain was there to stay; no one could have predicted its sudden fall. English, therefore, was Brodsky's only path to success. After his acceptance of the Nobel Prize in 1987, however, the surrounding hype was soon followed by the cataclysmic transformations caused by the collapse of the Soviet empire, and the brutality and the walls created by the Cold War were airbrushed out of common memory and soon forgotten by many. Brodsky's triumphant return to Russia—not in person but in print—came to be seen as a historic necessity, which it patently was not. In more than one way, in fact, Brodsky's Russian success was the result of the success of his English translations, even though in America he also managed to publish five new collections of poetry in Russian. He had, after all, been awarded the Nobel Prize for his work in both languages. But, for various reasons, neither Russians at home nor those who had emigrated were ever able to appreciate the importance of his translations for his world reputation.

Rubin's recollections of that memorable occasion at the close of 1979, when the three of them went over the final proofs of *A Part of Speech*, match Walcott's account. The book had been too long in preparation; now they faced the publisher's deadline and worked under enormous time constraints. Given the situation, it was fortuitous that Walcott and Brodsky were on an equal footing. It took Walcott with his own strong personality and temperament to counterbalance Brodsky's belligerence. Rubin remembered serving as a buffer between the two poets with their big egos and quick tempers:

> It was quite extraordinary and wild. Derek would say that there is a problem with English and suggest something. Brodsky would reject it. I would intervene and try to explain to Derek why Brodsky would not accept it. A heavy silence would follow and it seemed we were stuck. Then *I* would suggest something—then Derek and Brodsky would jump at me and call me stupid. . . . There was a lot of good humor, but also a lot of swearing and attacks. Everybody understood what was at stake and contributed to a great achievement.[26]

When *A Part of Speech* finally came out in 1980, it was rapturously received. The ground had been prepared by people like Henry Gifford, a British scholar of Russian literature, who had earlier reviewed the 1977 Russian version of *A Part of Speech*, positing that "the best poetry from America in recent years is the work of this Russian."[27]

THE EXILE'S ACHIEVEMENT

Gifford's 1980 review of the American collection was no less ecstatic. His review's title, "Idioms in Interfusion," derived from the prophetic observation he had made in 1978 in reviewing the Russian version: "A poet writing in another language is reborn into a second, parallel life, and the two lives will interfuse."[28] Now, in his assessment of the English translation, Gifford suggested that "the volume was not unworthy of the original," because a team of translators had worked under Brodsky's watchful eye; he concluded: "Every poem in the book reads as if English had been its first home."[29] This was, of course, far from true; Brodsky himself admitted in the author's note that, as a result of his reworkings, some of the translations had lost their smoothness. Yet in promoting the new book, Gifford felt compelled to be hyperbolic. He also echoed Brodsky's criticism of the Pulitzer Prize–winning poet Anthony Hecht for adding some extra lines to his translation of "Lullaby of Cape Cod." Gifford did not know, however, that Hecht, whom a book critic once described as "maybe the most accomplished master of technique since Auden,"[30] had written a letter to Brodsky in which he justified his translating method. Hecht had argued that any attempt of his "to mimic the poem's formal features would mean a ruthless sacrifice of many of the most splendidly imaginative features of the poem that make it the astonishing achievement that it is."[31] Gifford's review ended with a suggestion that Brodsky should be "considered 'a corresponding member' of the company of English and American poets."[32] This was exactly the kind of thing that Brodsky had longed to hear.

Amid the general chorus of praise, the dissenting voice of Robert Hass, an American poet of distinction, was notable. A translator of Miłosz's poetry, Hass was aware, as he wrote in a review in the *New Republic* eloquently titled "Lost in Translation" (December 20, 1980), of "the haunting literature of exile being made in our midst." Though he had been anticipating a new book of poetry by Brodsky in English, such hopes were thwarted when Hass found that "for the most part reading *A Part of Speech* is like wandering through the ruins of a noble building." As a poet with a background in Slavic studies, Hass grasped the hazards of translation. In America, a metrical poem smacked of dated poetics, whereas "in Russia it suggests the moral force of an art practiced against the greatest personal odds." Hass provides several examples of unnatural diction in the book where the translators had struggled with tone. As a result, Brodsky's poems either had "that tediously bouncy rhythm produced by clever young men . . . set to make a splash" or sounded "like an 18th-century hack rewriting Shakespeare." Hass was quick, however, to exonerate the author himself: "Brodsky, of course, cannot be held responsible for this carnage." He lauded the title cycle "A Part of Speech," believing it had been translated solely by Brodsky, when, as discussed in chapter 6, Daniel Weissbort had played a significant role; commended single translations by Wilbur, Kline, Walcott, Myers, and McDuff; and referred to "Lullaby of Cape Cod" as a poem of extraordinary interest, despite Anthony Hecht's translation rendering it "full of tasteless and hackneyed writing." Indeed, Hass's conclusion that "our hope must be that Joseph Brodsky, like Nabokov and Samuel Beckett, becomes his own translator," was bound to be very encouraging for the Russian poet.

Another crucial review of *A Part of Speech* came from Czesław Miłosz, who later that year was awarded the Nobel Prize in Literature. As a fellow Slav, he enlightened American readers about Brodsky's unique stature in the Russian context, explaining that "he does not resemble those Russian immigrants who stay in their Slavic shell and are mistrustful of the evil West."[33] Instead, Miłosz showed that Brodsky's roots lay in the pre–World War I era of European cosmopolitanism and that "Brodsky takes over where young Osip Mandelstam and young Anna Akhmatova were stopped."[34] Miłosz accurately portrayed Brodsky's style as "a peculiar brand of modernism: innovation within strict metrical patterns,"[35] which did not mean, however, that Brodsky followed tradition slavishly. "Brodsky's colloquialisms, slang expressions," he wrote, "would seem to call for the freedom of William Carlos Williams's spoken rhythm. Instead . . . Brodsky observes rules of craftsmanship going back to the late eighteenth-century poet Derzhavin."[36] At the same time, Miłosz specified that behind Brodsky's poetry there is a real experience of the twentieth century, with its political terror and totalitarianism; and that Brodsky's attachment to tradition, as well as his practice of poetry-as-vocation, was driven by an adherence to the higher cause of preserving "continuity in the world more and more afflicted by oblivion."[37] An expatriate himself, Miłosz reminded American readers how much was inevitably lost in translation. In the pages of the *New York Review of Books* he quoted the last two lines, in transliterated Russian, of the poem "1972," translated by Myers and Brodsky, to show that the translation, although "successful on the whole, does not convey the soaring movement of the last stanza."[38] Miłosz also drew the attention of his article's readers to the connection between the formal qualities of Brodsky's poems and the way they are manifested in his live performances: "Those who have heard him read his poetry know how closely its scansion corresponds to its ardor and restrained vehemence."[39] Incidentally, like Gifford, Miłosz also partially vindicated Kline in quoting more from his translations than from those done by others. Perhaps Miłosz simply wanted to pay justice to the poems included in the first part of *A Part of Speech*, titled "A Song to No Music," which were written in syllabo-tonic meters while Brodsky still lived in Russia. Yet it was the approval of people like Miłosz, Gifford, and Monas, among others, that cemented the idea in some corners that Kline was Brodsky's ideal translator.

One of Miłosz's favorite poems in the collection was Hecht's translation of "Lullaby of Cape Cod," which Miłosz called "a long meditation on displacement" and one of Brodsky's strongest poems "in affirmation of endurance":

> He accomplished what previous generations of Russian émigré writers were unable to do: to make the lands of exile, however reluctantly, their own, to take possession through the poetic word. He uses the metaphor of a stranded fish which adapts itself "to some deep, cellular wish," and wriggles toward the bushes.[40]

One can see Miłosz projecting onto Brodsky his own practice of making America, "however reluctantly," his home. Miłosz, who had shared his own portion of endurance in his 1972 "consolatory letter" to Brodsky, found in his Russian counterpart an able disciple. In conclusion, Miłosz expressed a desire that *A Part of Speech* might help "to secure for him the undisputed standing he deserves as a major poet, thanks to his work in English, which *in a considerable number of lines comes close to the original* in conciseness and strength [italics mine]."[41] As opposed to Gifford, Miłosz was extremely measured in his praise of the translations, showing perhaps the fundamental mistrust of translation peculiar to most poets.

A PART OF SPEECH AND ITS REPERCUSSIONS

Miłosz's and Brodsky's hopes soon came true. The book, which Brodsky had so actively shaped, alongside many other translators and poets, gave the final push to his American and world reputation, accelerating his success. Opportunities came pouring in. In 1981, he received a "genius grant" from the MacArthur Foundation and was offered a six-month residency as a fellow at the American Academy in Rome. He could finally realize his youthful fantasy of a prolonged sojourn in Italy. This stay resulted in some of his best poems, prose pieces, and a theater play.[42] Brodsky was living his wildest dream. Indeed, in September 1979, even before the publication of *A Part of Speech*, he sent Carl Proffer a postcard from Sicily, where he had gone to receive a prestigious literary award, emphasizing that his success was quite unprecedented for someone with his background and origins: "Not bad for a little Jewish boy from [the] SU."[43] Proffer, who had known Brodsky in the Soviet Union, was well aware that back home all the odds had been against him. For one, Nadezhda Mandelstam had reminded the Proffers in a 1973 letter that the only thing Brodsky would have been guaranteed, had he stayed in Russia, was more persecution:

> Give my love to Brodsky and tell him not to be an idiot. Does he want to feed the moth once more? We have no mosquitoes for such as he because he deserves only the North of our country. So let him be happy where he is, he ought to be it. And he will learn the language which he had longued [*sic*] for all his life. Did he master English? If not, he is crazy. I would have mastered it even in my age which is 73.[44]

Nadezhda Mandelstam pointed out that Brodsky's longing for English had taken root well before his American incarnation. She must have traced an affinity between his and Osip Mandelstam's longing for world culture. Brodsky did not disappoint her. He had understood soon enough, even when he still worried about retaining his Russian, that mastering English was his main path to success. As opportunities arrived, he embraced them one by one, working at an incredible pace: writing new poems in Russian and translating them; composing new essays and poems directly in English; giving scores of interviews and poetry readings; attending conferences; and roaming the globe. Brodsky was hungry to catch up on foreign travel to make up for the deprivation of the Soviet years. He relished each opportunity, and his travels were inspirational. Many of his poems and essays written in the West are, in fact, travelogues and diaristic in nature.[45] As Miłosz astutely observed, Brodsky was in a privileged position as a Russian poet, being surrounded by new worlds as yet "unnamed in Russian."[46] All this happened atop his regular university teaching, his support of Russian friends who began pouring into the United States with the third wave of emigration, his active intervention in the fates of friends persecuted in Russia, and his response to such political events as martial law in Poland. This incredible achievement was duly recognized. In 1986, his collection of essays *Less Than One* received the National Book Critics Circle Award for criticism. By the time *To Urania*, his next poetry collection in English, appeared in 1988, causing a backlash that raised serious questions about his competence in English, he had already been awarded the Nobel Prize in Literature the year before. The Nobel Prize proved a useful antidote to self-doubt.

SUPREME CONFIDENCE AND ITS UNDESIRED EFFECTS

Indeed, in his two subsequent collections in English, Brodsky increasingly took to translating his verse on his own. In *To Urania*, three-quarters of the poems consisted of his self-translations and poems written directly in English; only one-fifth was translated in collaboration with somebody else, and just a handful by other translators. In his last collection, *So Forth* (1996), the numbers tilted even further toward Brodsky's complete control over the English destiny of his verse, with 90 percent consisting of Brodsky's self-translations and poems he composed directly in English.[47] The reality was that as Brodsky became increasingly proficient in English, he saw more clearly the limitations of translators. Since modern literary education does not include the mastery of formal verse composition in either England or in America, the availability of translators who could fully understand his Russian poems—their linguistic variety and density, their allusiveness both intellectually and in the popular culture of the Soviet period—and could render them in complex English-language verse was vanishing to nonexistent. Though Brodsky may have been unable to recognize that his own command of English was at times still inadequate, he was right that there was no one else who could do it. Besides, as Brodsky became increasingly prominent on the American literary scene, it became more difficult to picture senior poets, his peers, devoting their time to translating his verse; in the case of *A Part of Speech*, they had been eager to support a young, unknown, persecuted poet. Finally, with the passage of years, he no longer wanted to argue, even collegially, with poets he liked and respected. It seemed best, all around, to do the translation himself. With his achievement, however, came greater self-assurance. True, his English was evolving at a rapid pace, but some associates, such as Rubin, were becoming concerned that its quality might be lagging behind his ever-growing confidence.

Rubin remembered one particular episode that revealed the role of Brodsky's personality in the question of his English. Despite improvements, Brodsky still consulted his trusted friends and associates who were native speakers. Rubin recalled arguing with Brodsky on one such occasion about an unidiomatic usage in one of his prose pieces. Exasperated by Brodsky's intransigence, Rubin turned for support to Masha Vorobiova, Brodsky's translation associate, neighbor, and devoted friend, who also happened to be present: "Masha! Masha! You can't say this. You know that this is awful. This is unacceptable."[48] Masha, who had spoken English since her teenage years, replied with a little hesitation: "Well . . . maybe it's possible. . . ."[49] With that, Rubin realized the strength of Brodsky's power of suggestion: "Even the people, especially his friends whom he relied on for things like this . . . no longer could tell whether it was English or Brodsky-speak. It was becoming acceptable."[50] At the same time, Rubin admitted that through his idiosyncratic usage, Brodsky was coining his own idiolect in English:

> You know, it's a very fascinating phenomenon. . . . I was recently glancing . . . at Danny Weissbort's book. And even he, sort of, recognizes that *Joseph had an influence on the English language* [italics mine]. That's really, I think, one

> of the things that he'd be most proud of, that would mean the most to him. I don't know . . . if anyone ever mentioned this: another thing that meant a tremendous amount to him was when his essays were accepted in the annual collection *The Best American Essays* of the century. That was like a Nobel Prize. I mean he was just over the moon: "American essays!" Anyway, to some extent he was changing the language in the way he used it.[51]

Rubin acknowledged Brodsky's desire to leave a mark on the English language itself, and witnessed his joy when his English essays received a distinction that would have made a native speaker proud.[52] Yet Rubin, cautious by nature, was concerned that Brodsky might be crossing the line: "I kept in my head the idea that you had to be careful not to let him run roughshod over you and insist that this was OK that he was creating a new language. There is a boundary there. At least no . . . boundary that I could define, but that I felt."[53]

The complication extended to his poetry and was multiplied by the difficulty inherent in poetry translation. The translating modality for *To Urania* was initially the same as for *A Part of Speech*. The translators, the "hired hands," would receive their interlinears and toil on their drafts, which Brodsky would subsequently rework. Having taken such an active part in revamping the translations in *A Part of Speech*, supplying new rhymes and making other substantial changes, it was easy for Brodsky to forget that many of the lines he later reshuffled had been initially shaped by skilled native speakers of English, such as Robert Lowell. In fact, Weissbort was not the only one to lament the shadow of invisibility that Brodsky cast over his fellow translators in his desire to mold his poems in English to his will. Myers similarly observed:

> At first, I was content to have "with the author" attached to these versions. I see this appears at the end of "Christmas 1971" ["December 24, 1971"] though the thing is all mine except for the last line. I suppose this is why people think I actually worked with Joseph. But when the poem had been greatly changed, I felt disinclined to share the billing.[54]

Indeed, because of the ever-increasing number of eccentricities in Brodsky's revisions, some translators like Myers began to feel uneasy, as he says, about having their names attached: "It wasn't my non-existent fastidious ego a-squeaking . . . Eventually, . . . we agreed that I would furnish some sort of fairly sophisticated armature or *polufabrikat* [half-finished product] which Joseph could mold to his will."[55] This shift in the way of working accelerated Brodsky's forays into self-translation. By the end of the 1980s, he had essentially become his own principal translator. Yet, as Weissbort observed, it was not until *So Forth* (1996), his last and posthumously published collection in English, that "Brodsky was ready to come out of the closet . . . as his own translator."[56] During the preceding period, however, his growing confidence had meant that when he began molding even the semi-finished *polufabrikaty*, as Myers called them, to his will, he had begun taking greater risks, such as including more linguistically questionable material. As Myers pointed out:

> Joseph wanted to write like a master in English, rather than a novice under tutelage, but the exasperating obstacles of mimetic translation proved insuperable in too many cases. . . . One wonders if the pressures of his everyday existence caused him to underestimate the vast amount of time needed for the task he had set himself. This is not to deny the presence of dazzling lines, indeed whole passages in *So Forth* and elsewhere—episodes which give an additional thrill to readers when they encounter these diamonds among the unpolished gems and rough-hewn stone. The very awkwardness of these episodes focuses my mind on what Joseph is saying; they become, in a way, nodes of creative tension.[57]

It is fascinating that while pointing to the stylistic awkwardness of Brodsky's self-translations, Myers also defends this very lack of polish, maintaining that it helped focus attention "on what Joseph is saying." In his review of Brodsky's *To Urania*, Walcott argued along similar lines that the unpolished, rough bits in English somehow provided access to the essence of his poetry: "Brodsky wishes the book to be read as English verse, not as translated Russian. This has its difficulties, its knots, but one is grateful that the knots are there, that the rough nap of the lines is not smoothed over by the flatiron of an even English diction . . . The kind of translation that turns Doctor Zhivago into Omar Sharif."[58] But there is clearly a contradiction here; while opposing an Omar Sharif type of smoothness, Brodsky emphatically wished his book to read as English verse—which was impossible precisely because of the lack of smoothness.

"STUBBORNLY YOURS": THE REASONS BEHIND THE OBSTINACY

It seems that the real reason why Brodsky didn't want his translations to sound just like English poetry was that the originals themselves had a distinct quality. In other words, he wanted the "uncommon visage"[59] of his muse to be visible even in his English translations. As much was suggested by his then editor and future literary executor, Ann Kjellberg, when she defended him from the first attacks of his British detractors:

> If English must be bent and stretched a bit to accommodate the highly condensed and nuanced forms available to the writer in Russian—forms which

> are as intrinsic to his sensibility as his subject-matter or imagery—then, I feel, this is a development we should only applaud in a language that is in danger of falling asleep in the well-worn furniture of its rules.[60]

In a conversation with me, Kjellberg acknowledged that the vitality and texture Brodsky introduced to something that had seemed flat and simple in earlier translation versions sometimes took her breath away. So it seemed worth it to her to endure his solecisms. But hers was a special position. Those who were less involved with Brodsky showed less openness to the eccentricities of his English. The line between innovation and blunder was hard enough to define in prose, let alone poetry. The freshness and innovation risked being mistaken for grammatical or idiomatic ineptitude. Myers, for one, wished that Brodsky had allowed some skillful native speaker to review and fix his translations:

> The obduracy that was in his character would have engendered a certain pride and made any admission of failure out of the question. He could, after all, have got some American wordsmith/poet to go over these translations and at least iron out errors in idiom and word-usage. Whatever the reasons for his decision not to do so, the question recurs to me—why didn't his editors intervene?[61]

Assessing in retrospect the damage that had been posthumously inflicted upon Brodsky's English reputation from the merciless attacks of his British compatriots, Myers showed surprise that none of Brodsky's American editors or friends had intervened. The problem was that even when someone attempted to intervene, Brodsky often ignored their advice. Thus, one of the major American poets of his generation, the ever-sardonic Mark Strand, remarked to me with a chuckle that he and Brodsky would sometimes read freshly written poems to each other over the phone. While Brodsky would give Strand advice on *his* poems, he rarely listened to what Strand had to say in return about his.[62]

That Brodsky refused to listen to the advice of native speakers had to do with his personality, which operated in resistance mode. What others described as his stubbornness, Miłosz thought was one of the most admirable traits of Brodsky's poetic persona. In fact, Miłosz traced resemblances between Brodsky and Lev Shestov, the early twentieth-century Russian-Jewish philosopher exiled to France, describing both with the same set of adjectives—"haughty, scornful, austere."[63] Miłosz thought it fortunate that Brodsky was so obstinate because he believed that therein lay the source of his resistance and endurance: "For were he more pliable and polite he would not have been able to maintain the purity of his refusal."[64] Yet when it came to his translations, Brodsky's refusal was directed not at the totalitarian state or a hostile existential order, but at the advice of well-intentioned friends and associates.

Still, from Brodsky's vantage point, this obduracy was justified. In his translations, he aimed at re-creating the same bond between meaning and sound as existed in the originals. Although those harmonies were often based on unusual prosodic principles, his translations could not be easily "fixed" without breaking those harmonies, which were always a matter of aesthetic choice. Weissbort reached a similar conclusion: "Since his command of English grammar and idiom was not always what one would have wished, I wondered if it might not be possible discreetly to 'fix' his versions. I discovered that they couldn't be altered without seriously damaging the sound structure."[65] In trying to "correct" the translations, Weissbort realized that he would have to redo them, which would not have made sense, since Brodsky had already rejected and reworked Weissbort's translations in the past.

THE MARTIANS & CO. ON THE ATTACK

The backlash came from British poets who did not mince words and were not disposed to cut their displaced counterpart, with his linguistic quirks, any slack—especially after he had been awarded the Nobel Prize. The sight of an Eastern European intruder stealing the applause filled them with righteous indignation. Given Brodsky's interest in the inanimate and his penchant for seeking a cosmic perspective on terrestrial matters, it is ironic that the movement of poets seeking to inflict the greatest damage on him was dubbed the Martian School of Poetry. Its members included Christopher Reid and Craig Raine.

The title of Reid's 1988 review of *To Urania*, "Great American Disaster," appealed to a century-old British anti-American bias.[66] The implication was that the American critics and poets who had endorsed Brodsky lacked taste and refinement. Had Reid limited himself to singling out examples of Brodsky's unidiomatic English, his review might have passed for fair criticism. But this was obviously not his intention. As the title suggests, disaster was the only type of greatness Reid was willing to concede to Brodsky. In a magisterially patronizing manner, Reid schooled Brodsky as someone "who has yet to achieve his mastery in English" and mocked him as a schoolmaster: "The first thing he needs to acquire if he wants to make progress, is an ear."[67] Reid claimed that "tone-deafness afflicts both self-translations and original poems," citing the example of two light-verse, Audenesque poems, "A Martial Law Carol" and "The Berlin Wall Tune." Both, according to Reid, demonstrated that Brodsky's "musical aspirations were destined to be cruelly thwarted."[68] In fact, Brodsky had written the first poem upon learning of the imprisonment of his two Polish friends Wiktor Woroszylski (1927–1996) and Adrzej Drawicz (1932–1997), writers and Solidarity activists, following the imposition of martial law in Poland in December 1981.[69] "A Martial Law Carol" was then smuggled into their prison, where the poem's addressees were able to read it. As for the effectiveness of his English, it was measured in this case by its real-life impact: the poem succeeded in boosting his friends' morale. Here we have the opening stanza:

> One more Christmas ends
> soaking stripes and stars.
> All my Polish friends
> are behind steel bars,
> locked like zeros in
> some graph sheet of wrath:
> as a discipline
> slavery beats math.[70]

The poem assured them that people in the West would now learn of their plight, giving them the hope and strength to get through their ordeal. Venclova recalled, "Joseph used to state that this fact gave him more pleasure than the Nobel Prize."[71] Woroszylski and Drawicz surely did not care if the English was idiomatic or not. The poem's statements in Russian-inflected English perhaps rendered them even more powerful for his Polish friends.

What seemed to irk Reid even more than the inadequacies of Brodsky's English was that Brodsky was unlike him and his Martian colleagues in ways essential to Brodsky's very identity. Reid could not stand Brodsky's "portentously authoritative manner" or his belief that a poet is a "vessel of incontrovertible truths"; and he was irritated that Brodsky refused to "forget the exalted nature of his vocation."[72] Ironically, the qualities Reid found so loathsome were the same ones that his fellow Eastern European, Miłosz, cherished most in Brodsky.

In his much more favorable review of Brodsky's posthumous collections *So Forth* and *On Grief and Reason*, Michael Hofmann downplayed the viciousness of his colleagues' attacks, ascribing their hostility to their artistic differences: "For all his modesty and clutter, Brodsky isn't an empirical English type of poet. Perhaps that's why Christopher Reid and, following him, Craig Raine, didn't get on with him."[73] There might be even more at play here, however, than aesthetic differences. British identity, in contrast to American, does not assume the immigrant as part of its essential makeup. Brodsky may have realized, if only unconsciously, that America would be more welcoming to a poet from Eastern Europe and more open to his voice.

He may have sensed that in America, he would not encounter the snobbery exemplified in the Reid-Raine critique. After all, this was the same crowd who thought America had ruined Auden. But not only did Reid speak condescendingly of Brodsky, infantilizing him and belittling his talent, he also deployed tactics, later taken up by Raine, to undermine Brodsky's work that hinted at the sort of antisemitism that Philip Roth, for example, identified as lurking in the British literary elite of the day.[74] In the years since, anglophone writers of differing ethnicities, usually colonial subjects, have struggled to be accepted as fully English, and there has been more open condemnation of the provincialism that marked the Martians and like-minded figures. Indeed, it took someone with Walcott's colonial experience of British class snobbery to be sensitive to the barriers erected around "Englishness" as well as to the antisemitic undertones in the British attacks against Brodsky.[75]

Two weeks after the appearance of Reid's review, Donald Davie, another British poet, who, unlike Reid, knew some Russian, doubled down on the attacks. The title of his piece in the *Times Literary Supplement* seemed at least outwardly more subtle: "The Saturated Line."[76] The insinuation here was that Brodsky packed his poems with too many metaphors and tropes, which, although they might have worked in Russian, did not let the poems "breathe" in English. Davie's conclusion, however, was not very different from the main thrust of Reid's piece: "History supplies hardly one instance of a poet writing to any purpose in anything but his native tongue."[77]

The globalized, multilingual reality of the last three decades, which has given rise to translingual literary studies, among other things, challenges such nativist axioms.[78] Furthermore, there is an uncanny parallel between Davie's deterministic statement that "history supplies hardly one instance of a poet" writing purposefully in a language not his mother tongue and the similarly reductive reasoning of the Soviet judge, Savelieva, who—years earlier—had sentenced Brodsky to five years of Arctic labor on the grounds that "history supplies hardly one instance of a poet" not belonging to the state-sanctioned Union of Soviet Writers. Indeed, Brodsky would tell his friends that the Soviet and the British critiques were the same: he did not respect the language and tradition, he forced it in new directions, he was an upstart. The only difference, it seems, was in the real motivation behind the hostility directed at him in each case. While the fear of creative independence outweighed even that of direct political opposition in totalitarian regimes, which explains Savelieva's guilty verdict, Davie's real grudge against Brodsky lurked in his final remarks: "The award of the Nobel Prize in 1987, when he was no more than forty-seven years old, may reasonably be thought not only premature but unkind."[79]

Brodsky, who had seen far worse written about him in the Soviet press, was now in a much better position to deal with such vitriol. He was basking in the ultimate acceptance that came with the Nobel Prize; his friends Walcott and Heaney reviewed *To Urania* in prestigious venues, showing a much more sympathetic attitude toward his idiosyncratic English. Still, Reid's and Davie's reviews might have bruised his ego, as most bilingual writers occasionally experience insecurities vis-à-vis their "new language of writing."[80] This was especially the case for Brodsky, given that he had an accent in English, as mentioned earlier. He also understood on some level that British English was more traditional and continuous with poetic heritage, and he believed that it was more prestigious. In fact, as Myers recalled: "Despite an ironclad certainty when it came to his gifts, including his confidence in his own translations, Joseph could nevertheless evince an odd insecurity at times. On one occasion, he was to address the British Academy in London, and confessed that he was in a panic about it."[81]

Thus, while Kjellberg responded to Reid's piece with a concise and dignified letter to the editors, pointing out the laughable nature of his reductive approach to poetry,[82] Brodsky drafted a rebuttal to Davie mimicking the venomous style of his British opponents: "I genuinely regret Mr. Davie's finding my poems 'oversaturated.' Next time around I'll try to water them down to his liking—to the consistency of tea."[83] In the end, he wisely opted to let it go at that. At least while he was alive, the damage to his reputation from those attacks remained negligible.

POET LAUREATE VERSUS PRESIDENT-ELECT

It was not just the Nobel Prize that helped Brodsky put such trifles in perspective. Clio, the muse of history, had her own astonishing surprises in store. Brodsky's arch-nemesis, the Soviet empire, the ogre from Auden's poem "August 1968," was about to expire.[84] By 1989, collections of Brodsky's poems had begun to appear in Russia for the first time. In a matter of months, he was signing contracts to publish his entire oeuvre in Russia, which was the beginning of his poetry's triumphant return to his country of origin. His Russian friends and relatives, whom he had not seen for almost two decades, started arriving in America on visits. Russian television crews camped on his doorstep, vying for interviews to be broadcast on Russia's central channels. Brodsky was living up to one of the cardinal myths linked to his given name—the biblical Joseph sold by his brothers to Egypt but ultimately embraced by them in his adopted home. Unlike his biblical prototype, Brodsky had not been sold into slavery but thrown out of his homeland, as it were, and into freedom. Yet his Russian brethren, too, had to seek him out now in the land of his exile, where he had achieved great success against all expectations. The poetic justice he had prophesized in "December in Florence" was delivered during his lifetime, although no one could have predicted it would happen so soon. His triumph was made possible exclusively because of what he had achieved in his adoptive country, and there was still more to come.

In 1991, the Librarian of Congress appointed him America's poet laureate. Mark Strand, who had served in the same position the year before, remembered that Brodsky was initially quite nervous about this nomination.[85] Having become an American citizen in 1977, Brodsky was the first poet with an accent in English to be appointed US Poet Laureate, and perhaps he dreaded an uproar similar to the one created by his British reviewers. Nevertheless, Brodsky accepted the role in the spirit of a civil servant, hoping to repay the country toward which he felt an immense gratitude. At the same time, learning so soon after the collapse of the USSR that he had been appointed poet laureate of the United States—the erstwhile USSR's archrival—must have felt like poetic justice for the cruelty inflicted on him and his parents by the Soviet state.[86] In his new capacity, Brodsky advocated for a federally subsidized program that would distribute millions of inexpensive paperback anthologies of American poetry to supermarkets and hotel rooms. He strongly believed in language's ability to liberate the mind and, by extension, poetry's power to improve the spiritual climate of a nation. In the end, his ideas did not gain much traction.[87]

At the beginning of his tenure, Brodsky, along with twenty other distinguished American poets, was solicited by the *Washington Post* to write a poem commemorating the inauguration of President-elect Bill Clinton. His poem, titled simply "To the President-Elect," appeared in December 1990 in a magazine feature honoring the inauguration. Brodsky rose to the occasion, silencing his doubters, although his poem differed substantially both in tone and structure from the numerous other poems published in the same issue by his American counterparts.[88] In this poem, Brodsky followed the "hum" of the iambic tetrameters of Robert Frost's poem "Provide, Provide." It is fascinating to see how he manages to repurpose not only the meter of Frost's poem but also its tone to suit the needs of a very different occasion. Frost's "Provide, Provide" is above all a reflection on a fall from grace, not through any notorious vagaries of fate but rather through such predictable human developments as old age, mismanagement, and physical decay:

> The witch that came (the withered hag)
> To wash the steps with pail and rag,
> Was once the beauty Abishag,
>
> The picture pride of Hollywood.
> Too many fall from great and good
> For you to doubt the likelihood.[89]

Differently from its Horatian models, which treated Fortune's whims as a calamity to which one should stoically submit, Frost advocates making practical provisions ahead of what he interprets as the natural course of events. The penultimate stanza of the poem contains, as mentioned, Brodsky's favorite aphorism: "No memory of having starred / Atones for later disregard, / Or keeps the end from being hard."[90] This seems to be a modification of a famous aphorism uttered by Francesca da Rimini in Canto V of Dante's *Inferno*: "There is no greater pain than to recall the happy time in misery."[91] Brodsky takes up the topic of a fall from grace but reverses the order, opening his poem instead with a depiction of the moment of utmost glory and personal achievement in the life of his protagonist:

> You've climbed the mountain. At its top,
> the climbing and the mountain stop.
> A peak is where the climber finds
> his biggest step is not mankind's.[92]

The slightly awkward last line of the stanza alludes to Neil Armstrong's quip upon landing on the moon. By insinuating that the addressee's personal success was not a big step for humanity, Brodsky shows an unprecedented irreverence toward the holder of political power, especially in an inaugural poem. It reflects the tension between poetry and politics so characteristic of his own life, but also points to the traditional Russian rivalry between tsar and poet—the former dominating his subjects' lives and the latter vying for their hearts and minds. Curiously, Brodsky projects this Pushkinian rivalry embedded in Russian history onto a most unlikely figure—a democratically elected American president:

> Proud of your stamina and craft
> you stand there being photographed
> transfixed between nowhere-to-go
> And us who give you vertigo.[93]

If there is one thing that earns the president the poet's respect, it is the "stamina and craft" they hold in common. However, in keeping with his general contempt for any type of political power as well as his belief in literature's superiority over politics,[94] Brodsky shows that, between the two of them, it is the poet who can predict the future, the poet who knows that the only way from the top is downhill. With a morbid glee, in the spirit of Hardy's famous motto—"if way to the Better there be, it exacts a full look at the Worst"[95]—the poet foretells the president's looming decline:

Well, strike your tent and have your lunch
before you stir an avalanche
of brand new taxes whose each cent
will mark the speed of your descent.[96]

The last stanza is noteworthy as Brodsky blends here the meter and flow of the iambic tetrameters of Frost's poem with his own technique of long-woven, prose-like stanzaic constructions, which he had learned as a young poet from John Donne. Thus, grammatically, the stanza consists of a single sentence, which leads to a maximum number (three) of enjambments in this stanza. Still, rhythmically, its flow is impeccable. If anything, Brodsky's poems show, as demonstrated here, that his ear in English was remarkable, confirming the hypothesis put to Miłosz by the American poet Kenneth Rexroth: "Anyone who has an ear for one language will have an ear for them all."[97] At the same time, the contrast between Brodsky's "To the President-Elect" inspired by Frost's "Provide, Provide" and Frost's own inaugural poem, "For John F. Kennedy His Inauguration,"[98] written in an almost Elizabethan style, could not be greater. This indicates that in his irreverence toward authority, the American poet laureate Joseph Brodsky remained essentially Russian. The contrast between Frost's poem and Brodsky's might also reflect the differences, as understood by Brodsky, between the two presidents-elect. At the same time, Brodsky apparently had not set out to write a poem that was nearly as serious as Frost's. He wrote it quickly and with a touch of humor.

Chapter Ten

The Critical Assessment

FROM THE PERSPECTIVE of most native English speakers, many of the liberties Brodsky took in English were unacceptable. It did not take a clique of ill-disposed British poets, with proprietary feelings about the English language and bitterness about an outsider's success, to suggest that Brodsky's poems in English were deficient. Even Richard Wilbur, who sympathized with Brodsky's plight and respected him as a poet, was not, finally, prepared to advocate for Brodsky's English. "I think Joseph was wonderful in his command of English, but I don't think he was a good poet in that language"[1] was the only comment I could obtain during a brief exchange with him after a poetry reading. Wilbur's position precluded further discussion. Or should one avoid taking an irritable remark at a poetry reading as the poet's last word? Perhaps Wilbur was simply tired of constant questions about Brodsky, who had garnered, during his lifetime, a level of recognition well beyond what most poets achieve.

GLASS HALF FULL

Yet there were other native speakers, certainly less authoritative than Wilbur, who were prepared to allow room for "Brodsky-speak" in English, providing him when he was alive with the affirmation he craved. Thus, Mary Mortimer-Maddox, the ex-wife of Scottish poet Alastair Reid, wrote a letter in which she praised Brodsky's self-translation of an elegy that had just appeared in the October 1993 issue of the *Times Literary Supplement*.[2] The letter provides an interesting insight into the phenomenon:

> Dear Joseph,
>
> I was sent your poem "Elegy" from the *TLS* and I wanted to comment on it. It is gutsy. Both in the subject matter and in the translation (no matter that I don't know Russian). I think that *you have allowed a new genre to come into being, it will be by the sheer force of your talent and your personality* [italics

> mine]. There is no way anyone can say that this poem reads like an English-language poem, and yet it is far better than most of the translations which have been done of your poems from the Russian. It is in a sense a heresy, for is there anything more sacred than the language itself in a poem? . . . And you have changed / or challenged . . . that . . . intrinsic truth.[3]

Mortimer-Maddox's letter seems to confirm Rubin's contention about the role of personality permeating the phenomenon of the anglophone Brodsky. After all, he had by then published his essays on Tsvetaeva and Mandelstam, as well as on Auden, Frost, and Hardy, in which he described his unique perspective on how prosody worked in the poems of his great Russian and English language predecessors. His essays provide invaluable insights into the motivation behind the visible results of the creative process. Admirers of his talent and expertise in poetic craft were eager to excuse the imperfections of his own English poems and translations.

An account by Melissa Green as a young and promising poet, and disciple of Walcott, reveals that she went through her own internal struggle between an urge to gratify Brodsky's enthusiasm for inventiveness in his second language and an awareness of the shortcomings of some of his English-language work:

> Sometimes he was so pleased with the inventiveness of his own rhymes that he would call to share them with me . . . Joseph . . . called at an ungodly hour to read an English language poem he'd just written. "Listen, listen," he'd say before reading me the poem, afterwards chuckling, "Good, good, pretty good stuff, yeah?" He took great delight in English idioms, and at moments I would gulp in distress and find myself meekly observing that the idiom he liked so much, which sounded so new and rich to his Russian ear was the equivalent of, say, a child's nursery rhyme, and in his poem sounded ridiculous. But if he didn't always catch the silliness of an expression as it sounded to a native speaker, he could tease out what was beautiful and original in a cliché.[4]

Green pinpoints the problem that occasionally arose in Brodsky's poetry composed directly in English. She identifies Brodsky's failure to recognize that phrases which sounded new and rich to his Russian ear came across very differently to a poet whose native language was English. There was indeed something endearingly childlike in his yearning for recognition from those around him, especially since he had already achieved a lot of recognition. This complicates Proffer Teasley's suggestion that the reason "his translations were not seriously criticized until after his death" was that he was both "influential and vengeful."[5] It seems, instead, that the "sheer force of his personality,"[6] as Mortimer-Maddox put it, coupled with his ambition to impress those around him, mesmerized many of his contemporaries, winning them over so thoroughly that they were willing to oblige him—and not because he had browbeaten them. And it was not only his essays in English that impressed them. As Melissa Green further attested, his "incantatory recitations" in Russian made similarly lasting impressions on his audiences who did not know Russian:

> The day I met Joseph Brodsky, he was reading at BU. I wasn't prepared for it. None of us were. Standing before a large window overlooking the Charles River, he rocked back and forth like a pendulum, his incantatory recitation in Russian calling to mind the chant of a cantor in medieval Constantinople. His poems tolled as from a great bronze bell, and we were inside the bell, his voice the hammer that made the heavy bronze boom. The air echoed as we sat stunned. I watched people thronging to Brodsky's side and saw how he snapped the filter from his cigarette and then lit it, looking out at the Charles.[7]

For Brodsky, it must have all been déjà vu. Back home his detractors had been legion. Indeed, those who disapproved did not always belong to Soviet officialdom. But the official rejection was overwhelming. Thus, when in 1969 the London Poetry International sent him an invitation to participate in the festival, the reply from the Union of Soviet Writers, the docile voice of Soviet policy, was rather brief: there is no such poet called Brodsky—only an ex-convict by that name. At the same time, his hometown brimmed with young admirers who lionized him. In a way, the situation repeated itself in the United States; native speakers took his side and defended his right to shape his English poems as he wished. They replaced his admirers in Russia who had celebrated him as their poet, official or not. In America, as in Russia, he captivated his audiences with charismatic performances and garnered widespread admiration, despite the presence of those, often adopting the position of "authority," who disapproved of his poetry. This neatly fit his conception of a continuity between his Russian and American incarnations.

Thus, David Samoilov (1920–1990), a poet from an older generation and by no means a Brodsky fan, who found the style of his entire poetic group too irreverent and provocative for his taste, remembered a Brodsky recital back in Russia: "Brodsky reads poorly by any standard—brokenly, mispronouncing 'r's,' adding a nasal twang, running the lines together, shaking his head—and yet he does this with such conviction that it comes out superbly and stays forever in your memory."[8] Curiously, Samoilov, a Jewish poet himself, disparaged Brodsky's accent, his famous Jewish "r," while grudgingly acknowledging the effectiveness of his recitals. Despite the idiosyncrasies of his diction and complete disregard for all the reigning Soviet canons of poetic performance, Brodsky was able to dominate and mesmerize his audiences. Miłosz believed there was something shaman-like about Brodsky's poetic gift.[9] Perhaps Brodsky assumed that since he had persuaded his Russian audiences to accept his Jewish "r," his American audiences would similarly acquiesce to his Russian accent in English. But while his poetic performances in Russian captivated Americans, the magic often vanished when, in his later period, he recited his English translations. For example, during a reading in 1994 at Queens College, someone from the audience asked him why the originals and the translations did not sound the same, and whether this difference was due to special qualities of the Russian language. Brodsky replied:

> No, I think it has to do with my abilities as a reader of English. I am not that good. Actually, on paper you may find the qualities for which you praise the Russian, you may find them in English as well. I am just simply a lousy reader [in English]. It interferes. I can read somebody else's poems rather well in English, but myself is difficult.[10]

When the thrill was gone, he used persuasion.

THE CLOWNS DEMOLISH THE CIRCUS

Brodsky's personal high point, his peak of "nowhere-to-go-from-here," overlapped with the end of the Soviet Union. This gave him an opportunity to reflect on the death of the Soviet Union and the coming end of the century and millennium, which both intrigued and titillated him, especially because he feared he might not live long enough to watch the story play out.[11] He also felt measured enthusiasm about the new developments in Russia; the victory had come a little too late and was bittersweet. While visiting Ann Arbor, Michigan, in October 1992, Brodsky commented on the dissolution of the Soviet Union: "It's a positive thing. Both positive, negative, neutral, idiotic, pleasant, hopeful and full of dejection."[12] For one thing, "those who have loved me more than themselves are no / longer alive"[13]—namely his mother and father, who could neither share in the triumph of the Nobel Prize nor reunite with their son, having passed away in 1983 and 1984, respectively.

Brodsky wrote a short poem titled "MCMXCV," the year in Roman numerals. The year 1995 turned out to be his last full calendar year; he lived only twenty-eight days into 1996. Brodsky wrote the poem in Russian and translated it himself into English. By now the translations did not lag much behind the originals:

> The clowns are demolishing the circus. The elephants have run off to India;
> tigers sell, on the sidewalk, their stripes and hoops,
> under the leaky cupola, there is hanging, off the trapeze,

as in a wardrobe, the limp tuxedo
of a disillusioned magician . . .[14]

"MCMXCV" can be read as an epitaph on the Soviet empire. The "circus" has collapsed, and it is the clowns who have remained in charge. There is a sense that the old Soviet apparat (whoever used to run "the circus") at least had the power to terrify, but now no one is left but the clowns. By the same token, the "limp tuxedo / of a disillusioned magician" suggests that the old, discredited slogans of communist ideology, though still on display, now fail to impress: it is "hanging, off the trapeze." Similarly, the image of tigers selling their stripes and hoops on the sidewalk evokes images of the former empire's impoverished subjects desperately selling off the remainder of the empire's spoils on sidewalks from Moscow to Berlin.

But "MCMXCV" can also be read as an epitaph on the twentieth century, or even on the civilization of the past millennium, as well as on the poet's own disintegrating body. Its English version, in particular, allows one to trace an intertextual connection with Yeats's poem "The Circus Animals' Desertion," which describes with a similar clinical detachment, and not without a certain masochistic glee, the disintegration of the aging poet's poetic laboratory:

Winter and summer till old age began
My circus animals were all on show,
Those stilted boys, that burnished chariot,
Lion and woman and the Lord knows what.
. . .
Now that my ladder's gone
I must lie down where all the ladders start
In the foul rag and bone shop of the heart.[15]

While Yeats's poem was written in ottava rima, Brodsky chose free verse as the form for his poem. Presumably, structureless vers libre better corresponded to the subject matter of the poem, featuring a general dismantling. Curiously, in the absence of rhymes, Brodsky introduced a different type of alternative parallelism, with the repetition midpoem of the opening image of clowns demolishing the circus:

. . . In the arena,
knee-deep in sawdust, *clowns*, wildly wielding
sledgehammers, *demolish the circus* [italics mine].[16]

On the whole, it seems that the greater presence of free verse, or less-structured metrical forms, in Brodsky's later poems contributed to more fluidity in translation. At that time, when Brodsky was really struggling to master the English medium, his Russian poetics become more complex.[17] As a result, the English and the Russian seem to merge more.

The first part of Auden's elegy "In Memory of W. B. Yeats," which Brodsky had discovered years earlier during his Arctic exile, was also composed in free verse. Auden used images of an Irish landscape as an extended metaphor for various body parts of a dying poet, also an allusion to Yeats's "The Circus Animals' Desertion":

> The provinces of his body revolted,
> The squares of his mind were empty,
> Silence invaded the suburbs,
> The current of his feelings failed . . .

In "MCMXCV," Brodsky extended his dialogue with both of these poets, showing once again faithfulness to the favorite Auden poem of his youth. Even when he wrote a poem in free verse, it was never an escape from tradition but a continuation of a poetic dialogue with his predecessors.

THE POET'S PURGATORY

Among his friends, Miłosz was most surprised by the hostile reactions to Brodsky after his death. Miłosz believed that they were led by those who thought Brodsky's fame was blown up for political reasons during the Cold War. Being a poet, Miłosz came up with a nobler image to describe the phenomenon: "It seems to me every poet after death goes through a purgatory . . ."[18]

The attack from the Martian poet Craig Raine proved to be especially devastating to Brodsky's reputation. Raine's review of Brodsky's last prose and poetry collections appeared just months after the latter's premature death from a heart attack. It was inauspiciously titled "A Reputation Subject to Inflation." The wounds were fresh: Brodsky's family, friends, and admirers were still in mourning when Raine set out to do exactly what his title promised—to deflate the reputation of the dead poet, who was now unable to respond. The review's subtitle, "The Nobel Prize–Winning Poet Joseph Brodsky Excelled Only in Mediocrity,"[19] clarified Raine's intentions from the start. He wanted to demolish not only Brodsky's English-language reputation but all of his work. If anything, Raine's piece showed that Brodsky had been right in rejecting the Nabokov comparisons: "Far from being the equal or rival of Nabokov, Brodsky was unable to achieve more than a basic competence in his adopted language."[20] This was an absurd comparison. As Elizabeth Beaujour had pointed out, Nabokov "spoke English with the same ease as Russian since infancy" because "bilingualism was an intrinsic part of the quintessentially Russian aristocratic childhood."[21] Pushkin too was perfectly bilingual, composing his first poems in French. Tsvetaeva and Nabokov were, in fact, trilingual, which was not unusual in their milieu. Brodsky, on the other hand, was born in Stalinist Russia and had to work against historic forces that rendered the mere idea of his transformation into an English-language poet utterly inconceivable. So, to have applied unattainable standards from a different epoch to him was misleading, to say the least. Raine's main grudge, like Davie's, was against Brodsky's immense success, which he sought to diminish by calling it "shrewd career management."[22] When Raine compares Brodsky to Merdle, the fraudulent financier from Dickens's novel *Little Dorrit*, a character embedded in antisemitic tropes, it raises once again the specter of prejudice. Thus, as pointed out by a scholar of Victorian literature: "Merdle combines the ostensible vulgarity of the Jew—too interested in his own business, not detached enough in his manner—with the Jew's purported predilection for gambling, chicanery, and, most importantly, speculation, the form of financial enterprise most powerfully associated with Jews in antisemitic discourse."[23] For Raine, even calling Brodsky a "charlatan" and a fraud felt too generous. Thus, Raine concluded that Brodsky was "*a world-class mediocrity*—bluffing but uncertain of his feel for the English language on which his international reputation was so precariously founded [italics mine]."[24] Astonishingly, in his own book of essays published some years later, Raine repeated the same abuse, apparently trying to boost his career and claim to fame around his role as the dead poet's baiter.[25]

The question as to why this hostility toward the English-language Brodsky struck such a chord so broadly is more intriguing than it might at first seem. For it is beyond any doubt that Brodsky's English-language poetry has not been well received in English-speaking literary and academic circles, even among those who championed him during his lifetime.[26] To begin with, there was truth in the purely objective criticism of his English. Neither his essays nor his self-translations are written in "plain American, which dogs and cats can read,"[27] as Walcott put it. Those who had previously cringed at the latest Brodsky poem or self-translation in a prestigious publication might have felt vindicated at last. No one had explained to them why they should read a poet with an accent. Or, if someone had tried, like Kjellberg in her rebuttal of Reid, their voice could now be easily ignored. Similarly, it no longer rang true to them when Hofmann argued that a major Russian poet embracing the English poetic tradition was a unique case, and that Brodsky had "made himself an anarchic gift to his adopted language."[28] Hofmann's arguments about the insuperable challenges of rhymed and metered translation from the Russian of such a complex poet as Brodsky did not work either; nor did his claim that "it is only by some miracle that this writing exists in

English at all."[29] Miłosz himself expressed serious doubts that Brodsky or Mandelstam could be translated into English.[30] But Brodsky's own dogged insistence on the possibility of translation ultimately worked against these arguments. The tide had turned against him. And it was not just a matter of Raine, the sinister clown from his poem, who drove the meanest nail into Brodsky's coffin. Nor is it the fate of every poet to suffer a posthumous purgatory.[31]

Conclusion

THE REASON neither the clashing opinions on Brodsky's English translations nor the more sophisticated arguments from translation studies have been able, so far, to explain the phenomenon of Brodsky in English is that the issue has never been solely a question of Russian-English poetry translation. What was really at stake was the translation—or transplantation—of the poet himself.

Poetry for Brodsky was a dialogue with his predecessors. But to guarantee his self-respect as a poet in a new country, he also needed to win over his contemporaries. His reputation preceded him: persecution at home, exile, endorsements from Akhmatova and then Auden. But to rely on that alone would have been too easy. He wanted to work for his survival as a poet in exile, to earn and shape his reputation himself in the new linguistic milieu.

This involved summoning his ability to captivate audiences with his skillful melodic recitations. It involved drawing the attention of his peers to his extraordinary command of his adoptive language. It involved showcasing his knowledge of the secrets of poetic craft. And since for Brodsky the poet was only a mouthpiece of language, it also involved becoming a vehicle of the poetic truths hidden therein. Ultimately, it involved demonstrating his ability to coin this language. It was this—and not just an accurate or faithful translation of his poems—that Brodsky needed in order to feel truly at home in his adoptive country.

To gain the respect and admiration of his peers, Brodsky also sought to translate his very identity as a poet, which went well beyond the questions of poetry translation. Feeling at home in America meant calling a fellow poet in the middle of the night to recite a freshly composed work in their shared language, in the hope of impressing them with a recent invention, be it a self-translation or a line written directly in English. This was his true ambition, and he was quite successful in fulfilling it. The achievement was especially impressive since English was the language he chose, learned, and cultivated as an adult, working against the grain of cultural disinheritance. Whatever could not be achieved through a command of his adoptive language was compensated for by the sheer force of his personality, his powers of persuasion, and his charm. His actual English translations, essays, and "occasionally a poem"[1] could thus be regarded almost as a bonus, a byproduct of the larger self-translation of Iosif Brodskii from Leningrad into Joseph Brodsky, poet laureate of the United States.

Bilingual readers and scholars are an ideal audience for his self-translations. Like Nabokov's version of *Eugene Onegin*, the self-translations represent another valiant attempt to square the circle of Russian-English poetry translation; ultimately, they also provide an infinite trove for bilingual observation and comparative study, even though this was clearly not part of Brodsky's original intention. As to his poems written directly in English, they exhibit a uniquely Russian "anxiety to be influenced," a desire to establish a connection with a foreign model through imitation and pastiche. When the physical, living person was gone, much of his English verse, and to a degree his self-translations, lost their raison d'être. Brodsky had perhaps anticipated this himself. No wonder he was not interested in translating his English poems into Russian. It is as if his American reputation had to be consistently nourished by his strong presence and continual effort to demonstrate what he could accomplish in English. After all, the authoritative role of a poet was his own import into American culture. With his departure, life could go back to normal. Many must have felt a respite from his moral imperatives. The Cold War was over, and American poets could again resume their marginal role in society.

Exile was Brodsky's central myth but also a lived reality. He experienced it twice and each time had to reconquer his fear. At twenty-four, he thought he might be prevented from realizing his potential, as had Mandelstam and Vvedensky of the previous generation.[2] At thirty-two, having reached the zenith of his poetic powers, he feared that the fountain might dry up when he was separated from its magic source, the Russian language spoken on streetcars and in grocery stores; he feared his muse would become mute. In each case he embraced his condition. It helped that he had longed for English all his life, as Nadezhda Mandelstam put it, and that his destiny in English had begun to preoccupy him even in Leningrad.

In America, Brodsky launched himself into teaching without any previous experience—and was scared. How could he, with his broken English, teach Americans their own literature? He soon realized that, even in his imperfect English, he could speak to poetry's lived purpose, explaining the subject matter better than many of his colleagues. In the Soviet Union reading literature, especially British and American works, had been a matter of resistance to totalitarianism. There, it equaled freedom. But it could never acquire such an existential value for his new colleagues in America. The same applied to his translations. At first, Brodsky considered only their literal accuracy; but then he felt that the music had to be restored too, and more effectively than the commissioned translators seemed able to deliver. After all, he was the author, and the translations had to please him before they could please anyone else.

In his "Lullaby of Cape Cod," Brodsky compared himself in the aftermath of his forced emigration to the United States to a fish stepping on dry land with no choice but to learn to walk: "Yet just because shoes exist and the foot is shod / some surface will always be there, some place to stand, / a portion of dry land."[3] The word "stifling" appears in the poem more than a dozen times. But the fish prevails; it "struggles against suffocation" and, against all odds, stays alive out of water. It would be unfair to expect the fish to climb trees. In Russia, poetry was the antidote to suffocation, and there was a strong element of continuity in Brodsky's endeavor. Music, meter, and rhyme were central to his experience of poetry, and he left no doubt in his address to future translators as to how he wished to be rendered into other languages. He was undeniably doctrinaire in his convictions; but in contrast to his detractors, he was devoted to a higher cause. He believed that independence and liberation, no less than enslavement, occurred through language and poetry. Literature could provide, if not a guarantee, at least a vaccine against unfreedom. He had lived through some of the great traumas of the twentieth century and witnessed the subjugation of an entire nation through the language of ideology. He cared for the cause of intellectual and spiritual freedom and hoped that his poetry might play a part in the liberation of the mind: hence, his Nobel lecture and his "immodest proposal," in a nod to Jonathan Swift, that poetry be distributed to hotel rooms.[4] The preservation of poetic meter and rhyme was part of building a bulwark against the disintegration of civilization, of poetic tradition, and of historic and artistic memory. Brodsky was an autodidact who had learned from his masters as well as from books. Memory was Akhmatova's main tool of political resistance. The memory of people whose lives had been canceled by the ruthless state machine, as well as of lines of censored poetry, helped her preserve her artistic and human dignity. Brodsky's ambition was similarly not for himself but for language, whose servant he regarded himself to be. His translators were the unsung victims of his doctrinaire attitudes, but many of them understood his grand vision and accepted his right to be difficult. He had earned it. And he succeeded where no other poet or translator had; he translated Brodsky-as-poet, in his entirety, with all his quirks, attitudes, and the accent, into another language and culture.

Brodsky's long and winding road of becoming an English-language author had begun in a Leningrad classroom, with a huge portrait of Joseph Stalin looming over the blackboard, where a Jewish boy failed to learn English from a Jewish woman. What followed were decades of passionate, independent study of English, which entailed the absorption, imitation, and translation of English-language poetic models into Russian and, later, of his own poems into English. His transplantation, which he interpreted as a continuation of space where English became merely a continuation of Russian by other poetic means, resulted in the unique process of translating his poetry into English, as well as in occasional poems and essays written directly in his second language. In the end, by applying his charisma, genius, and persuasion, he became by hook or by crook a part of speech in English as well as in Russian: "What gets left of a man amounts / to a part. To his spoken part. / To a part of speech."[5]

Appendix A

An Interview with Barry Rubin, New York City, February 2007

Barry Rubin was professor of Russian from the 1960s to the 1990s at Queens College CUNY, where Masha Vorobiova was a colleague for a period of time. Both were fluent in English and Russian and were friends and associates of Joseph Brodsky. This interview was conducted in English.

ZAKHAR ISHOV: When did you first meet Brodsky?

BARRY RUBIN: When he emigrated in June 1972, came to Vienna, and spent some time with Auden. And then Carl Proffer, who was at the University of Michigan, got him a job there. I was at Queens College of the City University of New York, which has five senior colleges in the university combined. We offered him a visiting lectureship for a semester. We were doing very well, and our department was prominent at the time, with about nine full-time faculty, which in Russian was very large for this country—and we didn't even have a graduate program. But we had probably several hundred students, which was a lot at that time [the early 1970s]. This was before the so-called *tret'ia volna* [the third wave of Russian emigration], which came in the late 1970s. So we offered Brodsky a semester teaching at Queens, which he accepted. I don't know what the arrangement was at Michigan or how long he had planned to stay there. But he was anxious just to see the country, and he wanted to be in New York.

ZI: Moving on to translations: how did you get involved in those?

BR: I guess I should preface my remarks. I lived in New York for twenty-five years or so—most of the period that Brodsky lived there too—and had been living there for some years when he came. So I saw a lot of him in New York, hundreds of times, under many circumstances, parties, working together, and so forth. It was very easy, just a matter of getting on the subway. And then in 1989, I moved to Pennsylvania, where I am now, and it made it much more difficult. Our contacts became infrequent. We spoke on the phone, but it was not the same. So I saw much less of him. By this time, he was already doing his own translations—of his poems mainly. He was writing essays—those exclusively in English. When he first came, his English essays were very rough.

ZI: Were you aware of Brodsky's translation collaboration with George Kline?

BR: There is something very sad in the relationship between him and Joseph. There was no one more devoted to Joseph, his success, and his work, even personally. And Kline was extremely important. He came up with *Selected Poems* at the moment when it needed to exist.

ZI: Not to mention the Auden foreword he had procured.

BR: Well, there would not have been something to write a foreword to had he not done those translations. And I think the book had not come out yet, when he came to Queens.

ZI: It was published in December 1973.

BR: We used a version of it for his readings when he came to Queens. We used those translations even before they were published. George gave us permission to use them publicly. I did a lot of readings of the English versions at that time. Brodsky was doing readings all over the place. I remember that he was invited once to do a reading in Plattsburgh, New York, which has a branch of the State University of New York (SUNY). Somebody on the faculty there was a close friend of Masha Vorobiova. I am sure you have heard of her.

ZI: Yes, most certainly. But to return to Kline for a second. Why did you think the whole situation was sad?

BR: Joseph was very loyal but not as loyal as George. Joseph was extremely loyal to many friends. But the complication here was his sense of his poetry. He was torn between his personal loyalty [to George Kline] and his loyalty to his poems, his loyalty to the language. And he equated his poems with the language. He was always talking about how language spoke to him and how important language was for the evolution of mankind. Language was speaking through him; Russian was coming out through him. So he was faced with a dilemma: how can you be loyal to someone if you think it will be detrimental to your poetry, to its truth. . . . And sometimes he just had to go the other way and say: "Can't do it." What disturbed me sometimes was that Joseph was a bit careless about how he handled those things. I didn't object to his principles but to the way he carried them out.

ZI: In one of the letters from Nancy Meiselas, she refers to George trying to "peddle" translations of "Cape Cod Lullaby" and "December in Florence," showing little respect for George.

BR: Oh, that's bad. But you have to understand that Nancy was reflecting what she picked up from Joseph. She started with an open mind but then absorbed those vibrations from Joseph. Whatever George was doing, the result was that they were trying to squeeze him out.

ZI: Then there was that episode between Hecht and Kline, an altercation about who was going to translate "Lullaby of Cape Cod."

BR: There was a lot of unnecessary stuff. None of that had to happen. Instead of saying upfront, "George, don't do it," Joseph would give that work to somebody else. George was very devoted to him and Joseph wanted to recognize his debt to him. So in trying not to hurt him, he would put things unclearly, which made matters even worse. . . . Of course, we changed the title, because it comes from "Lullaby of Birdland." That's why he called it "Lullaby." It's a jazz tune. But this is not clear from the Russian title. And when I asked Joseph what the origin was, he said "Lullaby of Birdland." I said we should call it "Lullaby of Cape Cod" rather than "Cape Cod Lullaby" to suggest the connection there. And that's the way it went. I am mentioning it because that's the direction in which I was pushing him: to find out what the references were in Russian and try to suggest them in English.

ZI: I noticed, studying the translation drafts and the correspondence, that Brodsky would often commission several people to do the same translation.

BR: Oh, yes. You could see how some people might get upset because of the amount of effort they had put in, to then have him say, "Well, thanks, sorry." [*laughs*] It didn't matter that you had worked for six months and put a part of your soul in this.

ZI: Were you aware of the falling-out between Joseph and Weissbort?

BR: You know, I have just started to read Weissbort's book [*From Russian with Love*], and I was a little surprised at how Weissbort had dealt with it . . . in his own way, I guess. I imagine that was because his relationship with Joseph was so important to him and so influential. When you read the book, you see how much thought he put into it about the relationship and the meaning of it all. . . . I was here in New York at the time, trying to get this book [*A Part of Speech*] put together and hearing Joseph walking around, saying "Danny is upset, but . . . what can I do?" What I did not appreciate at the time was Weissbort's perspective. I knew what the principle was, and I could objectively understand why Weissbort would be upset. But I did not have a sense of what Weissbort was actually doing. I saw the work of all the people contributing to that volume. And everybody labored over it. . . . I probably said this a long time ago about the translation by David Rigsbee. The first publication appeared in *Vogue*.[1] Now, if you look at the translation in *A Part of Speech*, and you look at the translation in *Vogue*, they're totally different. [*laughs*] That was a special case, in a sense, because Rigsbee, I don't think, knew Russian very well. He was working, I guess, with the *podstrochniki* [the interlinear translations]. And I went over the translations. Nancy Meiselas was the editor. She did the business aspect. She would write the letters and then forward the stuff to people. She would send me published translations, and my job was to say "OK, is this acceptable or are there problems with it?" And the strange thing with Rigsbee was that it had already been published, and I thought it would be easy. But when I looked at the poem, I realized that the meaning of the poem, the literal meaning, was totally wrong.

ZI: How did you manage to win Brodsky's trust in this delicate issue?

BR: Oh, it was fast. The translation was so far from the mark in terms of interpretation of images and the meaning of certain phrases. We are not even talking about the poetic aspects but about the literal meaning.

ZI: But had Joseph looked at it himself?

BR: No. [*laughs*] That's the point. I handed him this list, and I said, "All these things are wrong." It made no sense. You ask yourself, how did this get published? But Brodsky did not care at the time. It was one of the first things published in English after George Kline's book. It was probably in the mid-1970s, when Joseph had a very good relationship with Alex Liberman.[2] He would publish anything. [*laughs*] He was like Roger Straus. Joseph would say, "Here is the poem," and he would just publish it.

ZI: But Howard Moss from the *New Yorker*—was he any different?

BR: Ah, Howard Moss was a poet and a poetry editor. First of all, Howard Moss would not accept anything that was not good. If there was something strange about the meaning, he would question it. And if there was something that he thought did not work in terms of the sound, he would also question it. That was his profession. But Alex was the artistic director of *Vogue*. He was not the poetry editor. I don't think there was a poetry editor. *Vogue* was not a literary magazine. Have you looked at any of those issues of *Vogue*? [*laughs*] . . . And so Joseph would have David Rigsbee send a poem to *Vogue*, and Alex would say "Great." He was not going to take the trouble of looking at the original and comparing it with the translation. That was not his job. So I looked at the poem, and I told Joseph that it was all wrong. And we had to go back to the poem to get the meaning right. I then sent Rigsbee the corrections, saying all these things are incorrect, please deal with it. You have to retranslate it, and that's what he did, as far as I recall.

ZI: You yourself did translations of Brodsky's poems. How did it go?

BR: Yes, I did "San Pietro," and I did . . . "Homage to Yalta." It went well.

ZI: It seems that you did more interlinear translations for the translators who did not know Russian. Did Brodsky give you feedback on the interlinears?

BR: Yes, all the time. I asked him questions about all the poems in *A Part of Speech*. He would tell me anything I asked about. What I did first was to make sure that it all made sense. Is it logical, are there references? For instance, in "The End of a Beautiful Era," which was also translated by Rigsbee, there were references to the *Igor Tale* [a medieval Russian epic]. And there are some very difficult things that nobody understands exactly, and Joseph was quoting the stuff. But how do you translate it into English if nobody knows what the old Russian means? So, as long it was acceptable logically and he could accept it, we could work around it. We had trouble with one longer poem, "Lullaby of Cape Cod," translated by Anthony Hecht. It was much too long. Joseph said, "No, no, no, that's too long, please revise it," and Hecht said, "I am finished with it. And if you don't like it, I'm going to publish it in my own collection." Which he did. [*laughs*] How did he get away with it? Because Weissbort could not do it, and Hecht was somebody whom Joseph respected as a poet. And then we attempted it ourselves. I said, "Joseph, let's you and I try to do something just to show that it is possible to do this, keeping to the same structure, the same form." So we did a few stanzas. Obviously, Hecht was not interested in working on it anymore and was happy with his translation. Joseph finally went along with it.

When he, Derek, and I worked on the final text of *A Part of Speech*, we went through the whole text, we went through the galleys. The goal was to sit down and look at every poem and see whether there was anything Joseph was unhappy with, for whatever reason. Derek was there as the arbiter of English, and I was there as an intermediary who could explain Joseph to Derek and what Joseph had in mind when he was upset, or when he did not accept what Derek said. It was quite extraordinary and wild. Derek would say that there is a problem with English and suggest something. Brodsky would reject it. I would intervene and try to explain to Derek why Brodsky would not accept it. A heavy silence would follow and it seemed we were stuck. Then *I* would suggest something—then Derek and Brodsky would jump at me and call me stupid. . . . There was a lot of good humor, but also a lot of swearing and attacks. Everybody understood what was at stake and contributed to a great achievement. [*laughs*] This was in the apartment of Bill and Pat Strachan, who was an editor at Farrar, Straus and Giroux. They were in the country, and we used their apartment for the whole day. Derek has never forgotten. If you ever see him, ask him about our session and he will go on. It's extraordinary that it made such an impression on him as well.

ZI: You also translated Brodsky's prose, his Nobel lecture, among other things.

BR: Right. Most of his first book reviews were published in the *New York Review of Books*.

ZI: "Beyond Consolation." The review of translations of Mandelstam by Burton Raffel. That was the least diplomatic one.

BR: Well, one of the lines he used was mine.

ZI: Really?

BR: Yes. It was something like "he [Raffel] has to be stopped before he attempts more." It was pretty horrible. And Raffel had translated Nikolai Gumilev before he translated Osip Mandelstam. The chutzpah. The complete poetry of Gumilev and Mandelstam. He had a Russian collaborator who was very big at the time . . . Anyway, those I was translating. Brodsky's English was very rough and had to be heavily rewritten. He made many grammatical mistakes, used expressions that you could not use. . . .

Years later, of course, he was getting better. [*laughs*] And he would give a draft to his various friends to read and to comment on. And he gave me a draft of something—I don't remember what it was. I was, I think, in his apartment [on Morton Street], and Masha [Vorobiova] was there. I was extremely frustrated and argued with him. I did not hesitate to argue with him. I would say, "Joseph, this cannot be said, this is just awful, you can't say it." And in my frustration, I turned to Masha. Now Masha was not a native speaker, but she had been speaking English since her teenage years. And I said, "Masha! Masha! You can't say this. You know that this is awful. This is unacceptable." But Masha was a pussy cat, right? Not a tiger. So she said, "Well . . . maybe it's possible . . ." [*laughs*] And that was the moment I realized the power of suggestion and of persuasion that Brodsky had. Even the people, especially his friends whom he relied on for things like this, there was a certain amount of . . . how to describe it? Not brainwashing, but you started to . . . you no longer could tell whether it was English or Brodsky-speak. It was becoming acceptable.

You know, it's a very fascinating phenomenon. And people have recognized this, even the people who I would be surprised to hear say this. For example, I was recently glancing—I guess in anticipation of meeting you—at Danny Weissbort's book. And even he, sort of, recognizes that Joseph had an influence on the English language. That's really, I think, one of the things that he'd be most proud of, that would mean the most to him. I don't know if I have ever mentioned this to you, or if anyone ever mentioned this: another thing that meant a tremendous amount to him was when his essays were accepted in the annual collection *The Best American Essays*.

ZI: Yes, that was in 1986.

BR: That was like the Nobel Prize. I mean, he was just over the moon. American essays! Anyway, to some extent, he was changing the language in the way he used it. But I kept in my head that idea that you had to be careful not to let him run roughshod over you and insist that this was OK that he was creating a new language. There is a boundary there. No definable boundary that I could point to, but I felt it. I said that I had to rely on my own sense of what was new and acceptable and what was new and unacceptable. Something where one could say: he had gone too far. I thought that Masha had given in. The word is "browbeat." He had browbeaten her. After all, Masha lived next to him and the influence there was huge. I mean she treated his skill and his genius as sort of divine, almost unchallengeable. As long as he was asking for feedback, she would give him feedback. But as soon as he started pushing back and rejecting the feedback, she would say, "Oh, I guess it's OK." But I thought that I would be doing a disservice to him if I didn't resist.

ZI: And how would he react?

BR: He would argue. [*laughs*] One of the dictionaries he used—I can visualize it in his apartment, and you might have seen the pictures. On his desk he had the *Chambers Dictionary*. I'd never even heard of it. It's not used in this country. And he would use words from that volume. I would look at him and say, "It's not right, Joseph." And he would say, "But I can say this." I said, "Yes, but it's so British. You don't want to be that British." . . . To tell you one last thing about the translations, I remember occasions when he would come up with something in English that he liked better than the Russian. That makes sense. He had a different image. The English words stimulated something else, and he said, "Yeah, yeah, that's good." But it was certainly different from the Russian, and a person who knew Russian, a native speaker, would say this is definitely not a translation. No, it was not. And that's fine. It all depends on the definition of translation, what your expectations are. So someone who doesn't have the author's authority might say, "Well, I have done a lot of reading on theories of translation, and it is thought that a translation has to be faithful to the author's intentions." And people say, you've got to be faithful. Faithful to the author's intentions. But who knows what Dostoevsky intended? Who knows what Pushkin intended? Or Aeschylus? When you are working with a living author, it's a totally different thing. . . . There is an interesting book . . . on Nabokov's auto-translations and on how he approached his translations . . .

ZI: Well, Nabokov was also a character.

BR: Yes, he was very fanatical about language and was extremely nasty about other translators. . . . Before I forget. As a memento. *Na pamiat'*. Here is a tape recording. [Brodsky's] last reading at Queens, 1994. He reads for about forty minutes in English, and then a couple of poems in Russian. And then he answers questions, and his answers to questions were very interesting. I asked one of the questions, you'll hear it. I asked, "Have you ever translated any of your English poems into Russian?" At first he got angry—I thought he was going to hit me. [*laughs*] He said, "Why should I? No, no." But then it led to an explanation of why he wrote poems in English.

ZI: That's interesting. What did he say?

BR: That it was a special kind of activity, a special challenge for him, a certain feeling. He said that when he first started writing in English, it was kind of fun. He was not sure he could do it. He wrote them on special occasions. But there was also a kind of emotional reason why he did it that he explained. But he made it clear that as a result, it was not worth his effort to translate them into Russian. Because of the reason he had done them [i.e., because it was a special challenge for him]: he had gotten the sense of achievement already and did not care that these poems appeared in Russian.

On that recording you can already hear that he was not strong. He was not visibly ill, but, you know, his general heart condition had taken a toll on him. He'd get tired. He still smoked. He never gave up smoking. I drove him home after that reading, as a matter of fact. It was easy to get to Manhattan, maybe half an hour to Morton Street from Queens. We drove about half a mile, and he had me stop at a drugstore to buy some cigarettes. He only wanted one. He left the pack in the car, and I kept it for years. That kind of business did not help. And his cardiologist was a very cool guy. His name was Ron Drusin, an American. Ron became a good friend. He came to all Joseph's parties. I remember Ron once asking, maybe after Joseph's first bypass surgery, if he wanted to smoke. That's it—he did not get upset about it. There is only so far you can control a person. . . . Joseph always thought that smoking was a kind of passage to his muse, a kind of contact. He was not a drinker. He drank, but he was not a drunk. The people he knew, all the Russian émigrés, they would drink a lot. Yuz Aleshkovsky, for example. Joseph did a lot of promotion for Yuz's book. He built the careers of so many people, dozens of them besides Yuz. Have you ever looked at Yuz's stuff in English, like *Ruka*? I think two or three things of his were translated. Brodsky would go to Roger Straus and say, "Roger, this is great stuff." And Roger would say: "OK." [*laughs*] Michael Glenny was a very prominent British translator into English of mainly the Soviet stuff. He made a living from it. Very few translators I know make a living from it. He was the only one. . . . Tamara Glenny was his daughter. She acquired Russian growing up and was commissioned to translate Aleshkovsky. It was unbelievably difficult and kind of an unrewarding task. I mean, the humor there is so specific. It's hilarious in Russian, but when you translate it—what? It makes no sense; it's totally flat. [*laughs*] And Joseph would write those wonderful comments trying to sell it. He'd say, "The most brilliant humorist in Russian history." Or whatever. He never skimped with praise.

Appendix B

An Interview with Derek Walcott, New Haven, October 27–28, 2007

Derek Walcott was awarded the Nobel Prize in Literature in 1992. He was a professor of English and creative writing at Boston University from 1981 to 2007. The interview took place in New Haven, Connecticut, where Walcott spent time as a consultant on the production of one of his plays at the Yale Repertory Theater.

> A lot of us have had to defend Joseph in his translation into English. Many English poets say: "He is not an English poet and he can't be one, but he tries to be one." I don't think he tries to be one: he existed in an acerbated situation in which he was Russian, but he was writing in English. But his respect for the avoidance of English cliché led to his poetry being something new in English. And there were idiots who didn't see the good thing that was happening to English poetry by his struggles with what was inarticulate for him, to express it metrically. So that was his great endeavor. And what I heard tonight made me extremely happy. Because I heard very good poets reading Brodsky evenly. The even tone of Mark Strand and the even tone of Adam [Zagajewski], who are two different poets, were reading Brodsky as if they were coming out of this one voice. I think this fulfilled something which I have known for years. That if you gave the poems time, if you give the Brodsky translations time, the way you allow a patina to happen in a painting, the way you let it develop, the poems age into what they were always. There is a greyness and greatness into which they mature—certainly for me tonight. But the fact that the poets approaching the poetry approached it without any creational or any political identity, but as separate human beings, separate poets reading this produced a very calm joy. That's what I felt: serene, calm justification of Joseph's English poetry.
>
> —Derek Walcott, American Academy in Rome, "Tribute to Joseph Brodsky," March 18, 2011

ZAKHAR ISHOV: There is a generally bad reception of Brodsky's poems in English, his self-translations. Most of the people I spoke to in Russia don't even know Brodsky wrote poetry in English. In my work, I have tried to show the artistic merit of those translations without quixotically denying the fact that there were some problems with their English.

DEREK WALCOTT: He spoke perfect English grammatically . . . it was almost his second tongue. I don't think it is fair or kind to say that Brodsky did not know English or did not understand the practice of English.

ZI: In preparing my dissertation, I studied the Russian-English metrical contrasts, and I came to the conclusion that in translating from Russian into English, Brodsky tried to convey the real rhythm, the phonetic realizations of the respective verse meters of his poems. If we take the same verse meter in Russian and in English, it would sound different. Let's look at one example, the poem "Clouds":

> O summer clouds
> of the Baltic, I swear,
> you are nowhere
> to be outclassed . . .

DW (reads the poem): Well, it scans . . . what's the problem?

ZI: You are, of course, a better expert as far as English verse goes. To me it seems, though, that Brodsky is trying to convey here all the nuances of the rhythm of the original, and it is one of his most beautiful poems in Russian. But I wonder whether it works in English.

DW: Do you have the Russian poem here?

ZI: (recites):

> О, облака
> Балтики летом!
> Лучше вас в мире этом
> я не видел пока . . .

> O, oblaka
> Baltiki letom!
> Luchshe vas v mire etom
> ia ne videl poka . . .

DW: I have got the meter.

ZI: But you've got the meter because you just heard it in Russian. The question is whether you can arrive at this meter just from reading it in English. In English, you don't hear the Russian sound, so you reconstruct it from your experience of English poetry, right?

DW: Well, as meter it seems to me very consistent.

ZI: Brodsky corrected and revised . . . it was important to him. And many translators were upset at his revisions. Weissbort, for example, sent him very angry letters in 1979, reproaching him for the changes he had undertaken and claiming that Brodsky did not understand poetry translation into English.

DW: That is very second-rate.

ZI: Why do you think it is second-rate?

DW: Weissbort is injured because he feels his translations are being rebuked by Joseph because Joseph feels they were not up to what he wanted. Joseph's discontent with his translators led to a lot of quarrels. He even had a hard time with Tony's [Hecht] "Cape Cod Lullaby" translations. Brodsky said that there were many extra lines which Tony added to his verses that he didn't like. Well, I myself think that "Cape Cod" is a terrific thing, and Tony did what he did.

ZI: But here we are touching upon the nub of the problem. Brodsky insisted on mimetic translation, on rendering the exact form of the original, and the question is whether it was a good method. Of course, it was *his* idea about translation, and he tried to implement it. But in the example of "Cape Cod," we see that Anthony Hecht did not produce a replica version of the poem, but it works in English, and you say it's a good poem.

DW: As a poem, yes, but there might be a scholar who would say that it is not a Brodsky poem. The extra lines that Tony added are not in the original. But because it is designed in rhyme, he took some extra lines. I guess Joseph's argument would be that it shouldn't have happened, that "Cape Cod Lullaby" really isn't his but is Tony's, and that the extra lines shouldn't be there. I think it is permissible. For the reader it works, but for the author himself it doesn't.

ZI: So here we have the source of the conflict: a different reception of the translation by the author and by the reader. What do you believe Brodsky thought of his own self-translations?

DW: I think we have to examine Joseph's ambition in terms of his translations. And I think his ambition was huge in terms of his undertaking, and for some people it seems pompous and pretentious and unjustified. That's why I think some people are nasty in terms of their judgment. They are virtually saying, "Keep him away from any idea of being an English poet," which is obviously not what he wanted to be. He was not trying to be an English poet. He was someone trying to bring both elements into one language, which he himself was shaping with considerable respect for both languages. And his attitude was: if in the process of translation from Russian into English, the poet encountered something that deviated from Russian, for him it was permissible. He told me that. Well, that's not a conceited man, that is not somebody who cherishes his work so much that he doesn't want somebody violating it. What he is upset about is when the poetry is inadequate—that's what I think it is when he complains about any translator. It is not up to the standards of his poetry; it may be linearly, linguistically accurate, but tonally it is below the level of what he has created. Now, what Joseph creates is very complex, sometimes very difficult to be up to, very difficult to understand. It becomes completely difficult to understand in Russian as well as in English. But I think that in English he becomes really difficult to understand, not because of his inadequacy in English but rather because he is a difficult, intellectual poet. So it's the same thing if you transfer that into English. Well, somebody might say, "But that's not the English instinct in the language." My response to that is: must I be literate, must I be polite? My response to that is that it is something *I* had to go through as a writer . . . it is snobbery. It's based on snobbery; it's based on looking at Joseph as an immigrant, an immigrant into English poetry. And you can't separate that from an attitude about class. . . . Well, I can go as far as I want and say: I can allow myself to feel so persecuted that I'd say he is a Jewish immigrant into English poetry. The idea of the immigrant, that's the idea of me who is being reviewed as someone who is not a part of the fucking club.

ZI: Well, this explains a good part of the animosity against Brodsky. But at the same time, Donald Davie wrote in his review of *To Urania* that history has hardly produced examples of poets breaching the linguistic gap, and that there is Conrad and Nabokov, but not a poet. You can breach the language gap in prose, but not in poetry.

DW: OK, to repeat: Joseph is an extremely difficult poet. I am sure he is difficult in Russian. Is he not?

ZI: Yes, he is.

DW: Intellectually complex, sometimes even hard to work out what the metaphor is. That's the Russian poetry; that is his poetry. For someone to criticize him on that basis, that person should presume to be a Russian critic, not an English critic, first of all. Reading the Russian, saying "Ah, this is difficult to understand," right? Joseph's attitude to that was often stubborn. "No, no," he would say, "it's difficult, but it's not difficult." That was his stance, which was sometimes impenetrable and could be irritating to people (not for me), and I could understand that. But we are talking of Russian. A Russian would be telling him what we are saying. The point is, if you say it is difficult in Russian, it has every right to be difficult in English. You can't be so pompous and so proprietary as to say it is not supposed to be difficult in English.

ZI: No, that's clear.

DW: It's not clear to the reader, it may be clear to you. It's not clear to those who criticize. It's not even clear to other poets. I am talking about privilege, and what we are discussing in terms of Joseph's translations is privilege. Does he have the privilege to write English verse that is complicated to understand? Because what they believe is that what he is doing is not only perverse but that it is also peremptory, that he is taking over something that they have to defend. They have to defend English verse, modern or whatever, against an intruder. What is the act of the intruder? The crux of the matter is that question: What is the intruder trying to do? The intruder is trying—that's my understanding of it—to bring into the English language of poetry, not into the English crumpets and flats, to try to bring into that aesthetic, which might be traditional in a way, but just to introduce certain concepts that are there, have existed before, and he is not even inventing them, he is trying to follow a track. And the track that he is following, let's say, is the metaphysicals [the English metaphysical poets of the seventeenth century]. Let us just say that. Because Joseph hated surrealism, as I do. We are talking about metaphysics. We are talking about introducing into poetry, via Auden, questions of logic, questions of rhetoric, questions which may be scientific in their content, their context, or their theory. But to introduce that as part of the texture of the English verse. None of these people do that, or think it is part of poetry. I used to think so myself. The influence of Joseph on me is widening the subject, the intellectual subject of the poetry. And his position on it is that it is an intellectual occupation. It may have emotions in it or . . . whatever, even anything encroaching on sentimentality—he himself was sentimental in a great way, and pathetically sentimental sometimes, but that is what comes with the emigrant's stance as well—that was a part of poetry that has gone out. He was not careering, he was not making a career out of what he was doing. It was just that thought had gone out of the language [of poetry].

ZI: T. S. Eliot made the same point when praising the metaphysicals, saying that after them, thought left English-language poetry.[1]

DW: But Joseph was doing that during the immediate context of our time. American poetry did not do it because in the argument there has to be a frame. In Joseph's argument, there is a melodic frame. That's not the style and design of contemporary poetry in English—consequently, the intrusion of saying that this poem should be able to include what his critics felt to be condemnable. All immigrants are old-fashioned; Joseph loved the dated clichés. Joseph would use the equivalent of slang that had not survived. But he liked the slang, and he puts it in his verse, not because he is archaic but because he likes the vernacular. You know what I am saying? So if he says "23-skiddoo" or "what about you, baby?" it's funny. You think that he is a Russian in a plaid shirt and bad pants, and he has bad breath and he has glasses, and he comes in and that is how he says "23-skiddoo." Like Borat. That's like making Joseph into Borat. That's what they are virtually doing. It's like moving around in London, where the poets just smooch each other, or here where the vanity of the club is something. I am glad I am not a part of it—They are going to write about each other, talk about each other. So he is going to get slandered because he is not a part of the club. They have a perfect point in saying it is difficult and that's not English. It's not English in the way they want it. But there are many parts, even in Conrad in prose, for example, where critics would say somebody would have put it much simpler. So it is then your choice to say whether this is overheated, inflated, inflamed prose like Conrad's as opposed to, say, the prose of someone who is monosyllabic like Orwell. Yes, you could say that. Or Henry James, you can say that he is pompous, bloated, and, in a sense, if you want, you can say that this is what Joseph is trying to do because he is so excited about English; he has the excitement of the immigrant, and he is playing with the language. Yes, that is part of it, that's certainly a part of it, but that's OK.

ZI: What's interesting is that Brodsky wrote a lengthy response to Weissbort where he says that his main concern was not so much the accuracy of the translations but the sense of their linguistic dignity. Brodsky also adds a phrase saying that "today is not the last day of writing in English." So, somehow, what he had in mind was a bigger project. He also said that form in poetry as opposed to free verse represents a more courageous attitude, that free verse is cowardly. What do you make of these statements, especially of Brodsky's mention of the English translations' linguistic dignity in light of his critics' accusations of his verse being un-English?

DW: What Joseph said about English and American poetry is that English poets are more interesting because they are more interested in the design of the poems, and that American poets were not interested in the structure, stanzaic structure, for instance, of poetry. And obviously, the other one was harder, and it is not entirely cowardly, but it's a kind of laziness, I think, and a kind of taking it for granted that you do not have to earn the craft in the same way as you would have to earn it if you were doing something technical. So he had no respect, in a way, for free verse, and he admired structure and design, which is tougher.

ZI: But he wanted to influence the trends in English poetry. Isn't it presumptuous on the part of a non-native speaker?

DW: The one thing that everybody would see about Joseph in Russian and in English was his ambition. But his ambition was not a personal ambition, it was an ambition for poetry. Not for him. People do not understand that; they can't conceive of it because they are in a setup in which the hierarchies are thin, have to do with clubs, the reviews, the people you know. Joseph referred to Auden as Wystan—he was a friend. He was not dropping names when he spoke about Auden. And he spoke about Spender in the same sort of way. His insistence was on the idea of gentlemen in terms of conduct.

ZI: This is a line from your "Italian Eclogues" in memory of Joseph: "A conduct whose meter and poise were modelled on Wystan's." . . . In 2004 I met with Natasha Spender, and when I asked about Brodsky's self-translations, she said something which I have a feeling reflects Spender's opinion: "Brodsky could never get the accent right, like Stravinsky in his collaboration with Auden on the librettos." She was probably referring to Brodsky's manner of reciting his poetry. When you hear Brodsky read in English, he does things that are peculiar to Russian; he omits stresses on semantic words. And then he said that on paper his translations look better. I, for one, think that his self-translations are aimed at his own reading: they have to be read by Brodsky. So my question is, do these translations survive him as poetry?

DW: Nobody reads poetry like that in English, not in the contemporary manner. In the bass it is different. It's liturgical in tone. The language we have to read Brodsky is in English. We don't read Russian. Its survival depends a lot on translation. But because he did so much of his own translation, that makes him permanent; even as a curiosity it makes him permanent because he is not leaving much for someone else to do. Let me explain something about the interlinears that you would get from Joseph. Interlinears from Joseph on a poem in Russian would have the same shape. First of all, I don't think he would have happily allowed free verse translations of his poetry. That would be a betrayal of his design. But a lot of American poets have done it to some great poets. Lowell did it, Galway Kinnell did it, a lot of people have done it and changed the meter so that it is not the meter, exactly, of Villon, which I think is totally unfair and wrong. And the argument could be: "Well, this is America, now this is the American language, and this is the feel of Villon." Wrong! And that includes Lowell. It has to be the meter of whatever is in Villon. So at least you get a sense of the ballad, if they are ballads. If I were talking to Joseph now, we would probably go into a whole long discussion about the death of the ballad, of the apparent death. These forms do not die. When they are revived, they sound fresh. Which was another of Brodsky's aims: to revive those poems or to invent poems as a part of the visible structure of building something. You see the structure in front of you. This is a considerable contribution to twentieth-century poetry. And there are a lot of great poets in the twentieth century who don't show you a visible construction of the poem in front of your eyes—including Miłosz, including people who don't have stanzaic shape, necessarily. I think that Joseph and I agreed strongly on the idea of stanzaic shape, on the idea of the stanza, simply because as an artist working in that particular craft, you expect an enormous amount of material to construct what you are doing, and you make all the material accessible. You don't need to leave out rhyme, you don't need to leave out . . . whatever. What is the point of that? And that's why he [Joseph] describes that as cowardice, but I would describe it as laziness, or laziness when it is conceit.

The American poet believes that he is inventing so much that he need not do things that are old-fashioned and European. And that leads to a disaster. That leads to a thinness and barrenness of American poetry, continuing now in the universities. Joseph taught at a university, and he was very high on recitation, which is a terrific thing. And I do the same thing on recitation as part of the rhythm in poetry. And when you have to memorize something that is free verse, and it doesn't have the rhythm that you want to preserve, you don't want to do it. So there is a point there.

ZI: So do you think it is all a matter of fashion, and that what happened to John Donne and the poets of his school was that they had been out of fashion for almost three hundred years before they were rediscovered? Do you think the same thing might happen to Brodsky's English poetry, that it might be rediscovered?

DW: I don't have the feeling that it has been buried, or not read, or dismissed, or forgotten. Is that his situation in Russia? I don't know.

ZI: Well, in Russia he is read and revered. But there is another extreme; there is almost too much of it. There is a cult, but chiefly because he was a

Nobel laureate. Because of the difficulty that you mentioned, there was a slim stratum of readership that appreciated and sought his poetry at the time when it was prohibited. Back then his readers also risked persecution when they reproduced his work in samizdat, and this is now widely forgotten. On the other hand, I don't think that this mass appreciation is really genuine. Also, in Russia they know very little or nothing of his English poems. Because they have his Russian originals, his English verse seems to be something secondary. This has been a part of my PhD project, to make Russians aware of how important his English translations were for him. Whereas here in America, whomever I have met, and I mean people at the universities who have to do with poetry, they would say that Brodsky was not supposed to translate himself, that he was the worst translator of himself, that his poetry does not scan in English. Yet his English translations and the poems written directly in English are important contributions to the English language. To say the least, they raise important questions about the practice and possibility of poetry translation from Russian into English.

DW: I wouldn't recommend Joseph as a model to an English poet. I would not recommend him in terms of design. I would absolutely recommend him in terms of the content and the intellectual force, as well as many essential aspects of poetry. But although I might say to myself about another English poet, "It's OK to imitate Auden, it's OK to imitate Spender," I would say it is not a good idea to try to imitate Brodsky because he is an extremely individualistic poet. His style is very personal, almost diaristic in terms of what he puts down. You'd have to live his life to write like him, literally. You don't have to do this with other poets. Certain poets, I would say, you would not recommend as models because to a young poet they have things that might look like virtues. But there is obscurity in Brodsky, and that is the aspect of Brodsky that people jump on and criticize. But there are also astonishing metaphysics, astonishingly beautiful things that happen in the poem that you cannot copy—the wit in the poem which is so remarkable. That fantastic image he has [in "Lullaby of Cape Cod"] of a guy coming home one night, and he talks about the cockroach mob in the basin, then he compares the mob to the gladiators, but what is really astonishing is that he calls the spigot "Caesar's crown." I mean that's just mind-blowing for any poet that he should do that as a metaphor. It is good enough to have the cockroach as a mob in the basin, waving their antennae, but then you go beyond that and say that the person who flushes them down is Caesar, and that Caesar's crown is like the top of the spigot. Well, this is what metaphor is; it has its own narrative on top of the other thing that is going on.

ZI: Let me ask you whether you think Brodsky was evolving as an English-language poet. His witty Audenesque light-verse poem "To the President-

Elect" suggests he was, and I've realized that his self-translations were good training. So it seems he was evolving as an English-language poet and may have been interrupted in his bigger project.

DW: This is a very good question. But what if I ask you if you think that the Russian poetry was getting Anglicized, whether Brodsky was leaving the Russian language?

ZI: I don't think so. What is clear is that Brodsky was experimenting a lot with Russian verse.

DW: Do you think that his English had much influence on the Russian?

ZI: Well certainly, but I don't think his Russian ever left him.

DW: Did you ever check whether that Venice book was written in English?

ZI: Oh, *Watermark*? Yes, it was written in English.

DW: And then it was retranslated into Italian. Well, if he did write *Watermark* in English, then what was happening to him had happened to Nabokov and to Conrad. Something "other" enters the English language. You see, Brits are not joking with their snobbery; they don't meddle with their class system. I've been to England and have friends there, so I know. They can become very reluctant to accept. . . . It's like having black blood in you, or Jewish. They still haven't [accepted] . . . Rosenberg. Do you know him, Isaac Rosenberg, a Jewish poet who died in World War I? Sassoon wrote an introduction to his book. But there was always a little mark of astonishment that Jewish Rosenberg would be admitted into the company of Edward Thomas or Wilfred Owen. And the antisemitism is still there; we know that. The core of America has never confronted the reality that American literature in the twentieth century is Jewish literature, written by Jewish Americans. . . . Joseph was beautifully treated in America, and he loved it, not because of appropriation but because it had that openness—and I am not contradicting myself. The openness in viewing him as a Jewish-Russian poet was self-complimentary. You compliment yourself if you entertain him well. You know what I am saying? There is that danger. If normally I persecute you, and then you come from the Balkans, and you come here, and I treat you well, then that means I have never persecuted you. Joseph adopted this country similar to the way Auden had America, and this sensibility of circling in language is identical. Why is the relationship between Brodsky and Auden toward America identical? It's because of the language. Because Auden opened perception to admit everyday things and to make verse out of those everyday things more than Eliot had done. Or to make political journalism part of poetry that was never there before. Journalism was there for journalists, and then "1 September 1939" is a political editorial. Maybe that's why Auden did not ultimately like it.

ZI: You don't approve of Auden's dropping this poem from later editions, do you?

DW: No, because I think sometimes the first version has to be the one you have, and even if you correct it and you think you make something tougher, the heart isn't there. That's a very touching poem, and what Auden probably didn't like was to touch people in the wrong way, in a way that appeared to him to be a trick.

ZI: Brodsky, on the other hand, insisted on the poet's ability to make his statements inevitable, conveying weight to poetical statements because of the form, because of the sound and their unity, which produce the effect of inevitability. Whereas Auden had his reservations, saying that the poet shouldn't abuse these effects. I think what you've just said is very interesting. Brodsky's worship of Auden is well known, and yet it is not quite clear what united these so outwardly different poets. Auden is British, Anglo-Saxon, and Brodsky is Russian-Jewish.

DW: I don't think that Auden was socially a snob.

ZI: But there is such a difference in their cultural backgrounds, their sensibilities.

DW: Craig Raine was a snob. Auden was not a snob. First of all, Auden is probably the great twentieth-century poet because of his range alone, that's enough. So in terms of scale, he is a major poet. It is inevitable that he would be an influence. But in private, in his choices. . . . Joseph always tried to make a distinction between aesthetics and ethics. And he considered the aesthetical even more powerful than the ethical. So Auden has been an influence on me, on everybody, because of what he seized on, not in the hereditary poetical way but by the observations that were there in parts in Eliot and in other influences, for example in German influences. But the language is as strong as if one were living in Shakespeare's period and were influenced by Shakespeare. I don't think that Joseph was ashamed of his affinity with Auden.

ZI: On the contrary.

DW: Which is terrific. Because in our time we don't accept that, we don't want to identify, because we all have egos. It would be like saying Raphael was Leonardo's friend. Two great painters living separately. Or Picasso was Georges Braque's friend. Or Auden was Brodsky's friend. That's the level of company you are privileged to be in. Just to know them and so on. I never knew Auden, but for Joseph his friendship with Wystan was a very respectful and an intimate one.

ZI: Let me rephrase my previous question: Do you think his English translations will survive the challenge of time?

DW: Your question is whether they will survive on the basis of his own translations? I think there will be many that will not survive because a lot of them are too syntactically tortured and stubborn in some ways. They may not be read for that reason, but they may be read academically or historically. But what is good in them, the good ones, the ones that survive, obviously these are going to remain as long as . . . well, as a part of English poetry.

ZI: Yes.

DW: You see, that's the difficulty. It's not read as English poetry. That's what they are claiming, the people in the club: "This is not English poetry."

ZI: But Brodsky insisted that they should be read as English poetry, that these translations should stand on their own as a part of the English language.

DW: It would be hard to disentangle and to understand what is English and what is part of the Russian.

ZI: Not exactly.

DW: Yes, it is. Because he is intellectual in English. We are dealing with the incomprehension of what he is saying intellectually. It can be exasperating not to be able to understand. His argument is: it's not that I am so difficult, it's that you are not thinking well. And that's a very good argument.

ZI: But if we say that what matters is the thought, the intellectual force and the depth of his metaphors, but not the form. . . .

DW: No, no, no. That's part of the admiration. The reason it is wound up like that is because of the form. The reason why it's difficult is because of the shape. But because you cannot understand doesn't mean that the shape has to be condemned.

ZI: You know, prosody in Russian is not as daring as it is in English.

DW: I don't think you can read Joseph as a master of English prosody. That's not there. Nor could he have claimed that.

ZI: But wasn't his project to show the merits of the form and the possibilities it opens as a device for modern English poetry?

DW: No, I don't think that was his intention. I don't think he had that kind of ambition—to be a great English poet. He would have been an idiot to try to do that.

ZI: . . . not to be a great English poet, but to show that you can do these things in English.

DW: He would have had to say that he wanted to be a great English poet. And he didn't. He wanted to be able to show that in English you could achieve the same vibrations that you could in Russian. That's what he was trying to do. Or he wanted to bring into English poetry the same vibrations. But even that was not his ambition. It was his work. This is an individual work we are talking about. He was not doing it for English poetry. He was doing it for himself. He was not a novelist. He was not doing a novel, he was not doing a play, he was not doing something public. He was doing something extremely private, which he had to resolve for himself. So the first satisfaction was his own satisfaction. He was trying to write English that would satisfy him before it satisfied a reader. Let me just summarize it all in two lines: You don't admire Brodsky for English metrics, what you admire is the fact that he could achieve it as a Russian poet. When it is achieved, it is beautiful in English as English. And that can be brought into beauty by a good poet translator. So you see Joseph's translators had to be poets. That's why it is the poet's problem. It's the problem of both of them. Someone you should talk to is Glyn Maxwell. He is a younger poet who likes Brodsky, who has been translating Brodsky. Another poet who is translating Brodsky into Italian is Matteo Campagnoli.

ZI: Can we talk a bit more about Brodsky's translations? Why do you think he didn't want them to sound smooth in English?

DW: The feeling of a poem in translation can be awkward. But I think what it does . . . I think for another poet . . . is that it adds knots to a thing which is too smooth. And that is what the origin of any wood is. It's not, by nature, smooth. You look for the knots in the creation. If you are reading John Donne, you are trying to work out something that is, in a way, awkward. The awkwardness is because of the intellectual in the poems. I learnt that from Joseph. I learnt not to be complicated, but not to be too smooth from the beginning. Critics are not going to accept that because what they want is a repetition of standard English poetry from a Russian. Well, you are not going to get that. You should not want that. What you should want is a Russian's idea of the translation of English poetry, and a Russian's idea of what he likes in English. And that same love of English creates Conrad, and it creates Nabokov, and it creates other writers. Now because it is poetry, because it is metaphysical, it is intellectually complicated. You see, Joseph reminded me that the poet has to think. I was in a relaxed kind of mood. Having experience in the craft, I was relaxing in terms of creativity. And what I had to rediscover was that concentration, which doesn't come easy. It should not be allowed to come easily.

ZI: At the same time, Brodsky insisted on maintaining the form of the originals in translation. Let's take iambic pentameter . . .

DW: If I did a line in translation, he would say, "this is too iambic; what's needed is something less fluent."

ZI: Something that troubles the rhythm.

DW: Not discord, but better to work from discord than overmelodic poetry because the overmelodic iambic line, especially, has too many echoes of tradition in it, which constricts individuality a little too much. Particularly in his case. I may be wrong, but because of the length of the Russian line compared to the compression of the iambic line, what he wanted to have was a combination in which you would be able to use the Russian equivalent to bring to light the Russian originality of what he had and to transfer the difficulty that is in the Russian, even metrical difficulty, into the English version, which is what I very highly respected. Now when you get a translation like that by Dick Wilbur . . .

ZI: "Six Years Later" . . .

DW: Yes, that's good. I don't know how close that is metrically to the Russian.

ZI: It is very close. What I have discovered in an effort to get a grasp of prosodic theory is that Brodsky was trying to deliver the rhythm of the original more than, strictly speaking, trying to convey its metrical scheme. Iambic pentameter in Russian and English sound different because Russian typically displays omissions of stress and in English . . .

DW: Russian has also feminine rhymes.

ZI: Traditional Russian verse has an alternation of feminine and masculine rhymes. And this also was problematic.

DW: You see, Joseph's concept of translation was not a transliteration from Russian. It was as if he provided the translator with a poem on which he or she the translator could orchestrate from the Russian, including making his or her own metaphors within the poem. He did not mind. He would even look forward to saying "Oh, change that. I accept that as part of your feeling of the poem." I was amazed at that: on the one hand, he would be extremely precise; on the other, he would also say, "You have the liberty to do what you want."

ZI: What do you make of the criticism, often leveled at Brodsky's self-translations, that he returns to poetic devices that are no longer in current use in English-language poetry?

DW: I don't come from America, so that doesn't bother me at all. I am enthusiastic about it. But there are a lot of people who hate the design of Joseph's poems. The rhymes in his poems and the enjoyment of rhyme are not part of the American spirit, you know. I think he had a hard time with an American audience. Whereas people like Dick Wilbur and Mark Strand, they enjoy it.

(Walcott in the company of his partner Sigrid Nama and some other friends.)

DW: Joseph Brodsky had a lot of translators. So he invited me and Barry Rubin, a professor at Queens who knows Russian, to do a translation. We were staying at the house of Pat Strachan, who was at Farrar, Straus and Giroux. Joseph came to the apartment, and we were going to translate. . . . We were looking through the proofs, these were the last proofs. Each of us was proposing something, and the other guy would say . . . nah. You know, Joseph was very dismissive too, very exact in terms of the rhythm being right. He did not want it to sound too much like English poetry, like a common meter. He worked like hell. I don't know what time it was, but by the end or somewhere in the middle, Joseph got tired and he said, "Fuck you, fuck you, fuck me, and fuck poetry!" Of the whole poem, in about six hours, he did about three lines. I don't know the rhythm of translators, but I would imagine that is the kind of rhythm they go by. It's an unappreciated occupation, underappreciated.

(Walcott was asked whether he had translated poetry himself.)

DW: No. When I was much younger, I tried it a couple of times . . . but no.

ZI: But you translated the Brodsky poem "Letters from the Ming Dynasty."

DW: The thing about Joseph's translations is that he used to translate himself into what he called an "interlinear," a line-by-line translation from Russian into English. But it wasn't just crude prose. It was as metrical as he could make it and sometimes even with rhymes. So when you have in a book "translated by Derek Walcott," I tell people that I read it, I didn't translate it, for Joseph did all his interlinears. No, I have to say this because it was part of what he was doing . . . in one or two lines he liked that translation a lot, and like any real poet, he enjoyed rhyme and off-rhyme in the poem. . . . Once I did a change on a Richard Wilbur translation . . .

ZI: I think you did that on the plane.

DW: I was with Joseph on the plane? I can't remember that. Joseph lived on Morton Street in New York, very close to where we live now. It's very hard to pass there. I would go to his apartment. We'd go and talk a lot. He was absolutely terrific on English poetry. He knew it. He liked Hardy a lot and Auden completely.

Sigrid Nama: I wanted to add something not about the poetry so much but on Joseph. Joseph was a poet first of all and very generous with other poets. He wanted everybody to get known within the limelight. He was a catalyst in that sense. And that is why he came up with the idea that there should be a poetry book next to the Bible in every hotel room, and that you should be able to get poetry magazines at the checkout counter in the grocery stores. But also, the conferences where poets came together, like the Getty conference, and he got the whole world of poetry together to know each other. Because, you know, people in the same profession do know each other, but you have to have occasions to come together.

DW: I remember one incident. I was going up to teach at Columbia one morning. On the way up, I picked up the *New Republic*. I opened the *New Republic*, and there is this fantastic poem by Adam Zagajewski, "To Go to

Lvov." You know it? I say to myself, Jesus. So I take it to the class, and I read it in the class. It's magnificent. Later I call Joseph: "Joseph, do you know a guy called Adam Zagajewski?" He says, "Derek, I brought him to Farrar & Straus." And then the other thing: we were in Rotterdam at a conference. And before that, I had gotten a bunch of poems from the PEN conference. And these Russians were coming over, Alexander Kushner and some other guys. And they sent me some poems to read. The translations were so bad! I said I won't read that stuff, I can't read it. They are too bad, the translations. So Joseph and I sat together and looked at half of the poems I refused to read. And Joseph and I began to translate Kushner, and from the first couple of lines I could see that the guy is good. . . . This is another story about translation.

Appendix C

An Interview with Mark Strand, New York City, July 2009

Mark Strand (1934–2014) has been recognized as one of the major American poets of his generation. He was named poet laureate of the United States in 1990 and was awarded the Pulitzer Prize in Poetry in 1999. The interview took place at his home.

> CHARLIE ROSE: Mark Strand, as a poet characterize Joseph Brodsky, define him, help us understand his poetic soul.
>
> MARK STRAND: Well, I don't know Russian, so I can't talk about him as a Russian poet. But as an English poet he was an exotic. He did things that no English or American poet born into the language would possibly do. The way he ordered language . . . to say unusual is an understatement. He made choices that none of us here would ever make. We are bound by word orders and structures that we grew up with and he wasn't. So that his poetry was at once a flagrant violation of whatever it was we had tried to do through our coming to terms with English poetry, and also a kind of miraculous step forward. I found him just, well, unbelievably gifted at invention. I mean there's no poet in England or America who would take the chances that Joseph took. No one sounds like him. It's as if he . . . I mean the English language was his toy. He had loved it, and he played with it in ways that are not possible for someone born into the language to. And underneath that play, of course, there's a huge moral dimension to his poetry—a dimension that draws on his experience, his exile, I mean his experience in the Soviet Union, having been sent to Archangel to a work camp, and his subsequent exile in the United States.
>
> —Mark Strand, interviewed by Charlie Rose, *The Charlie Rose Show*, March 19, 1996

ZAKHAR ISHOV: Let's start with Brodsky's translations and poems in English.

MARK STRAND: There has been a lot of criticism of his poems in English. American poets would like to believe they speak American. Usually in the conversational tone. I have found over the years that Brodsky's poetry strikes a very artificial note. I am thinking of the criticism: Robert Haas, for example. I have myself gone on record in saying that I find his poems in English very exotic. It's a different English.

ZI: Well, having studied many of his translation drafts in my dissertation on Brodsky's English self-translations, defended last year in Berlin, I show that Brodsky could be very creative in his translations. He often changed his original metaphors and invented new ones in English. And this arguably promoted his self-translations to the status of independent texts in English. Would you agree with that?

MS: Sure. It's his poems. He can do what he wants. [*laughs*] If you are the author of the originals, and you are translating them, you have a great deal more freedom than somebody who's just a translator. The idea is to re-create an English equivalent of a Russian poem, but not a word-for-word transliteration. Something that has the feel of the original and retains the idea of the original. But, you know, metrical changes, the possibilities of rhyme are different in different languages. Russian does not sound like English. So you can't make an English poem sound like a Russian. But you can make an English poem feel like a Russian poem.

ZI: Well, English and Russian are different. But at the same time, if you look back, and I think Brodsky very often looked back in terms of tradition, all European poetries adopted their metrics from Greek and Latin, and they were quantitative languages, and modern European languages are accentual. This means that poetry both in English and Russian has a common metrical matrix.

MS: But you know even in English, which is an accentual language, I mean it's measured in feet—unstressed—stressed—unstressed—stressed—but it is quantitative because it's the length of the unstressed syllable that determines the greater or lesser mechanical quality of the rhyme. In other words, if you rhyme with the same amount of stress each time, you are going to have doggerel. If you vary the penultimate unstressed syllable—only vary in length, because it's unstressed—you are going to hit the stress slightly differently. And this creates variation. You can rhyme, but you don't hit the rhyme with exactly the same force.

ZI: Can you give me an example?

MS: "It's been a long long day / Since you went away."

ZI: I see. I found this little book of photographs taken in Venice by the artist Ewa Zebrowski, *Remembering Brodsky*, from 2003, for which you wrote an endnote.

MS: Oh, yeah. I think I just dashed it out.

ZI: Well, and I found this quote by you where you say that Brodsky would give you advice on your poems:

> Joseph and I would read our poems to each other over the telephone and give each other advice. I always took his advice. Rarely, I believe, did Joseph ever take mine. His questions were mainly about usage. He was never sure how American or how British he wanted his poems to sound. On the page they could be trying either, but when he read them aloud, they sounded like English trying to be Russian. He would chant his poems, gravely intoning each line, allowing it to rise slightly and then trail off at the end. It was a little like hearing a dramatic recitation of the liturgy. The effect was mesmerizing.[1]

So what kind of advice would he give you on your own poems?

MS: He would say, "You should call this poem this." He would give me a title. I remember once I didn't use it, but twenty years later I thought, "he was right." I could have called the poem, instead of "The End," "The Stories of Cirrus and Cumulus." It was a line in the poem: "The stories of cirrus and cumulus come to a close." But it was usually, "You don't need to say that." Or he would drop a word. I would do the same with him. I'd say, "You can't say that in English."

ZI: But he was very stubborn.

MS: Veeery stubborn. [*laughs*] But it was not a studious examination of each other's poems. When you hear a poem over a telephone, something hits your ear and you say, "I don't think that sounds right." And he would say that to me.

ZI: Obviously, you treated each other as equals. Yet I remember reading somewhere your saying that Brodsky was a greater poet than yourself.

MS: Absolutely. Even though I can only read him in translation. I feel that he operates on a conceptual level that I can't. Just in creation of metaphor.

The invention of hypothesis—he hypothesized like that. [*snaps a finger*] The largeness of his world. There was Latin, and his historical poems.

ZI: Also his nativity poems.

MS: [*cringes*] No, I don't like them. I mean, I have read some of that stuff, but Joseph's infatuation with Christmas is not my thing. I am definitely an atheist. I mean poems that had to do with English poetry. Just his knowledge of English and American poetry. His knowledge of European poetry. His ability to write about almost anything.

ZI: But you did not include him in the 2005 book *100 Great Poems of the Twentieth Century*. [*laughs*]

MS: Because he was too young. I stopped in 1927. There is some mistake in there too. Some idiotic editor changed something.

ZI: But personally you would have chosen a Brodsky poem for the *100 Great Poems* book?

MS: I don't know which I'd choose.

ZI: A couple of years ago, I went to the Library of Congress and listened to a recording of you, Brodsky, and Rosanna Warren talking together on a panel when he was poet laureate.[2]

MS: Oh, yeah? What were we talking about? I don't remember.

ZI: About American poetry. It was a very witty discussion. There was a lot of laughter. Do you know this poem he wrote when he was poet laureate, "To the President-Elect"? [*Recites the poem*].

MS: It's fantastic.

ZI: So it works as an English poem after all?!

MS: Well, no American would write like that. Perhaps an English poet would. Americans don't do that.

ZI: Do you mean because of the British type of wit?

MS: No, it's wit, but also in kind of its own way, it's civic poetry. It's not vatic. Joseph registered knowing how he felt about the world and how the world felt about individual endeavor. He sometimes took a public view, and very often his poems were addressed to the public at large. Americans very often write as if they were addressing themselves. You read American poems and have a sense that you are overhearing a conversation someone is having with himself. Very often in Joseph's poetry, and certainly in Auden's, the poet is speaking to a large group.

ZI: Auden's "1 September 1939" would be an example.

MS: "I sit in one of the dives / On Fifty-second street." [*recites*]

ZI: In his conversations about Akhmatova, Brodsky explained that she was an enormous influence on him, but more of a personal influence than as a poet. He admired her as a poet, but she worked in a different aesthetics. Would the same be true of you and Brodsky?

MS: Yeah, I know. I have no interest in writing the way Brodsky writes. I was never influenced by his work. And I was rarely, only early in my career, influenced by Auden, who was a big influence on Joseph. I was influenced by Wallace Stevens. And I don't think Joseph was influenced at all by Stevens. Joseph liked Frost and Hardy, and Stevens was too exotic, too embedded in a particular kind of English for Joseph. No, I mean, I marveled at what I could understand of Joseph's poems, like that poem "Six Years Later." You know, it's so beautiful, but it would certainly not be anything that I aspire to.

ZI: That makes me think of your elegy "In Memory of Joseph Brodsky": "What remains of the self / Unwinds into a vanishing light . . ."[3]

MS: It's built on repetition. Also, he would always say, "et cetera, et cetera." His mind was always running ahead of the conversation.

ZI: So, you are saying that for you Brodsky was more of a great friend than a great poet?

MS: I believe he was a great poet, but I did not emulate his poetry.

ZI: In his essay in memory of Auden, Brodsky writes that Auden told him: "I have known three great poets, each one a prize son of a bitch." Meaning Yeats, Frost, and Brecht. And for you, who would be a great poet whom you knew as a great poet?

MS: Well, I knew Frost a little. I mean, I met him when I was at school. When he came to Yale, I took care of him for three days. I knew Robert

Penn Warren, who was great. I think Richard Wilbur was great. Joseph was great. The great poets I knew, they were nice people. [*laughs*]

ZI: Talking of greatness, you seem to be rather self-effacing about your poetry, right?

MS: Right. Well, it's not worthless. I am not saying that.

ZI: But Brodsky's attitude toward poetry, his sense of poetic authority was very different.

MS: He was very certain of himself. Of his opinions, of his aesthetic. It's a psychological difference. I was never sure of myself when I was young. People did not think I was a genius. People saw that Joseph was a genius all his life. If people keep telling you, "you are a genius," you will start believing it. I mean, I had ideas, but I guess I thought that most of my intelligence went into my work.

ZI: Yes, but what I am trying to say is that Brodsky had this enormous claim for poetry, that it is the greatest vocation, etc., and you don't have it.

MS: Joseph had a belief in poetry that exceeded anyone else's that I know of. He simply believed that poetry was the most important thing in the world. I never believed that.

ZI: Do you think it's a Russian thing?

MS: It might be a Russian thing. I attributed it to Joseph. I believe that poetry is important, but Joseph really sacrificed himself for poetry. I mean, there is a difference. I don't know of any single American poet who would do that. Somehow life is more important. For Joseph, poetry *was* life, and life was not more important than poetry. For instance, Joseph never gave up smoking. He could not write unless he smoked. Life is not worth anything if I cannot write; therefore, I cannot give up smoking. I don't know if I'd seen another person who would think in those terms. It's hard for an American to believe in poetry to the extent that Joseph did because very few people read it. I mean, it's not as if society affirms what you believe. In Russia he went out and saw people come to hear him read. People reading your poems, avidly passing them around as if they were the truth. It means something else.

ZI: Well, in Russia his popularity was strictly underground, and the poems were circulated in samizdat.

MS: I think that samizdat helped. Because (a) it was forbidden. And whenever something is forbidden, it increases its value. And it was from someone who had suffered from the regime. So, it had the authority of truth.

ZI: I remember in one of his letters to Brodsky written in the early 1970s, after Nadezhda Mandelstam's memoir had come out, Stephen Spender made quite a prophetic remark. He said that it seems that in Russia the regime fears a poem as if it might be dynamite, whereas in the West poets live in a vacuum ultimately writing for other poets. But he said that one day perhaps the same will finally happen also in Russia, i.e., that the situation of the poet in Russia will become as marginal as it is here.

MS: Which is true. That's the way it is. I mean, in Russia all the young people are not reading poetry. They are going to rock concerts. Do they read Joseph now in Russia? Probably not.

ZI: Well, in Russia he is a huge name because of the Nobel. In Russia it's always all or nothing. You are either a parasite, an enemy of the people, or this larger-than-life icon. . . .

I have one last question. Brodsky laid this great importance on poetic forms and tradition, whereas I get the impression from reading your poetry that you rely more on the cadence of spoken speech. Maybe I am wrong.

MS: You are right.

ZI: But you wrote this book on prosody.[4]

MS: Well, I wrote a little of it.

ZI: So how would you assess the importance of the prosodic forms?

MS: Every poet should know about traditional forms, and every poet should have experimented with them. Just the way every artist should know how to draw.

ZI: Derek Walcott, in his "Italian Eclogues," in memory of Brodsky, writes: "You refreshed forms and stanzas," crediting him with revitalizing those prosodic devices. The same thing that Auden did, right?

MS: Auden was part of the movement—all the restoration of forms. It happened in this country in the fifties. Deep investment in the form. Richard Wilbur, Anthony Hecht . . . all these people.

ZI: So it seems that it is like a fashion that comes and goes. First, they reject the form out of rebellion. But when they notice the desolation it has brought, they embrace it again.

MS: Not only that, but whatever they do in the way of revolutionary works of art becomes absorbed immediately into the mainstream. So what seemed like a revolution lasts about ten minutes. It's not a revolution then. It becomes a style.

Appendix D

A Memoir by Barry Scherr: "Brodsky in 1970"

Barry Scherr is a distinguished Professor Emeritus of Russian at Dartmouth College and author of the groundbreaking 1986 monograph Russian Poetry: Meter, Rhythm, and Rhyme. *Professor Scherr shared with me his memoir on meeting with Brodsky and graciously allowed me to include it in this book.*

I first met Brodsky when I was an exchange student in the Soviet Union. I can provide a few details regarding my seeing him, but you need to keep in mind that this was fifty years ago. Although I jotted down a few notes right afterwards—which I have now reread for perhaps only the second time since then—for the most part I need to rely on what is by now my no doubt imperfect memory of the time.

In 1969–70, the program that brought American scholars to the Soviet Union was the IREX exchange, which had just replaced the initial program (the Inter-University Committee on Travel Grants) that had been in place for about a dozen years. The largest group of participants on the IREX exchange that year was located in Moscow, and we were housed on the sixth and seventh floors of one wing at Moscow State University. It turned out that one of the other Americans had met Brodsky through someone else, and he mentioned to some of us that Brodsky had actually been in his room at the university. A while afterwards—this was already in late May, near the end of my time on the exchange—I went to Leningrad to obtain some materials for my research. That other American happened to make a research trip of his own to Leningrad at about the same time. Shortly after I arrived there, he asked me whether I would like to meet Brodsky, and of course I did. So the two of us went to his and his parents' place on Liteinyi Prospekt—that famous "room and a half"—on the evening of May 26, just two days after Brodsky's thirtieth birthday; we had a second visit on May 29.

He seemed at the time a bit older than thirty, but I initially focused less on his appearance (and his near constant smoking) than on his living space, which was not large but seemed even smaller, filled as it was with various items: suitcases and trunks piled high, a large box with Chinese characters, pictures and objects tucked in everywhere. He had a lot of books, of course; many of those—probably the majority—contained poetry, and a surprising number were in English. I remember only two of the photos, one of Akhmatova and one of Robert Frost, whom he greatly admired. He had two posters in English. The larger of the two must have been made for him by somebody; it began "WANTED DEAD (PREFERABLY) OR ALIVE IOSIF BRODSKIJ" and went on to list a series of crimes that he had supposedly committed in the United States. The other poster, smaller, said "BEWARE—SEX MANIAC." We drank the vodka that he offered, while he preferred the English gin that he had somehow obtained. At some point, either on that visit or the next one, Brodsky cooked omelets for us, but mostly he talked extensively about Russian and Western literature. He began, though, by referring to politics, saying that one is better off without it, that activists give up some part of themselves. He claimed not to understand American activists (again, this was 1970, when many American universities were in turmoil after the killings at Kent State), and he said that he did not like tendentiousness in literature of any sort. Just after that he commented that he was tired of seeing the Jewish question in American literature and did not like those who wrote about it.

That was a segue into his wide-ranging discussions regarding literary figures. He mentioned that Richard Wilbur was his favorite American poet (he had the same paperback of Wilbur's poetry that I happened to own), and he said that he liked many other American poets as well, both past and present. He called Robert Lowell (about whom he had complicated feelings) a bad poet, and he stated that he liked Auden (who had written the introduction to a book of Brodsky's poems in English) but not his philosophy on the role of the poet. He felt there were only two good Russian prose writers in the twentieth century, Nabokov and Platonov. Most of the good prose writers of the 1920s were only stylists; to be a great writer you had to offer some new spiritual idea—Nabokov's is that we are in the post-Christian era. He found Bulgakov to be imitative of Merezhkovsky, Andreyev, and others (this was when *Master and Margarita* was all the rage in the USSR). Probably because I mentioned that I was working on Aleksandr Grin, he offered an interesting comment to the effect that all of contemporary Russian prose can be said to have developed from Tolstoy's realism and Grin's romanticism—"unfortunately," Brodsky added. He thought Russian poetry was much better than its prose and went through many of the big names of the twentieth century (Mandelstam, Akhmatova, Tsvetaeva, Pasternak, and a few more). He also felt that some of the secondary figures, such as Zabolotsky and Kliuev, were just a notch below the others and certainly very fine poets. At one point he mentioned liking Dylan Thomas's poetry and expressed a desire to live in Ireland, for its green countryside, bad weather, and people who were poor, sentimental, and religious—all of which reminded Brodsky of Russia. Although he had mentioned not liking political literature, he had read and quoted from Robert Penn Warren's *All the King's Men*. In general, he seemed to have read widely in English literature, albeit the poetry far more than the prose.

During the second visit the focus was primarily on Russian poets, about whom in some cases he spoke at length. The one non-Russian poet he discussed in detail that evening was Cavafy. As with Wilbur, his bookshelf contained the very edition of Cavafy's poetry (translated from Greek into English) that I had bought for myself a few years earlier. He expressed his admiration for several specific poems by Cavafy, and later I was to sense an influence by Cavafy on some of Brodsky's works. He had mixed feelings regarding both Esenin and Mayakovsky. He found some of Esenin's poems to be excellent, but others relied too much, perhaps solely, on emotion. Mayakovsky, he felt, was a tragic figure, a person of enormous talent whose creative skills were undermined by his attempts to come to terms with the Bolshevik revolution. As for the best-known poets of the day in the West, he cordially disliked Voznesensky, saying that he hides his bad (artistic) qualities and political toadyism behind a creative mask. Yevtushenko, he found to be egotistical and hedonistic but at least open about those qualities (and thus, in his opinion, a more attractive figure than Voznesensky, even though he did not seem to care particularly for Yevtushenko's poetry). His most extensive remarks concerned Akhmatova. He talked in some detail of meeting her and said at one point that the six years during which he knew her were the best of his life. He also referred briefly to a number of younger poets, his contemporaries, whom he found especially interesting. I did not know them at the time, so I don't think I caught all the names, but they included some who I later realized were in my late colleague Lev Loseff's circle (Ufliand, Eremin), as well as Naiman, Velichansky (who had just published in *Novyi mir* a few months earlier), and Stanislav Krasovitsky (whom Brodsky said was older than the others, had gone mad for a while, and was generally unpublished). I suppose that most or all of this is what others heard when they visited him during those years. Toward the end of the evening, he read several of his poems ("Na smert' T. S. Eliota," "Podsvechnik," "Proshchaite, mademuazel' Veronika," and one or two others) with that particular way of reciting that he employed later as well. I believe it was after the second visit that he walked us partway to the Peter and Paul Fortress and encouraged us to spend the (almost white) night there, which we did, while he returned home.

I'll just mention two other items related to that evening. The first was his almost blithe disregard of any personal risk he might have faced by entertaining two American graduate students. Of course, that was the least of what he did in his day. Judging from the number of books published abroad on his shelves, to say nothing of various other foreign objects, it was clear he had met with people from other countries fairly often. As I mentioned, he had managed to get into Moscow State University (where entrance was supposedly by *propusk* [ID card] only), and I would assume he did so more than once. For all that he was no doubt under some kind of surveillance, he seemed almost oblivious to any personal threat—and for that matter it was in telling us about one or two escapades that he assumed an almost carefree affect. Perhaps because of his attitude we did not feel unsafe during the meetings—nor did we experience any consequences from the time we spent with him. The second item is that some years later, well after Brodsky had become settled in the United States, I had an opportunity to ask him about those (for me) memorable occasions when I had met him in his home and he recited several of his poems. I described those two evenings as best I could, hoping to find out what he had been thinking at the time. "No," he replied, "I don't recall ever seeing you in the Soviet Union."

Abbreviations

AAA	*An Age Ago: A Selection of Nineteenth-Century Russian Poetry*, trans. and ed. Alan Myers (New York: Farrar, Straus and Giroux, 1988).
APOS	Joseph Brodsky, *A Part of Speech* (New York: Farrar, Straus and Giroux, 1980).
"BC"	Joseph Brodsky, "Beyond Consolation" (a review), trans. Barry Rubin, *New York Review of Books* 21, no. 1 (February 7, 1974), http://www.nybooks.com/articles/9613.
CON	*Joseph Brodsky: Conversations*, ed. Cynthia L. Haven (Jackson: University Press of Mississippi, 2002).
CPE	Joseph Brodsky, *Collected Poems in English*, ed. Ann Kjellberg (New York: Farrar, Straus and Giroux, 2000).
FSG archives	"Brodsky General," Farrar, Straus and Giroux, Inc. records. Manuscripts and Archives Division, New York Public Library. Astor, Lenox, and Tilden Foundations.
JBP	Joseph Brodsky Papers, GEN MSS 613, Beinecke Rare Book & Manuscript Library, Yale University.
"LE"	Joseph Brodsky, "Learning English" (undated [1987]), Joseph Brodsky Papers, GEN MSS 613, Box 83, Folder 2014, Beinecke Rare Book & Manuscript Library, Yale University.
LOC	MSS84477, Joseph Brodsky Correspondence, Joseph Brodsky Papers, 1965–1972, Manuscript Division, Library of Congress, Washington, DC, 20540, http://hdl.loc.gov/loc.mss/mss.home.
"LTO"	Joseph Brodsky, "Less Than One," in *Less Than One*, 3–33.
LTO	Joseph Brodsky, *Less Than One: Essays* (London: Penguin Books, 1986).
"OGR"	Joseph Brodsky, "On Grief and Reason," in *On Grief and Reason*, 223–66.
OGR	Joseph Brodsky, *On Grief and Reason: Essays* (New York: Farrar, Straus and Giroux, 1996).

"Otherland"	Joseph Brodsky, "Language as Otherland," 1976, Joseph Brodsky Papers, GEN MSS 613, Box 123, Folders 2764–65, Beinecke Rare Book & Manuscript Library, Yale University.
"Room"	Joseph Brodsky, "In a Room and a Half," in *Less Than One*, 447–501.
"Shadow"	Joseph Brodsky, "To Please a Shadow," in *Less Than One*, 357–83.
SP	Joseph Brodsky, *Joseph Brodsky: Selected Poems*, trans. George L. Kline, foreword by W. H. Auden (London: Penguin Books, 1973).
"Spender"	Joseph Brodsky, "In Memory of Stephen Spender," in *On Grief and Reason*, 459–84.
"TA"	Joseph Brodsky, "Translating Akhmatova," *New York Review of Books* 20, no. 13 (August 9, 1973), http://www.nybooks.com/articles/9770.
"Visage"	Joseph Brodsky, "Uncommon Visage: The Nobel Lecture," in *On Grief and Reason*, 44–58.
W	Joseph Brodsky, *Watermark* (London: Penguin Books, 1992).
"Wilbur"	Joseph Brodsky, "On Richard Wilbur," *American Poetry Review* 2, no. 1 (January–February 1973): 52.

Notes

PREFACE

1. Joseph Brodsky, "A Guide to a Renamed City," in *Less Than One: Selected Essays* (New York: Farrar, Straus and Giroux, 1986), 69–94.

2. Nadezhda Mandelstam, *Vospominaniya* (Moscow: Soglasie, 1999), 296.

3. W. H. Auden, "In Memory of W. B. Yeats," in *W. H. Auden: Selected Poems*, ed. Edward Mendelson (New York: Vintage Books, 1979), 80.

INTRODUCTION

1. Robert Frost, "Conversation on the Craft of Poetry," in *Collected Poems, Prose & Plays* (New York: Library of America, 1995), 853.

2. Elizabeth T. McLaughlin, "Coleridge and Milton," *Studies in Philology* 61, no. 3 (July 1964): 569.

3. W. H. Auden, "Note," in *W. H. Auden Reading His Poetry*, nonmusic sound recording (London: Harper Collins Audio Publishers, 1955).

4. George Steiner, *After Babel: Aspects of Language and Translation* (Oxford: Oxford University Press, 1975), 241.

5. Dante Alighieri, *Il Convivio*, in *Le Opere di Dante* (Florence: Nella Sede Della Società, 1960), 155. Translation mine.

6. W. H. Auden, "Translation and Tradition: The Translations of Ezra Pound," in *The Complete Works of W. H. Auden, Volume III: Prose: 1949–1955* (Princeton, NJ: Princeton University Press, 2008), 388.

7. Quoted from Steiner, *After Babel*, 261. See also Roman Jakobson, "On Linguistic Aspects of Translation," 232–39 in *On Translation*, ed. Reuben A. Brower (Cambridge, MA: Harvard University Press, 1959), 238.

8. Yuri Lotman, *Universe of the Mind: A Semiotic Theory of Culture* (London: I. B. Tauris, 1990), 14–15.

9. W. H. Auden, *A Certain World: A Commonplace Book* (London: Faber and Faber, 1982), 366–67.

10. Lawrence Venuti, ed., *The Translation Studies Reader* (London: Routledge, 2000), 16.

11. Gilbert Highet, *The Classical Tradition: Greek and Roman Influences on Western Literature* (New York: Oxford University Press, 1957), 104.

12. Highet, *The Classical Tradition*, 105.

13. Highet, *The Classical Tradition*, 105.

14. Tomas Venclova, "Translations of World Literature and Political Censorship in Contemporary Lithuania," *Lituanus* 25, no. 2 (1979), http://www.lituanus.org/1979/79_2_01.htm.

15. James H. Billington, *Russia in Search of Itself* (Washington, DC: Woodrow Wilson Center, 2004).

16. Efim Etkind, *Russkie poety-perevodchiki ot Trediakovskogo do Pushkina* (Leningrad: Izdatel'stvo "Nauka," 1973).

17. Brian James Baer, *Translation and the Making of Modern Russian Literature* (New York: Bloomsbury, 2016). "Born in Translation" is, for example, the subtitle Brian Baer gave to the introduction to his book on the role of poetry translation in the genesis of modern Russian literature.

18. A. S. Pushkin, *Perevody i podrazhaniia*, ed. K. N. Atarova and G. A. Lesskis (Moscow: OAO Izdatel'stvo "Raduga," 1999).

19. Joseph Brodsky, "On Richard Wilbur," *American Poetry Review* 2, no. 1 (January–February 1973): 52.

20. Harold Bloom, *The Anxiety of Influence: A Theory of Poetry* (New York: Oxford University Press, 1997).

21. Michael Wachtel, *The Cambridge Introduction to Russian Poetry* (Cambridge: Cambridge University Press, 2004), 10.

22. Omry Ronen, *The Fallacy of the Silver Age in Twentieth-Century Russian Literature* (Amsterdam: Harwood Academic, 1996).

23. Katerina Clark, *Moscow, the Fourth Rome: Stalinism, Cosmopolitanism, and the Evolution of Soviet Culture, 1931–1941* (Cambridge, MA: Harvard University Press, 2011), 32.

24. Clark, *Moscow, the Fourth Rome.* See also Isaiah Berlin, "Why the Soviet Union Chooses to Insulate Itself," in *The Soviet Mind: Russian Culture under Communism* (Washington, DC: Brookings Institution, 2004), 90–97.

25. Arlen V. Bljum, *Zensur in der UdSSR. Archivdokumente 1917–1991*, vol. 1–2 (Bochum: Projekt-Verlag, 1999).

26. Maurice Friedberg, *Literary Translation in Russia: A Cultural History* (University Park: Pennsylvania State University Press, 1997), 33.

27. Joseph Brodsky, "Uncommon Visage: The Nobel Lecture," in *On Grief and Reason: Essays* (New York: Farrar, Straus and Giroux, 1996), 55.

28. Gerald S. Smith, "Russian Poetry since 1945," in *The Routledge Companion to Russian Literature*, ed. Neil Cornwell (London: Routledge, 2001), 197.

29. Czesław Miłosz, foreword to *Joseph Brodsky, Leningrad: Fragments*, ed. Mikhail Lemkhin (New York: Farrar, Straus and Giroux, 1998), 10.

30. Joseph Brodsky, *Watermark* (London: Penguin Books, 1992), 8.

31. Joseph Brodsky, "Author's Note" to *A Part of Speech*, in *Collected Poems in English*, ed. Ann Kjellberg (New York: Farrar, Straus and Giroux, 2000), 507.

32. Valentina Polukhina, "Angliiskii Brodskii," in *Iosif Brodskii: Tvorchestvo, lichnost', sud'ba: Itogi trekh konferentsii*, ed. Iakov Gordin (St. Petersburg: Zhurnal "Zvezda," 1998), 49–59. In 1998, Valentina Polukhina sent questionnaires to forty British poets concerning Brodsky's English.

33. For a summary of the reigning approaches on Brodsky's English, see Alexandra Berlina, "The American Brodsky: A Research Overview," *Resources for American Literary Study* 38 (2016): 195–211.

34. W. H. Auden, "Letter to Lord Byron," in *As I Walked Out One Evening: Songs, Ballads, Lullabies, Limericks, and Other Light Verse* (New York: Vintage Books, 1995), 49.

35. Joseph Brodsky, "To Please a Shadow," in *Less Than One*, 357–83. Incidentally, the poem "Letter to Lord Byron" happened to be Brodsky's favorite Auden poem.

36. Adrian Wanner, "Joseph Brodsky in English," in *The Bilingual Muse: Self-Translation among Russian Poets* (Evanston, IL: Northwestern University Press, 2020), 138–58. In fact, the number of poems Brodsky composed directly in English increased incrementally in each new English-language poetry collection of his.

37. Joseph Brodsky, "Less Than One," in *LTO*, 3.

38. Joseph Brodsky, "Infinitive," in *CPE*, 345.

39. Wanner, *Bilingual Muse*, 6.

40. Joseph Brodsky, "Learning English" (undated [1987]), Joseph Brodsky Papers, GEN MSS 613, Box 83, Folder 2014, Beinecke Rare Book & Manuscript Library (BRBL hereafter), Yale University.

41. Brodsky, "LE."

42. Brodsky, "LE."

43. Brodsky, "LE."

44. Brodsky, "LTO," 23.

45. Cathy S. Gelbin and Sander L. Gilman, *Cosmopolitanisms and the Jews* (Ann Arbor: University of Michigan Press, 2017). It is generally referred to in English as the "Doctors' Plot."

46. Joseph Brodsky, "Room," 469–70.

47. Irena Grudzinska Gross, "A Jewish Boy with a Head Full of Russian Rhymes," conference presentation, panel on "Joseph Brodsky: A Citizen of Empires," Association for Slavic, East European, & Eurasian Studies, Boston, November 24, 2013.

48. Brodsky, "LTO," 7–8. For a discussion of Brodsky's polemics with the Marxist dictum that "existence conditions consciousness," see Svetlana Boym, "Estrangement as a Lifestyle: Shklovsky and Brodsky," *Poetics Today* 17, no. 4 (Winter 1996): 513.

49. Brodsky, "LE."

50. Brodsky, "LE."

51. For a detailed analysis of the poem, see Alexandra Berlina, *Brodsky Translating Brodsky: Poetry in Self-Translation* (New York: Bloomsbury Academic, 2014), 172.

52. Brodsky, "Sextet," in *CPE*, 265–66.

53. Joseph Brodsky, "Roman Elegies," trans. Joseph Brodsky, in *CPE*, 274–75.

54. For a recent discussion of the creative potential of writing poetry "with an accent," see Wanner, *Bilingual Muse*, 26.

55. J. M. Coetzee, "Speaking for Language," *New York Review of Books* 43, no. 2 (February 1, 1996): 28.

56. Brodsky, "LE."

57. Brodsky, "LE."

58. Brodsky, "LE."

59. Brodsky, "Shadow," 382.

60. Joseph Brodsky, "In Memory of Stephen Spender," in *OGR*, 461.

61. Alan Myers, "The Handmaid of Genius: An Interview with Valentina Polukhina" (November 2003–September 2004), in Valentina Polukhina, *Brodsky through the Eyes of His Contemporaries* (Boston: Academic Studies, 2008), 516–40, here 525.

62. Brodsky must have written "Learning English" sometime around 1986, for he mentions in it having "spent nearly a third of his lifetime with English on his lips." The math would be correct in 1986 when Brodsky was 46 and had lived for 14 years, since 1972, in the United States.

63. Brodsky, "LE"; Eleonory Gilburd, *To See Paris and Die: The Soviet Lives of Western Culture* (Cambridge, MA: Harvard University Press, 2018), 5. Like most Soviet citizens, Brodsky's schoolteachers had been denied the freedom of movement and any opportunity to travel abroad because of travel restrictions and closed borders. Writing in English here takes on the symbolic importance of offering an imaginary, if probably posthumous, escape route for his teachers from a totalitarian situation.

64. Christopher Reid, "Great American Disaster," review of *To Urania*, by Joseph Brodsky, *London Review of Books* 10, no. 22 (December 8, 1988): 17–18.

65. Craig Raine, "A Reputation Subject to Inflation," *Financial Times*, November 16–17, 1996, xix.

66. Raine, "A Reputation Subject to Inflation," xix.

67. Donald Davie, "The Saturated Line," review of *To Urania*, by Joseph Brodsky, *Times Literary Supplement*, December 23–29, 1988, 14–15.

68. Michael Schmidt, "Time of Cold," review of *A Part of Speech*, by Joseph Brodsky, *New Statesman*, October 17, 1980, 25.

69. Reid, "Great American Disaster," 17.

70. Davie, "The Saturated Line," 14–15.

71. Raine, "A Reputation Subject to Inflation," xix.

72. Seamus Heaney, "Brodsky's Nobel: What the Applause Was All About," *New York Times Book Review*, November 8, 1987, 1, 63, 65.

73. Iosif Brodskii, "Grosh tsena russkosti, kotoruiu mozhno utratit" (press conference, Helsinki, August 1995), quoted in Gordin, ed., *Iosif Brodskii*, 50. Translation mine.

74. Bożena Shallcross, *Through the Poet's Eye: The Travels of Zagajewski, Herbert, and Brodsky* (Evanston, IL: Northwestern University Press, 2002), xv.

75. Shallcross, *Through the Poet's Eye*, xv.

76. Helen Benedict, "The Flight from Predictability: Joseph Brodsky," *Antioch Review* 43, no. 1 (Winter 1985): 20.

77. Brodsky, "LTO," 9.

78. Miłosz, foreword to *Joseph Brodsky, Leningrad: Fragments*, ed. Lemkhin, 10.

79. Brodsky, "LE."

CHAPTER ONE

1. Lev Losev, *Iosif Brodskii: Opyt literaturnoi biografii* (Moscow: Molodaia Gvardiia, 2006); Emily Lygo, *Leningrad Poetry 1953–1975: The Thaw Generation* (Bern: Peter Lang, 2010); Smith, "Russian Poetry since 1945."

2. Brodsky, "Visage," 55.

3. Brodsky, "Visage," 55.

4. Herman Ermolaev, *Censorship in Soviet Literature, 1917–1991* (Lanham, MD: Rowman and Littlefield, 1997), 10.

5. See Marianna Tax Choldin, *A Fence around the Empire: Russian Censorship of Western Ideas under the Czars* (Durham, NC: Duke University Press, 1985).

6. Isaiah Berlin, *Russian Thinkers* (New York: Viking, 1978), 18.

7. Sidney Monas, *The Third Section: Police and Society in Russia under Nicholas I* (Cambridge, MA: Harvard University Press, 1961), 289.

8. Stephen Spender similarly argued that "the difference between censorship in the West and in the communist countries is so great that it amounts, not to a difference in degree, but of kind." Stephen Spender, "Thoughts on Censorship in the World of 1984," in *Censorship: 500 Years of Conflict*, ed. William Zeisel (New York: Oxford University Press, 1984), 120.

9. Simon Karlinsky, "Evtushenko and the Underground Poets," in *Freedom from Violence and Lies: Essays on Russian Poetry and Music*, ed. Richard Taruskin, Thomas A. Koster, and Robert Hughes (Boston: Academic Studies, 2013), 229.

10. Henry Hardy, preface to *The Soviet Mind*, xx.

11. Michael Ignatieff, *Isaiah Berlin: A Life* (New York: Metropolitan Books, 1998), 161.

12. Berlin, *The Soviet Mind*, 6–7.

13. Ermolaev, *Censorship in Soviet Literature*, 99–139.

14. Ignatieff, *Isaiah Berlin*, 166–67.

15. Ermolaev, *Censorship in Soviet Literature*, 99.

16. Clark, *Moscow, the Fourth Rome*, 346.

17. See Serhii Plokhy, *The Gates of Europe: A History of Ukraine* (New York: Basic Books, 2015), and Anne Applebaum, *Iron Curtain: The Crushing of Eastern Europe, 1944–1956* (New York: Doubleday, 2012).

18. Isaiah Berlin, "The Arts in Russia under Stalin," in *The Soviet Mind*, 6–7.

19. Smith, "Russian Poetry since 1945," 197.

20. Georgii Kizeval'ter, *Vremia nadezhd, vremia illiuzii: Problemy istorii sovetskogo neofitsial'nogo iskusstva. 1950–1960 gody* (Moscow: Novoe literaturnoe obozrenie, 2018).

21. Nadezhda Mandelstam, *Kniga vtoraia* (Paris: YMCA, [1972] 1987), 412.

22. Ellen Hinsey and Tomas Venclova, *Magnetic North: Conversations with Tomas Venclova* (Rochester, NY: University of Rochester Press, 2017), 130–31.

23. Kizeval'ter, *Vremia nadezhd, vremia illiuzii*.

24. "The year 1956 shaped all of us with its message of . . . casting doubt upon everything" (translation mine). Gabriel Superfin, "Podvergat' vse somneniiu," in Kizeval'ter, *Vremia nadezhd, vremia illiuzii*, 143; Philip Boobbyer, "Vladimir Bukovskii and Soviet Communism," *Slavonic and East European Review* 87, no. 3 (July 2009): 453.

25. Joseph Brodsky, foreword to *Winter Dialogue*, by Tomas Venclova (Evanston, IL: Northwestern University Press, 1997), vii–xviii, here xii.

26. Brodsky, "Spender," 468.

27. See Stephen Spender, *The Thirties and After: Poetry, Politics, People (1933–75)* (London: Macmillan, 1978), 19.

28. Stephen Spender, "Conversation with Rajiv Mehrotra," in *The Spirit of the Muse: Conversations on the Journeys of Artists*, by Rajiv Mehrotra (Carlsbad: Hay House, 2011), 167.

29. Edward Mendelson, introduction to *Early Auden* (New York: Viking, 1981), xiv–xx.

30. Brodsky, "Visage," 55.

31. Nirman Moranjak-Bamburac, "Iosif Brodskij i akmeism," *Russian Literature* 40 (1996): 59–60.

32. Joseph Brodsky, "Translating Akhmatova," trans. Barry Rubin, *New York Review of Books* 20, no. 13 (August 9, 1973), http://www.nybooks.com/articles/9770; Joseph Brodsky, "Beyond Consolation," *New York Review of Books* 21, no. 1 (February 7, 1974), http://www.nybooks.com/articles/9613.

33. Mandelstam, *Kniga Vtoraia*; Kizeval'ter, *Vremia nadezhd, vremia illiuzii*.

34. Yuri Mal'tsev, "Rozhdenie samizdata," in *Volnaia russkaia literatura 1955–1975* (Frankfurt am Main: Possev-Verlag, 1976), 7–15.

35. Smith, "Russian Poetry since 1945."

36. Isaiah Berlin, "The Arts in Russia under Stalin," in *The Soviet Mind*, 1–27, here 8–9.

37. Ann Komaromi, *Uncensored* (Evanston, IL: Northwestern University Press, 2015). Samizdat ("self-published") was a network of hand-to-hand reproduction and circulation of ordinary typed copies of literary material that emerged during the communist period in Russia and in the Eastern Bloc, allowing artists to go around the strict Soviet censorship.

38. Nadezhda Mandelstam, *Hope Abandoned: A Memoir* (Harmondsworth, UK: Penguin Books, 1974), 21–22.

39. Liudmila Alekseeva, *Istoriia pravozashchitnogo dvizheniia v Rossii: Sovetskii period* (Moscow: Moskovskaia Khel'sinkskaia gruppa, 2016); Vera Lashkova, in *Svobodnye liudi: Dissidentskoe dvizhenie v rasskazakh uchastnikov*, ed. Aleksandr Arkhangel'skii (Moscow: Vremia, 2018), 135.

40. Smith, "Russian Poetry since 1945," 199; Lygo, *Leningrad Poetry 1953–1975*.

41. Losev, *Iosif Brodskii*, 49–54, 65–68.

42. Liudmila Shtern, *Brodskii: Osia, Iosif, Joseph* (Moscow: Izdatel'stvo nezavisimaia gazeta, 2001).

43. Diana Myers, "Joseph Brodsky, 1940–1996," in Volume 1, A–D, of *Censorship: A World Encyclopedia*, ed. Derek Jones (London: Fitzroy Dearborn, 2001), 355–57.

44. Hinsey and Venclova, *Magnetic North*, 180.

45. Hinsey and Venclova, *Magnetic North*, 163–64.

46. Cynthia L. Haven, ed., *Joseph Brodsky: Conversations* (Jackson: University Press of Mississippi, 2002), 9.

47. See Sergei Kovalev, "Sergei Kovalev," in Arkhangel'skii, *Svobodnye liudi*, 124.

48. Hinsey and Venclova, *Magnetic North*, 165.

49. Losev, *Iosif Brodskii*, 65–68.

50. Joseph Brodsky, "Aleksandr Sergeyevich Pushkin," in *An Age Ago: A Selection of Nineteenth-Century Poetry*, trans. and ed. Alan Myers (New York: Farrar, Straus and Giroux, 1988), 155.

51. Hinsey and Venclova, *Magnetic North*, 236.

52. Viktor Golyshev, "Tarusa: V epitsentre iskusstva," in Kizeval'ter, *Vremia nadezhd*, 46.

53. Anatoli Naiman, interview with Valentina Polukhina, in *Iosif Brodskii, Razmerom podlinnika* (Tallinn, 1990), 131. Translation mine.

54. Venclova and Hinsey, *Magnetic North*, 177.

55. Tomas Ventslova, "Brodskii—perevodchik Norvida," in *Sobesedniki na piru: Literaturovedcheskie raboty* (Moscow: Novoe literaturnoe obozrenie, 2012), 410–33, here 410.

56. Brodsky's pun on "camp" was widespread among the Soviet intelligentsia: the word "*lager'* " is used with its meaning as in "prison camp" or "gulag"—a taboo word in the Soviet context—rather than as in a socialist bloc ("*sotslager'* "), as used in the official jargon.

57. Anna Husarska, "A Talk with Joseph Brodsky," *New Leader* 70, no. 19 (December 14, 1987): 8–11.

58. Irena Grudzinska-Gross, "Pod vlianiyem? I. Brodsky i Pol'sha," trans. S. Zenkevich, *Staroe literaturnoe obozrenie* 2, 278 (2001): 1–9.

59. Frida Vigdorova and Michael R. Katz, "The Trial of Joseph Brodsky," *New England Review* 34, no. 3 (2014): 183–207, doi:10.1353/ner.2014.0022.

60. Aleksander Wat, *My Century: The Odyssey of a Polish Intellectual* (New York: W. W. Norton, 1988), 199.

61. Smith, "Russian Poetry since 1945," 199.

62. Smith, "Russian Poetry since 1945," 199.

63. Irina Paperno, *Stories of the Soviet Experience: Memoirs, Diaries, Dreams* (Ithaca, NY: Cornell University Press, 2009), 49.

64. See Ventslova, "Brodskii—perevodchik Norvida," 268–69.

65. Tomas Ventslova, "'Sreten'e': Vstrecha v Peterburge," in *Sobesedniki na piru*, 269.

66. Carl R. Proffer, *The Widows of Russia* (Ann Arbor, MI: Ardis, 1992), 44. Akhmatova encouraged them to include at least one woman in their poetic group, recommending Natalya Gorbanevskaya. This, however, never happened. See Venclova and Hinsey, *Magnetic North*, 177.

67. Tomas Venclova, "Joseph Brodsky and Anna Akhmatova: A Meeting in a Poem," a talk at the Einstein Forum, Berlin, April 22, 2003.

68. Venclova, "Joseph Brodsky and Anna Akhmatova."

69. Venclova, "Joseph Brodsky and Anna Akhmatova."

70. Venclova, "Joseph Brodsky and Anna Akhmatova."

71. Viacheslav V. Ivanov, "Vstrechi s Akhmatovoi," *Znamia* 6 (1989): 199–209.

72. Proffer, *Widows of Russia*, 45.

73. Proffer, *Widows of Russia*, 13–61; Ventslova, "'Sreten'e': Vstrecha v Peterburge," 267–86.

74. "At his graduation, Pushkin was singled out by Gavrila Romanovich Derzhavin, the most honored poet of the preceding generation; this was a symbolic moment in the history of Russian literature in which the baton, as it were, was passed from one epoch and one style to another." Brodsky, "Aleksandr Sergeyevich Pushkin," in *AAA*, 155.

75. Brodsky was equally surprised to hear Nadezhda Mandelstam's name mentioned before meeting her in person in 1962, admitting: "I didn't know that she existed." Joseph Brodsky, "Nadezhda Mandelstam (1899–1980): An Obituary," in *LTO*, 146.

76. Hinsey and Venclova, *Magnetic North*, 198.

77. Hinsey and Venclova, *Magnetic North*, 204.

78. Hinsey and Venclova, *Magnetic North*, 247.

79. Brodsky, foreword to *Winter Dialogue*, by Venclova, x; Yuri Tynianov, *Archaisty i novatory* [*Archaists and Innovators*] (Leningrad, 1929).

80. Brodsky, foreword to *Winter Dialogue*, by Venclova, xii.

81. Venclova, "Joseph Brodsky and Anna Akhmatova."

82. "And be punished under a foreign code of conscience." Auden, "In Memory of W. B. Yeats," 80.

83. Hinsey and Venclova, *Magnetic North*, 247–48.

84. Komaromi, *Uncensored*, 9.

85. Hannah Arendt, "The Answer of Socrates," in *The Life of the Mind, Volume One, Thinking* (San Diego, CA: Harcourt Brace Jovanovich, 1978), 173.

86. Iakov Gordin, "Nashe delo—pochti antropologicheskoe" ["Our Goal Is Almost Anthropological"], in *Vozhidanii varvarov: Mirovaia poeziia v perevodakh Iosifa Brodskogo* [*World Poetry in Translation by Joseph Brodsky*], ed. Aleksei Purin (St. Petersburg: Zhurnal "Zvezda," 2001), 6.

87. Ignatieff, *Isaiah Berlin*, 158.

88. Hinsey and Venclova, *Magnetic North*, 202.

89. "Brodsky considered her among the best, and the only specialist on the same intellectual and artistic level as Pushkin himself." Hinsey and Venclova, *Magnetic North*, 193.

90. Vladimir Veidle, "Pushkin i Evropa," in *Pushkin v russkoi filosofskoi kritike: Konets XIX–XX vek*, ed. R. A. Gal'tsev (Moscow: Universitetskaia kniga, 1999), 417.

91. V. N. Toporov, "K otzvukam zapadnoevropeiskoi poezii u Akhmatovoi (T. S. Eliot)" ["On Echoes of Western European Poetry in Akhmatova (T. S. Eliot)"], *International Journal of Slavic Linguistics and Poetics* 16 (1973): 157–76.

92. Hinsey and Venclova, *Magnetic North*, 202.

93. See Ernest Hemingway, *For Whom the Bell Tolls* (New York: Charles Scribner's Sons, 1940). Hemingway titled his novel *For Whom the Bell Tolls* after a sermon by John Donne, quoting from it in the epigraph to his novel.

94. George L. Kline, introduction to *Joseph Brodsky: Selected Poems*, trans. George L. Kline, foreword by W. H. Auden (London: Penguin Books, 1973).

95. Joseph Brodsky, "Elegy for John Donne," in *SP*, 38.

96. Viacheslav V. Ivanov, "Brodskii i metafizicheskaia poeziia," in *Izbrannye trudy po semiotike i istorii kul'tury*, vol. 2 (Moscow: Iazyki Russkoi kul'tury, 2000), 769. Translation mine.

97. Anatolii Naiman, "Rasskazy o Anne Akhmatovoi," in *Konets pervoi poloviny XX veka* (Moscow: Khudozhestvennaia literatura, 1989), 72–73.

98. Hinsey and Venclova, *Magnetic North*, 245.

99. Wat, *My Century*, 200.

100. David M. Bethea, *Joseph Brodsky and the Creation of Exile* (Princeton, NJ: Princeton University Press, 1994), 226–27.

101. Georges Nivat, *Aleksandr Solzhenitsyn* (St. Petersburg: Vita Nova, 2014), 159–73.

102. "Men of genius like Meyerhold the producer and Mandel'shtam the poet, and of talent like Babel', Pil'nyak, Yashvili, Tabidze, the then recently returned London émigré Prince D. S. Mirsky, the critic Averbakh (to take the best-known names alone) were 'repressed,' that is, killed or done away with in one way or another." Berlin, "The Arts in Russia under Stalin," in *The Soviet Mind*, 6–7.

103. Wat, *My Century*, 199–200.

104. Tomas Venclova, *Aleksander Wat: Life and Art of an Iconoclast* (New Haven, CT: Yale University Press, 1996).

105. Wat, *My Century*, 199–200.

106. Hannah Arendt, "Personal Responsibility under Dictatorship," *The Listener*, August 6, 1964, 195

107. Ermolaev, *Censorship in Soviet Literature*, 99–139.

108. Roberta Reeder, Efim Etkind, and Yakov Gubanov, "The Crimes of Joseph Brodsky," *New England Review* 20, no. 3 (Summer 1999): 95–135, https://www.jstor.org/stable/40243738.

109. Catharine Nepomnyashchy, *Abram Tertz and the Poetics of Crime* (New Haven, CT: Yale University Press, 1995).

110. Nivat, *Aleksandr Solzhenitsyn*.

111. Vigdorova and Katz, "The Trial of Joseph Brodsky."

112. Joseph Brodsky and George L. Kline, "Elegy for John Donne," *Russian Review* 24, no. 4 (October 1965): 344, https://www.jstor.org/stable/126920.

113. Hinsey and Venclova, *Magnetic North*, 147–48.

114. Under international pressure, Brodsky's five-year term was eventually commuted to two years.

115. That is, "a-Soviet" as in "anti-political." Lidiia Chukovskaia, "Iosif Brodskii," in *Iz dnevnika: Vospominaniia* (Moscow: Vremia, 2010), 228. Translation mine.

116. Brodsky and Kline, "Elegy for John Donne," 341–44.

117. W. H. Auden, foreword to *SP*, 12.

118. Hannah Arendt, *The Origins of Totalitarianism* (New York: Harcourt, Brace, 1951), 331–32.

119. Venclova and Hinsey, *Magnetic North*, 245.

120. "On Brodsky's example one can see particularly well the difference between the official Soviet poets such as Evtushenko, Voznesensky etc., on the one hand, and the underground poets, on the other." Mal'tsev, "Rozhdenie samizdata," 293.

121. Karlinsky, "Evtushenko and the Underground Poets."

CHAPTER TWO

1. Liudmila Sergeeva, "Konets prekrasnoi epokhi," in *Zhizn' okazalas' dlinnoi* (Moscow: Izdatel'stvo AST, 2019), 161.

2. Susan Sontag, afterword to *Joseph Brodsky, Leningrad: Fragments*, ed. Lemkhin, 201.

3. Joseph Brodsky, "You've forgotten that village lost in the rows and rows," trans. Daniel Weissbort with the author, in *CPE*, 107.

4. Brodsky, "Shadow," 361.

5. Coetzee, "Speaking for Language," 28.

6. See my discussion around Efim Etkind's publication of *Brodski ou le procès d'un poète* (1988) in Zakhar Ishov, "'Post-Horse of Civilisation': Joseph Brodsky Translating Joseph Brodsky" (PhD diss., Freie Universität Berlin, 2008), 72–74, https://d-nb.info/1023579340/34 .

7. Brodsky, quoted in *CON*, ed. Haven, 8.

8. "All in all, as I now think back, that [exile to the North] was one of the best periods in my life . . ." Solomon Volkov, *Conversations with Joseph Brodsky: A Poet's Journey through the Twentieth Century*, trans. Marian Schwartz (New York: Free Press, 1998), 82.

9. See Irena Grudzinska Gross, *Czesław Miłosz and Joseph Brodsky: Fellowship of Poets* (New Haven, CT: Yale University Press, 2009), note 3, 305.

10. Iosif Brodskii, *Otkrytki* [*Postcards*] (St. Petersburg: Muzei Anny Akhmatovoi, 2002).

11. Joseph Brodsky, "Letter No. 1, January 15, 1965, Norenskoe," MSS84477, Joseph Brodsky Correspondence, Joseph Brodsky Papers, 1965–1972, Courtesy of the Manuscript Division, Library of Congress, Washington, DC, https://hdl.loc.gov/loc.mss/eadmss.ms011073.

12. Joseph Brodsky, "Letter No. 2, January 23, 1965, Norenskoe," LOC.

13. Joseph Brodsky, "Letter No. 3, January 31, 1965, Norenskoe," LOC.

14. Joseph Brodsky, "Letter No. 5, undated, 1965, Norenskoe," LOC.

15. Joseph Brodsky, "Letter No. 4, March 20, 1965, Norenskoe," LOC.

16. Joseph Brodsky, "Letter No. 8, April 26, 1965, Norenskoe," LOC.

17. Joseph Brodsky, "Letter No. 10, May 17, 1965, Norenskoe," LOC.

18. Brodsky, "Letter No. 10, May 21, 1965, Norenskoe," LOC.

19. Brodsky, "Shadow," 366.

20. Brodsky, "Letter No. 11, May 21, 1965, Norenskoe," LOC.

21. Sidney Monas, "Words Devouring Things: The Poetry of Joseph Brodsky," *World Literature Today* 57, no. 2 (Spring 1983): 214, https://www.jstor.org/stable/40137818.

22. Anthony Hecht, introduction to *A Part of Speech*, by Joseph Brodsky (London: Oxford University Press, 1997), ix.

23. W. H. Auden, *Forewords & Afterwords* (New York: Random House, 1973), 7.

24. Humphrey Carpenter, *W. H. Auden: A Biography* (London: George Allen and Unwin, 1981), 55.

25. Mendelson, *Early Auden*, xiv–xx.

26. "Brodsky found a group of like-minded poets not in Russian or European contemporary poetry, but in English poetry written three hundred years prior." Mikhail Kreps, *O poezii Iosifa Brodskogo* (Ann Arbor, MI: Ardis, 1984), 27. Translation mine.

27. Derek Walcott, "Italian Eclogues" (for Joseph Brodsky), *New York Review of Books* 43, no. 13 (August 8, 1996): 18.

28. Brodsky, "Shadow," 361–62.

29. Susan Sontag, "Joseph Brodsky," in *Where the Stress Falls: Essays* (New York: Farrar, Straus and Giroux, 2001), 330.

30. Czesław Miłosz, "A Struggle against Suffocation," review of *A Part of Speech*, by Joseph Brodsky, *New York Review of Books* 27, no. 13 (August 14, 1980): 24.

31. Sergeeva, "Konets prekrasnoi epokhi," 142–46.

32. Andrei Sergeev, "O Brodskom," in *Omnibus: Roman, rasskazy, vospominania, stikhi* (Moscow: Novoe literaturnoe obozrenie, 2013), 426–64.

33. Venclova and Hinsey, *Magnetic North*, 236.

34. Joseph Brodsky, "On Grief and Reason," in *On Grief and Reason: Essays* (New York: Farrar, Straus and Giroux, 1996), 223–66. Brodsky taught classes on Frost at the University of Michigan and at Mount Holyoke, as well as once in Paris, and dedicated a lengthy essay to his poetry.

35. Brodsky, "OGR," 224.

36. Brodsky, "Wilbur," 52.

37. Brodsky, "OGR," 225–26.

38. W. H. Auden, introduction to *The Faber Book of Modern American Verse*, ed. W. H. Auden (London: Faber and Faber, 1956), 13.

39. Auden, introduction to *Faber Book of Modern American Verse*, 17.

40. Dana Gioia, David Mason, and Meg Schoerke, eds., *Twentieth-Century American Poetics: Poets on the Art of Poetry* (New York: McGraw-Hill, 2004), 12.

41. Joseph Brodsky, "Autumn in Norenskaia," in *Collected Poems in English*, ed. Ann Kjellberg (New York: Farrar, Straus and Giroux, 2000), 9.

42. W. H. Auden, "Rimbaud," in *Collected Shorter Poems 1927–1957* (London: Faber and Faber, 1969), 126.

43. Hinsey and Venclova, *Magnetic North*, 230.

44. Joseph Brodsky, "Letter No. 11, June 7, 1965, Norenskoe," LOC. Translation mine.

45. Joseph Brodsky, "Letter No. 12, June 8, 1965, Norenskoe," LOC. Translation mine.

46. Joseph Brodsky, "Letter No. 13, 1965 [August], Norenskoe," LOC. Translation mine.

47. Friederike Kind-Kovacs, *Written Here, Published There* (Budapest: Central European University Press, 2014). *Tamizdat*—in Russian, a publication "over there"—was an unsanctioned publication in the West named by analogy with samizdat, or self-publishing.

48. See Ivan Tolstoi, "Brodskii protiv tamizdata," *Radio Liberty*, May 24, 2015, https://www.svoboda.org/a/27033961.html.

49. Gleb Struve, "Letter to Boris Filipoff," February 18, 1965, personal correspondence, Boris Filipoff Papers, GEN MSS 334, Box 13, Folder 335, BRBL, Yale University.

50. Tolstoi, "Brodskii protiv tamizdata."

51. Brodsky, "Letter No. 8, April 26, 1965, Norenskoe," LOC. Translation mine.

52. Iosif Brodskii, *Stikhotvoreniia i poemy* (Washington, DC: Inter-Language Literary Associates, 1965).

53. George L. Kline, "Joseph Alexandrovich Brodsky," a biographical note in *The Living Mirror: Five Young Poets from Leningrad*, ed. Suzanne Massie (Garden City, NY: Doubleday, 1972), 225.

54. George L. Kline, "A History of Brodsky's *Ostanovka v pustyne* and His *Selected Poems*," *Modern Poetry in Translation* 10 (Winter 1996): 8–19, here 11.

55. Hinsey and Venclova, *Magnetic North*, 231.

56. Hinsey and Venclova, *Magnetic North*, 231. That is how Brodsky met Venclova and his other Lithuanian friends for the first time.

57. Hinsey and Venclova, *Magnetic North*, 230.

58. *CON*, ed. Haven, 8.

59. Sergeev, "O Brodskom," 432.

60. Clarence Brown, introduction to *Osip Mandelstam: Selected Poems* (New York: Atheneum, 1974), xvii.

61. Friedberg, *Literary Translation in Russia*, 79.

62. Clare Cavanagh, *Lyric Poetry and Modern Politics: Russia, Poland, and the West* (New Haven, CT: Yale University Press, 2009); Czesław Miłosz, *The Captive Mind* (New York: Vintage Books, 1981), 190. The Soviet situation of the 1930s was largely replicated in the late 1940s and early 1950s in Poland. Thus, in *The Captive Mind*, Czesław Miłosz cited the case of Delta [Konstanty Ildefons Gałczyński, 1905–1953], one of Poland's most favored and popular poets who, after falling out of grace with the Communist Party, was commissioned to do a translation of *A Midsummer Night's Dream* by a state publisher. "Nothing should be wasted . . . in a socialist economy," Miłosz commented sardonically.

63. Viktor Kulle, "'Tam, gde oni konchili, ty nachinaesh . . .': O perevodakh Iosifa Brodskogo," *Russian Literature* 37 (1995): 267–88. See also Yasha Klots, "The Poetics and Politics of Joseph Brodsky as a Russian Poet-Translator," in

Contexts, Subtexts, and Pretexts: Literary Translation in Eastern Europe and Russia, ed. Brian James Baer (Amsterdam, PA: John Benjamins Publishing Company, 2011), 187–204.

64. Gordin, *Vozhidanii varvarov*, 5–8.

65. See Michael Wachtel, "Joseph Brodsky chitaet Iosifa Brodskogo: *Chast' rechi* i poetika perevoda," in *Sub Rosa: In honorem Lenae Szilard*, ed. Denise Atanaszov-Szokolova (Budapest: ELTE BTK, 2005), 594–603.

66. Ivanov, "Brodskii i metafizicheskaia poeziia," 777.

67. Hinsey and Venclova, *Magnetic North*, 245.

68. Joseph Brodsky, "The Azadovsky Affair," *New York Review of Books* 28, no. 15 (October 8, 1981), https://www.nybooks.com/articles/6877.

69. Hinsey and Venclova, *Magnetic North*, 230.

70. Philip T. Grier, "George L. Kline, 1921–2014," *Slavic Review* 74, no. 1 (Spring 2015): 233–35.

71. Iosif Brodskii, *Ostanovka v pustyne* (New York: Chekhov Publishing Co., Columbia University, 1970).

72. Kline, "A History of Brodsky's *Ostanovka v pustyne* and His *Selected Poems*."

73. Kline, "A History of Brodsky's *Ostanovka v pustyne* and His *Selected Poems*."

74. James M. Edie, ed., *Russian Philosophy*, with the collaboration of George L. Kline (Chicago: Quadrangle Books, 1965).

75. Kline, "A History of Brodsky's *Ostanovka v pustyne* and His *Selected Poems*," 9–10.

76. George L. Kline, "Translating Brodsky," *Bryn Mawr Now* (Spring 1974): 8–9.

77. Brodsky and Kline, "Elegy for John Donne," 341–44.

78. George L. Kline, "Iosif Aleksandrovich Brodskii," in *The Modern Encyclopedia of Russian and Soviet Literature*, vol. 3, ed. Harry B. Weber (Gulf Breeze, FL: Academic International, 1979), 130.

79. Brodsky, "Room," 447–501.

80. Barry P. Scherr, "Brodsky in 1970" (see Appendix D).

81. Scherr, "Brodsky in 1970."

82. Carl R. Proffer, "Notes for a Memoir of Joseph Brodsky," in Carl R. Proffer, *Bez kupiur: Literaturnye vdovy Rossii: Zametki k vospominaniiam of Iosife Brodskom*, trans. Vladimir Babkov and Viktor Golyshev (Moscow: Izdatel'stvo ACT/ Corpus, 2017), 200–201.

83. Kline, "A History of Brodsky's *Ostanovka v pustyne* and His *Selected Poems*," 10.

84. Kline, "A History of Brodsky's *Ostanovka v pustyne* and His *Selected Poems*," 10.

85. Auden, foreword to *SP*, 9.

86. Lev Loseff, "To a Friend: In Memoriam: *Na smert' druga*, from *Chast'*

rechi," in *CPE*, 517. Brodsky's 1973 elegy in memory of the Moscow poet Sergei Chudakov was in response to a false report of his death.

87. "Wystan [Auden] . . . wrote the introduction to my *Selected* and must have realized that my 'Verses on the Death of T. S. Eliot' is based on his 'In Memory of W. B. Yeats.'" Brodsky, "Spender," 469–70.

88. David M. Bethea, "Exile, Elegy, and Auden in Brodsky's 'Verses on the Death of T. S. Eliot,'" *PMLA* 107, no. 2 (March 1992): 232–45.

89. Auden, "In Memory of W. B. Yeats," in *Selected Poems*, 82.

90. Brodsky, "Verses on the Death of T. S. Eliot," in *SP*, 101.

91. Auden, foreword to *SP*, 9–11.

92. Kline, "A History of Brodsky's *Ostanovka v pustyne* and His *Selected Poems*," 15.

93. Kline, "A History of Brodsky's *Ostanovka v pustyne* and His *Selected Poems*," 15.

94. Kline, "A History of Brodsky's *Ostanovka v pustyne* and His *Selected Poems*," 15–16; Joseph Brodsky, *Elegy to John Donne, and Other Poems*, trans. and ed. Nicholas Bethell (London: Longmans Green, 1967).

95. Kline, "A History of Brodsky's *Ostanovka v pustyne* and His *Selected Poems*," 16.

96. Brodsky, "Shadow," 376.

97. Hinsey and Venclova, *Magnetic North*, 147–48; Catharine Theimer Nepomnyashchy, "The Trials of Abram Tertz," in *Abram Tertz and the Poetics of Crime* (New Haven, CT: Yale University Press, 1995), 1–39.

98. Sergei Dovlatov, quoted in Alexei Yurchak, *Everything Was Forever, Until It Was No More: The Last Soviet Generation* (Princeton, NJ: Princeton University Press, 2005), 127.

99. Joseph Brodsky, "Memorial for Carl R. Proffer" (lecture, New York Public Library, New York City, April 1, 1985), unpublished, JBP, GEN MSS 613, Box 123, Folders 2772–2773, BRBL, Yale University.

100. Kline, "A History of Brodsky's *Ostanovka v pustyne* and His *Selected Poems*," 11.

101. Kline, "A History of Brodsky's *Ostanovka v pustyne* and His *Selected Poems*," 10.

102. Kline, "Translating Brodsky," 8–9.

103. Kline, "Translating Brodsky," 8–9.

104. Joseph Brodsky, "Six New Poems," trans. George L. Kline, *Unicorn Journal*, no. 2 (1968): 20–30.

105. Joseph Brodsky, "Letter to George Kline," Easter 1969, JBP, GEN MSS 613, Box 19, Folder 50, BRBL, Yale University. The letter was written on Easter 1969 on the margins of a manuscript of the English publication: "Joseph Brodsky, *Six New Poems*, translated by George L. Kline." I have translated the first half of the quote from the Russian, while the expression "Forever yours, Jo-

seph," as well as the rest of the quote starting with "Excuse me, please, my terrible English," were originally in English.

106. Joseph Brodsky, "Notes on Translation of 'Nature Morte' by George Kline," January 1972, in George L. Kline Private Archive.

107. Kline, "A History of Brodsky's *Ostanovka v pustyne* and His *Selected Poems*," 17.

108. Kline, "A History of Brodsky's *Ostanovka v pustyne* and His *Selected Poems*," 17.

109. George L. Kline, "Note on the Translation," in *SP*, 18.

110. Joseph Brodsky, "Letter to Diana Myers," Leningrad, June 12, 1969, Joseph Brodsky Papers, Collection Number 88072, Box 1, Folder 3, Courtesy of the Hoover Institution Archives. Translation mine.

111. Tomas Venclova, email to Zakhar Ishov, May 12, 2019.

112. Joseph Brodsky, "Letter to Diana Myers," Leningrad, April 12, 1969, Joseph Brodsky Papers, Collection Number 88072, Box 1, Folder 3, Hoover Institution Archives.

113. See Nila Friedberg, *English Rhythm in Russian Verse: On the Experiment of Joseph Brodsky* (Berlin: Walter de Gruyter, 2011).

114. T. S. Eliot, *The Varieties of Metaphysical Poetry* (London: Faber and Faber, 1993), 138.

115. Mario Praz, *John Donne* (Turin: Edizioni S.A.I.E., 1958), 87.

116. Praz, *John Donne*, 269.

117. Barry P. Scherr, "To Urania," in *Joseph Brodsky: The Art of a Poem*, ed. Lev Loseff and Valentina Polukhina (New York: Palgrave, 1999), 100.

118. Igor' Pomerantsev, "Iosif Brodskii: Khleb poezii v vek razbroda" (1981), *Arion*, no. 3 (1995), http://magazines.russ.ru/arion/1995/3/dialog.html. Translation mine.

119. Hinsey and Venclova, *Magnetic North*, 230–50.

120. Joseph Brodsky, "Letter to Carl Proffer," November 6, [1971], JBP, GEN MSS 613, Box 11, Folder 315, BRBL, Yale University.

121. Kline, "Iosif Aleksandrovich Brodskii," 130.

122. See Romas Katilius, Joseph Brodsky Papers, M1960, Box 7, Folder 1, Courtesy of the Department of Special Collections, Stanford University Libraries.

123. See Proffer, *Bez kupiur*, 200–201.

124. Golyshev, "Tarusa: V epitsentre iskusstva," 46. Translation mine. On May 10, 1972, Brodsky was summoned to the exit visa and emigration agency OVIR. The high-ranking KGB officer who met him there "offered" him a choice: either emigrate or face renewed persecution at home. See also Proffer, *Bez kupiur*, 200–201.

125. Monas, "Words Devouring Things," 214.

CHAPTER THREE

1. Daniel Weissbort, *From Russian with Love: Joseph Brodsky in English* (London: Anvil Press Poetry, 2004), 9–10.

2. Joseph Brodsky, "Letter to Lev Loseff," August 2, 1972, Lev Loseff Papers, Joseph Brodsky, Correspondence Outgoing, Box 1, Folder 7. Courtesy of the Bakhmeteff Archive, Rare Book & Manuscript Library, Columbia University Libraries (hereafter RBML, Columbia).

3. Grudzinska Gross, *Czesław Miłosz and Joseph Brodsky*, 188–89.

4. Kline, "A History of Brodsky's *Ostanovka v pustyne* and His *Selected Poems*," 18–19.

5. Joseph Brodsky, "Letter to Lev Losev," January 15, 1974, LLP, JB, Box 1, Folder 6, RBML, Columbia. Translation mine.

6. Veidle, "Pushkin i Evropa," 419.

7. Proffer, *Bez kupiur*, 274–75.

8. Joseph Brodsky, "Elegy," in *W. H. Auden: A Tribute*, ed. Stephen Spender (London: Weidenfeld and Nicolson, 1975), 243. Brodsky would later regret having published this elegy, which he wrote just fifteen months into his American transplantation under social pressure, and would distance himself from it as too conventional an imitation of Auden, whose work would continue to shape him as a poet. Here are the opening lines of the poem:

> The tree is dark, the tree is tall,
> to gaze at it isn't fun.
> Among the fruits of this fall
> your death is the most grievous one.
>
> The land is bare. Firm for steps,
> It yields to a shovel's clink.
> Among next April's stems
> your cross will be the unshaken thing.
>
> Seedless it will possess its dew
> humiliating grass.
> *Poetry without you*
> *equals only us.* [Italics mine.]

9. Brodsky, "Shadow," 357.

10. Joseph Brodsky, "Letter to Diana Myers," Leningrad, 1972, JBP, Collection Number 88072, Box 1, Folder 5, Hoover Institution Archives. In his early letters from America to Diana Myers, Brodsky spoke of a "psychological anesthesia." See also Proffer, *Bez kupiur*, 262.

11. Joseph Brodsky, "A Reading," Boston University, April 9, 1995, in Grudzinska Gross, *Czesław Miłosz and Joseph Brodsky*, 7.

12. Brodsky, "A Reading," 1–8.

13. See Andrzej Franaszek, *Miłosz: A Biography* (Cambridge, MA: Belknap Press of Harvard University Press, 2017).

14. Grudzinska Gross, *Czesław Miłosz and Joseph Brodsky*, 1–2.

15. Grudzinska Gross, *Czesław Miłosz and Joseph Brodsky*, 2.

16. Brodsky, "Room," 482.

17. Brodsky, "Room," 478.

18. Fausto Malcovati, interview by Zakhar Ishov, November 26, 2011. Translation from the Italian mine.

19. Joseph Brodsky, "Lullaby of Cape Cod," in *CPE*, 120.

20. Brodsky, "Lullaby of Cape Cod," 120.

21. Liza Henderson, "Poetry in the Theater: An Interview with Joseph Brodsky," *Theater* 20, no. 1 (February 1, 1988): 51–54.

22. Joseph Brodsky, "Letter to Elvira Katilene and Romas Katilius," March 1974, JBP, M1960, Box 5, Folder 8, Department of Special Collections, Stanford University Libraries. Translation mine.

23. Brodsky, "Letter to Elvira Katilene and Romas Katilius."

24. Brodsky, "Letter to Lev Losev," January 15, 1974.

25. "His exile came as a shock to Brodsky, which brought about a reaction—rage." Proffer, *Bez kupiur*, 270. Translation mine.

26. Czesław Miłosz, "A Letter to Brodsky," December 26, 1984, in Grudzinska Gross, *Czesław Miłosz and Joseph Brodsky*, 236.

27. Czesław Miłosz, "Nobel Lecture," December 8, 1980, https://www.nobelprize.org/prizes/literature/1980/milosz/lecture/.

28. David M. Bethea, "Brodsky's and Nabokov's Bilingualism(s): Translation, American Poetry, and the *Muttersprache*," *Russian Literature* 37, no. 2–3 (1995): 157–84, here 157.

29. Bethea, "Brodsky's and Nabokov's Bilingualism(s)," 157. See also Ellendea Proffer Teasley, *Brodsky Among Us: A Memoir* (Brighton, MA: Academic Studies, 2017). A recent attempt to revisit this parallelism in a Brodsky memoir by Proffer Teasley is the case in Bethea's point. Proffer Teasley insists that "burning ambition" was as much Brodsky's own trait as it was Nabokov's. It seems, however, that she understands ambition in the narrow sense of careerism, which, strictly speaking, applies neither to Nabokov nor to Brodsky.

30. See Alexander Dolinin, "Nabokov as a Russian Writer," in *The Cambridge Companion to Nabokov*, ed. Julian W. Connolly (Cambridge: Cambridge University Press, 2005), 62.

31. Ann Kjellberg, "His English: Ann Kjellberg on Brodsky's Self-Translations," 2015, The Book Haven, Stanford University, http://bookhaven.stanford.edu/2015/04/his-english-ann-kjellberg-on-brodskys-self-translations/.

32. See Iosif Brodskii, "Pis'mo Viktoru Golyshevu" (1977), in *Portfel': Literaturnyi sbornik*, ed. Aleksandr Sumerkin (Dana Point, CA: Ardis, 1996), 69.

33. Joseph Brodsky, "A poem on a postcard from Venice to Roger Straus," undated, JBP, GEN MSS 613, Box 14, Folder 385, BRBL, Yale University.

34. See Nancy Meiselas, "Letter to George Kline," September 19, 1978, Box 41, "Brodsky General," Farrar, Straus and Giroux, Inc. records. Courtesy of the Manuscripts and Archives Division, New York Public Library, Astor, Lenox, and Tilden Foundations.

35. Meiselas, "Letter to George Kline," September 19, 1978.

36. Meiselas, "Letter to George Kline," September 19, 1978. See Roger Straus, "Letter to Joseph Brodsky," September 25, 1977. Box 41, Farrar, Straus and Giroux archives (hereafter FSG archives).

37. George L. Kline, "Working with Brodsky," *The Paintbrush* 4, no. 7–8 (Spring and Autumn 1977), 25.

38. Joseph Brodsky, "Letter to George L. Kline," April 22, 1973, JBP, GEN MSS 613, Box 8, Folder 209, BRBL, Yale University.

39. Nancy Meiselas, "Letter to Brodsky," (undated [1975]), JBP, GEN MSS 613, Box 10, Folder 258, BRBL, Yale University.

40. Joseph Brodsky, "Twenty Sonnets to Mary Queen of Scots," in *CPE*, 226; Brodsky, "Lullaby of Cape Cod," 116–29.

41. Nancy Meiselas, "Letter to Barry Rubin," April 12, 1976, Box 41, FSG archives.

42. Kline, who was one of the ten translators working on *A Part of Speech*, ended up translating eleven out of fifty-five poems for the collection, but three of them had earlier appeared in *Selected Poems*. See Ishov, "Post-Horse of Civilisation."

43. Brodsky, "Lullaby of Cape Cod," 117.

44. Barry Rubin, interview by Zakhar Ishov, New York City, February 7, 2007. (See Appendix A.)

45. Alan Myers, "Letter to Brodsky," July 15, 1972, JBP, GEN MSS 613, Box 10, Folder 270, BRBL, Yale University.

46. Stephen Spender, "Bread of Affliction," review of *Selected Poems*, by Joseph Brodsky, *New Statesman*, December 14, 1973, 915–16.

47. Spender, "Bread of Affliction," 915.

48. Spender, "Bread of Affliction," 915.

49. Kline is referring to Joseph Brodsky, "You're coming home again. What does it mean?," in *SP*, 33.

50. George L. Kline, "Letter to Brodsky," January 9, 1974, JBP, GEN MSS 613, Box 8, Folder 209, BRBL, Yale University.

51. Dana Gioia, "*A Part of Speech* by Joseph Brodsky," *Hudson Review* 33, no. 4 (Winter 1980–81): 611.

52. See Box 41, FSG archives.

53. Rubin, interview by Ishov. (See Appendix A.)

54. Rubin, interview by Ishov.

55. Kline, "Working with Brodsky," 27.

56. Nancy Meiselas, "Letter to Joseph Brodsky," March 1, 1977, Box 41, FSG archives.

57. George L. Kline, "Letter to Anthony Hecht," London, May 6, 1977, Box 41, FSG archives.

58. Anthony Hecht, "Letter to Nancy Meiselas," October 27, 1977, Box 41, FSG archives.

59. George L. Kline, "Letter to Brodsky," June 18, 1977, JBP, GEN MSS 613, Box 8, Folder 209, BRBL, Yale University.

60. David Montenegro, "An Interview with Joseph Brodsky," 1986, in *CON*, ed. Haven, 113.

61. Derek Walcott, "Magic Industry," review of *To Urania*, by Joseph Brodsky, *New York Review of Books* 35, no. 18 (November 24, 1988): 35–39.

CHAPTER FOUR

1. Joseph Brodsky, "Vtoroe Rozhdestvo na beregu," Russian-language version, 1971, JBP, GEN MSS 613, Box 68, Folder 1779, BRBL, Yale University.

2. "Since the time when I started to write poetry more or less seriously, I have tried . . . to compose a poem on every Christmas as kind of a birthday wish." Iosif Brodskii, "Rozhdestvo: Tochka otscheta: Beseda Iosifa Brodskogo s Petrom Vailem," in *Rozhdestvennskie stikhi* (Moscow: "Nezavisimaia Gazeta," 1997), 58. Translation mine.

3. Zakhar Ishov, "Joseph Brodsky and Italy" (PhD diss., Yale University, 2015).

4. Brodsky, *W*, 42–43.

5. Kline, "Working with Brodsky," 25.

6. Joseph Brodsky, "A Letter to George Kline," May 20, 1976, JBP, GEN MSS 613, Box 68, Folder 1780, BRBL, Yale University.

7. Brodsky, "A Letter to George Kline," May 20, 1976 (annotations made by Brodsky).

8. Joseph Brodsky, "The Child of Civilization," in *LTO*, 126.

9. Ovid, *Tristia. Ex Ponto* (Cambridge, MA: Harvard University Press, 2002). For a discussion of the connection between Ovid and Pushkin, see Zakhar Ishov, "Joseph Brodsky's 'December in Florence': Re-interpreting Exile in the Company of Dante," *Australian Slavonic and East European Studies Journal* 31, no. 1–2 (2017): 121–63.

10. Brodsky, "The Child of Civilization," 126.

11. Joseph Brodsky, "Assignments" (undated), JBP, GEN MSS 613, Box 126, Folders 2823–2824, BRBL, Yale University.

12. Brodsky, "Assignments."

13. See Wanner, *Bilingual Muse*, 19.

14. Brodsky, "A Letter to George Kline," May 20, 1976.

15. Kreps, *O poezii Iosifa Brodskogo*, 13.

16. Brodsky, "TA."

17. Brodsky, "A Letter to George Kline," May 20, 1976 (annotations made by Brodsky).

18. Brodsky, *W*, 42–43.

19. Cynthia L. Haven, *The Man Who Brought Brodsky into English: Conversations with George L. Kline* (Boston: Academic Studies, 2021), 101. According to this recently published book of conversations between Kline and Cynthia Haven, in his last years Kline seemed to claim that many of the changes Brodsky made to his drafts of "A Second Christmas . . ." had been first suggested by Kline himself. Apparently, Kline, who was outwardly accepting of Brodsky's revisions and rejections of his work, was, over time, trying to revise the story of his relationship with Brodsky, to enhance the image of his contribution. However, even in this final attempt to rewrite the history of their collaboration, Kline had to admit that, when it came to the rhyme "unfrozen/horizon," the authorship clearly belonged to Brodsky. Haven, *The Man Who Brought Brodsky*, 89.

20. Brodsky, "A Letter to George Kline," May 20, 1976.

21. Viktor Žirmunskij, *Introduction to Metrics: The Theory of Verse*, trans. C. F. Brown (The Hague: Mouton, 1966), 45–46. Zhirmunsky not only departed from Andrey Bely's pioneering work on the study of rhythmical variations within Russian poetry, but also went beyond Bely's "subjective evaluations of rhythmical types."

22. Žirmunskij, *Introduction to Metrics*, 80.

23. Viktor Zhirmunskii, *Teoriia stikha* (Leningrad: Sovetskii pisatel', 1975), 237. Translation mine.

24. Scherr, "To Urania," 94.

25. Brodsky quoted in *CON*, ed. Haven, 161.

26. Etkind, *Russkie poety-perevodchiki ot Trediakovskogo do Pushkinu*, 204–5.

27. Hecht, introduction to *APOS*, x.

28. Michael Wachtel, "The Russian Caesura: Rhythm, Syntax, and Semantics," in *"A Convenient Territory": Russian Literature at the Edge of Modernity, Essays in Honor of Barry Scherr*, ed. John M. Kopper and Michael Wachtel (Bloomington, IN: Slavica, 2015), 21–40.

29. N. N. [Anatoly Naiman], "Zametki dlia pamiati" (1964), in *Ostanovka v pustyne*, by Iosif Brodskii (St. Petersburg: Pushkinskii fond, 2000), iv–v. Naiman's note came out anonymously. See Kline, "A History of Brodsky's *Ostanovka v pustyne* and His *Selected Poems*."

30. Praz, *John Donne*, 268. Translation from the Italian mine.

31. Eliot, *Varieties of Metaphysical Poetry*, note 33, 57.

32. Eliot, *Varieties of Metaphysical Poetry*, 138.

33. Eliot, *Varieties of Metaphysical Poetry*, 175.

34. Derek Walcott, interview by Zakhar Ishov, New Haven, CT, October 27, 2007. (See Appendix B.)

35. Brodsky, "Visage," 58.

36. Eliot, *Varieties of Metaphysical Poetry*, 51.

37. Brodsky's reference to the "undines" here is slightly mysterious, for they occur neither in the original nor in Kline's translation drafts.

38. Brodsky, "A Letter to George Kline," May 20, 1976.

39. Walcott, interview by Ishov. (See Appendix B.)

40. Scherr, "To Urania," 94.

41. Joseph Brodsky, "On 'September 1, 1939' by W. H. Auden," in *LTO*, 304–56, here 306.

42. See Hor. Carm. 1.11. Translation from Latin mine in collaboration with Antonina Kalinina. The original is quoted from http://www.horatius.ru/index.xps?2.111.

43. William Butler Yeats, "The Second Coming," in *The Variorum Edition of the Poems of W. B. Yeats*, ed. Peter Allt (New York: Macmillan, 1957), 402.

44. Capital letters stand for a feminine ending, and lowercase letters stand for a masculine ending (e.g., aBaB). The stresses in each line are in bold, and their number per line is given in parentheses.

45. Quoted in Scherr, "To Urania," 100.

46. Brodsky, "A Letter to George Kline," May 20, 1976. Re: "the/a": The choice of definite versus indefinite article is extremely difficult for native speakers of Russian, even someone like Brodsky, since Russian does not use them.

47. Myers, "The Handmaid of Genius," 528.

48. Joseph Brodsky, "Write a poem about the future" (Student Assignment, undated), JBP, GEN MSS 613, Box 126, Folder 2824, BRBL, Yale University.

49. See Brodsky's early poems, such as "Nature Morte" and "1972," in *CPE*, 48, 67.

50. Joseph Brodsky, "An Interview between Joseph Brodsky and Czesław Miłosz," in *Czesław Miłosz: Conversations*, ed. Cynthia L. Haven (Jackson: University Press of Mississippi, 2006), 116–17.

51. See Robert Frost, "Etherealizing" and "Why Wait for Science," in *Robert Frost: Collected Poems, Prose, & Plays* (New York: Library of America, 1995), 358–59.

52. Donald Rayfield, introduction to *The Eyesight of Wasps: Poems*, by Osip Mandelstam, trans. James Greene (London: Angel, 1989), 19–34.

53. Incidentally, this practice intersects with one of Nikolai Gumilev's translation "commandments." He advocates retaining at least one of the words in a rhyme pair. For a discussion of Gumilev's "commandments," see pages 95–96.

CHAPTER FIVE

1. Isaiah Berlin, "A Great Russian Writer," in *The Soviet Mind*, 41.

2. Bethea, *Joseph Brodsky and the Creation of Exile*, 68.

3. Berlin, "Great Russian Writer," 44–45.

4. Brodsky, "TA."

5. See Katharine Hodgson, Joanne Shelton, and Alexandra Smith, eds., *Twentieth-Century Russian Poetry: Reinventing the Canon* (Cambridge: Open Book, 2017).

6. Caryl Emerson, "Word Wars," *Chronicle of Higher Education* 63, no. 22 (January 29, 2017), SB11; Stanislav Shvabrin, *Between Rhyme and Reason: Vladimir Nabokov, Translation, and Dialogue* (Toronto: University of Toronto Press, 2019); Wanner, *Bilingual Muse*.

7. Proffer Teasley, *Brodsky Among Us*, 69.

8. Brodsky, "TA."

9. Brodsky, "TA."

10. Stanley Kunitz, "A Note on the Translations," in *Poems of Akhmatova*, trans. Stanley Kunitz with Max Hayward (Boston: Little, Brown, 1973), 33.

11. Brodsky, "TA."

12. Brodsky, "TA."

13. Anna Akhmatova, *The Complete Poems of Anna Akhmatova*, trans. Judith Hemschemeyer (Somerville, MA: Zephyr, 1990).

14. Stanisław Barańczak, *Ocalone w tłumaczeniu* [*Saved in Translation*] (Kraków: Wydawnictwo a5, 2004), 27. Translation from the Polish mine with the help of Magda Heydel.

15. Paperno, *Stories of the Soviet Experience*, 51.

16. "Dear Mr. Caine, . . . A certain 'beguiling beauty' you are discerning in them is the beholder's argument. . . . *To me, those translations are just mercenary trash*" [italics mine]. Joseph Brodsky, "Letter to the Editor Caine," "C" general 1972–1995, JBP, GEN MSS 613, Box 3, Folder 79, BRBL, Yale University.

17. Richard Wilbur, "The Art of Poetry, No. 22," interview by Peter A. Stitt, Helen McCloy Ellison, and Ellesa Clay High, *Paris Review*, no. 72 (Winter 1977), http://www.theparisreview.org/interviews/3509/the-art-of-poetry-no-22-richard-wilbur.

18. Brodsky, "TA."

19. Robert Lowell, "A Reading," sound recording of reading at the Poetry Center of the 92nd Street "Y," New York City, December 8, 1976 (Caedmon, 1978).

20. Proffer Teasley, *Brodsky Among Us*, 68.

21. Brodsky, "TA."

22. Proffer Teasley, *Brodsky Among Us*, 73.

23. Brian Boyd, *Vladimir Nabokov: The American Years* (Princeton, NJ: Princeton University Press, 1991), 136.

24. Vladimir Nabokov, "Problems of Translation: *Onegin* in English," *Partisan Review* 22, no. 4 (Fall 1955). Republished in *Theories of Translation: An Anthology of Essays from Dryden to Derrida*, ed. Rainer Schulte and John Biguenet (Chicago: University of Chicago Press, 1992), 143.

25. Walter Benjamin, "Die Aufgabe des Übersetzers," in *Sprache und Geschichte: Philosophische Essays*, ed. Rolf Tiedemann (Stuttgart: Philipp Reclam, 1992), 60.

26. For example, the Leningrad writer Sergei Dovlatov rarely used two words in a single sentence that started with the same letter. See Petr Vail, "Brodskii o Dovlatove," *Russian Literature* 47 (2000): 383–87.

27. W. H. Auden, "An Unpublished Interview (1953)," *The Harvard Advocate*, "W. H. Auden 1907–1973," special issue, 1973, 32.

28. Gioia, Mason, and Schoerke, eds., *Twentieth-Century American Poetics*, 6.

29. Joseph Brodsky, "The Power of Poetry": the two Nobel Prize winners Joseph Brodsky (1987) and Derek Walcott (1992), at the Gothenburg Book Fair, September 9, 1993, Library of Congress, Sound Division.

30. Walter Benjamin, "The Task of the Translator," in *Illuminations: Essays and Reflections*, ed. Hannah Arendt (New York: Schocken Books, 1969), 75.

31. Brodsky, "TA."

32. Brodsky, "TA."

33. Ivanov, "Brodskii i metafizicheskaia poeziia," 769. Translation mine.

34. Friedberg, *Literary Translation in Russia*, 79.

35. Friedberg, *Literary Translation in Russia*, 7.

36. Friedberg, *Literary Translation in Russia*, 3.

37. Ivanov, "Brodskii i metafizicheskaia poeziia," 769. Translation mine.

38. See Friedberg, *Literary Translation in Russia*.

39. Nikolai Gumilev, "On Translation of Poetry," in *On Russian Poetry*, ed. and trans. David Lapeza (Ann Arbor, MI: Ardis, 1977), 38.

40. Nadezhda Mandelstam, *Hope Abandoned*, trans. Max Hayward (New York: Atheneum, 1974), 86.

41. Brodsky, "BC."

42. Berlin, *The Soviet Mind*, 130–65; Michael David-Fox, "What Is Cultural Revolution?," *Russian Review* 58, no. 2 (April 1999): 181–201.

43. Mandelstam, *Hope Abandoned*.

44. Venclova and Hinsey, *Magnetic North*, 245.

45. Proffer Teasley, *Brodsky Among Us*, 68.

46. Brodsky, "Visage," 55.

47. Venclova, "Joseph Brodsky and Anna Akhmatova."

48. Venclova, "Joseph Brodsky and Anna Akhmatova."

49. Hans Christoph Buch, "Nachmittag eines Nobelpreisträgers: Begegnung mit Joseph Brodsky," in *Übung mit Meistern: Begegnungen und Gespräche* (Berlin: Aufbau-Verlag, 1996), 90–91. Translation mine.

50. Brodsky, "BC."

51. Brodsky, "BC."

52. Brodsky, "Wilbur," 52.

53. Brodsky, "Wilbur," 52.

54. "The cleverness of phrase and the delicious aptness of Wilbur's poems sometimes mask an unwillingness or inability to think or feel deeply." James Dickey, *Babel to Byzantium* (New York: Farrar, Straus and Giroux, 1968), quoted from the Poetry Foundation website: biography of Richard Wilbur, https://www.poetryfoundation.org/poets/richard-wilbur.

55. Brodsky, "Wilbur," 52.

56. Brodsky, "Wilbur," 52.

57. Brodsky, "Wilbur," 52.

58. Brodsky, "Wilbur," 52.

59. Brodsky, "Wilbur," 52.

60. Brodsky, "Wilbur," 52.

61. Richard Wilbur, "Letter to Rhoda Schwartz," September 9, 1972, JBP, GEN MSS 613, Box 17, Folder 445, BRBL, Yale University.

62. Ishov, "Post-Horse of Civilisation," 88–91.

63. William Carlos Williams, "The Poem as a Field of Action," in *Twentieth-Century American Poetics*, ed. Gioia, Mason, and Schoerke, 51–57.

64. Williams, "The Poem as a Field of Action," 51.

65. Williams, "The Poem as a Field of Action," 48.

66. Brodsky, "Visage," 55. Coetzee commented: "Aesthetics, he says, is the mother of ethics, in the sense that making fine aesthetic discriminations teaches one to make fine ethical discriminations. . . . (At moments like this Brodsky finds himself closer to . . . Vladimir Nabokov, than he might wish to be.)" Coetzee, "Speaking for Language," 29.

67. Williams, "The Poem as a Field of Action," 55–56.

68. Williams, "The Poem as a Field of Action," 46.

69. Williams, "The Poem as a Field of Action," 56.

70. Williams, "The Poem as a Field of Action," 56.

71. Williams, "The Poem as a Field of Action," 56.

72. Mendelson, *Early Auden*, xiv–xx.

73. Mendelson, *Early Auden*, xx.

74. Mendelson, *Early Auden*, xx.

75. Brodsky, "TA."

76. Elżbieta Tosza, *Stan serca: Trzy dni z Josifem Brodskim* [*The State of the Heart: Three Days with Joseph Brodsky*] (Katowice: Ksianznica, 1993), 43, quoted from Grudzinska Gross, *Czesław Miłosz and Joseph Brodsky*, 237.

77. Bethea, *Brodsky and the Creation of Exile*, 52–60. Thus, Bethea points out a connection between Eliot's and Brodsky's reception of Dante. See also Nataliya Karageorgos, "'A List of Some Observations': The Theory and Practice of

Depersonalization in T. S. Eliot and Joseph Brodsky," *Slavic and East European Journal* 63, no. 3 (Fall 2019): 408–30.

78. T. S. Eliot, "Tradition and the Individual Talent," in *The Sacred Wood: Essays on Poetry and Criticism* (London: Methuen, 1976), 49–52.

79. Tomas Ventslova, "Dva interv'iu Valentiny Polukhinoi s Tomasom Ventslova," in *Sobesedniki na piru*, 289. Translation mine.

80. See W. H. Auden, "Doggerel by a Senior Citizen," in *As I Walked Out One Evening*, 204. It is evident in the context of Auden's poem that the superior artistic standards he had in mind were those of his artistic predecessors.

81. Eliot, "Tradition and the Individual Talent," 49–52.

82. Brodsky, "TA."

83. Daniel Weissbort, "Battle over Translation," reply by David McDuff, *New York Review of Books* 29, no. 14 (September 23, 1982), https://www.nybooks.com/articles/1982/09/23/battle-over-translation/.

84. Vladimir Ufliand, "Ose Brodskomu" ["To Iosif Brodskii"], in *Rifmovannye uporiadochennye teksty* (St. Petersburg: Russko-Baltiiskii informatsionnyi tsentr Blits, 1997), 276. Translation mine with James Stotts.

85. W. H. Auden, foreword to *A Mask for Janus*, by W. S. Merwin (New Haven, CT: Yale University Press, 1952), ix–x.

86. Brodsky, "TA."

87. Brodsky, "TA."

88. Brodsky, "BC."

89. Brodsky, "BC."

90. Patricia Blake, introduction to *Writers in Russia: 1917–1978*, by Max Hayward, ed. Patricia Blake (London: Harvill, 1983), lxiv.

91. W. H. Auden, foreword to *Antiworlds and The Fifth Ace*, by Andrei Voznesensky, trans. W. H. Auden [and others], ed. Patricia Blake and Max Hayward (New York: Basic Books, 1967), vi.

92. Brodsky, "TA."

93. Jay Parini, "About W. S. Merwin," Modern American Poetry, http://www.english.uiuc.edu/maps/poets/m_r/merwin/life.htm.

94. W. S. Merwin, "On Open Forms," in *Naked Poetry: Recent American Poetry in Open Forms* (Indianapolis, IN: Bobb-Merrill, 1969), 270.

95. See "W. S. Merwin," Poetry Foundation, https://www.poetryfoundation.org/poets/w-s-merwin.

96. Brodsky, "TA."

97. "I hold the fort alone, everybody sides with the Indians." Joseph Brodsky, "Letter to Alan Myers," January 7, 1979, JBP, GEN MSS 613, Box 10, Folder 272, BRBL, Yale University.

98. *Czesław Miłosz: Conversations*, ed. Haven, 195.

99. *Czesław Miłosz: Conversations*, ed. Haven, 189–90.

100. "Dear Joe,

I've just had a letter from a Dorothy Connell in England asking me to help with some Iranian translations (I know not even a character of Iranian) and saying that you had suggested me and given her my address. I'm delighted, of course. . . . I thought you had views about my translations that would have precluded the recommendation, but I'm very happy that it's not so." William Merwin, "Letter to Brodsky," October 18, 1985, JBP, GEN MSS 613, Box 10, Folder 259, BRBL, Yale University.

101. Joseph Brodsky and Derek Walcott, " 'Form in Poetry,' moderated by Bengt Jangfeldt," *Kenyon Review* 23, no. 2 (Spring 2001): 193.

102. Walcott, "Magic Industry," 35.

103. See Dolinin, "Nabokov as a Russian Writer," 117–29.

104. Joseph Brodsky, "Letter to Jonas Modig," April 27, 1989, South Hadley, MA, quoted from "A Photocopy in Bengt Jangfeldt's archive."

105. Alan Myers, "Letter to Joseph Brodsky," January 13, 1979, JBP, GEN MSS 613, Box 10, Folder 270, BRBL, Yale University.

106. Stephen Spender, "Letter to Brodsky," August 9, 1973, JBP, GEN MSS 613, Box 14, Folder 379, BRBL, Yale University.

107. Czesław Miłosz, "A Letter to Brodsky," February 4, 1974, JBP, GEN MSS 613, Box 10, Folder 263, BRBL, Yale University.

108. D. M. Thomas, introduction to *Requiem and Poem Without a Hero*, by Anna Akhmatova, trans. D. M. Thomas (London: Paul Elek, 1976), 17.

109. Yves Bonnefoy, "On the Translation of Form in Poetry," *World Literature Today* 53, no. 3, "An Homage to French Poet Yves Bonnefoy" (Summer 1979): 374.

110. Friedberg, *Literary Translation in Russia*, 5–6. Curiously enough, Tsvetaeva, whom Brodsky worshipped as one of the twentieth-century greats, tried to translate Russian poetry equimetrically into French, as Brodsky later did into English, but her translations were even less popular in France than Brodsky's in the English-speaking countries. See Wanner, *Bilingual Muse*, 79–114.

111. Brodsky, "TA."

112. Brodsky, "BC."

113. Brodsky, "BC."

114. See Shvabrin, *Between Rhyme and Reason*, 333.

115. Nadezhda Mandelshtam, foreword to *Eyesight of Wasps*, 11.

116. Myers, "Handmaid of Genius," 534.

117. Brodsky, "BC."

118. Weissbort, "Battle over Translation."

119. Stanley Kunitz, "Translating Anna Akhmatova," in *Translating Poetry: The Double Labyrinth*, ed. Daniel Weissbort (London: Macmillan, 1989), 110.

CHAPTER SIX

1. Daniel Weissbort, "Letter to Brodsky," November 14, 1972, JBP, GEN MSS 613, Box 17, Folder 440, BRBL, Yale University.

2. Daniel Weissbort, "Letter to Brodsky," May 3, 1974, JBP, GEN MSS 613, Box 17, Folder 440, BRBL, Yale University.

3. Weissbort, "Letter to Brodsky," May 3, 1974.

4. Weissbort, "Letter to Brodsky," May 3, 1974.

5. For a discussion of Brodsky's use of accentual verse, see G. S. Smith, "The Versification of Joseph Brodsky, 1990–1992," *Modern Language Review* 97, no. 3 (July 2002): 653–68.

6. See Nancy Meiselas, "Letter to Weissbort," July 27, 1976, Box 41, FSG archives.

7. See Wachtel, "Joseph Brodsky chitaet Iosifa Brodskogo: *Chast' rechi* i poetika perevoda," 595.

8. Joseph Brodsky, "Postcard to Daniel Weissbort," 1977, JBP, GEN MSS 613, Box 17, Folder 441, BRBL, Yale University.

9. Joseph Brodsky, "Letter to Meiselas," February 15, 1977, Ann Arbor, Box 41, FSG archives.

10. See Zakhar Ishov, "The Battlefield of Translation: Joseph Brodsky and Daniel Weissbort," *Wiener Slavistisches Jahrbuch* 6 (2018): 122–42.

11. Joseph Brodsky, "Postcard to Daniel Weissbort," 1978, JBP, GEN MSS 613, Box 17, Folder 441, BRBL, Yale University.

12. Joseph Brodsky, "Letter to Alan Myers," November 4, 1978, JBP, GEN MSS 613, Box 10, Folder 272, BRBL, Yale University.

13. Weissbort, *From Russian with Love*, 24.

14. Weissbort, *From Russian with Love*, 24.

15. Daniel Weissbort, "Letter to Brodsky," November 26, 1979, JBP, GEN MSS 613, Box 17, Folder 440, BRBL, Yale University.

16. Daniel Weissbort, "Letter to Brodsky," November 29, 1979, JBP, GEN MSS 613, Box 17, Folder 440, BRBL, Yale University.

17. Joseph Brodsky, "Letter to Daniel Weissbort," December 3, 1979, JBP, GEN MSS 613, Box 17, Folder 440, BRBL, Yale University.

18. Brodsky, "Letter to Daniel Weissbort," December 3, 1979.

19. I am grateful to one of the manuscript reviewers for making this point. Incidentally, in his discussion with Brodsky titled "Form in Poetry," Walcott had also predicted a return of formal verse in English-language poetry. See Brodsky and Walcott, "Form in Poetry," 188.

20. W. H. Auden, introduction to *Selected Poetry and Prose of Byron*, quoted in Anthony Hecht, *The Hidden Law: The Poetry of W. H. Auden* (Cambridge, MA: Harvard University Press, 1993), 174.

21. Brodsky, "TA."

22. Brodsky, "Letter to Daniel Weissbort," December 3, 1979.

23. Daniel Weissbort, "Letter to Brodsky," December 10, 1979, JBP, GEN MSS 613, Box 17, Folder 440, BRBL, Yale University.

24. Thus, in his Nobel lecture Brodsky described himself as "someone rather private . . . someone who all his life has preferred his private condition to any role of social significance." Brodsky, "Visage," 44.

25. Auden, foreword to *SP*, 11.

26. Osip Maksimovic Brik, *Two Essays on Poetic Language* (Ann Arbor: University of Michigan Press, 1964), 25.

27. Henderson, "Poetry in the Theater: An Interview with Joseph Brodsky," 51–54.

28. Weissbort, *From Russian with Love*, 24.

29. In his discussion of Weissbort's translation of a different poem from the same cycle, "I was born and grew up in the Baltic marshland," Wachtel pointed out how essential for Brodsky was the rhythmical impulse of the original poem. See Wachtel, "Joseph Brodsky chitaet Iosifa Brodskogo: *Chast' rechi* i poetika perevoda," 600.

30. Brodsky, "Letter to Daniel Weissbort," December 3, 1979.

31. Weissbort, *From Russian with Love*, 39.

32. Brodsky, "Letter to Daniel Weissbort," December 3, 1979.

33. Proffer Teasley, *Brodsky Among Us*, 73–74.

34. Weissbort, "Letter to Brodsky," December 10, 1979.

35. See interview with Barry Rubin, 2007 (Appendix A).

36. Brodsky, *CPE*, 507.

37. See *CON*, ed. Haven, 73–74.

38. Weissbort, *From Russian with Love*, 38.

CHAPTER SEVEN

1. Richard Wilbur, "Translating Joseph Brodsky's 'Six Years Later,'" 2005, Web of Stories, http://www.webofstories.com/play/richard.wilbur/28.

2. It seems that there was no intentional connection between the prominence of the number six in this poem and its title, "Six Years Later." The poem initially appeared as "Sem' let spustia" ["Seven Years Later"]. See also Brodsky, *CPE*, 508. The title had to be changed because it was pointed out to Brodsky how far apart were instances of the second of January falling on a Tuesday.

3. Walcott, "Magic Industry," 35–39.

4. Interview with Barry Rubin, 2007. (See Appendix A.)

5. Weissbort, *From Russian with Love*, 38.

6. Joseph Brodsky, "Six Years Later" (1968), English interlinear translation by Barry Rubin (undated), JBP, GEN MSS 613, Box 65, Folder 1618, BRBL, Yale University.

7. Joseph Brodsky, "Six Years Later" (1968), English translation by Richard Wilbur, 1979, JBP, Box 65, Folder 1620, BRBL, Yale University.

8. Zhirmunskii, *Teoriia stikha*, 238.

9. Richard Wilbur, "A Letter to Joseph Brodsky," May 13, 1977, JBP, GEN MSS 613, Box 17, Folder 445, BRBL, Yale University.

10. Wilbur, "A Letter to Joseph Brodsky," May 13, 1977.

11. Wilbur, "A Letter to Joseph Brodsky," May 13, 1977.

12. Wilbur, "Translating Joseph Brodsky's 'Six Years Later.'"

13. Wilbur, "Translating Joseph Brodsky's 'Six Years Later.'"

14. "Joseph Brodsky, The Art of Poetry, No. 28," interview by Sven Birkerts, *Paris Review*, no. 83 (Spring 1982): 82–126; quoted in *CON*, ed. Haven, 73–74.

15. Richard Wilbur, "A Letter to Joseph Brodsky," April 26, 1982, JBP, GEN MSS 613, Box 17, Folder 445, BRBL, Yale University.

16. Richard Wilbur, "A Talk about Translation," in *The Catbird's Song: Prose Pieces 1963–1995* (New York: Harcourt Brace, 1997).

17. Wilbur, "A Letter to Joseph Brodsky," April 26, 1982.

18. Wilbur, "A Letter to Joseph Brodsky," April 26, 1982.

19. Brodsky, "Six Years Later," 1968, trans. Rubin.

20. Brodsky, "Six Years Later," 1968, trans. Wilbur.

21. Joseph Brodsky, "Six Years Later," in *APOS*, 4.

22. Kunitz, "A Note on the Translations," 33.

23. Brodsky, "Six Years Later," in *APOS*, 3.

24. Birkerts, "Joseph Brodsky, The Art of Poetry," 74.

25. Weissbort, *From Russian with Love*, 38.

26. Weissbort, *From Russian with Love*, 38.

27. Brodsky, "Shadow," 378.

28. See Voznesensky, *Antiworlds*.

29. See Karlinsky, "Evtushenko and the Underground Poets," 229–40.

30. Venclova and Hinsey, *Magnetic North*, 187.

31. See Blake, introduction to *Writers in Russia: 1917–1978*, lxiii.

32. Venclova and Hinsey, *Magnetic North*, 156.

33. Venclova and Hinsey, *Magnetic North*, 204.

34. Venclova and Hinsey, *Magnetic North*, 244.

35. Iosif Brodskii, "Neizvestnoe interv'iu: Razgovor poeta s Elizabet i Khaintsem Markshteinami," *Colta*, October 23, 2013, https://www.colta.ru/articles/literature/907-iosif-brodskiy-neizvestnoe-intervyu. Translation mine.

36. Proffer, *Bez kupiur*, 274–75.

37. Proffer, *Bez kupiur*, 275.

38. Karlinsky, "Evtushenko and the Underground Poets," 238.

39. Brodsky, "Shadow," 377.

40. Brodsky, "Shadow," 377.

41. Joseph Brodsky, "Letter to Daniel Weissbort," December 3, 1979, JBP, GEN MSS 613, Box 17, Folder 440, BRBL, Yale University.

42. Proffer Teasley, *Brodsky Among Us*, 76–77.

43. Joseph Brodsky, "Letter to Lowell" (undated), in "Fond Iosifa Aleksandrovicha Brodskogo," Otdel rukopisei, Rossiiskaia Natsional'naia Biblioteka, St. Petersburg, Fund 1333, File 446. Translation mine.

44. Since Brodsky is asking Lowell for Auden's address, one can assume that it was written sometime in early 1968, before Kline had gotten in touch with Auden, which was in early 1969.

45. See Michael Wachtel, "Translation, Imitation, Adaptation, or Mutilation? Robert Lowell's Versions of Boris Pasternak's Poetry," and "Addendum: Boris Pasternak's 'The Wedding' and Robert Lowell's 'The Landlord,'" in *Novoe o Pasternakakh*, ed. Lazar Fleishman (Moscow: "Azbukovnik," 2017), 532.

46. Proffer Teasley, *Brodsky Among Us*, 75.

47. Bethea, *Joseph Brodsky and the Creation of Exile*, 235–36.

48. Clarence Brown, "The Best Russian Poetry Written Today," *New York Times Book Review*, September 7, 1980, 11.

49. Monas, "Words Devouring Things," 214.

50. See Joseph Brodsky, interview by Tom Vitale, "A Conversation with Joseph Brodsky," May 5, 1984, New York City, broadcast in part on "The Moveable Feast," National Public Radio, published in *Ontario Review* 23, article 3 (Fall–Winter 1985–86).

51. Birkerts, "Joseph Brodsky, The Art of Poetry," 93.

52. Ann Kjellberg, email to Zakhar Ishov, May 24, 2014.

53. See Ishov, "Joseph Brodsky and Italy."

54. Birkerts, "Joseph Brodsky, The Art of Poetry," 93.

55. Monas, "Words Devouring Things," 214.

56. See Ishov, "Joseph Brodsky's 'December in Florence.'"

57. See Zakhar Ishov, "Introduction to Poetry in the Form of Poetry: Dante Read by Mandelstam," *Slavic & East European Journal*, forthcoming.

58. Berlina, *Brodsky Translating Brodsky*, 30.

59. "December in Florence" will often be referred to simply as "December" hereafter.

60. See Denis Akhapkin, "Perechityvaia 'Dekabr' vo Florentsii,'" *Zvezda* 5 (2020): 135–56.

61. Iosif Brodskii, *Chast' rechi* (Ann Arbor, MI: Ardis, 1977).

62. Czesław Miłosz, "Nobel Lecture," December 8, 1980, https://www.nobelprize.org/prizes/literature/1980/milosz/lecture/.

63. Ishov, "Joseph Brodsky's 'December in Florence.'"

64. See Giuseppe Mazzotta, "Why Did Dante Write the Comedy? Why and How Do We Read It?," in *Dante Now*, ed. Theodore J. Cachey (Notre Dame, IN: University of Notre Dame Press, 1995), 63–79.

65. Mazzotta, "Why Did Dante Write the Comedy?"

66. Vyacheslav Ivanov, "Unstressed Intervals in Brodsky's 'Dol'niki,'" *Elementa* 2, no. 3/4 (1995): 277–84.

67. Joseph Brodsky, "Note to 'Dekabr' vo Florentsii,'" English interlinear translation by Barry Rubin, JBP, GEN MSS 613, Box 56, Folder 1075, BRBL, Yale University.

68. Eliot, "The Possibility of a Poetic Drama," in *The Sacred Wood*, 58.

69. Eliot, "The Possibility of a Poetic Drama," 54–55.

70. Brodsky, "On 'September 1, 1939' by W. H. Auden," 326.

71. "Joseph Brodsky, interview by John Glad," College Park, Maryland, April 1979, quoted in Weissbort, *From Russian with Love*, 72.

72. Barry Scherr, *Russian Poetry: Meter, Rhythm and Rhyme* (Berkeley: University of California Press, 1986), 160; Ivanov, "Unstressed Intervals in Brodsky's 'Dol'niki.'"

73. See Gerald S. Smith, "Notes on Prosody," in *The Garland Companion to Vladimir Nabokov*, ed. Vladimir E. Alexandrov (New York: Garland, 1995), 37–43.

74. Brodsky, foreword to *AAA*, xviii.

75. Henderson, "Poetry in the Theater."

76. See Zhirmunsky, *Teoriia stikha*, 237.

77. Zhirmunsky, *Teoriia stikha*, 426.

78. Brodsky, interview by Tom Vitale, "A Conversation with Joseph Brodsky."

79. Robert Lowell, introduction to *Imitations* (New York: Farrar, Straus and Giroux, 1979), xiii.

80. Thus, Edmund Wilson suggested that *Imitations* (1961) was "really an original sequence by Robert Lowell of Boston." See "An Interview with Edmund Wilson," *New Yorker*, June 2, 1962, 118–28.

81. George Steiner, "To Traduce or Transfigure: On Modern Verse Translation," *Encounter* 27, no. 2 (1966): 52.

82. Vladimir Nabokov, "On Adaptation," in *Strong Opinions* (London: Weidenfeld and Nicolson, 1974), 281–82.

83. See Michael Wachtel and Craig Cravens, "Nadezhda Iakovlevna Mandel'shtam: Letters to and about Robert Lowell," *Russian Review* 61, no. 4 (October 2002): 529–30.

84. Wachtel and Cravens, "Nadezhda Iakovlevna Mandel'shtam," 529–30. For a discussion of the specific liberties Lowell took in his translations of Pasternak as well as other European poets, see Wachtel, "Addendum: Boris Pasternak's 'The Wedding' and Robert Lowell's 'The Landlord.'"

85. See Osip Mandelstam, *Sobranie sochinenii v dvuch tomakh: Stikhotvoreniia* (Washington, DC: Inter-Language Literary Associates, 1964).

86. Gleb Struve, "Letter to *Time*," January 6, 1966, personal correspondence, Boris Filipoff Papers, GEN MSS 334, Box 13, Folder 335, BRBL, Yale University.

87. Blake, introduction to *Writers in Russia: 1917–1978*, lxiii.

88. Blake, introduction to *Writers in Russia: 1917–1978*, lxiii.

89. Blake, introduction to *Writers in Russia: 1917–1978*, lxiii–lxiv.

90. Joseph Brodsky, "Dekabr' vo Florentsii," English translation by Barry Rubin, drafts, undated, JBP, GEN MSS 613, Box 56, Folder 1075, BRBL, Yale University.

91. Joseph Brodsky, "Dekabr' vo Florentsii," English translation by Robert Lowell, draft, undated, JBP, GEN MSS 613, Box 56, Folder 1073, BRBL, Yale University.

92. Wachtel, "Translation, Imitation, Adaptation, or Mutilation?," 598.

93. Nabokov, "On Adaptation," 282.

94. Scherr, "To Urania," 94.

95. Joseph Brodsky, "Dekabr' vo Florentsii," English translation by Brodsky, drafts, JBP, GEN MSS 613, Box 56, Folder 1071, BRBL, Yale University.

96. Lowell, introduction to *Imitations*, xi.

97. Brodsky, "Dekabr' vo Florentsii," trans. Lowell.

98. Peter Porter, "Satire with a Heart," *The Observer*, December 14, 1980, 28.

CHAPTER EIGHT

1. Brodskii, *Chast' rechi*.

2. Joseph Brodsky, "Letter to Efim Etkind," August 17, [1976], JBP, GEN MSS 613, Box 4, Folder 126, BRBL, Yale University.

3. "George Kline has been a highly skilled, sensitive and knowledgeable scholar-translator, almost a poet." Monas, "Words Devouring Things," 218.

4. George L. Kline, "Letter to Joseph Brodsky," November 4, 1978, JBP, GEN MSS 613, Box 8, Folder 209, BRBL, Yale University.

5. Myers, "The Handmaid of Genius," 528.

6. Joseph Brodsky, "A Letter to Alan Myers," November 4, 1978, JBP, GEN MSS 613, Box 10, Folder 272, BRBL, Yale University. Brodsky uses an unusual transliteration of the Russian expletive «ёб» [usually, yob].

7. Myers, "The Handmaid of Genius," 529.

8. Myers, "The Handmaid of Genius," 528.

9. Myers, "The Handmaid of Genius," 531.

10. Myers, "The Handmaid of Genius," 528.

11. Osip Mandelstam, "Fourth Prose," in *The Noise of Time: The Prose of Osip Mandelstam* (San Francisco: North Point, 1986), 181, quoted in Irina Surat, "Where Did 'Stolen Air' Come From?," *Russian Studies in Literature* 53, no. 1 (2017): 89–101.

12. Joseph Brodsky, "Letter to Alan Myers," January 7, 1979, JBP, GEN MSS 613, Box 10, Folder 272, BRBL, Yale University.

13. George L. Kline, "Letter to Nancy Meiselas," July 27, 1979, Goose Pond, Box 41, FSG archives.

14. Kline, "Letter to Nancy Meiselas," July 27, 1979.

15. Kline, "Letter to Nancy Meiselas," July 27, 1979.

16. Henderson, "Poetry in the Theater."

17. Žirmunskij, *Introduction to Metrics*, 171.

18. Scherr, *Russian Poetry*, 126.

19. Scherr, *Russian Poetry*, 142. See also Ivanov, "Unstressed Intervals in Brodsky's 'Dol'niki.'"

20. Žirmunskij, *Introduction to Metrics*, 171.

21. Žirmunskij, *Introduction to Metrics*, 171.

22. Žirmunskij, *Introduction to Metrics*, 163–64.

23. Žirmunskij, *Introduction to Metrics*, 205.

24. Alan Myers, "Letter to Weissbort," in "His Own Translator: Joseph Brodsky," by Daniel Weissbort, *Translation and Literature* 7, no. 1 (1998): 105.

25. See Zakhar Ishov, "Brodsky and Benjamin," *Przekładaniec: A Journal of Literary Translation* 30, ed. Magda Heydel (2015): 9–32.

26. Carol Jacobs, "The Monstrosity of Translation," *MLN* 90, no. 6 (December 1975): 756.

27. "A bird, as you know, is very often a bard, since technically speaking, both sing . . . a poet may be delegating certain aspects of his psyche to the bird." Brodsky, "OGR," 98.

28. See Mazzotta, "Why Did Dante Write the Comedy?," 63–79.

29. Joseph Brodsky, "Language as Otherland," 1976, JPB, GEN MSS 613, Box 123, Folders 2764–2765, BRBL, Yale University.

30. "Otherland."

31. Dante Alighieri, *The Divine Comedy*, vol. 3, *Paradiso*, Canto XVII, trans. and ed. John D. Sinclair (London: Oxford University Press, 1971), 244–45.

32. Joseph Brodsky, "Dekabr' vo Florentsii," English translation by Alan Myers, drafts, 1978, JBP, GEN MSS 613, Box 56, Folder 1074, BRBL, Yale University.

33. Sontag, afterword to *Brodsky, Leningrad: Fragments*, ed. Lemkhin, 203–4.

34. Joseph Brodsky, "A Writer Is a Lonely Traveller, and No One Is His Helper," *New York Times Magazine*, October 1, 1972, 11, http://www.nytimes.com/1972/10/01/archives/says-poet-brodsky-ex-of-the-soviet-union-a-writer-is-a-lonely.html.

35. Brodsky, "Otherland."

36. Brodsky, "Otherland."

37. The addition of "frozen" in the second line of Brodsky's translation may have been suggested by the notion of mirrors (*zerkala*) from the same line in the original.

38. Myers, "Letter to Weissbort," in Weissbort, "His Own Translator: Joseph Brodsky," 105.

39. Weissbort, "His Own Translator: Joseph Brodsky," 106.

40. See Scherr, *Russian Poetry*, 160; Ivanov, "Unstressed Intervals in Brodsky's 'Dol'niki'"; Friedberg, *English Rhythm in Russian Verse*.

41. Weissbort, "His Own Translator: Joseph Brodsky," 107.

42. Weissbort, "His Own Translator: Joseph Brodsky," 107.

43. Weissbort, "His Own Translator: Joseph Brodsky," 109.

44. Brodsky, "Letter to Alan Myers," January 7, 1979.

45. Joseph Brodsky, "Letter to Alan Myers," November 4, 1978, JBP, GEN MSS 613, Box 10, Folder 272, BRBL, Yale University.

46. Weissbort, "His Own Translator: Joseph Brodsky," 106.

CHAPTER NINE

1. Birkerts, "Joseph Brodsky, The Art of Poetry," 95.

2. See Bethea, *Joseph Brodsky and the Creation of Exile*, 235–36; Brown, "The Best Russian Poetry Written Today," 11.

3. Monas, "Words Devouring Things," 218.

4. *CON*, ed. Haven, 149.

5. Mikhail L. Gasparov, "The Semantic Halo of the Russian Trochaic Pentameter: Thirty Years of the Problem," *Elementa* 2, nos. 2, 3–4 (1996): 191–214.

6. Zhirmunsky, *Teoriia stikha*, 436. Translation mine.

7. *CON*, ed. Haven, 148–49.

8. W. H. Auden, "1 September 1939," in *Another Time* (London: Faber and Faber, 1940), quoted from https://poets.org/poem/september-1-1939.

9. Brodsky, "Visage," 44.

10. Brodsky, "An Immodest Proposal," in *OGR*, 206. Brodsky once argued that these lines by Frost ought to enter the bloodstream of every US citizen.

11. Auden, *Selected Poems*, 81.

12. Brodsky, interview by Vitale, "A Conversation with Joseph Brodsky."

13. The poets discussed in *On Grief and Reason* (1996) are those Brodsky taught in the last decade of his life and felt most strongly in that period.

14. Elizabeth Klosty Beaujour, "Bilingualism," in *The Garland Companion to Vladimir Nabokov*, ed. Vladimir E. Alexandrov (New York: Garland, 1995), 37–44.

15. Brodsky, interview by Vitale, "A Conversation with Joseph Brodsky."

16. Eugenia Kelbert, "Joseph Brodsky's Supralingual Evolution," in *Das literarische Leben der Mehrsprachigkeit: Methodische Erkundungen*, ed. Till Dembeck and Anne Uhrmacher (Heidelberg: Universitätsverlag Winter, 2016), 148.

17. Birkerts, "Joseph Brodsky, The Art of Poetry," 85.

18. William Baer, "Derek Walcott," in *Fourteen on Form: Conversations*

with Poets (University Press of Mississippi, 2004), ProQuest Ebook Central, https://ebookcentral.proquest.com/lib/uu/detail.action?docID=840348.

19. Interview with Derek Walcott, 2007. (See Appendix B.)

20. Myers, "The Handmaid of Genius," 528–30.

21. Polly Platt and W. H. Auden, "Interview: W. H. Auden," *The American Scholar* 36, no. 2 (Spring 1967): 267.

22. Henderson, "Poetry in the Theater," 53.

23. Brodsky, "Letter to Elvira Katilene and Romas Katilius," March 1974. Translation mine.

24. The most prominent of them were the editor Vladimir Maramzin, the literary critic Mikhail Kheifets, and the translation and French literature scholar Efim Etkind. See Joseph Brodsky, "An Appeal for Vladimir Maramzin," *New York Review of Books*, September 19, 1974, https://www.nybooks.com/articles/1974/09/19/an-appeal-for-vladimir-maramzin/.

25. Lev Loseff, "Chapter Ten: Illness," in *Joseph Brodsky: A Literary Life*, trans. Jane Ann Miller (New Haven, CT: Yale University Press, 2011), 247.

26. Interview with Barry Rubin, 2007. (See Appendix A.)

27. Henry Gifford, "The Language of Loneliness," *Times Literary Supplement*, August 11, 1978, 902–3.

28. Gifford, "The Language of Loneliness," 902–3.

29. Henry Gifford, "Idioms in Interfusion: Review of 'A Part of Speech,'" *Times Literary Supplement*, October 17, 1980, 1159.

30. William Baer, "Anthony Hecht," in *Fourteen on Form*.

31. Anthony Hecht, "Letter to Nancy Meiselas," December 28, 1977, JBP, GEN MSS 613, Box 6, Folder 170, BRBL, Yale University.

32. Hecht, "Letter to Nancy Meiselas," December 28, 1977.

33. Czesław Miłosz, "A Struggle against Suffocation," *New York Review of Books* 27, no. 13 (August 14, 1980): 23.

34. Miłosz, "A Struggle against Suffocation," 23.

35. Miłosz, "A Struggle against Suffocation," 23.

36. Miłosz, "A Struggle against Suffocation," 23.

37. Miłosz, "A Struggle against Suffocation," 23.

38. Miłosz, "A Struggle against Suffocation," 25.

39. Miłosz, "A Struggle against Suffocation," 23.

40. Miłosz, "A Struggle against Suffocation," 24.

41. Miłosz, "A Struggle against Suffocation," 25.

42. Ishov, "Joseph Brodsky and Italy."

43. Joseph Brodsky, "Postcard to Carl Proffer," September 19, 1979, JBP, GEN MSS 613, Box 11, Folder 315, BRBL, Yale University.

44. Nadezhda Mandelstam, "Letter to Carl Proffer," February 1973, JBP, GEN MSS 613, Box 192, Folder 4197, BRBL, Yale University.

45. Sanna Turoma, *Brodsky Abroad: Empire, Tourism, Nostalgia* (Madison: University of Wisconsin Press, 2010).

46. Miłosz, "Nobel Lecture."

47. Natasha Rulyova, *Joseph Brodsky and Collaborative Self-Translation* (New York: Bloomsbury Academic, 2020), 76.

48. Interview with Rubin, 2007. (See Appendix A.)

49. Interview with Rubin, 2007.

50. Interview with Rubin, 2007.

51. Interview with Rubin, 2007.

52. See Elizabeth Hardwick and Robert Atwan, eds., *Best American Essays 1986* (New York: Ticknor and Fields, 1986). Three of Brodsky's essays appeared in the 1986 volume. He was also included in the volumes published in 1993 and 1995.

53. Interview with Rubin, 2007. (See Appendix A.)

54. Myers, "The Handmaid of Genius," 530.

55. Myers, "The Handmaid of Genius," 530.

56. Weissbort, "His Own Translator: Joseph Brodsky," 104.

57. Myers, "The Handmaid of Genius," 536–37.

58. Walcott, "Magic Industry," 35.

59. "Uncommon visage" was how Brodsky himself referred to the uniqueness of his poetic voice after a line in a Baratynsky poem. See Brodsky, "Visage."

60. Ann Kjellberg, "Brodsky's English," *London Review of Books* 11, no. 2 (January 19, 1989), https://www.lrb.co.uk/the-paper/v11/n02/letters#152305.

61. Myers, "The Handmaid of Genius," 536–37.

62. Mark Strand, interview by Zakhar Ishov, New York City, July 9, 2009. (See Appendix C.)

63. Miłosz, "Nobel Lecture."

64. Miłosz, "Nobel Lecture."

65. Daniel Weissbort, "'Something Like His Own Language': Joseph Brodsky," *PN Review 142*, 28, no. 2 (November–December 2001), https://www.pnreview.co.uk/.

66. Reid, "Great American Disaster," 17–18. See also Stephen Spender, *Love-Hate Relations: A Study of Anglo-American Sensibilities* (London: Hamish Hamilton, 1974).

67. Reid, "Great American Disaster," 17.

68. Reid, "Great American Disaster," 17.

69. Joseph Brodsky, "A Martial Law Carol," in *CPE*, 271.

70. Brodsky, "A Martial Law Carol," 271.

71. Hinsey and Venclova, *Magnetic North*, 348–49.

72. Reid, "Great American Disaster," 17–18.

73. Michael Hofmann, "On Absenting Oneself: A Review," *Times Literary Supplement*, January 10, 1997, 6–8.

74. English antisemitism is a major theme of Roth's novel *The Counterlife*. See Philip Roth, *The Counterlife* (New York: Farrar, Straus and Giroux, 1987). See also Bryan Cheyette, "English Anti-Semitism: A Counter-Narrative," *Tex-*

tual Practice 25, no. 1 (2011): 15–32. Roth and Brodsky shared a publisher in Roger Straus and a common circle of friends in New York. In his later years, Roth was a habitue of Brodsky's midtown haunt, the Russian Samovar.

75. Interview with Walcott, 2007. (See Appendix B.)

76. Davie, "The Saturated Line," 14–15.

77. Davie, "The Saturated Line," 14–15.

78. See Yasemin Yildiz, *Beyond the Mother Tongue: The Postmonolingual Condition* (New York: Fordham University Press, 2012); see also Wanner, *Bilingual Muse*.

79. Davie, "The Saturated Line," 15.

80. See Eugenia Kelbert, "Acquiring a Second Language Literature: Patterns in Translingual Writing from Modernism to the Moderns" (PhD diss., Yale University, 2015), 66.

81. Myers, "The Handmaid of Genius," 538.

82. Kjellberg, "Brodsky's English."

83. Joseph Brodsky, "On Donald Davie," 1988, a draft, JBP, GEN MSS, Box 94, Folder 2291, BRBL, Yale University.

84. In "August 1968," Auden commented on the invasion of Czechoslovakia by Soviet tanks: "The ogre does what ogres can." Spender later referred to Auden's eight-liner as "a terse authoritative summation of the invasion in words that have the axe-edge of a public execution." Stephen Spender, "Wystan Hugh Auden, 1907–1973," *The Harvard Advocate* 108, no. 2–3, special issue, "W. H. Auden 1907–1973" (1974): 61.

85. Interview with Strand, 2009. (See Appendix C.)

86. Incidentally, Venclova remembered that shortly before his forced emigration from Russia, Brodsky expressed a wish to be appointed, once he made it to the United States, as a literary consultant to the Library of Congress in the hope that such an appointment would annoy the Communist Party bosses back home. See Tomas Ventslova, "O poslednikh trekh mesiatsakh Brodskogo v Sovetskom Soiuze" ["On Brodsky's Last Three Months in the Soviet Union"], in *Iosif Brodskii i Litva* [Joseph Brodsky and Lithuania], ed. Ramunas Katilius (St. Petersburg: "Zvezda," 2015), 347.

87. Brodsky managed to inspire, however, at least one enthusiastic young man, Andrew Carroll, who tried to start a foundation called the American Poetry and Literacy Project to organize the distribution of free poetry books to the general public. See David Streitfeld, "Book Report," *Washington Post*, November 23, 1997, https://www.washingtonpost.com/archive/entertainment/books/1997/11/23/book-report/a4ff86b6-988f-4610-ae81-6663102d5f03/.

88. See Kevin Sullivan, "Well-Versed in Politics? Lyrical Advice for Clinton from Some of America's Premier Poets," *Washington Post*, December 13, 1992, https://www.washingtonpost.com/archive/lifestyle/1992/12/13/well-versed-in-politics-lyrical-advice-for-clinton-from-some-of-americas-premier-poets/b081fe34-6cf5-4168-8ccc-b893da00a1d0/.

89. Robert Frost, "Provide, Provide," in *Selected Poems* (London: Penguin Books, 1955), 197.

90. Frost, "Provide, Provide," 197.

91. Dante Alighieri, *The Divine Comedy*, vol. 1, *Inferno*, Canto V, trans. and ed. John D. Sinclair (New York: Oxford University Press, 1971), 79.

92. Joseph Brodsky, "To the President-Elect," in *CPE*, 492.

93. Brodsky, "To the President-Elect," 492.

94. "Language and, presumably, literature are things that are more ancient and inevitable, more durable than social organization." See Brodsky, "Visage," 47.

95. Thomas Hardy, "In Tenebris II," in *The Essential Hardy*, ed. Joseph Brodsky (Hopewell, NJ: Ecco, 1995), 99.

96. Brodsky, "To the President-Elect," 492.

97. Ewa Czarnecka and Aleksander Fiut, "Between Poetry and Prose," in *Conversations with Czesław Miłosz* (New York: Harcourt Brace Jovanovich, 1987), 316–17.

98. Robert Frost, "For John F. Kennedy His Inauguration," in *Robert Frost's Poems*, ed. Louis Untermeyer (New York: Washington Square, 1964), 276–77.

CHAPTER TEN

1. Richard Wilbur, conversation with Zakhar Ishov, New Haven, CT, December 9, 2007.

2. Joseph Brodsky, "Sweetheart, losing your looks, go to live in a village," in *CPE*, 399.

3. Mary Mortimer-Maddox, "Letter to Brodsky," November 19, 1993, JPB, GEN MSS 613, Box 10, Folder 265, BRBL, Yale University.

4. Melissa Green, "The Linen Way," *Parnassus: Poetry in Review* 33, nos. 1–2 (2013): 277–97, 430.

5. Proffer Teasley, *Brodsky Among Us*, 76.

6. Mortimer-Maddox, "Letter to Brodsky," November 19, 1993.

7. Green, "The Linen Way," 430.

8. David Samoilov, "O Brodskom," in *Pamiatnye zapiski* [Memorable Notes] (Moscow: "Mezhdunarodnye otnosheniia," 1995), 439.

9. "I envy the inventiveness of Brodsky in this aspect of poetry. Nobody used before him such rhymes in Russian as he did. That's why I say that he was a shaman, because he was under an influence of poetic inspiration. Those things were not contrived, not done in accord with reflection. I'm sure it's received as a gift of a daimon." Miłosz, quoted in *Czesław Miłosz: Conversations*, 198.

10. Joseph Brodsky, "Reading at Queens College," February 28, 1994. Barry Rubin kindly shared this recording with me.

11. "The century will soon be over, but sooner it will be me." See Joseph Brodsky, "Fin de Siècle," in *CPE*, 387.

12. Elizabeth Wallace, "Poet Brodsky Visits 'Home': 'Russia's like the Wild

West,'" *Ann Arbor News*, October 20, 1992, https://aadl.org/aa_news_19921020-poet_brodsky_visits_home.

13. Joseph Brodsky, "In Italy," in *CPE*, 340.

14. Joseph Brodsky, "MCMXCV," in *CPE*, 455.

15. W. B. Yeats, "The Circus Animals' Desertion," in *Collected Poems* (London: Picador, 1985), 391.

16. Brodsky, "MCMXCV," 455.

17. See Smith, "The Versification of Joseph Brodsky, 1990–1992."

18. Miłosz, quoted in *Czesław Miłosz: Conversations*, 193–94.

19. Raine, "A Reputation Subject to Inflation," xix.

20. Raine, A Reputation Subject to Inflation," xix.

21. Beaujour, "Bilingualism," 37.

22. Raine, "A Reputation Subject to Inflation," xix.

23. See Deborah Epstein Nord, "Dickens's 'Jewish Question': Pariah Capitalism and the Way Out," *Victorian Literature and Culture* 39, no. 1 (2011): 35.

24. Raine, "A Reputation Subject to Inflation," xix.

25. See Craig Raine, *In Defence of T. S. Eliot* (London: Picador, 2000).

26. See David-Antoine Williams, "Tête-à-tête, Face-à-face: Brodsky, Levinas, and the Ethics of Poetry," *Poetics Today* 30, no. 2 (Summer 2009): 209, doi10.1215/03335372-2008-008.

27. Walcott, "Magic Industry," 37.

28. Hofmann, "On Absenting Oneself," 7–8.

29. Hofmann, "On Absenting Oneself," 7–8.

30. Miłosz, quoted in *Czesław Miłosz: Conversations*, 194.

31. In the wake of Russia's unprovoked and brutal full-scale invasion of Ukraine on February 24, 2022, controversy surrounding a poem by Brodsky has resurfaced online and in academic circles. The poem, which speaks condescendingly of Ukraine's independence, was read by Brodsky, in Russian, at Queens College, City University of New York, in 1994. Although it was never published, the poem has circulated widely on the internet and been rightfully condemned for expressing colonialist Russian attitudes. The issue of this poem lies outside the scope of the present study, which was completed before the February 2022 invasion. Nonetheless, future Brodsky studies should include a full evaluation of its political and cultural implications, as I am doing in current research.

CONCLUSION

1. Brodsky, "Shadow," 357.

2. Alexander Vvedensky (1904–1941) was a St. Petersburg poet. Along with Daniil Kharms, Vvedensky became a major figure in the short-lived underground avant-garde group OBERIU (an abbreviation for "the Union for Real Art"). He found himself on the receiving end of political persecution in the

1930s and died on a prison train in 1941. Today he is regarded as one of the most influential Russian poets of the twentieth century.

3. Brodsky, "Lullaby of Cape Cod," 124.

4. Brodsky, "An Immodest Proposal," 198–211.

5. Brodsky, "A Part of Speech," in *CPE*, 114.

APPENDIX A

1. Brodsky's poem "A Song to No Music" first appeared in *Vogue* in February 1975 in David Rigsbee's translation under the title "Singing without Music." It was subsequently revised with the author. See *CPE*, 508.

2. Alex Liberman was married to Tatiana du Plessix and was the stepfather of her daughter, Francine du Plessix Gray, who was rumored to be the daughter of Mayakovsky. They were close friends with Gennady Shmakov, who was close friends with Mikhail Baryshnikov. It is unclear how established all these relationships were at the time of the Rigsbee translation, but it became an important set of relationships in Brodsky's life. Another connection with the magazine was Edith Gross, who was Brodsky's neighbor at 44 Morton Street and was an editor at *Vogue*. She might have been responsible for publishing Brodsky's work in *Vogue*.

APPENDIX B

1. Similarly, Brodsky used to quote Pushkin on Baratynsky, in relation to Derek Walcott: "He is alone among us for he thinks."

APPENDIX C

EPIGRAPH: Charlie Rose, "Remembering Joseph Brodsky: Three poets—Tomas Venclova, Anthony Hecht, and Mark Strand—remember former poet laureate Joseph Brodsky," *The Charlie Rose Show*, March 19, 1996, https://charlierose.com/videos/15770.

1. Ewa Monika Zebrowski, *Remembering Brodsky* (Montréal: E. M. Zebrowski, 2003), 11.

2. See "Remembering Joseph Brodsky," https://charlierose.com/videos/15770: "Charlie Rose: How did he feel about becoming poet laureate?. . . . You were his predecessor. Did Brodsky have any misgivings about this honor bestowed on him?

Mark Strand: He was a little worried that American poets might feel here was an interloper—you know, a Russian had come over to be a poet laureate. But he had become an American citizen. Why should not an American citizen, even if he was born in Russia, be a poet laureate? He certainly knew more about

American poetry than just about anyone I'd encountered. He was a little worried about the backlash, and there wasn't really any backlash that I know of."

3. Mark Strand, "In Memory of Joseph Brodsky," in *New Selected Poems* (New York: Alfred A. Knopf, 2009), 234.

4. Mark Strand and Eavan Boland, eds., *The Making of a Poem: A Norton Anthology of Poetic Forms* (New York: W. W. Norton, 2000).

Index

Page locators in *italics* indicate tables.